DEVELOPMENT AND SECURITY
IN SOUTHEAST ASIA

The International Political Economy of New Regionalisms Series

The *International Political Economy of New Regionalisms Series* presents innovative analyses of a range of novel regional relations and institutions. Going beyond established, formal interstate economic organizations, this essential series provides informed interdisciplinary and international research and debate about myriad heterogeneous intermediate level interactions.

Reflective of its cosmopolitan and creative orientation, this series is developed by an international editorial team of established and emerging scholars in both the South and North. It reinforces ongoing networks of analysts in both academia and think-tanks as well as international agencies concerned with micro-, meso- and macro-level regionalisms.

Development and Security in Southeast Asia

Southeast Asia

Volume III: Globalization

Edited by

DAVID B. DEWITT
York University, Canada
CAROLINA G. HERNANDEZ
University of the Philippines, Philippines

ASHGATE

Published by
Ashgate Publishing Limited
Gower House
Croft Road
Aldershot
Hants GU11 3HR
England

Ashgate Publishing Company
Suite 420
101 Cherry Street
Burlington, VT 05401-4405
USA

Ashgate website: http://www.ashgate.com

British Library Cataloguing in Publication Data
Dewitt, David B. (David Brian), 1948-
   Development and security in Southeast Asia
   Vol. 3: Globalization David B. Dewitt and Carolina G.
   Hernandez. - (The international political economy of new
   regionalisms)
   1. National security - Asia, Southeastern 2. Globalization
   3. Asia, Southeastern - Economic conditions - 20th century
   I. Title II. Hernandez, Carolina G.
   327.5'9

Library of Congress Control Number: 2001091161

ISBN 0 7546 1792 0

Printed and bound in Great Britain by Antony Rowe Ltd.,
Chippenham, Wiltshire

Contents

PART III: COUNTRY CASE STUDIES

VOLUME I: THE ENVIRONMENT

PART I: INTRODUCTION

PART II: CASE STUDIES

VOLUME II: THE PEOPLE

PART I: INTRODUCTION

PART II: CASE STUDIES

List of Tables

List of Contributors

EDITORS

David B. Dewitt is Professor of Political Science and since 1988, Director of the Centre for International and Security Studies, York University, Toronto.

Carolina G. Hernandez is President, Institute for Strategic and Development Studies, Inc. (ISDS) and Professor, Department of Political Science, University of the Philippines, Diliman, Quezon City.

AUTHORS

Amitav Acharya is Professor of Political Science on leave from York University, Toronto and currently Deputy Director of the Institute of Defence and Strategic Studies in Singapore.

Leonora C. Angeles is Assistant Professor of Women's Studies and Community and Regional Planning at the University of British Columbia in Vancouver, Canada.

Kusnanto Anggoro is Research Staff, Department of International Affairs, Centre for Strategic and International Studies, Jakarta. He obtained his Bachelor of Science from the Department of Electrical Engineering, Bandung Institute of Technology, and graduated from the Faculty of Social and Political Science, University of Indonesia, Jakarta. He earned his Ph.D. in International Politics from Glasgow University, United Kingdom.

David Capie is a Postdoctoral Researcher at the Institute of International Relations at University of British Columbia, Canada and teaches at the George Washington University/Ford Foundation Program for International Studies in Asia (PISA) in Hanoi, Vietnam.

Maria Socorro Gochoco-Bautista is a Research Fellow, Institute for Strategic and Development Studies, Inc. (ISDS) and Rosa S. Alvero Professor of Economics at the University of the Philippines, Diliman, Quezon City.

Herman Joseph S. Kraft is a Ph.D. candidate of Political Science at York University in Toronto and Assistant Professor, Department of Political Science, University of the Philippines, Diliman, Quezon City.

Pierre P. Lizée is Associate Professor of Political Science at Brock University, Canada, where he is also the co-director of the Program in International Political Economy.

Amado M. Mendoza, Jr. is a Research Fellow, Institute for Strategic and Development Studies, Inc. (ISDS) and Assistant Professor, Department of Political Science, University of the Philippines, Diliman, Quezon City.

Hadi Soesastro is the Executive Director of the Centre for Strategic and International Studies (CSIS Jakarta) and lectures at the University of Indonesia.

Rizal Sukma is currently Director of Studies at the Centre for Strategic and International Studies (CSIS Jakarta) and visiting lecturer at the Post-Graduate Faculty at the University of Indonesia.

Acknowledgements

It is a pleasure to acknowledge the institutions that provided the support so essential to undertaking a somewhat unusual multifaceted research program. The Canadian International Development Agency (CIDA) reached beyond its traditional focus when it agreed to explore in what ways the expanded discourse on security in the post-cold war world might be relevant to their primary mandate of development. In cooperation with the Ottawa-based International Development Research Centre (IDRC), funding was received to bring together experts from throughout Southeast Asia (SEA) and from Canada to undertake some exploratory work. We are most thankful to Ann Bernard, then of IDRC, and Norm Macdonnell of CIDA, who shepherded us through the early stages and provided guidance and advice along the way.

CIDA generously agreed to fund the program, and we are grateful to the Asia Branch and to Jean-Marc Metevier, then Vice-President Asia and to Susan Davies, then Regional Director, for their support. Brian Hunter, Senior Economist did much more than serve as our principal contact and project manager. He offered sustained intellectual support, took an individual interest in each and every researcher, and never failed to challenge and to provoke. Indeed, had either of us encountered economists like Brian when we were students it is quite likely that we would now be in his, rather than our profession.

The Canadian embassies in Manila and in Jakarta provided in-country support throughout the program. We are particularly thankful to Ambassador Stephen Heeney and Mr Stewart Henderson, both in Manila during the start and early part of the Development and Security in Southeast Asia (DSSEA) Program, and to Ambassador Gary Smith, then in Jakarta, for their assistance. We would be remiss if we did not acknowledge the intellectual encouragement offered by General Jose T. Almonte, ret., then National Security Adviser to Philippine President Fidel V. Ramos, who insisted that we were exploring questions that to him, were fundamental to a better understanding of the challenges facing the nations of SEA. Since leaving government many of his public statements continue to reflect his unique sense of obligation to humanist values, the obligation of government to its people, and the necessity for the peoples of SEA to forge a new consensus in its common fight against poverty and injustice.

Three research centers carried the bulk of the administrative and organizational responsibilities for the DSSEA program. Our colleagues at the Centre for International and Strategic Studies (CSIS) in Jakarta, especially Hadi Soesastro and Clara Joewono who managed all the field research, conferences, and echo seminars which took place in Indonesia. Hadi served both as the Chair of the Task Force on Globalization for the DSSEA program and as the Indonesia country coordinator. A man of remarkable intellect and kindness, it is always a pleasure and honor to work with him. Clara provides all of us with a model of humility, modesty, and graciousness even in the face of extremely trying and, at times, dangerous circumstances. She is a remarkable stabilizing force, and has an exceptional knowledge of the politics of Indonesia and, more generally, SEA. It is a pleasure to acknowledge, with thanks, our good friend and colleague, Jusuf Wanandi, who ensured that CSIS Jakarta was always available to assist us throughout the life of the program.

The Institute of Strategic and Development Studies, Inc. (ISDS), Manila, served not only as the coordinating center for all the Philippine-based DSSEA activities, but also took on the primary responsibility for the *DSSEA Update*, a publication which emerged as an unanticipated major aspect of our program. It is a pleasure to acknowledge the devotion and extraordinary efforts that Crisline Torres, Josefina Manuel, Maria Ela Atienza, and Rowena Layador have brought to this program. Their unflagging support and commitment made the complications and challenges of running a multiyear, international program manageable, even during the most trying political circumstances. We also wish to note the important help received in the final stages of preparing the manuscript for publication: Myla Tugade who did the layout, Dona Dolina who assisted with transforming the materials into the Ashgate format, and Amado Mendoza, Jr. and Ruth Lusterio-Rico who assisted the final editing of the second and third volumes, respectively.

The Centre for International and Security Studies (CISS), York University (Toronto) assumed the lead role in handling all the administrative and financial details of the program, from negotiating the contracts first with CIDA and IDRC and then with each of the researchers, through to providing the accounting and preparing the annual reports. Heather Chestnutt and Joan Broussard not only managed all these technical details with their characteristic combination of efficiency, effectiveness, and accuracy, but also monitored the quality of the DSSEA activities, provided advice to the program co-directors, and often served as the first lifeline to the researchers as they each faced what often would seem as unique challenges in undertaking field work. Without fail Joan and Heather would solve whatever problems occurred and thereby ensured that each scholar was able to pursue his or her research unencumbered by administrative or other problems. Their skills and knowledge make directing this complex research and outreach program much easier and more pleasant than it otherwise would have been.

Our final thanks must go to those colleagues who provided the intellectual guidance and strength of this program. Paul Evans, now of the University of British Columbia, but formerly a colleague at York University, was a principal motivator behind launching this effort, and together with us and Amitav Acharya engaged CIDA and the IDRC in the initial ideas of linking development with security. Tim Shaw of Dalhousie University not only was a participant in the pilot study, but also convinced us that we should transform a difficult and eclectic set of research papers into a somewhat more coherent book project. We thank him for his unfailing encouragement and his personal commitment to these volumes. And of course, the last word goes to our colleagues, those whose chapters you are about to read and to those many scholars, policy makers, and members of non-government organizations who joined us in this endeavor. The authors of the following chapters are a remarkable group of scholars, some senior and with deserved international reputations, others just starting off on what we are certain will be important careers. This was an unusual program that each of them agreed to join, and we are thankful and appreciative of their contributions. We also must point out the special roles played by Jennifer Clapp, Peter Dauvergne, Hadi Soesastro, and Jorge V. Tigno, each of whom served as principal guide to their colleagues on their respective task forces. Without their participation, our task as co-directors would have been much more difficult and far less pleasant. We thank them.

David B. Dewitt and Carolina G. Hernandez
Toronto and Manila

List of Abbreviations

AFTA	ASEAN Free Trade Area
APEC	Asia Pacific Economic Cooperation
ARF	ASEAN Regional Forum
ASEAN	Association of Southeast Asian Nations
ASEAN AMM	Foreign Ministers Meeting
ASEAN ISIS	Institutes of Strategic and International Studies
ASEAN SOM	Senior Officials Meeting
BAIDS	Balanced Agro-industrial Development Strategy
CARP	Comprehensive Agrarian Reform Program
CBM	Confidence Building Measures
CSCAP	Council for Security Cooperation in Asia Pacific
DAR	Philippine Department of Agrarian Reform
DOLE	Department of Labor and Employment – Philippines
DSSEA	Development and Security in Southeast Asia
DTI	Philippine Department of Trade and Industry
EOI	Export-Oriented Industrialization
EPZ	Export Processing Zone
FDI	Foreign Direct Investment
FUNCIPEC	Front Uni National Pour Un Cambodge Indépendent, Neutre, Pacifique, et Coopératif
GATT	General Agreement on Tariffs and Trade
GDP	Gross Domestic Product
GNP	Gross National Product
GSP	Generalized System of Preferences
GTEB	Garments and Textiles Exporters Board
ICW	Indonesian Corruption Watch
IMF	International Monetary Fund
MNCs	Multinational Corporations
NFA	Philippine National Food of Authority
NGOs	Non-government Organizations
NIE	Newly-industrialized Economies
NPA	No Permanent Address
OECD	Organization for Economic Cooperation and Development
PO	People's Organization
PECC	Pacific Economic Cooperation Council
PEZA	Philippine Economic Zone Authority
REER	Real Effective Exchange Rate
SEIFI	Semiconductor Electronics Industry Foundation, Incorporated

SEA	Southeast Asia
TAC	Treaty of Amity and Cooperation
TIPI	Texas Instruments Philippines Incorporated
TNCs	Transnational Corporations
TNI	Indonesia's Armed Forces
UNDP	United Nations Development Programme
UNESCO	United Nations Educational, Scientific, and Cultural Organization
UNIDO	United Nations Industrial Development Organization
UNTAC	United Nations Transitional Authority in Cambodia
US	United States
WTO	World Trade Organization
ZOPFAN	Zone of Peace, Freedom and Neutrality

Map Showing Location
of Study Area

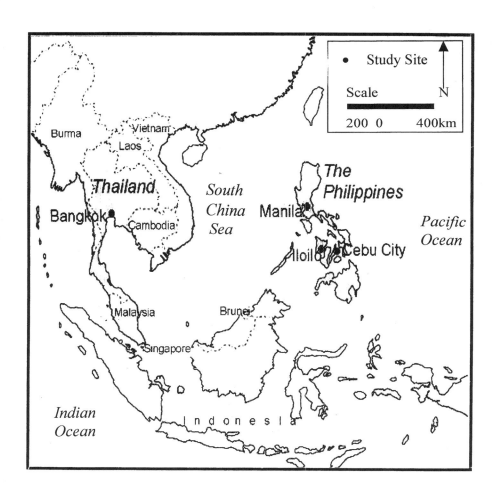

PART I
INTRODUCTION

Chapter 1

Defining the Problem and Managing the Uncertainty

David B. Dewitt and Carolina G. Hernandez

Introduction

Development and Security in Southeast Asia (DSSEA) has as its core the question of the relationship between government and civil society in their efforts to define and to pursue security, broadly defined. Thus, the DSSEA research program at the outset posits a tension between how government and its instruments understand and pursue security and how people and the communities that they comprise understand and seek their own particular security interests. It is based on the premise that the process of development is, essentially, a partnership between official agencies, the private sector, and people, and that the issue of security is found across levels of social, economic, and political organization and is intimately entwined with the challenges posed by the dynamics of (mis)managing development. Moreover, our approach to development and security explicitly acknowledges the potential importance of the tensions between local and external factors across levels of authority, production, and distribution.

Governance, whether in terms of an explicit 'social contract' or implicitly as the control, management, and allocation of public resources (including goods and services) and, in some cases, intruding into and distorting the relationship between the public and the private, is at the heart of the overarching challenges linking development with security in SEA. A subset of this focus is the underlying realization of the importance of human resource development. Consequently, the concept of social capital runs throughout all the specific projects pursued within this research program and reported in these three volumes.

The DSSEA program is concerned with the attainment of three goals: (1) identifying and understanding the linkages between security and development through conducting case studies across levels of state-society relations, as well as comparatively within the region; (2) developing enhanced theoretical and conceptual understanding of these complex linkages both to further our knowledge and to improve our abilities to develop practical instruments in support of improved human well being; and (3) using the acquired knowledge and information for empowerment and change. This volume, along with the accompanying other two, reports the results of empirical research conducted primarily in Indonesia and the Philippines by scholars from these two countries and Canada.

The three volumes represent research organized around the complementary themes of environment and resources, globalization, and people and communities, with each connected through the common concern on the linkages between the dynamics of development and the challenges to security.[1] The approach is based on two underlying assumptions: (1) that the model of development on which the rapid economic expansion of SEA has been articulated is not sustainable because it involves dynamics of social and political inequality bound to cause its demise over the long term; and (2) that the language of security provides the best vocabulary through which these problems can be delineated, debated, and resolved. Supporting these two assumptions are the ideas of human security and social capital, the former, while acknowledging the primacy of the state, focuses on the well being of the individual and her community, and the latter referring to the extent to which community-based organizations and civil society more generally are engaged participants in forms of local and national political and economic decision-making.[2]

Defining the Problem

In the post-cold war era, the concepts of both development and security have been transformed to meet new strategic realities. Development has long been recognized as a non-linear process often accompanied by unintended consequences; it also is no longer presumed to be either benign or necessarily a public good. On the other hand, development is increasingly argued to be inherently linked with freedom, as 'a process of expanding the real freedoms that people [ought to] enjoy'.[3] Within this broader understanding, the economic, social, and political are entwined into a composite which provides the foundation for such personal and community freedom and, hence, also enhanced security.

Security no longer is defined simply as defense of one's national territory by armed forces against military threat. Neither threat nor risk to the state or its people come only from military forces or groups prepared to engage in violence but also from many other factors which cross boundaries, penetrate society, and challenge the capacity of the state to regulate entry and exit. Further, security is more than protecting the state or even the governing regime as important as both of those may be. Today, security also is viewed as a descriptor of community and individual life; that the authorities have a responsibility to ensure personal safety and well being, just as the integrity of communities and their sense of their own future needs confirmation. The question of agency – the instruments responsible for the security of people and institutions – therefore, likely involves more than only the military and the police, and as such also becomes entwined with the concerns about the agents for development.[4]

Neither development nor security as policies can be achieved through unilateral means. Both are dependent on a mix of short-, medium-, and long-term factors located in the interstices between the individual, the society, the state, and the inter-state systems. Yet relatively little is understood about the linkages, never mind casual relations, which bind these two core components of national expression. The DSSEA program addresses aspects of these linkages. Most concretely, our interest is to locate the strong and weak links between some of the complex dynamics of development and the challenges of security. We situate this effort initially within the paradigm of the nation-state, but explicitly acknowledge that many non-state and sub-state actors, as well as the attendant social forces, may turn out to be the defining variables in this exercise. Indeed, as it turns out almost all of the case studies in this project explore the linkages between government, the private sector, and civil society.

Non-military threats to security seem to be crowding the policy agenda of nations throughout the world. Particularly after the attacks against the United States on 11 September 2001, the rise of terrorism, whether domestic or international, has hugged the headlines of national and international media and assumed the status of a major security concern in countries the world over. The alarming global spread of the devastating disease acquired immunodeficiency syndrome (AIDS) threatens the security of individuals as well as entire nations. The rate of ecological damage rapid economic development creates is wreaking havoc of immense proportions with devastating consequences for our collective futures whether in terms of biodiversity or simply making less land either habitable or productive. Non-renewable resources have been exploited to the point of making them a focal point of international competition and even war, while individuals and their communities become increasingly vulnerable and insecure to the globalized forces of extraction, production, and distribution. Access to and management of 'strategic resources' including water continues to command bilateral and multilateral attention. Disputes over fish stocks have brought allies and partners to the point of diplomatic brinkmanship, while communities at home suffer from resulting massive unemployment and its consequent social dislocation.

Markedly different from the Western concept of security based essentially and primarily on the state's military and defense capability, East Asian concepts view security in a comprehensive, multidimensional, and holistic manner. The five non-communist states of Indonesia, Malaysia, the Philippines, Singapore, and Thailand which together formed the original core of the Association of Southeast Asian Nations (ASEAN), have viewed security in these terms since the Association's founding in August 1967.[5] Believing that a nation's security begins from within, Indonesia stressed the primacy of domestic security by solving internal sources of security threats such as communist insurgency, ethnic tensions, economic malaise, and social divisions within its far-flung archipelago, creating in the process a condition of national resilience.[6] According to the Indonesian view, one subsequently and implicitly supported by the rest in ASEAN, when all the states in the region achieve national resilience, there would be no security problems they could export to their neighbors. The result would be a community of confident and secure nation-states, resilient to extra-regional threats, and hence, better able to promote and to sustain regional stability and security.[7]

The Malaysian concept of comprehensive security emphasized non-military sources of security threats. It was seen as 'inseparable from political stability, economic success, and social harmony'.[8] As with national resilience, security threats were seen as originating primarily from within the state. This conception was in large measure due to the presence of domestic insurgencies and the problems engendered by the task of nation building in multiethnic societies with great disparities in wealth and income among their constituent ethnic communities. While the inter-ethnic violence of 30 years ago has not reappeared, the 1997 Asian financial crisis and the controversy surrounding Prime Minister Mahathir Mohamed's continuing efforts to retain political dominance have introduced a level of domestic tension and unease not witnessed for a number of decades. The vulnerability of developing states and their governments to the fortunes of 'performance legitimacy' can be seen throughout the region, though Malaysia, as well as Thailand and Singapore, has been sufficiently resilient to withstand the havoc experienced in Indonesia.

Singapore developed a similar notion of security. Viewed in terms of 'total defense', it is also multidimensional, holistic, comprehensive, and begins from within. The Philippines and Thailand also adopted similar conceptions of security making for an ASEAN-wide acceptance of comprehensive security in SEA by the 1980s, though this is now under severe strain since the expansion to the ASEAN-10 coming almost simultaneously with the shock of the 1997-98 Asian financial meltdown.

While security in the cold war era focused an external threats to states and relied primarily on military means, including the establishment of a network of bilateral and multilateral military alliances focused on nuclear deterrence, a new concept of security mechanism launched by former Canadian Secretary of State for External Affairs, Joe Clark, emphasized an evolving inclusive regionalism and multilateralism as a complement to bilateralism, mutual reassurance instead of nuclear deterrence, and the use of both military and non-military means to promote security in recognition of the multifaceted nature of threats to security. Cooperative security as the notion came to be known, is a complementary mechanism to comprehensive security in dealing with a post-cold war environment increasingly challenged by non-military threats to the security of individuals, communities, societies, and nation-states as well as the international system.[9]

This Canadian contribution has been complemented by the more recent articulation of human security. Initially given wide attention as a result of the United Nations Development Programme (UNDP) *Report on Human Development*,[10] it was adapted by then Canadian Foreign Minister Lloyd Axworthy to frame Canada's articulation of how, when, where, and why Canada and like-minded countries should be prepared to intervene to protect and make safe individuals and communities from the ravages of war, whether domestic or international, the threats to their safety and well being from systemic challenges, as well as to enhance their security in the face of man-made or natural calamities. In Axworthy's language, 'human security entails taking preventive measures to reduce vulnerability and minimize risk, and taking remedial action where prevention fails'.[11] One of the critical aspects of this approach is the acknowledgement that security not only is multifaceted but that it is both a process and an objective which calls on responsible actions by both governments and others. In this construction, security is no longer a state-centric phenomenon; nor can it be achieved merely by employing the traditional instruments of the state. Indeed, in many situations it is its very reliance on the state and its dominance in defining the meaning of security that renders people, communities, and other states insecure.[12]

Most of the regimes in Southeast Asia (SEA) are – or were until recently – authoritarian; their legitimacy has been sustained either by force or by remarkable levels of economic development. Failure, as dramatically witnessed by the 1997 financial crisis and the ensuing upheaval in Indonesia, severe economic downturn in Thailand and South Korea along with the tensions experienced by Malaysia and the Philippines, has eroded support, even among elites, and challenged the foundations of some governing regimes. The stark alteration in the economic well being of these countries and the capacity of the governments to distribute, even minimally, the benefits that previously accrued through economic expansion, has shaken their political and social structures. Though the general resilience of the political, military, and economic classes to such pressures has been notable in spite of the precipitous decline of specific families, the inter-ethnic domestic tensions released have threatened the security of the state as well as many of its communities. Moreover, the precarious raw materials and resource-based economic system, laid vulnerable to the financial upheavals combined with the impact of the globalization of production and marketing which affects commodity pricing, has exacerbated the already uncertain situation faced by poorly educated workers and migrant labor, creating both domestic and cross-border tensions.

Sustainable development is not possible in an unstable domestic environment. Ironically, however, economic development has unleashed a set of dynamics generating social, economic, and political change, including increasing popular participation in the economy and in the society, increasing access to education and information, increasing mobility of peoples, along with the rise of a middle class. If the experiences of Taiwan and South Korea in Northeast Asia and more recently Thailand and the Philippines in SEA are relevant in this discussion, demands for greater political participation, liberalization, and democratization are likely to occur in other parts of Eastern Asia. Resistance on the part of governing elites to accommodate these demands, whether dramatically as in Indonesia or more cautiously in Malaysia, can lead to political instability of the sort that undermines sustainable development and domestic security itself. In this context, sustainable development also encompasses the creation of domestic and inter-state institutions that have the specialized knowledge and skills to regulate, to manage, and to facilitate stable political pluralism, economic development, and social equity. Thus, sustainable development is more than merely attaching specific conditions to economic change; it is also the evolution of a responsible civil society in which there exists a consensus concerning the benefits that accrue from institutionalizing good governance, resource management, and social equity. It provides an approach to achieving 'development as freedom' enunciated so passionately by Amartya Sen.

Since well before the UN-sponsored World Commision on Environment and Development (Brundtland Commission) published their 1987 report, *Our Common Future*, scholars, journalists, and non-governmental organizations had been raising serious concerns over the relationship between economic development, environmental consequences, and security. However, it was the Brundtland report that finally gave political meaning to the range of implications that were becoming ever more apparent, thereby moving ecology from the esoteric to center stage. The core concept around which the analysis and recommendations evolved was sustainable development, defined as the ability 'to ensure that [development] meets the needs of the present without compromising the ability of future generations to meet their own needs'. For this to be achieved, policy, behavior, and analysis among all sectors of society – government, industry, individuals – would have to come to terms with the implications of the nature of the 'interlocking crises' to be faced.[13]

Although some wrote on the probable connections between economic development, environmental degradation, and politics, few explored these linkages with any scientific rigor, and fewer with questions of security explicitly in mind.[14] While the ending of the cold war has not had a marked affect on the realities of this complex set of issues – if anything the 'facts on the ground' may be worse – it has led to an increased awareness of and concern with development and security. The 1992 Earth Summit and its adoption of *Agenda 21* gives some indication that political leaders are becoming more aware of the core significance of the environmental-economic-political linkages for their own countries if not the globe, although this does not mean that a consensus has been achieved concerning appropriate action.[15] Indeed, recent environmental summits in Kyoto and The Hague have underlined the extent to which state and private sector interests continue to coalesce in ways which impede significant progress on global environmental norms and regulations. Undoubtedly, while much of this has to do with the domestic politics of participating countries, it also is a reflection of the pervasive impact of the forces of globalization and the uncertainties attendant among the public, the private sector, and governments about how to address this market phenomenon which, in so many ways, impacts upon environmental and ecological issues.

The linkage between sustainable development and the environment is relatively well-known and has formed the basis of much discussion since the Brundtland Commission, as well as efforts at encouraging both standards and policy since the United Nations 1992 Conference on Environment and Development (UNCED). Over the last few years, the relationship between sustainable development (or aspects of it) and security has become a focus for research, for it encapsulates the tensions between the demands for economic growth, political stability, and individual and collective rights. Depending upon the context and the mix of choices, some scholars have pointed to the causal linkages between environmental degradation – often caused by resource depletion, improperly managed industrial development, and human displacement – and conflict. The scale of conflict can vary from interpersonal violence to challenges to governmental authority, from internal disturbances to regime repression, from revolution to interstate violence. Unsustainable and mismanaged economic activities which degrade the environment, aggravate human relations, and exacerbate intra-state as well as inter-state relations can lead to social upheaval, challenging the security of the individual, of the community, of the country, and potentially of the region.

Both problems and opportunities abound. Over the three decades prior to the 1997 financial crisis, SEA had been the locus of remarkable economic development. The stability of governing regimes was tied to performance legitimacy. The costs, however, were profound, including depletion of scarce resources, deterioration of marine and land environments, population migrations, and inadequately controlled rapid urbanization. Domestic as well as territorial problems, including current secessionist efforts, can be linked to policies fostering specific forms of economic growth in a vacuum of political representation, a fundamental political unwillingness to redress the inequitable redistribution of economic benefits, and the presence of an emerging and demanding civil society. Due to accompanying environmental scarcities and degradation, already difficult domestic situations carried the potential to exacerbate points of tension with neighboring states.[16]

What was evident from both the research literature as well as the regular and reputable journalistic accounts well before the 1997 financial crisis was a sense that the then current economic developments, especially those viewed as evidence of the mismanagement of development, could compromise if not severely undermine the security of these states, where security is understood as being 'essentially concerned with the maintenance of society's basic values; and with the institutions, such as legitimate political or legal system, which enable a country to sustain and defend the values its nationals regard as central to its independent existence'.[17] As the decade of the 1990s evolved, it also became clear that the growing insecurity of individuals and their communities could be ignored only at the peril of governing institutions. The previous decades of development strategies, as inequitable and incomplete as they might have been, had created sufficient awareness and heightened expectations that the authorities no longer could assume their citizens' compliance, especially as their own performance-based legitimacy was under threat.

The economy and the environment are separate but intertwined – and in some cases, integrated – systems. Though the causal relations are complex, and even more so when linking them to politics and to security, it is evident that to separate them in an arbitrary manner, as if decisions about one can be taken in isolation and with impunity concerning the others, is both wrong and foolhardy. 'Threats to the peace and security of nations and regions [and individuals] from environmental breakdown are potentially greater than any foreseeable military threat from conventional arms'.[18] There are no significant parts of the globe which have not suffered from environmental degradation, though not all are affected equally nor are all equally culpable. Nevertheless, almost without exception the causes are political and economic choices, at times made from afar and even with the best of intentions given the available options. The results are a combination of resource depletion, uneven distribution of benefits, displacement, debt, and often political instability, conflict, and violence, as well as the intensification of 'poor governance'.[19] SEA is repository of all these factors.

Local political, economic, and commercial decisions have environmental consequences that, as with acid rain and deforestation, have not only regional but global ecological impact. As MacNeill notes, 'If nations are to stop depleting their basic stocks of ecological capital, governments will need to reform those public policies that now actively encourage the infamous *de's*: *de*forestation, *de*sertification, *de*struction of habitat and species, *de*cline of air and water quality'.[20] In many places, these second-order phenomena aggravate already contentious resource-based contexts, where two or more countries draw on the same river system, fish from the same sea, or claim under-sea and under-seabed rights from the same location at a time when each has increased needs driven by, among other things, demography, development, and rapid unplanned and unmanaged urbanization.[21]   Much the same occurs with agricultural and grazing lands as well as with timber stands and mineral and ore deposits, though these usually are less state boundary questions initially and more likely to be tribal, clan, and other sub-state boundary problems.

Hence, for the DSSEA program, development makes sense only when understood in terms of sustainable development, a comprehensive concept with ecological, economic, social, and political dimensions. To be sustainable, economic development must be sensitive to its excessive demands on natural resources and its negative impact on the physical environment. Development, broadly defined, must also take into account the social dimension which includes the competing requirements of economic development and the preservation of social structures and cultural norms and values without which the survival of communities would be at risk. These include rights to ancestral lands without access to which tribal communities are likely to perish, and the capacity of both rural and urban dwellers to maintain their primary identities seriously diminished. The fruits of economic development need to be shared more equitably within the state's regions and peoples as well as across regions beyond the nation-state. The alternative would be economic deprivation for the powerless, a phenomenon that has often led to social tension and division within the society, and ultimately insecurity, conflict, and violence.

There is also a political dimension to sustainable development. Erosion of the ecological balance, uneven distribution of the economic pie, neglect or destruction of the rights of peoples, and other negative outcomes of the (mis)management of development results in eventual political decay, contributing to social tension and political turmoil that ties up the resources of the state as it reacts defensively to such challenges, dissipating state resources, fraying the social fabric, undermining the political legitimacy of ruling elites, and leading to violence. That this is at least partially a snapshot of what became the Asian financial crisis, the mirror image of the Asian economic miracle, is generally conceded. What remains in dispute are the appropriate responses more immediately as well as over the longer term.

The emergence of human rights, democratization, and the environment, in addition to economic development and market reforms, as issues in contemporary international relations that challenge the traditions of the inviolability of the sovereign state raises their potentials for engendering tensions and conflict between and among states. Examples within SEA are all too plentiful, not least of course the recent conflict and intervention in East Timor or the earlier hesitant involvement of ASEAN in the putative coup in Cambodia. The diplomatic tensions between the Philippines and Singapore in the mid-1990s must be seen not only in terms of uneven economic development within ASEAN but also in terms of divergences in their conceptions about human rights and democracy, about which Singapore ardently advocates a set of Asian values distinct from those in the West.[22] The protracted multilateral disputes around, in, and under the South China Sea are more than an issue of Chinese-ASEAN relations or bilateral security and defense politics. It is a set of issues that range from classic questions of boundary legitimacy to fundamental concerns about access to and control over the management of fish, mineral, and energy resources, and all the economic, social, and political factors linked with these productive and extractive sectors. Forest fires in Indonesia continue to undermine sustainable development and create threats to the well being of individuals both at home and abroad, thereby creating political demands which require governmental response with the potential for exacerbating relations between states in both bilateral as well as regional terms. Even the seemingly benign decision to allow Taiwanese entrepreneurs to introduce a non-Asian snail into Vietnam for commercial harvesting and sales is evolving into a serious threat to Vietnam's capacity to produce sufficient rice to feed its people. How that will play into the emerging regional interdependencies and competition, including the Mekong River project, remains uncertain but is at least instructive concerning the unintended consequences of economically driven decisions. Furthermore, both these examples (forest fires and snails), depending upon how they are handled, could undermine movement towards democratic and market reforms in various states in the region. Thus, understanding the complex linkages between the processes of development and their implications for the security of individuals at various levels of governance is an urgent imperative of our time, particularly where state-society relations remain biased in favor of the state.

DSSEA: The Research Program

The research was organized around three task force themes – environment, globalization, and people – that had been identified as principal factors in the development-security nexus. Our preference to understand these phenomena at least partially through human security and social capital concepts as a means to balance the privileged position of the state in both the security and development literature informed the selection of specific research projects, with the results of each task force presented in three volumes. The most significant findings and their policy implications are stated in each volume's overview chapter immediately following this one.

The program involved two additional activities beyond the conventional empirical research: echo seminars and a broader outreach effort. Echo seminars were designed to engage member of civil society (including other researchers), and the private sector, as well as local and national officials and politicians. The purpose was both to inform them of our work and to involve them, when possible, as participants. These meetings took place both in capital cities as well as in regional centers in the Philippines and Indonesia, at times drawing in excess of 150 local experts to a single session. Although the impact of these meetings on this initial research phase is difficult to measure, it is evident that the discussions and the ensuing contacts among interested parties has heightened awareness of the issues, stimulated opportunities for more intensive collaboration on future research, and in some locales invigorated policy development and political action. These meetings also made clear the extent to which, in both Indonesia and the Philippines, local activists and researchers have intensive knowledge and intuitive understanding of the security-development linkages, and a strong desire to have a role in policy formulation. Equally clear is the absence of positive dialogue between civil society and both the government and the private sector. The solitudes are striking given the profound long-term consequences and the fact that to address the security-development nexus requires involvement of all the principal stakeholders. Further outreach was undertaken through the regular publication and wide distribution of the *DSSEA Update*, designed to inform the various participants in the program, to engage the wider governmental audience throughout SEA and within ASEAN, and to encourage as well as to facilitate the involvement of civil society.

While both the *DSSEA Update* and our echo seminars were very well received, our three-year program confirmed what conventional wisdom has long asserted: that the differences in perceptions as well as policy preferences and priorities between researchers from universities and the institutions of civil society in Manila and Jakarta and the elites from the political and private sector are striking; and even more so from non-governmental experts and locals from provincial arenas. Although echo seminars often provided very positive encounters between researchers, activists, private sector representatives and government officials, our research tended to confirm the embedded nature of the dilemma: that development as defined by some combination of government policy and private sector interests undermined security as defined by individuals and their communities.

Much of the discourse of disagreement revolved around the different points of departure and of purpose: a government-defined security of national well being and the capacity to deal with threat focused on the harnessing of state capacity, whether in terms of military security or economic security, in support of regime stability. This became increasingly evident in the shadow of the 1997 financial crisis, where domestic political, communal, and economic matters and the importance of regional interstate political and economic relations highlighted the inside/outside duality of managing national security. Security was threatened both by domestic instabilities and by external factors at times beyond the control of the government. On the other hand, locally-defined security was premised on the capacity individuals, families, and communities to ensure well being, to be free of fear and of want, and to find ways to better manage the personal and inter-communal consequences of the intervention of government and the private sector in their daily lives. Whether the issue was the availability of food at fair and constant prices or protection from environmental degradation or the challenges introduced through the phenomenon of globalization, locals understood the multi-layered nature of security even as they were alienated from the process. Their extraordinary vulnerability was exacerbated and highlighted by the incapacity of the government to address the national-level security challenges in the wake of the 1997 financial crisis.

The DSSEA Research Program, begun before the financial crisis, found itself caught up in the spiral of events precipitated by the financial meltdown throughout much of SEA. Though requiring some adjustment by a number of the researchers, what the crisis did offer was a sudden opportunity for fieldwork that could track the local and regional impacts of the ensuing events. The chapters offered in these three volumes present insights into how different sectors of society weathered not only the chronic challenges of development and their impact on facets of security, but how the unanticipated acute changes were managed. To what extent were the local-through-national forces of security able to respond? How did this dramatic economic dislocation that posed fundamental challenges to the political integrity of the governing regimes affect the processes of development, and to what extent did any of this heighten insecurity? How resilient were the political, social, and economic forces that underpin much of the development ethos and are the building blocks of government policy and are reflected in the criteria of performance legitimacy? Do we now know something new about the linkages between development and security because this research program was able, by chance, to factor in the crash of 1997?

Managing the Uncertainty

Even before the 1997 financial crisis, it was evident to scholars and practitioners alike the SEA was in the midst of some profound transformations in state-society relations. Although still struggling with the extremes of wealth and poverty while encumbered by the twin scourges of authoritarian politics and corruption, civil society was increasingly a force for social, economic, and political change, at times challenging but also often in partnership with government and the private sector. Moreover, the forces of globalization along with the actions of regional and global organizations, especially financial institutions, had an ever growing impact on the range of policy options available, while introducing new issues around productive competitiveness and market vulnerability. For most of SEA, this period of economic growth, although not equitably distributed, did usher in a period of heightened expectations and confirmed the model of 'performance legitimacy' as one of the templates by which regime success was assessed.

Yet even at this time the uncertainty of what dramatic economic change could bring was evident in the inability of most governments to address the social dislocations and political discord fostered by the all too often mismanagement of development strategies. From the individual to community through to the state levels, the basic issue should have been how to manage the uncertain outcomes brought forth by the actions of interventionist governments, the role of medium-and large-scale private enterprise, the pervasive results of globalization, and the profound impact of the international financial markets on local conditions. As challenging as all these would have been in more cohesive, well off and structurally-integrated societies, when imposed upon polities which were divided by ethnicity, religion, language, loyalties, and wealth differentials, and already under stress from profound environmentally induced dislocations, the only certainty was insecurity.

The research reported in these three volumes attests to the intimate relationship between the process of development and the perceived sense of well being and security, whether of the individual or the nation. Further, this scholarship identifies the importance of governments recognizing that in their pursuit of wealth (especially if it is linked with more equitable distribution of well being), power, and political stability, taking seriously their obligations to view civil society as partners in development is essential for overall security and even to regime survival, unless the preference is a return to authoritarian or totalitarian rule. To ensure that security is a positive outcome of economic development requires that other aspects of development, including social and political freedoms, were strengthened. Our research testifies to the centrality of this assertion. Whether in land management, agricultural production or resource practices, or the challenges faced by labor in response to the changing nature of globalized competition, development cannot occur solely as an economic phenomenon blind to the issue of its two-sided impact on the individual, the community, or the nation. The improvement of economic well being, as Amartya Sen declared, is not the sole criterion of development; it need not nor should it occur at the cost of individual or community security. Indeed, it should be synonymous with enhancing the security of the nation and its government through the process of empowering citizens and ensuring their well being.

The chapters in these three volumes report on original research undertaken in an effort to better understand the intricate relationship between the human desire for security and, concomitantly, its expression through seeking an improved standard of living. Too often we uncovered examples where the pursuit of economic change as the dominant and clearly too narrow expression of development policies compromised the desire for security. The overview chapters that begin each of these volumes offer a number of insights and policy recommendations which attempt, in a very modest way, to address this tension between the dynamics of development and the desire for security. Though we began this project with an overriding sense of wanting to explore how development intersected with inter-state security, what has emerged from this research is a profound refocusing on the sub-state levels of security as the engine of change. From this perspective, inter-state and regional security can only be strengthened when each national community is secure in its place and its sense of a welcome future. Ironically, this harkens back to the earliest thinking within ASEAN when the ideas of comprehensive security and national resilience as the guides for national development strategies provided a rationale also for arguing the need for each country to pursue these twin goals and, out of that would emerge a secure, stable, and increasingly prosperous region. In some interesting and unanticipated ways, this research project tends to confirm that early intuitive position. Although it is too early to suggest that regional security in fact would be a natural derivative of successful country-by-country development (in the fuller Amartya Sen terms), it is likely that it would allow the dynamics of cooperative security arrangements to emerge as an effective approach to the management of inter-state and inter-regional relations.[23]

Notes

1   The two project co-directors authored a draft paper which set out the assumptions and the conceptual direction of the project. This was revised and published as Acharya, A., Dewitt, D. B., and Hernandez, C. G. (1995), 'Sustainable Development and Security in Southeast Asia: A Concept Paper', *CANCAPS Papier Number 6*, August. Much of the conceptual discussion in this chapter is drawn from this paper though informed by the results of the ensuing research program. In this regard it is a pleasure to acknowledge the ongoing

contributions to our thinking by our academic colleagues in the DSSEA program, and to Brian Hunter, Senior Economist, Asia Pacific Branch, Canadian International Development Agency, who, while supporting our work, actively confronted and challenged us throughout this effort.

2   This language is partially paraphrased from an undated Fall 1999 discussion brief, *Development, Security, and Post-Crisis Reconstruction in Southeast Asia*, prepared by Pierre Lizee as he responded to our request for DSSEA researchers to reflect on this project.

3   Sen, A. (1999), *Development as Freedom*, Alfred A. Knopf, New York, pp.3.

4   Amartya Sen explores these issues in much detail. See his *Development as Freedom*.

5   These five were joined by the admission of Brunei Darussalam in 1984 and then in 1995 Vietnam was admitted and in 1997 Laos and Myanmar, followed in 1998 by Cambodia. See Acharya, A. (2001), *Constructing a Security Community in Southeast Asia*, Routledge, London.

6   While useful as political rhetoric and ideological orthodoxy in Indonesia's and ASEAN's formative years of nation-building and regional consolidation, comprehensive security and resilience clearly fell to the forces of revisionism, fundamentalism, corruption, mismanagement of development, and economic inequities most recently and cruelly seen both in the East Timor struggle and the protracted domestic violence and ongoing expressions of secessionism or autonomy. Nevertheless, in principle these ideas of comprehensive security and national resilience so widely shared among the original five ASEAN partners afford a clear and well-reasoned statement about the inherent linkages between economic progress, well being, governance, regional cooperation, and security.

7   We are not offering any judgement on the validity of these assertions, nor on any causal connections these might have with the political, social, or economic realities which are the histories of the countries and communities of contemporary Southeast Asia. Rather, the point here is to identify the security-relevant doctrines and ideologies which have been articulated and employed by the leaders of these countries as they faced the challenges of nation-building and regime survival.

8   Malaysian Prime Minister Mahathir Mohamad as cited in Acharya, *Constructing a Security Community in Southeast Asia*, 2001, pp.4.

9   For an overview of these ideas see Dewitt, D. B. (1994), 'Common, Comprehensive, and Cooperative Security in Asia Pacific', *The Pacific Review*, vol. 7, no.1.

10 United Nations Development Program (UNDP) (1994), *Human Development Report 1994*, Oxford University Press, New York.

11 Department of Foreign Affairs and International Trade (1999), *Human Security: Safety for People in a Changing World*, Government of Canada, April, pp.5.

12 For a most interesting statement on human security, see Almonte, J. T. (2000), *A Human Agenda for ASEAN*, remarks drawn from his presentation at the 'Inaugural Meeting of the ASEAN People's Assembly', Batam Island, Indonesia, 24-26 November 2000, distributed as *PacNet 1*, 5 January 2001, CISIS/Pacific Forum, Honolulu.

13 The World Commission on Environment and Development (1987), *Our Common Future*, Oxford University Press, Oxford, chapter 1.

14 *Ibid.*, chapter 11, did address aspects of the relationship between development, peace, conflict, and security. A more recent statement by the principal author of the Brundtland Report is MacNeill, J. (1989), 'Strategies for Sustainable Economic Development', *Scientific American* 261, September; also in still more developed form, see MacNeill, J., Winsemius, P., and Yakushiji, T. (1991), *Beyond Interdependence: The Meshing of the World's Economy and the Earth's Ecology*, Oxford University Press, New York. See also Holmberg, J., Bass, S., and Timberlake, L. (1991), *Defending the Future: A Guide to Sustainable Development*, International Institute for Environment and Development,

London. Among the earlier pieces which challenged the cold war definition of security, see Ullman, R. H. (1983), 'Redefining Security', *World Politics*, vol.8, no.1; and Mathews J. T. (1989), 'Redefining National Security', *Foreign Affairs*, vol.68, no.2, Spring. An important contribution to this literature was an article which provided the first public report of a large and ongoing research program exploring the causal connections between environment and conflict; see Homer-Dixon, T. (1991), 'On the Threshold: Environmental Changes as Causes of Acute Conflict', *International Security*, vol.16, no.2, Fall.

15 For a view which clearly challenges the now orthodox view of sustainable development as expressed in *Our Common Future* as well as *Agenda 21*, see Crovitz, L. G. (1994), *The Asian Manager: Asian Imperatives and Western Perspectives in Sustainable Development*, a paper presented at the 'Asian Institute of Management Conference', Manila, Philippines, 17 February 1994.

16 For relatively early statements which foreshadowed much of this, see Lonergan, S. (1994), *Environmental Change and Regional Security in Southeast Asia*, Project Report No. PR 659, Directorate of Strategic Analysis, Ottawa, March; and Myers, N. (1993), *Ultimate Security: The Environmental Basis of Political Stability*, W. W. Norton, New York; and MacNeill, *et. al.*, (1991), 'Environmental refugees' has become a significant factor of both cross-border and internal tensions and conflict in many parts of Eastern Asia, both north and south.

17 Harris, S. (1994), 'Enhancing Security: Non-Military Means and Measures II', in B. Nagara and K.S. Balakrishnan (eds), *The Making of A Security Community in the Asia-Pacific*, ISIS Malaysia, Kuala Lumpur, pp.191.

18 MacNeill, J. (1991), 'Strategies for Sustainable Economic Development', chapter 10.

19 See a superbly focussed discussion on this issue by Jones, S. 'Promoting Human Rights', in Nagara and Balakrishnan (eds), *The Making of a Security Community*, 1994, pp.344-46.

20 MacNeill, *et. al.*, *Beyond Interdependence: The Meshing of the World's Economy and the Earth's Ecology*, 1991, pp.23.

21 There is a growing literature, some anecdotal but much increasingly scientific, which describes and begins the difficult process of explaining the causal relationships between environment, ecology, economic development, land tenure, social construction, displacement, violence, etc. In addition to the previous citations, see for example, Homer-Dixon, T. F. (1999), *Environment, Scarcity, and Violence*, Princeton University Press, Princeton, N.J.; Kaplan, R. (1994), 'The Coming Anarchy', *The Atlantic*, February; Homer-Dixon, T. F., Boutwell, J. H. and Rathjens, G. W. (1993), 'Environmental Change and Violent Conflict', *Scientific American*, February; Homer-Dixon, T. F. (1994), 'Across the Threshold: Empirical Evidence on Environmental Scarcities as Causes of Violent Conflict', *International Security*, Summer; Homer-Dixon, T. F. (1994), 'The Ingenuity Gap: Can Poor Countries Adapt to Resource Scarcity?', University of Toronto ms., April; Ruckelshaus, W. D. (1989), 'Toward a Sustainable World', *Scientific American* 261, September; and Westing, A.H. (ed.) (1986), *Global Resources and International Conflict: Environmental Factors in Strategic Policy and Action*, Oxford University Press, New York. On the important issue of maritime environments, see, for example, Townsend-Gault, I. (1994), 'Testing the Waters: Making Progress in the South China Sea', *Harvard International Review*, Spring; and his *Ocean Diplomacy, International Law, and the South China Sea*, preliminary draft paper presented at the 'Eighth Asia Pacific Roundtable', Kuala Lumpur, June 1994; and 'Part IV: SLOCs and Maritime Security', in Nagara and Balakrishnan (eds) (1994), *The Making of a Security Community*.

22 Hernandez, C. G. (1995), *ASEAN Perspectives on Human Rights and Democracy in International Relations: Divergencies, Commonalities, Problems, and Prospects*, Center for Integrative and Development Studies, University of the Philippines, Quezon City.

23 One can consider the difficulties which the expanded ASEAN-10 now faces as evidence of what continued national asymmetries coupled with substantial domestic underdevelopment and insecurity within a number of Southeast Asian countries can do to any efforts to create an improved sense of security or consolidate a more effective regional mechanism to manage uncertainty.

References

Acharya, A. (2001), *Constructing a Security Community in Southeast Asia*, Routledge, London.

Acharya, A., Dewitt, D. B., and Hernandez, C. G. (1995), 'Sustainable Development and Security in Southeast Asia: A Concept Paper', *CANCAPS Papier Number 6*, August.

Almonte, J. T. (2000), *A Human Agenda for ASEAN*, paper presented at the 'Inaugural Meeting of the ASEAN People's Assembly', Batam Island, Indonesia, 24-26 November 2000, distributed as *PacNet 1*, 5 January 2001, CSIS/Pacific Forum, Honolulu.

Crovitz, L. G. (1994), *The Asian Manager: Asian Imperatives and Western Perspectives in Sustainable Development*, paper presented at the 'Asian Institute of Management Conference', Manila, Philippines, 17 February 1994.

Department of Foreign Affairs and International Trade (1999), *Human Security: Safety for People in a Changing World*, Department of Foreign Affairs and International Trade, Government of Canada, April, pp.5.

Dewitt, D. B. (1994), 'Common, Comprehensive, and Cooperative Security in Asia Pacific', *The Pacific Review*, vol. 7, no. 1.

Harris, S. (1994), 'Enhancing Security: Non-Military Means and Measures II', in B. Nagara and K.S. Balakrishnan (eds), *The Making of A Security Community in the Asia-Pacific*, ISIS Malaysia, Kuala Lumpur, pp. 191.

Hernandez, C. G. (1995), *ASEAN Perspectives on Human Rights and Democracy in International Relations: Divergencies, Commonalities, Problems, and Prospects*, Center for Integrative and Development Studies, University of the Philippines, Quezon City.

Holmberg, J., Bass, S., and Timberlake, L. (1991), *Defending the Future: A Guide to Sustainable Development*, International Institute for Environment and Development, London.

Homer-Dixon, T. F. (1991), 'On the Threshold: Environmental Changes as Causes of Acute Conflict', *International Security*, vol. 16, no. 2, Fall.

Homer-Dixon, T. F. (1994a), 'Across the Threshold: Empirical Evidence on Environmental Scarcities as Causes of Violent Conflict', *International Security*, Summer.

Homer-Dixon, T.F. (1994b), *The Ingenuity Gap: Can Poor Countries Adapt to Resource Scarcity?*, University of Toronto ms., April.

Homer-Dixon, T. F. (1999c), *Environment, Scarcity, and Violence*, Princeton University Press, Princeton, N.J.

Homer-Dixon, T. F., Boutwell, J. H. and Rathjens, G. W. (1993), 'Environmental Change and Violent Conflict', *Scientific American*, February.

Jones, S. 'Promoting Human Rights', in B. Nagara and K.S. Balakrishnan (eds), *The Making of A Security Community in the Asia-Pacific*, ISIS Malaysia, Kuala Lumpur, pp.344-46.

Lonergan, S. (1994), *Environmental Change and Regional Security in Southeast Asia*, Project Report No. PR 659, Directorate of Strategic Analysis, Ottawa, March.

MacNeill, J. (1989), 'Strategies for Sustainable Economic Development', *Scientific American*, no. 261, September.

MacNeill, J., Winsemius, P., and Yakushiji, T. (1991), *Beyond Interdependence: The Meshing of the World's Economy and the Earth's Ecology*, Oxford University Press, New York.

Mathews J. T. (1989), 'Redefining National Security', *Foreign Affairs*, vol. 68, no. 2, Spring.

Myers, N. (1993), *Ultimate Security: The Environmental Basis of Political Stability*, W.W. Norton, New York.

Ruckelshaus, W. D. (1989), 'Toward a Sustainable World', *Scientific American*, no. 261, September.

Sen, A. (1999), *Development as Freedom*, Alfred A. Knopf, New York, pp.3.

The World Commission on Environment and Development (1987), *Our Common Future*, Oxford University Press, Oxford.

Townsend-Gault, I. (1994a), *Ocean Diplomacy, International Law, and the South China Sea*, preliminary draft paper presented at the 'Eighth Asia Pacific Roundtable', Kuala Lumpur, June 1994.

Townsend-Gault, I. (1994b), 'Part IV: SLOCs and Maritime Security', in B. Nagara and K.S. Balakrishnan (eds), *The Making of A Security Community in the Asia-Pacific*, ISIS Malaysia, Kuala Lumpur.

Ullman, R. H. (1983), 'Redefining Security', *World Politics*, vol. 8, no. 1.

United Nations Development Programme (UNDP) (1994), *Human Development Report 1994*, Oxford University Press, New York.

Westing, A. H. (ed.) (1986), *Global Resources and International Conflict: Environmental Factors in Strategic Policy and Action*, Oxford University Press, New York.

Chapter 2

Globalization, Development, and Security in Southeast Asia: An Overview

Hadi Soesastro

Globalization as a Response to Globalization

Globalization is not a new phenomenon. The world has experienced several waves of globalization over the past few centuries. While this may be true, globalization is a process that cannot be taken for granted. Even developed countries and established societies feel compelled to look for ways to enable them to deal effectively with the 'new globalism', as characterized by the rise in the importance and influence of international financial markets.[1]   For the countries in Southeast Asia (SEA), globalization definitely is a totally new experience. All Southeast Asian countries, with the exception of Thailand, are young nation-states, having gained independence only within the past half a century. For these countries, the integrity of the nation-state is a primary concern. Globalization is seen as posing a major challenge, often even perceived as posing a threat, to the integrity of these young nation-states. However, the older members of Association of Southeast Asian Nations (ASEAN), the main regional vehicle that brings together all ten Southeast Asian nations, have not sealed themselves off from the present wave of *economic globalization.* They have been more cautious with respect to globalization in the cultural, social, and political fields. The older ASEAN members refer to Brunei, Indonesia, Malaysia, the Philippines, Singapore, and Thailand. To different degrees, these countries are participants in today's economic globalization process. In fact, it can be argued that until the onset of the financial crisis in 1997 they have been among the *active* participants in economic globalization.

Various indicators have been used to describe an economy's degree or depth of integration into the world economy. For instance, the World Bank's (WB) index of integration consists of four components, namely the ratio of trade to gross domestic product (GDP); a creditworthiness rating; the ratio of foreign direct investment (FDI) to GDP; and the share of manufactured goods to total exports. According to this measure, Malaysia and Singapore have the highest index of integration among the Southeast Asian countries. Thailand has shown the most rapid rise in its integration index during the decade until the mid-1990s. The older members of ASEAN have seen much improvement in all four components of the index. However, the most remarkable development has been in the continuing increase of the ratio of trade to GDP and the share of manufactured goods in total exports. Vietnam, one of the new members of ASEAN, which has begun to open up its economy about a decade ago has followed closely the pattern of its ASEAN neighbors.

In all these countries, it was not the business community that has been at the forefront of the globalization process. Rather, the governments have been the initiator and promoter of economic globalization as they adopt policies aimed at integrating their economies into the world economy, initially through export-oriented development, supported by an increased use of FDIs. Gradually they began to open up their home markets for goods and services. This is a familiar story by now and needs no further elaboration. What has often been overlooked is the fact that this policy of globalization has been pursued in tandem with a policy for promoting regional economic cooperation. The wisdom of doing so rests on the belief that each member would be better off by joining forces with other regional economies in the effort to integrate its economy into the world economy rather than to go it alone. Hence, economic regionalism in SEA has been outward oriented rather than inward oriented. Given that Southeast Asian countries trade mostly with countries outside the region, with intra-Southeast Asian trade accounting for no more than one-fifth of the region's total trade, it is only logical that they have adopted the concept of 'open regionalism'.

Southeast Asian countries have pursued their economic globalization by liberalizing their economies, each at a different pace, either being guided by their commitments in the World Trade Organization (WTO) or Asia Pacific Economic Cooperation (APEC) or ASEAN Free Trade Area (AFTA). The AFTA agreement has spelled out end dates for achieving a free trade area with import tariffs being reduced to zero to five per cent for most items. The newer members of ASEAN have been given a longer time frame. Some ASEAN countries have introduced a policy of subsequently multilateralizing their AFTA tariff preferences, i.e., to apply the lower tariffs to non-ASEAN countries as well, a policy that clearly reflects the principle of open regionalism. Of course, implementation of these policies has not been as smooth as often portrayed. In each country, the governments are faced with opposition to liberalizing the economy from various interest groups. In many of these countries, the powerful interest groups are those with close connection to the government itself. With 'crony capitalism' encroaching into the 'developmental state', internal resistance tends to become stronger and more difficult to dismantle. These interest groups have a way of sealing themselves off from the effects of globalization that they do not like, although this cannot always be effective. The political economy of protection and protectionism takes on a different nature in different societies. An 'effective' state can resist pressures from domestic as well as international interest groups. Regional arrangements become all the more desirable if they can help contain pressures from domestic interest groups. At the other end, it is almost universally the case that weaker, marginalized, groups in society cannot make their voices heard and they have no muscle to influence government policy.

An earlier examination of ASEAN members' globalization policy shows that governments, as initiators and promoters of the policy, have given attention and efforts mostly to the so-called 'first-order' adjustments.[2] First-order adjustments involve the process of opening up the economy to the forces of globalization. These adjustments are undertaken to enhance the economy's international competitiveness, which they believe is a prerequisite for taking part in and fully benefiting from globalization. These first-order adjustments include policies that are aimed primarily at increasing the attractiveness of the ASEAN economies as a production platform for the global market. Until the onset of the crisis, it is generally believed that these countries have been rather successful in undertaking their first-order adjustments. But they have been less successful in undertaking 'second-order' adjustments, namely in coping with domestic economic, social, and political changes that come as a consequence of economic opening up, which affect perceptions and conditions of security at various levels, the individual, the community, the state, as well as the region. However, this disappointing record in undertaking second-order adjustments has been overshadowed by the hyper-growth macroeconomic 'miracle'. In a sense, the financial crisis has been a blessing in disguise as it has helped to reveal the many shortcomings of the development policies pursued by the Southeast Asian countries. In fact, as will be discussed later, much more has been revealed and this revelation points to the need for a total rethinking of 'development' and 'security'.

This brief excursion provides the background for the research on the links between globalization, development, and security that has been undertaken under the Development and Security in Southeast Asia (DSSEA) project. The Globalization Sub-group of the research has taken the following understanding as points of departure:

1. Southeast Asian countries believe that they can benefit from participating in the economic globalization process. They have consciously adopted globalization policies. Thus, globalization is understood as both an evolving *structural condition* of the world economy and a *conscious national policy* (Amitav Acharya) or as both a *description* of a state of affairs and a *prescription* for strategy and policy (Rizal Sukma). In SEA, globalization (as a policy or strategy) is largely seen as a response to globalization (as a condition or state of affairs).

2. The governments have been at the forefront in the globalization process; they are the main initiators and promoters of the policy of economic globalization. In other words, globalization in SEA tends to be state-led. Governments believe that involvement in economic globalization would enhance economic deliveries by the state (regime) that in turn would strengthen the legitimacy of the state (regime).

3. The policy of globalization has been pursued in tandem with, perhaps supported by, the policy of strengthening regional economic cooperation, also promoted by governments. Governments have encouraged and facilitated the involvement of the business sector but they attempt to maintain control over the nature of economic interactions and transactions through various regional inter-governmental schemes.

4. In pursuing the globalization policy, governments have given attention mostly to 'first-order' domestic adjustments—the process of economic opening up with the main objective of increasing international economic competitiveness.

5. They have not given sufficient attention, beyond the rhetoric, to the need to undertake 'second-order' adjustments, namely to cope with domestic economic, social and political changes that have come about as the country undertakes economic globalization. This suggests that globalization as a response to globalization has been pursued only partially.

The financial crisis unfolded while the research was undertaken. This gives additional insights into the fundamental problems of globalization, even though the crisis is not caused solely by globalization. As a result of the crisis, in some Southeast Asian countries serious questions have been raised about the benefits of economic globalization. Some have argued that the appropriate policy now should be one of 'de-globalization'.[3] Malaysia's Prime Minister has introduced selective short-term capital controls with the aim of sealing off the economy from the volatility of short-term capital movements. This policy has been ridiculed at the beginning but may have brought about some qualified success, at least in the short term. Yet rather than retreating from globalization, the region as a whole is officially still on track towards greater economic integration into the world economy. In fact, as a way to overcoming the crisis ASEAN economic and finance ministers have renewed their pledge to continue with economic liberalization, including in the financial sector. Simon Tay has proposed a reorientation from a 'globalization from above' to a 'globalization from below'.[4] This is a relevant point in SEA where globalization has been initiated and promoted mainly by governments largely for the benefit of the state rather than its citizens.

There is greater recognition, however, that economic liberalization cannot be left to chance, but needs to be pursued in accordance with some blueprint about the appropriate sequencing of the liberalization. In addition, indicators of economic performance can no longer be confined to traditional macroeconomic fundamentals but will have to take into account such factors as legal certainty, public and corporate governance, and even involvement in regional cooperation. These are now included in the concept of 'enhanced fundamentals' of an economy.[5] Furthermore, it has become clear that consistent and coherent economic policies are key to maintaining market confidence, which in a globalized world plays an important role in the successful performance of an economy. These have been the main economic lessons of the current economic and financial crisis and should be taken seriously by the Southeast Asian countries in their continued participation in the globalization process. The crisis has also shown that the absence of sufficient social safety nets and effective social policies has aggravated the human misery and the adverse impact of the economic crisis on human security, especially of the weak and the poor.

From an economic perspective, the most immediate challenge for policy is in the area of international financial management that addresses problems of exchange rate policy and capital account management at the national or regional level as well as issues of a new international financial architecture. The basic issue, or more precisely dilemma, for national policy is clearly expressed in the so-called 'impossible trinity' of simultaneously achieving a high degree of sovereignty, financial stability, and abundant capital inflows. Hence, nations must decide on the kind of trade-off that they are willing to make. If regional cooperation can effectively overcome sovereignty problems, countries can better assure inflows of capital while maintaining stability. Southeast Asian countries will sooner or later be confronted with the need to make a decision on this issue. They can opt to each go on their own or decide to work together. In choosing the latter option, they will need to give up the principle of maintaining absolute national sovereignty. This will not be an easy decision as many

ASEAN members still strongly believe that ASEAN is essentially a 'sovereignty-enhancing' regional arrangement.

Maria Soccoro Gochoco-Bautista, the only other economist in Globalization Sub-group, consisting of 10 researchers, has examined the problems of financial liberalization in the Philippines in great depth, showing why the monetary authorities failed to adopt a consistent and coherent exchange rate policy. The main point of the study is to show the importance of good governance and the acceptance of market discipline when tapping global financial markets. This requirement is not easily fulfilled as the state, in its attempt to deliver on its economic goals, by regaining control over aspects of economic policy which globalization seems to have taken away, tends to resort to the use of state powers rather than market methods. In many instances, the state has given in to pressures from big business. Financial management issues are much more remote to the public than, for instance, environmental or employment issues. Thus, financial policy tends to be dominated by a very small group in the society. Yet, in the globalized world financial instability has become a major threat to human security. How, then, can the people, or civil society in particular, take part in the discourse on financial matters?

Financial matters will be high in the regional and national economic agenda in the years to come. They pose a major challenge to development and security policies. However, bigger challenges are perhaps to be found in the political and social fields. Political scientists and students/experts on international relations in the Globalization Sub-group author the other chapters in this volume. Leonora C. Angeles has focused her analysis on the impact of the globalization of production on the welfare and security of Filipino workers, especially female workers, in export manufacturing industries. She raised the concern that the globalization of production tends to transform states into 'entrepreneurial agents' that are overly concerned with maintaining favorable business climate for international capital by curbing the activities of labor unions and other social movements. How can this tendency be counterbalanced?

The critical literature on globalization sees this process essentially as one that serves the interests of capital and the capitalist class. According to this view, globalization has dramatically changed the relation of states to the international economy. Previously states could be seen as gatekeepers, insulating the domestic economy from the negative influences of the international economy. At present, the policies of the state have been reduced to those of entrepreneurial agents transmitting the exigencies of the globalizing economy of international production onto the domestic economy. Is a reorientation towards policies of insulation a viable option? In a negative sense, this reorientation would involve a return to inward-oriented policies. In a more positive sense, Vervoorn defines 'insulation' as a strategy for regaining control over personal or local affairs lost through globalization.[6] Angeles seems to support such a positive view of insulation. She argues that as developing countries and late industrializers try to ride on the wave of production globalization, a host of policies and measures need to be adopted. These include social capital building and improvement of governance. In essence, it requires democratization of the political environment.

A third study on the Philippines documents and explains the process of differentiation of perception and response to globalization, economic liberalization, and industrialization on the part of the popular movements and non-elite groups. Amado Mendoza, Jr. has shown that various groups from among the popular movements have adjusted to the economic reforms undertaken as part of the structural adjustment programs under the auspices of the International Monetary Fund (IMF). These groups have 'constructively engaged' the government to make the reform process a humane, pro-poor one. They also have been able to extract commitments from the government to adopt policies in favor of sustainable development and gender equity. They have skillfully used international initiatives on environment, development, population, human rights, and gender to obtain these governmental commitments. Within non-elites, there is a diversity of perception of the impact of globalization and economic liberalization on their security. However, they see initiatives such land conversion processes that threaten the livelihood and viability of rural communities or infrastructure projects that displace urban poor communities as 'development aggression' in that development creates a threat to the human security of individuals, families, neighborhoods, and local communities.

The two case studies of Indonesia focus on the political consequences of the economic globalization process. Rizal Sukma discusses the security *problematique* of globalization and development facing the Indonesian state. The attempt by the state to seek material gains from economic globalization may help the state to retain its role as the principal agent of development. This role is crucial for the state as it helps sustain the security and legitimacy of the regime. However, economic globalization may bring about such political consequences as manifested in the rise of new groups in the society that demand greater political participation, and the absorption of new ideas such as human rights. The financial crisis in Indonesia has deepened and has turned into a severe economic crisis and a political crisis of unprecedented proportion because of mishandling and serious lack of good governance. In essence, it was a failure on the part of the regime to undertake the necessary political reform to cope with the non-economic challenges of globalization. This situation, as Sukma sees it, clearly shows that Indonesia has failed miserably in its struggle to cope with the globalization process. Its inability to manage and cope with the social and political consequences of economic globalization has resulted in the weakening of regime legitimacy, the collapse of the political order, and the breakdown of security at all levels—regime security, societal security, and even personal security. This was clearly evident during 1998 and 1999 until the formation of the new government under the democratically elected Abdurrachman Wahid.

While the abrupt change in government has opened up the way for a democratic transition, Sukma argues that this will not automatically lead to democratic consolidation. Post-Soeharto Indonesia is in a delicate process of negotiation among various contending political forces that in the end could result in either a return to authoritarianism or democratic consolidation. A more frightening prospect is the progressive deterioration in the social and political situation of the country that results in a 'failed' state. A clear lesson can be drawn from the rapid deterioration experienced in Indonesia: that regime security in the name of development, but at the expense of political participation, risks producing a failed state.

In the Indonesian context, as shown by Kusnanto Anggoro, this nexus of development and regime security has been reinforced by the dominant role of the military in political life within the concept of its dual function. Nation building and state building have become the most important objectives that the military has committed itself to defend. As stated by Anggoro, it is natural to expect that national integrity, state authority, and regime legitimacy are most prominent in military thinking of national security and have become the obsession of the military. The threat to national security as visualized by the military occupies a whole spectrum of dangers. A most recent addition to this list is 'global interaction'. Indonesia's latest Defense White Paper points to the need to take globalization into the country's strategic calculation. It is not specific in identifying what globalization entails beyond stating that it is an external dynamic that influences internal politics. Captured by its own understanding of the development and security nexus, the military accepts the benefits from economic globalization while it is extremely suspicious about the non-economic aspects of globalization. With the financial crisis, the military has become more cautious about globalization in general as it strongly subscribes to some of the most ridiculous conspiracy theories about the causes of the crisis. Until then, it has adopted, what Anggoro calls, a 'flexible response' to globalization. Yet, while they support the government's policy of economic globalization they are not sure what to do about non-economic globalization. On that, they have resorted to the use of rhetoric but if this fails to meet their objective they have not hesitated to use force. The era of political reform in Indonesia has challenged the military's dual function. Developments in the past few years, however, show that the military may be the institution in the country that has the most difficulty adjusting to changes. Therefore, democratic consolidation in Indonesia is not necessarily around the corner.

The failure of the military in Indonesia to adjust to changes can be traced back to its inability to participate in discourse on many new concepts and ideas. One powerful concept and idea that has spread across the globe as globalization advances is human rights. Its rapid spread can only be understood to mean that indeed it is a universal idea. It is a concept, as is globalization, which will have significant bearing on the development and security nexus as perceived by governments and the ruling elite in many Southeast Asian countries. Herman Kraft's chapter addresses the pertinent question of whose security is the state advancing—that of the regime or that of the people—in the context of the human rights discourse in the region. He rightly points out that in many developing countries, human rights policies are framed within the development and security nexus where the focus is on the survival of the state by enhancing the stature of the regime in power with its citizens. In turn, this sows the seeds of political dissent, which is not tolerated by the state.

The security of the regime is still a powerful argument for protection against the forces of globalization and democratization. Globalization can be used as an excuse to strengthen a country's political identity and integrity, which often translates into an authoritarian, paternalistic—essentially a non-democratic—system. The promotion of 'Asian values' by some leaders in SEA some time ago can be seen as an attempt to justify adopting an open economic policy but maintain heavy state control over political, social, and cultural developments. However, it is exactly the lack of democratic political institutions and stalled democratization that often become serious obstacles for resolving internal communal conflicts in a non-violent manner.

Pierre Lizée addresses this issue by pointing to the somewhat paradoxical impact of globalization on issues of conflict and conflict resolution. Any 'peace building' effort must equate the pursuit of peace with that of democratization. Globalizing dynamics challenge the validity of the state as a site of political affiliation and, to that extent, they undermine the legitimacy of the very structures through which democratization can be pursued and developed. He further contends that globalization often invites as a reaction the reconstruction of social identities around communal lines that hamper the development of a system of rights of the individual and, consequently, that of democracy. Lizée makes the point that international (or regional) peace-building efforts and operations are at the intersections of these two contradictory tendencies. They reflect the consensus of the international community on the need to help societies, torn by protracted conflict, reach a new social contract able to foster some measure of justice and democracy. However, these efforts take place in an environment shaped by the global forces that often act as obstacles to that very goal. The case study on the international intervention in Cambodia in early 1990s shows the difficulties encountered during that operation that have a bearing on the way operations of social reconstruction should be conducted. International efforts in East Timor at present can still go wrong both because of the way in which Indonesia has left that territory but also because of a serious lack of internal mechanisms within the local East Timor communities to settle their differences in a non-violent manner. There have been calls for greater efforts by regional actors, such as ASEAN, to help settle conflicts in their own backyard. It is yet not clear how far ASEAN will take up the challenge of initiating peace-building efforts in East Timor. If and when it does, it will have to link peace-building and democracy-building. Lizée shows that 'constructive intervention' can work. The two concepts of social capital and human security can provide a framework through which ASEAN can articulate a coherent and effective peace-building doctrine in this context.

In fact, this concept can be extended to ASEAN cooperation in general beyond efforts to help resolve internal conflicts. This will require a change of mindset on the part of ASEAN leaders. The challenge faced by ASEAN to change its institutional culture, described as 'the 'ASEAN way', in order to meet the challenges of globalization, is the focus of David Capie's paper. Based on the idea of 'sovereignty-enhancing regionalism', the ASEAN way has thus far proved to be resilient to the economic and political forces unleashed by globalization. The new members of ASEAN appear to be at the forefront in defending this kind of regionalism although some older conservative members are also hesitant to allow ideas of constructive intervention to seep into the organization. It remains to be seen how ASEAN can sustain its sovereignty-enhancing regionalism if this means an extension to the region of the protection of state sovereignty, which in practical terms is none other than the security of the regime. This is analogous to the extension of national import-substitution protectionist policies to the region through the establishment of a discriminatory regional free trade area or a customs union.

It is legitimate for ASEAN countries to resort to regional cooperation arrangements to reassert the power of the state in coping with the social and economic impacts of globalization, especially to protect the poor and the weak. The state must have the capability to develop, manage, and secure the financing of social safety net programs. However, this reassertion of power by the state through regional cooperation can often be misused to protect the state from the need to open up politically. Regional cooperation must not reinforce the *prevailing structure* of the development and security nexus that tends to justify and sustain authoritarian regimes.

The research on regional responses to globalization contained in this volume points to the potential role of regional arrangements in SEA and the wider Asia Pacific region (for example, APEC) to influencing the nexus between development and security. Amitav Acharya's chapter takes a cut at the linkage between development and security at the regional level and examines how globalization, as manifested in greater economic interdependence, and the recent Asian crisis are impinging upon regional security. The author argues that a rethinking of globalization in the region that has been prompted by the dramatic political and security impact of the Asian economic crisis will lead to the formulation of economic policies more sensitive to political and security considerations. Yet at the same time he also observes that globalization can have the effect of empowering the forces of democratization within the societies. This will enhance regional peace and stability as regional cooperation moves away from being an exclusively state-centric and elite-driven process to one that has a broader social basis.

Policy Recommendations

1. **The state needs to redefine the nexus between development and security, away from one that is of a state-centric nature.**
   The Globalization Sub-group of the DSSEA project concludes that the globalization process has very significant implications on development and security in the region. Globalization, narrowly defined, refers to economic globalization, namely the integration of global markets, whereas globalization in its broadest sense involves cultural, social, and political influences as well. Indeed, in formulating the project outline it immediately became clear that globalization, even in its narrow sense alone, creates complex policy problems for both development and security in developing societies, especially where state building and nation building are seen as uncompleted tasks.

The state continues to play a dominant role in the national development process and the security of the state is regarded as the most important prerequisite for the nation's integrity. Thus, the first task of inquiry is to examine the effects of globalization on the policies and behavior of the state in addressing development and security problems and challenges. The dominant concept of development and security in most of SEA is state-centric. The linkage between development and security in such developing societies as in SEA at present still rests with the (dominant) role and position of the state. How will globalization affect this development and security nexus? Will it weaken the role of the state in development and at the same time help dismantle its monopoly over national security? Or will it instead further reinforce the state's dominant position as it reasserts itself in the wake of the perceived 'threat' of globalization? Will this create greater incompatibilities in the pursuit of state security and human security, namely the security of its citizens?

Herman Kraft in his chapter rightly points out that the 'duality' of security and development in SEA is a historical legacy of the fragile post-colonial state structures that emerged in the wake of the Second World War. In some countries, this experience has been more traumatic than in others. Indonesia, for example, had gone through a period of secessionist movements, separatism, insurgencies, and ideological, ethnic, and religious conflicts for the first 20 years of its existence. State building and nation building have become the main preoccupation of the state. Security came to be defined strictly in terms of state building and nation building. During this period and even beyond that, the national security agenda of consolidating the state formed the core of the national agenda. The state set this agenda and defined all the parameters of national security that equated national security with the security of the state, and subsequently, the security of the regime. Tolerance for political dissent was low or totally absent. In the Indonesian case, the second traumatic event of the mid-1960s led to the recognition of the need for and importance of economic development. The disregard of and failure in undertaking economic development was seen as the most fertile ground for unrest, insurgencies, and other movements to challenge the legitimacy of the state.

The concept of *comprehensive security* was introduced to incorporate development as a major component of security. In this manner, development got defined within a state-centric security agenda. The state becomes the main, if not the sole, agent of development. The concept of the developmental state, adopted in most of East Asia, further reinforced the dominance of the state. The need for order and security in order to be able to pursue development has produced the much-heralded 'virtuous circle' of development-security-development. However, the belief in this virtuous circle has also created a 'vicious circle' of a state-centric development and security nexus.

2. **To be able to effectively ride on the wave of globalization, there is no substitute to strengthening domestic and local institutions as well as domestic political reforms.**
   Globalization can affect both that virtuous circle and the vicious circle in the development and security nexus. National economic development that increasingly relies and taps on the global economy through the broadening and deepening of economic integration becomes subject to volatile and increasingly autonomous movements in the global economy. The vulnerability of and the risks faced by the national economy depend upon the strength and health of domestic institutions as well as involvement in regional and international arrangements. Economic development based on the policy of globalization bears great costs if insufficient adjustments are made. Many countries in SEA have failed to undertake 'second-order' adjustments.

Rodrik has called this the second stage of reform, essentially pointing to the need for political and social reform that would help create effective institutions of conflict management.[7]   These institutions are a necessary complement to economic globalization. There is also the need to improve channels through which non-elites can make themselves heard and to bring them into decision-making councils. Furthermore, the provision of social insurance (social safety nets) is an equally important component of economic globalization. Finally, the economic globalization policy that Southeast Asian countries are likely to pursue cannot achieve popular legitimacy unless they are perceived to be the result of a broader deliberation at the national level. Political participation is key to this process. The virtuous circle involving the mutual reinforcement of development and security can only be maintained if second-order adjustments or the second stage of reform is successfully undertaken. This being the case, the vicious circle of a state-centric development and security nexus can be broken, with development and security becoming more oriented towards the people.

Two questions need to be raised here. The first is perhaps rather semantic in nature but can be important conceptually. Is it correct to continue to talk in terms of first- or second-order adjustments or first or second stage of reforms, suggesting that there is a sequencing that begins with economic development and reform before undertaking political and social development and reform? This so-called 'grand sequencing' may be a fallacious concept.[8] Yet, how can economic and political reform be undertaken simultaneously without creating chaos as has happened in Russia? This relates to the second question of how this state-centric development and security nexus can be transformed smoothly and peacefully into a people-oriented one. Globalization can positively influence this transformation but the key to success is the presence of local actors.

Globalization has led the state to cede a greater role to the business sector in the development process. The process of economic liberalization, deregulation, and privatization since the early 1980s in SEA has provided a greater space for the business sector. This serves the state and regime well as the more active involvement of the business sector, local and international, helps sustain economic growth and in turn strengthen their legitimacy. At the same time, there is always a strong tendency on the part of the leadership to maintain control over the business community. A kind of collusion evolves in which the regime or political leadership provides privileges to groups of businesses who in turn would be committed to help uphold the regime. In the course of the development, independent business entities are being squeezed out. The emergence of crony capitalism in the region has its origins in the interest of the state to maintain political control over the business sector and to control the financial resources of the business sector. As the international business has much greater leverage than local business *vis-à-vis* the government, a more mutually beneficial relationship obtains as governments adopt more friendly policies towards FDIs and the operation of multinational enterprises. But this greater leverage is not often used to support development and security policies that are less state-centric. The business community, local and international, often prefers to deal with a strong state and a centralized government.

3. **Active participation of civil society is critical to the establishment of the national ownership of development and security policies.**

The above situation clearly underlines the importance of civil society. Civil society is, together with state and market, one of the three 'spheres' that interface in the making of democratic society.[9] In the words of Barber, civil society is 'an independent domain of free social life where neither governments nor private markets are sovereign'.[10]   Civil society has been also called the *private non-profit sector* or the *voluntary sector*. Walzer has argued about the important, perhaps critical, role of this 'third sector' in the democratization process in unambiguous terms: 'only a democratic state can create a democratic civil society; only a democratic civil society can sustain a democratic state'.[11]   Moreover, Wolfe believes that 'both democratic government and a free economy depend on virtues and values generated neither by the state nor by the market, but by civil society'.[12]

In the era of globalization, it is perhaps all the more important to establish the *national ownership* of development and security policy even as the policy of globalization is adopted. Within the nation, it is also important that the ownership of development and security policy rests with the people and not monopolized by the state. Here is where civil society has a critical role to play. The crisis has helped Southeast Asians discover the role of civil society in development. Thus far, it has been the 'missing link' in the social, political and economic 'space' that has been occupied predominantly by the state and the market. The notion of civil society as the third sphere suggests its emancipatory nature. The expansion of civil society is seen as the expansion of the space for moral, power-disinterested action.[13] It is the space of 'uncoerced human association'.[14]   Is it therefore possible for civil society to help develop harmonious relations between civil society and the state, producing a more 'civilized society'? Or are they bound to be in confrontation or competition with each other? Does the notion of civil society imply a relationship that works to limit the state's capacity to pervade and control society? Should civil society provide a check on the excesses of the state (and the market)? Should it reign in the state or should it oppose the state? These are definitely the most salient questions for SEA at present. Will civil society-state relations in SEA be structured largely by 'state corporatism' that has already made a deep imprint on state-market relations that are not easily dismantled? In many societies at present internal and external changes have led to a revisiting of the ideas of the relationship between state and society. The North-South Institute of Canada has identified five reasons for the renewed interest in civil society.[15] First, the dismantling—or the perception of it—of the welfare state in the industrialized countries has led to the expectation that the private non-profit sector will provide the services. Second, concerns about the decline of social capital, resulting from individualism in developed societies or caused by prolonged state domination in developing societies, have led to a desire to return to community spirit, volunteerism, and association forming. Third, the triumph of capitalism and the spread of the free market system necessitate a civil society that could assure greater equity. Fourth, the globalization of democracy leads to the need to foster a 'good governance' basket of attributes: formally democratic and administratively efficient practices, in addition to the counter-balancing efforts of civil society. Fifth, the collapse of sovereignty leads to the rise in global civil society. In addition to these, perceptions of donor countries or agencies that aid has failed have led to the promotion of civil society in the recipient societies by the donors. Civil society is seen as both an improved channel for aid and an important prerequisite for the termination of aid.

The above suggests that much is expected of civil society. It serves to promote democratization; in fact, it is seen as a prerequisite for democracy. Diamond identifies six functions of civil society in shaping democracy: (1) to act as a reservoir of resources to check the power of the state; (2) to ensure that the state is not held captive by a few groups; (3) to supplement the work of political parties in stimulating political participation: (4) to stabilize the state because citizens will have a deeper stake in social order; (5) to act as a locus for recruiting new political leadership; and (6) to resist authoritarianism.[16]

In addition, it is expected to provide services to the poor and underprivileged members of the society. In fact, it is also expected to provide for the social safety nets in a given polity. It should help assure sustainability by engaging in capacity building and human resources development. Furthermore, it is expected to facilitate economic liberalization. *And finally, it can thwart governments, particular groups, or political agendas as well as send political messages.*

It is thus legitimate to be concerned that civil society will likewise be overburdened. Therefore, it is important to view civil society in the context of the developmental challenges in individual societies. By its nature, voluntary organizations are somewhat unstructured; they are disparate and atomized. Occasionally they will engage in coalitions but most of the time they are fragmented. Is there need for these organizations to pool resources or should they remain disparate? Should priorities be set society-wide or should they be left to individual groups to decide? Is civil society to act mainly as 'mediating structures' whose main agenda is to promote social justice as proposed by Berger and Neuhaus?[17]

It is likely that the prevailing situation and environment in a society will influence the agenda and activities of organizations and movements as well as networks of organizations that constitute civil society. Both civil society organizations and agencies or foundations supporting the development of civil society have been preoccupied with two issues. First is the importance of the enabling environment for civil society to develop. This must rest on a belief in civil liberties. As Blaney and Pasha have argued, there must be 'a system of rights, constituting human beings as individuals, both as citizens in relation to the state and as legal persons in the economy and the sphere of free association'.[18] First and foremost, civil society must work to put and maintain such a system in place.

The second issue concerns the need to strengthen the management, funding, and human resources of civil society organizations so they are able to function effectively. Much attention has been given to the strengthening of non-governmental organizations (NGOs), but civil society includes organizations that are not NGOs in the sense commonly used. Peasants that organize themselves to defend their land rights or to demand for fair compensation for the land used for development projects are often overlooked.

4. **Regional and international cooperation among civil society organizations should be seen as an integral part of the regionalization and globalization policies pursued by Southeast Asian nations.**

Two other issues deserve equally serious attention. The first is the need for civil society structures that can absorb and mediate conflict. Civil society is not necessarily a harmonious sphere where there are no conflicts. Anthony Giddens noted this in his book, *The Third Way* where he also proposed that 'the state should also protect individuals from the conflicts of interest always present in civil society'.[19] This opens up an important question about the role of government in promoting civil society. Will the hand of the government necessarily produce state-led civil society?

Second is the importance of regional and international cooperation among civil society organizations to pool their resources in shaping international (and regional) public policies that in turn could influence national public policies. Networks of non-governmental organizations are playing an important role in the Asia Pacific region in shaping policies to promote regional cooperation and confidence building. They have been dubbed as the Second Track, because of their interaction with intergovernmental fora (First Track). Examples include the Institutes of Strategic and International Studies (ASEAN ISIS) that interact with the ASEAN Foreign Ministers Meeting (AMM) and the ASEAN Senior Officials Meeting (SOM). There is also the Pacific Economic Cooperation Council (PECC) that interacts with APEC, and the Council for Security Cooperation in Asia Pacific (CSCAP) that interacts with the ASEAN Regional Forum (ARF). All these regional non-governmental institutions have been initiated by civil society organizations, including academic institutions. PECC paved the way for the establishment of APEC. ASEAN ISIS promoted the idea of ARF and took the initiative to organize CSCAP as a second track organization for the ARF.

As stated earlier, the weakening of sovereignty has given rise to global civil society. In place of governments, civil society organizations are seen to be more representative of the populace. Civil society organizations may also assume the role of international watchdog over the actions of states on the international level. In many instances, they also take up issues that are traditionally seen as domestic matters (for example, the policies of the military regime in Myanmar, the process of reconciliation in Cambodia, and the one that needs to be set in motion in East Timor). In the Asia Pacific, this has given rise to a growing network of second track institutions. Although these non-governmental activities exist, there is a tendency on the part of governments in the region to create their own state-led civil society at the regional level. Woo suggested that the involvement of non-governmental actors in APEC fora has come about mainly as a result of collective state action.[20] He argues that APEC has not been receptive to the voices of the non-state sector except through associations or groups that it has officially sanctioned. He attributed this to such factors as the influence of ASEAN and Japan in the formation of APEC and the belief that the Asian miracle rests on the adoption of the corporatist development model. These factors may no longer hold today. It remains to be seen whether APEC will continue to promote a state-led civil society at the regional level when the development of civil society has gained greater momentum at the national level in many countries in Asia Pacific.

Strengthening civil society should become a priority in SEA. Until recently, civil society was an alien concept in Indonesia.[21] The Indonesian word used is *masyarakat madani*. This was originally used in Malaysia and was introduced into Indonesia by Anwar Ibrahim in 1994 during the second *Istiqlal* Festival in Jakarta. It was taken from the Arabic word *al-mujtamai al-Madani*, which in the Middle East has been used to convey the idea of civil society. However, this concept purports to include the civilization of the entire society, including the government. Consequently, the government has made civil society its business. Presidential Decree No 18/1999 of 24 February 1999 established a National Reform Team towards *Masyarakat Madani*. There are concerns that through this decree, the Indonesian state attempts to maintain full control of civil society organizations.

Civil society in Indonesia has been very weak. The main constraint has been political. The fall of Soeharto opened up a greater space for civil society. Although this has unleashed a democratization process, civil society continued to be seen by the transition government of Habibie as a serious threat to its survival as civil society was at the forefront in the opposition against the Habibie government and its continuation in power. Buchori believes that civil society will survive and gradually develop in Indonesia, but the process of leadership transfer will critically influence this prospect.[22] Hikam is of the opinion that the role civil society organizations in Indonesia will increase because of the current global and national trends towards 'debureaucratization' and decentralization of decision-making processes in society.[23]

While the concept of civil society may be new to Indonesians, NGOs are not a new phenomenon in Indonesia.[24] Many traditional institutions have functioned as 'social empowerment agencies'. As described by Eldridge, the main role of NGOs in Indonesia is to enhance the capacity for self-management among less advantaged groups, enabling them to deal with government agencies and other powerful forces on more equal terms.[25] A more recent development in Indonesia is the emergence of 'issue-oriented NGOs'. They have arisen in response to the concentration of power and the 'top-down' approach in development under Soeharto's New Order governments. These issue-oriented NGOs have gained prominence due to their efforts to provide alternatives to the society beyond the state's framework and strategy of development.

The active involvement of civil society in the change of government and in demanding reforms in all fields, including governance, has built a momentum towards expanding the space for civil society. Civil society has also participated actively in assuring that the recent general elections were conducted fairly and freely. Various election monitoring groups have been set up to prevent a recurrence of the practice of vote rigging by the state apparatus and the government party. The Indonesian Corruption Watch (ICW), the Indonesian Transparency Society, and the Urban Poor Consortium are important civil society efforts that have emerged during this transition period. It is important to note that these activities have arisen in response to the increased threat to human security during the same period. The Urban Poor Consortium recognizes the critical role of social capital in empowering the society, especially the weak and the poor. They have already made positive achievements, but they also continue to be harassed by the state. Some legal or constitutional guarantee may be necessary to allow civil society in Indonesia to grow.

5. Southeast Asian countries should adopt policies to promote the development of a tripartite governance structure.

The guarantee by the state of a space for civil society in development is an important feature in the Philippines. The sphere of civil society participation in governance has widened with the process of democratization that has been unleashed by the overthrow of the Marcos government. A study by Magno shows that in the environmental sector NGOs have become legitimate players in influencing decision-making at various levels of governance. At the national level, NGOs have various institutional openings.[26] These openings include the establishment of an NGO desk that addresses NGO participation in the development programs of the Department of Environment and Natural Resources. There is also NGO representation in the Philippine Council for Sustainable Development that monitors the government's adherence to the environmental agreements reached at the 1992 Rio Summit. Environmental NGOs are also engaged in the implementation of national policies such as the National Integrated Protected Areas System (NIPAS) approach to biodiversity conservation. NGOs are given seats in Protected Area Management Boards that are tasked to undertake program planning and implementation in the respective sites.

At the local level, NGOs are guaranteed participation in local development councils under the 1991 Local Government Code. Here, NGOs can push for a sustainable development agenda in deliberative processes with the local government units. In Cagayan de Oro, a tripartite arrangement called Task Force Macajalar was formed in the mid-1990s to combat illegal logging. In the province of Misamis Occidental, joint government-citizen checkpoints have been set up to prevent transport of illegally cut timber products from the province. There is widespread realization in the Philippines that environmental management tasks previously undertaken solely by the state are more effectively undertaken through cooperative systems involving government, NGOs, and people's organizations (POs).

In Thailand, traditionally the state was very strong and civil society organizations were weak. Student organizations were the first civic groups that fought for democratization and social justice in October 1973. However, as the economy grew, civil society organizations became stronger and played more effective roles against the state power and the interest of the business community.[27] These organizations have been formed to check the government, the politicians, the bureaucracy, and other state mechanisms. As in other countries, most of them represent the interests of the poor, women, children, the underprivileged, and the rural people who are politically and economically weak and are unable to fight for themselves.

As in Indonesia, the crisis has provided greater opportunity to civil society to exert its role in pressing for reforms. The issue of good governance, both public and corporate, is now firmly placed in the Thai national agenda. This process had begun before the crisis. It was soon realized that the democratization in 1992 had not produced good government in the body politic as well as in the government administration. There was widespread corruption, as well as vote buying, and a serious lack of transparency. The Pro-Democracy group that opposed the military-supported government initiated the call for a new constitution. This initiative failed to garner support from the liberal political parties and the urban middle class. However, as political corruption became more serious and money politics became more deep-rooted, in late 1996 the National Assembly decided to set up a Constitutional Drafting Assembly (CDA). The CDA was composed of 99 members, 76 of whom were representatives of all provinces, and the remaining 23 were selected from among political scientists, public law experts, and former public service officials. The National Assembly agreed to relinquish its right to draft a new constitution to an autonomous drafting body in response to pressures from civil society. Several civic groups were effective in influencing the drafting. This led to the introduction of several new civil rights and expansion of existing rights and liberties already protected in the previous constitution. The urban middle class was strenuously campaigning for the endorsement of the draft. The new constitution was proclaimed in October 1997. It aims at enhancing the strength of civil society in Thailand in order to consolidate the democracy and to provide a mechanism for checks and balances.

SEA must develop a new pattern of governance. The vision for a new governance model must assure the full involvement of civil society and a strong and balanced partnership between the three sectors: state, market, and civil society. SEA has discovered the missing link in development, namely civil society, but it still has some way to go in strengthening it to become an equal partner in a kind of 'tripartite governance' for development and security in the era of globalization.

Notes

1 Bowles, P. (1998), 'Canada', in C. E. Morrison and H. Soesastro (eds), *Domestic Adjustments to Globalization*, Japan Center for International Exchange, Tokyo.

2 Soesastro, H. (1999), 'Domestic Adjustments in Four ASEAN Countries', in C. E. Morrison and H. Soesastro (eds), *Domestic Adjustments to Globalization*, Japan Center for International Exchange, Tokyo.

3 Bello, W. (1999), 'The Answer: De-Globalize', *Far Eastern Economic Review*, 29 April.

4 Tay, S. (1999), *Questioning Globalization*, paper presented at the 'Conference on Globalization and Regional Security', organized by the Asia-Pacific Center for Security Studies, Hawaii, 23-25 February 1999.

5 Soesastro, H. (1998), 'Long-term Implications for Developing Countries', in R. Garnaut and R. McLeod (eds), *East Asia in Crisis – From Being A Miracle to Needing One?*, Japan Center for International Exchange, Tokyo.

6 Vervoorn, A. (1998), *Re-orient – Change in Asian Societies,* Oxford University Press, Melbourne.

7 Rodrik, D. (1999), *The New Global Economy and Developing Countries: Making Oppenns Work*, Overseas Development Council Policy Essay No. 24, Overseas Development Council, Washington, DC.

8 Soesastro, 'Long-term Implications for Developing Countries', 1998.

9 United Nations Development Programme (UNDP) (1993), UNDP and Civil Society, UNDP, New York.

10 Barber, B. (1998), *A Place for Us: How to Make Society Civil and Democracy Strong*, Hill and Wang Publisher.

11 Walzer, M. (1997), 'The Concept of Civil Society', in M. Walzer (ed.), *Toward a Global Civil Society*, Berghahn, Oxford.

12 Wolfe, A. (1991), *Whose Keeper? Social Science and Moral Obligation,* University of California Press.

13 Diamond, L. (ed.) (1991), *The Democratic Revolution: Struggles for Freedom and Pluralism in the Developing World*, Perspectives on Freedom No. 12, Freedom House.

14 Walzer, M. (1992), 'The Civil Society Argument', in C. Mouffe, *Dimensions of Radical Democracy: Pluralism, Citizenship, Community,* Verso Books, London.

15 The North-South Institute (no date), *Civil Society and the Aid Industry*, Draft Working Paper, The North-South Institute.
16 Diamond, *The Democratic Revolution: Struggles for Freedom and Pluralism in the Developing World*, 1991.
17 Berger, P. L. and Neuhaus, R. J. (1996), *To Empower People: From State to Civil Society*, 2nd edition, AEI Press, Washington, DC.
18 Blaney, D. L. and Pasha, K. M. (1993), 'Civil Society and Democracy in the Third World: Ambiguities and Historical Possibilities', *Studies in Comparative International Development*, vol.28, no.1, Spring, pp.3-24.
19 Giddens, A. (1999), *The Third Way: The Renewal of Social Democracy*, Polity Press.
20 Woo, Y. P. (1998), *State-led Civil Society at the Regional Level: The Case of the APEC Study Centres*, paper presented at a 'Conference on APEC and Civil Society', organized by Universiti Sains Malaysia, Pulau Pinang, Malaysia, 5-6 October 1998.
21 Buchori, M. (1999), *Development of Civil Society and Good Governance in Indonesia*, paper presented at the 'Global ThinkNet Paris Conference on International Comparative Study on Governance and Civil Society', organized by Japan Center for International Exchange and Institut Francais des Relations Internationales, Paris, 18-19 March 1999.
22 *Ibid.*
23 Hikam, M. AS (1999), 'Non-Governmental Organizations and the Empowerment of Civil Society', in R. W. Baker, M. H. Soesastro, J. Kristiadi, and D. E. Ramage (eds), *Indonesia – The Challenge of Change*, Institute of Southeast Asian Studies, Singapore.
24 *Ibid.*
25 Eldrigde, P. J. (1990), 'NGOs and the State in Indonesia', *Prisma*, no.47, pp.34-56.
26 Magno, F. A. (1999), 'Social Capital and Environment Protection', *DSSEA Update*, no.5.
27 Bunbongkarn, S. (1999), *Governance and Civil Society in Thailand*, paper presented at the 'Global ThinkNet Paris Conference on International Comparative Study on Governance and Civil Society', organized by Japan Center for International Exchange and Institut Francais des Relations Internationales, Paris, 18-19 March 1999.

References

Barber, B. (1998), *A Place for Us: How to Make Society Civil and Democracy Strong,* Hill & Wang Publishers.
Bello, W. (1999), 'The Answer: De-Globalize', *Far Eastern Economic Review*, 29 April.
Berger, P. L. and Neuhaus, R. J. (1996), *To Empower People: From State to Civil Society*, AEI Press, Washington, D. C.
Blaney, D. L. and Pasha, M. K. (1993), 'Civil Society and Democracy in the Third World: Ambiguities and Historical Possibilities', *Studies in Comparative International Development*, vol. 28, no. 1, pp. 3-24.
Bowles, P. (1998), 'Canada', in C. E. Morrison and H. Soesastro (eds), *Domestic Adjustments to Globalization*, Japan Center for International Exchange, Tokyo.
Buchori, M. (1999), *Development of Civil Society and Good Governance in Indonesia,* paper presented at the Global ThinkNet Paris Conference on 'International Comparative Study on Governance and Civil Society' organized by Japan Center for International Exchange and Institut Francais des Relations Internationales, Paris.
Bunbongkarn, S. (1999), *Governance and Civil Society in Thailand*, paper presented at the Global ThinkNet Paris Conference on 'International Comparative Study on Governance and Civil Society organized' by Japan Center for International Exchange and Institut Francais des Relations Internationales, Paris.

Diamond, Larry (ed.) (1991), *The Democratic Revolution: Struggles for Freedom and Pluralism in the Developing World*, Freedom House.

Eldrigde, P. J. (1990), 'NGOs and the State in Indonesia', *Prisma*, vol. 47, pp. 34-56.

Giddens, A. (1999), *The Third Way: The Renewal of Social Democracy*, Polity Press.

Hikam, M. A. S. (1999), 'Non-Governmental Organizations and the Empowerment of Civil Society', in R. W. Baker, M. H. Soesastro, J. Kristiadi and D. E. Ramage (eds), *Indonesia— The Challenge of Change*, Institute of Southeast Asian Studies, Singapore.

Magno, F. A. (1999), 'Social Capital and Environmental Protection', *DSSEA Update*, no. 5.

Rodrik, D. (1999), *The New Global Economy and Developing Countries: Making Openness Work*, Overseas Development Council, Washington, DC.

Soesastro, H. (1998). 'Long-term Implications for Developing Countries', in R. Garnaut and R. McLeod (eds), *East Asia in Crisis—From Being A Miracle to Needing One?*, Routledge, London.

Soesastro, H. (1999), 'Domestic Adjustments in Four ASEAN Economies', in C. Morrison and H. Soesastro (eds), *Domestic Adjustments to Globalization*, Japan Center for International Exchange, Tokyo.

Tay, S. (1999), *Questioning Globalization*, paper presented at the 'Conference on Globalization and Regional Security', Asia-Pacific Center for Security Studies, Hawaii.

The North-South Institute (n.d.), *Civil Society and the Aid Industry*, Canada.

United Nations Development Programme (UNDP) (1993), *UNDP and Civil Society*, UNDP, New York.

Vervoorn, A. (1998), *Re-orient—Change in Asian Societies*, Oxford University Press, Melbourne.

Walzer, M. (1992), 'The Civil Society Argument', in C. Mouffe (ed.), *Dimensions of Radical Democracy: Pluralism, Citizenship, Community*, Verso Books, London.

Walzer, M. (1997), 'The Concept of Civil Society', in M. Walzer (ed.), *Toward a Global Civil Society*, Berghahn Books, Oxford.

Wolfe, A. (1991), *Whose Keeper? Social Science and Moral Obligation*, University of California Press.

Woo, Y. P. (1998), *State-led Civil Society at the Regional Level: The Case of the APEC Study Centers*, paper presented at the Conference on 'APEC and Civil Society', Universiti Sains Malaysia, Pulau Pinang, Malaysia.

PART II
REGIONAL CASE STUDIES

Chapter 3

Globalization, Interdependence, and Regional Stability in the Asia Pacific

Amitav Acharya

Introduction

The economic crisis that hit Asia from mid-1997 onwards not only spelled a premature end to the much-vaunted 'Asian economic miracle', but also called into serious question some of the traditionally held assumptions about the relationship between economic interdependence and international security. Until the crisis, governments and regional analysts viewed economic interdependence as a major positive force for regional stability. Its benefits were seen to lie in the creation of expanded channels of communication between elites and governments in the region, promotion of a sense of regional community, and more debatably, discouragement of conflict and war. 'The intricately interwoven economic ties binding states together', argued American scholar Robert Scalapino, 'will reduce incentives to resort to violence...Today and in the future, any war conducted with one's neighbors will penetrate deeply into the very marrow of one's own economic system'.[1]   While interdependence was acknowledged to have the potential to create its own sets of new political and security problems, such as those linked to 'trade wars' and competition for investment, it also contributed to a greater willingness among the governments to look for regional cooperation and conflict management mechanisms. One result of this was the creation of cooperative institutions, including the Asia Pacific Economic Cooperation (APEC) and the ASEAN Regional Forum (ARF), to manage problems of prosperity and peace in the Asia Pacific region.

But the Asian economic crisis creates a greater sense of pessimism about the alleged pacific effects of economic interdependence. Apart from giving further ammunition to the critics of interdependence who had argued that economic linkages were themselves not significant in promoting peace, the Asian crisis generated a host of security challenges for the region. Among other things, the crisis underscored a new reality about the economics-security linkage in the regional environment, one that focuses on the hitherto unexplored relationship between interdependence and globalization, the latter being a far more sweeping and powerful force than the former, and perhaps a more crucial determinant of regional peace and stability. The presumed benefits of interdependence in the political and security arena are under attack from the forces unleashed by globalization to an extent not acknowledged in the theoretical literature on interdependence that was based on the euphoria about the rise of largely trade-based interdependence during the early post-Second World War period.

The Asian economic crisis has been called by Manuel Montes (1998) as 'globalization's first major crisis'.[2] Caution is warranted in accepting this view. Some have argued, from a neo-classical economist's perspective, that the crisis resulted from insufficient globalization (in the sense of 'free-market' policies of national governments), rather than too much of it. Moreover, domestic social, political, and institutional factors have played a major role in the origins and development of the crisis. Nonetheless, economic globalization, no matter how vaguely defined, remains central to understanding the sources and implications of the crisis, including its political and security effects.[3] As one study puts it, the origin of the crisis has to be seen in the context of 'Southeast Asia's dependence on an impersonal and unpredictable global financial system in which the market's unyielding criticism of economic performance has immediate consequences'.[4]

The Asian economic crisis provides an interesting and rich backdrop to understand how the forces of globalization may influence and affect the results of economic interdependence that the region had experienced as a result of decades of impressive economic growth. It necessitates rethinking the relationship between globalization, interdependence, development, and security. This chapter addresses this task. It is divided into three parts. The first part provides a conceptual discussion of interdependence and globalization and their relationship with development and security issues in the Asia Pacific region. Of particular importance here are the arguments supporting the view that economic interdependence contributes to greater peace and stability in international relations. The second part looks at the effects of the Asian economic crisis on regional peace and stability. This is done with a view to assess whether the crisis, as a byproduct of economic globalization, actually undercuts the arguments concerning the pacific effects of interdependence and justifies the prevailing sense of pessimism about regional order in the Asia Pacific. The third part considers how the crisis is reshaping the thinking of regional countries regarding globalization and interdependence as tools of national security and regional order.

Interdependence, Globalization, and the Development-Security Nexus[5]

The term 'interdependence' is a broad and ill-defined concept in the theoretical literature on international relations. Its usage is even less precise when one looks at policy discourses in the Asia Pacific region.[6] In the academic literature, following the classic work on the subject by Robert Keohane and Joseph Nye,[7] the term is associated with a situation of 'mutual dependence' between two or more actors. In Asia Pacific policy debates, however, interdependence is often defined broadly and loosely as a convenient shorthand for economic linkages of all kinds across the region, especially horizontal flows, transactions, trade, and financial movements.[8] While academic theorists may distinguish simple 'interconnectedness' from genuine interdependence, the latter implying a reciprocal relationship of 'sensitivity' and 'vulnerability', the distinction tends to be blurred or ignored in academic and policy debates concerning economics and security in the Asia Pacific region.

The term globalization, on the other hand, is used in the region in two inter-related senses closely reflecting the usage of the term in the academic literature. The first is globalization as national policy, the conscious decision of governments to open up their economies to the global market forces, with a focus on liberalization of foreign investment. The second sense in which the term globalization is used in the region refers to it as an evolving structural condition (or state) of the world economy and political structure. While some see globalization in this sense as a primarily economic phenomenon, driven by the relatively unfettered movement of capital, including investments supporting transnational production as well as the whole range of financial flows,[9] others take a much broader view, accepting globalization as multidimensional with economic, political, security, cultural, and environmental dimensions.[10]

While the terms interdependence and globalization are often used in the region almost interchangeably, there are key differences. Three are especially noteworthy. First, while interdependence is more closely (but not exclusively) associated with relatively simpler forms of economic transactions, such as the volume of trade, globalization is seen as more closely (but not exclusively) associated with more fundamental economic linkages, such as transnational production. In policy discussions concerning regional security in the Asia Pacific, the term interdependence came to be used earlier than the term globalization, suggesting that the latter is viewed as a subsequent and more intense pattern of economic relationship. Second, globalization is more likely to be viewed not just as an economic phenomenon *per se*, but as a holistic notion combining economic, political, and cultural aspects. Interdependence, on the other hand, has a more specific, economic, connotation. Third, globalization is more clearly expected to produce a loss of the political autonomy of the state. While interdependence may or may not lead states to voluntarily accept limits to sovereignty in areas of economic decision-making, globalization is considered sovereignty-eroding.

In what ways does the relationship between interdependence and globalization influence the development and security nexus? The linkage can be summed up in three general propositions:

1. The growing interdependence of the Asia Pacific region reflects, and builds upon, decades of rapid economic growth.
2. Economic growth, in turn, is substantially the result of policies adopted by states to open up their economies to the forces of globalization. Globalization in this sense refers to the policies of a state to open up its economy to global market forces and adopt market-conforming developmental strategies.
3. Interdependence is closely linked to regional stability. Despite periodic outbreaks of economic rifts and tensions among trading partners, the relationship between interdependence and security is generally positive. Among the regional states, economic interdependence has generated a sense of common destiny and the realization of a common vulnerability to external dangers. It has contributed to the formulation of cooperative institutions and approaches to deal with these dangers.

The last argument, which is central to the study's analysis, is by no means unique to the Asia Pacific region. The view that economic interdependence promotes peace and stability has a long pedigree in political theory and philosophy. The most influential initial arguments[11] on this subject were made in the specific context of free trade. For example, the German philosopher, Immanuel Kant, argued that the 'spirit of commerce' was 'incompatible with war'. John Stuart Mill, the noted Utilitarian, found that commerce was 'rapidly rendering war obsolete, by strengthening and multiplying the personal interests which act in natural opposition to it'.[12] Richard Cobden, of the Manchester School of economic internationalists, credited free trade with 'breaking down the barriers that separate nations; those barriers behind which nestle the feelings of pride, revenge, hatred and jealousy'.[13] Cordell Hull, an architect of America's 'open door' policy during the inter-war years, put it more dramatically and unambiguously, 'If goods can't cross borders, soldiers will'.[14]

The perspective of free trade advocates was subsumed and advanced in more recent times by the arguments of interdependence theorists, such as Keohane and Nye in their 1977 classic, *Power and Interdependence: World Politics in Transition.* Taking a much broader view of the causes and effects of interdependence than the free trade advocates, the postwar interdependence theorists posited a positive correlation between economic interdependence and peace and stability, which may be summarized into the following five general arguments:

1. As economic interdependence rises, war becomes increasingly unnecessary because the key objectives of war, such as markets and resources, are already available on competitive terms to anyone who wants them.
2. As states become more dependent on imports and exports of indigenous production, they become vulnerable to disruption caused by war. Thus, any attempt to settle conflicts by war is likely to be self-injurious by causing disruption to the economy of the aggressor. Haas[15] argues that 'increased trade and cross-national investment, especially free trade and capital flows, result in a more highly articulated international division of labor; any disruption in that division of labor causes the belligerents to incur heavy losses of welfare; fearing such losses, countries are less willing to go to war'. Norman Angell points to the self-injurious nature of war in such a context: 'if credit and commercial contact are to be tampered with in an attempt at confiscation the credit-dependent wealth is undermined, and its collapse involves that of the conqueror; so that if conquest is not to be self-injurious it must respect the enemy's property, in which case it becomes economically futile'.[16]
3. Because of the greater fear of self-damage in using force, instruments other than military ones may become more effective and attractive. This means a greater emphasis on creating pacific means of conflict resolution, including multilateral regimes and institutions.
4. Pressure of economic competition forces states within a liberal international economic order to favor resource allocation to productive sectors than to defense, which is considered to be an unproductive sector. As Haas puts it, 'increasing popular demands for services on the part of the government limit the amount

available for armaments and war; any disruption of welfare services is resented and will cause domestic strife leaders prefer to avoid'.[17]

5. An open international economy based on free trade and investment creates a shared commitment to individualist, materialist and humanist values, thereby eroding the will of states to use force.[18]

The arguments concerning the pacific effects of interdependence have not remained unchallenged. Skeptics argue that the historical evidence for the liberal arguments is shaky; the era of free trade under British hegemony was also an era of massive expansion of imperialism and wars associated with it. Buzan,[19] in a major attack on the liberal position, argues that while a liberal system can provoke war, a mercantilist system can be quite benign. While liberals attribute the relative peace in the post-Second World War international system to growing interdependence, the skeptics cite factors other than free trade, such as the deterrent effects of nuclear weapons and the bipolar distribution of power during the cold war period. The main historical evidence cited by the skeptics against the liberals is the situation preceding World War I when close economic interdependence among the European powers, such as Britain and Germany, did not prevent military competition leading to the outbreak of war.

Skeptics also argue that economic interdependence, instead of reducing conflict among states, may actually aggravate or exacerbate tensions, undermine security ties, fuel trade wars, and may even lead to military confrontation. Three major negative perspectives on the linkage between economic growth, interdependence, and security may be identified. The first, which has adherents within a more pessimistic branch of the liberal school itself, holds that economic interdependence makes the domestic well being of states more vulnerable to external disturbances. A second negative perspective may be identified within the realist school.[20] This begins with the neo-mercantilist position that the welfare ('low politics') goals and methods of states are secondary to, and ultimately superseded by, security ('high politics') objectives. Interdependence, even if at a very high level, does not matter ultimately if and when it conflicts with the national security objectives of states. Accordingly, states in an interdependent regional or international economy will not forego the use of force against other states if the latter's actions are perceived to be damaging to the former's core national security interests,[21] such as sovereignty and territorial integrity. Similarly, states will not significantly lower their defense spending and military preparedness for the sake of more productive resource allocations in response to the pressure of economic competition. If anything, economic competition will feed political tensions and justify higher military spending. Furthermore, interdependence is rarely symmetrical and this becomes a powerful source of conflict. In this view, economic competition is one dimension of the condition of anarchy, which keeps the state-system locked into a perennial security dilemma.

In recent years, the realist skepticism concerning the positive impact of interdependence on security has been supported by the emergence of neo-mercantilist scenarios about the future of the global economy. Mercantilists believe that national security is best pursued through economic self-reliance. Applied to a regional context, it corresponds to the idea of regional trading blocs that promote intra-bloc economic liberalization while shielding the regional actors from unwelcome external competition. The underlying assumption is that intra-regional market integration and external protectionism create the conditions for maximizing the potential for growth and reducing the economic vulnerabilities of the regional actors. This conception of regional economic security is operationalized through measures, ranging from a free trade area to a customs and economic union that are theoretically not inconsistent with an open multilateral trade regime. If pursued to the extreme, they however lead to protectionist trade blocs. In recent years, the emergence of such regional trading blocs was foreseen by a number of scholars with the decline of the GATT system and the increasing 'regionalization' of global economic activity under the auspices of the three economic superpowers: the United States (US), Japan, and Germany.[22] Some neo-mercantilist scenarios have envisioned a tri-polar structure of world politics and economy consisting of an inward-looking European Union (EU); a Latin American trade bloc dominated by the US; and an East Asia trade bloc dominated by Japan.

The realist-mercantilist challenge to the pacific claims of interdependence makes two assumptions: first, with the end of the cold war, economic issues have assumed a higher salience than the traditional security problematic; and second, the liberal economic order which characterized the global political economy first under British and then American hegemony is facing a terminal crisis. A world divided into regional blocs is not only reflective of the emerging multi-polar system structure, but is also a logical response to the problem of economic insecurity faced by states in the post-hegemonic era.

A third challenge to the pacific claims of interdependence comes from the critical and neo-Marxist tradition.[23] This perspective focuses particularly on the consequences of globalization for intra- and inter-state relations. It views the globalization of production and finance as the chief locomotive of the world economy and identifies the political, economic, social, strategic, and ecological factors behind the mobility of capital (such as the search for cheap labor and lower environmental standards). The mobility of capital creates a global (or regional) economy, which is extremely hierarchical in terms of its economic and political organization. Such an economy features a high degree of domination and marginalization on a North-South axis. Growth tends to be uneven; its benefits are often distributed unequally. This leads to natural contradictions between the wealthy and the marginalized, both within and between states. The critical perspective on globalization highlights the potential for social conflict unleashed by transnational production, conflicts that may negate whatever benefits brought about by interdependence.[24] The political and security implications of globalization pit states against various forms of social movements, and takes the form of conflicts between the privileged economic and political elite on the one hand and the marginalized groups involving labor, women's groups, environmental movements, etc. on the other.

The Impact of the Asian Economic Crisis

Some analysts have viewed the Asian economic crisis as a 'defining event of the post-cold war international order'.[25] While this may be an overstatement, there is little question that the crisis will have a profound effect in reshaping the regional security order in the Asia Pacific. For a number of reasons, it challenges the political and security benefits of the region's growing interdependence since the post-Second World War period.[26]

Economic Competition and the Balance of Power

Since the late 1980s, a shared commitment to economic globalization has served as a stabilizing factor in the Asia Pacific regional balance of power. Interdependence forged through trade and investment dampened strategic rivalry and in recent times, even raised the possibility of a great power concert. But the Asian crisis poses new uncertainties about the balance of power involving the US, Japan, and China.

First, the crisis has reshaped the perceptions of China and Japan in the region. China has gained more political clout at the expense of Japan, thanks to its pledge not to devalue its currency[27] and its contribution to the IMF-led rescue packages for Thailand and Indonesia.[28] The crisis has also provided China with an opportunity to present itself as a force for regional stability and secure recognition from the US and other Asian countries as a 'responsible' regional power.

China's actions are shaped primarily by its own sense of vulnerability to the effects of the crisis. The crisis threatens China's markets in the region, an important source of its growth. In this sense, interdependence has been an important factor in inducing the sort of Chinese international behavior that is widely seen in the region to be positive and constructive. But there may be some damaging consequences of China's increased clout in regional economic and security affairs. Chipman (1998) argues that China's vocal criticism of Japan's failure to revive its own economy and its open, if cautious, pressure on the Indonesian government to deal with the plight of the ethnic Chinese are not only indicative of a new assertiveness, but also a retreat from its professed policy of non-interference in the internal affairs of other states.[29] If this is true, then China's neighbors are bound to be nervous.

Moreover, there have been some indications that China has sought to exploit the crisis to increase its political influence at the expense of the US. A report by the United States Institute of Peace (USIP) on the crisis underscored this by citing 'rumors of quiet Chinese warnings delivered to some Southeast Asian neighbors to guard against American 'hegemonic' ambitions' as indicated in its use of the IMF to demand greater economic and political liberalization.[30] Far more susceptible to Chinese political gains is the position of Japan. Its inability to stimulate its own economy (which has grown between one to two per cent for the last eight years), and address its banking crisis has been widely criticized in the region as a failure of leadership. Japanese leadership is also undermined conceptually, with the revealed dangers of the so-called 'Japan model' of government-business relations. Once seen as a major reason for the region's economic success, it is now blamed for breeding corruption and cronyism that contributed to the regional economic downturn.[31]

China's political gains from the crisis may be short-lived, however. The crisis underscores China's role as the main competitor of Asian countries that are reliant mostly on low-technology exports. Competition from China played a 'significant role', to cite a US Congressional Research Service report,[32] in undermining the export growth of Southeast Asian countries and hence, contributed to the economic crisis. With cheaper but more skilled labor force and greater investments in infrastructure, China has become a more attractive destination for Japanese and other foreign investments in Asia than many of the Southeast Asian countries. Apart from competing with Southeast Asian countries in the same export markets, China's currency devaluation in 1994 'directly undercut' the exports of Southeast Asian countries, especially Thailand, Malaysia, and Indonesia, thereby undermining their balance of payments and foreign exchange reserves and adding to their debt pressures. These realities may contribute to a more negative view of China's regional economic and political role if Beijing fails to keep its promise of not devaluing its currency.[33]

As with China, the Asian economic crisis has paradoxical effects on the attitudes of regional governments and peoples towards the US. While highlighting the extent to which the Asian countries are dependent on the US economy and security umbrella, the crisis has also bred some resentment in the region against the US. This relates to perceptions that the US did precious little to prevent the escalation of the crisis when the first signs of trouble appeared. There is also the belief that the US is using the International Monetary Fund (IMF) to open up Asian markets, which its economic diplomacy had failed to do previously. They see US pressure behind the IMF's unprecedented expansionist and interventionist role in regional economic affairs.

On the US side, a crucial factor affecting relations with Asia is the issue of trade deficit. The devaluation of the region's currencies has led to a flood of cheap Asian exports to the US. In the first half of 1998, US imports from East Asia, excluding Japan, rose 10 per cent, while Japan's trade surplus with the US jumped 24.7 per cent during August 1998 compared to the same period a year ago.[34] This has prompted American accusations that while it is making sacrifices to absorb imports from Asia to help its economies out of the crisis, Japan is hurting them and the US with its mounting trade surpluses.

A renewed phase of trade-related conflicts between US and East Asian nations, apart from fuelling greater protectionist sentiments in the US. Congress, may also test US security commitments in the region and create further uncertainties about the regional balance of power.[35] This prospect generates new insecurities for the region's weaker states. The ASEAN countries confront a shifting and unpredictable balance of power without 'the solid economic growth, which had underpinned both their national confidence and their defense purchasing power'.[36] To compound matters, the crisis affects their collective ability to moderate and manage the regional balance of power through cooperative institutions such as ASEAN and the ARF.

Inter-state Conflicts in Southeast Asia (SEA)

The economic downturn has generated strains in the bilateral ties within ASEAN. Particularly hit have been Singapore's relations with its neighbors, Indonesia and Malaysia. Until the economic crisis, nothing illustrated the use of economic interdependence as a tool of national security and regional stability more clearly than Singapore's professed pursuit of a 'prosper-thy-neighbor' policy. In 1995, Prime Minister Goh Chok Tong articulated this policy in the following terms:

Prosperous countries make good neighbors. The pursuit of economic growth leading to social stability within individual countries contributes to regional peace and stability. A more stable and peaceful region would in turn promote even more growth as foreign investment funds are increasingly attracted to the region. More growth means more trade with one another. It is a virtuous cycle of prosper-thy neighbor.[37]

Far from vindicating the 'prosper-thy-neighbor' logic, the regional economic downturn has highlighted tensions that reflect what Cooper (1968) has termed as the 'beggar-thy-neighbor' effect of interdependence (which occurs when a state's efforts to pursue its own interest damages the interests of others *coincidentally*).[38] Singapore-Malaysia relations have been poisoned by Malaysia's perception that Singapore is not interested in helping it out of the economic downturn by offering unconditional financial assistance that would have reduced its need for outside help with strings attached - see the chronology of Singapore-Malaysia relations in the annex. Former Indonesian President Habibie leveled the same charges against Singapore, who openly criticized Singapore as not being 'a friend in need'. Comparing the help Indonesia received from Japan, Malaysia, and others, Habibie claimed that while others were 'pro-active' in helping Indonesia, Singapore was 'pro-active in the negative direction'.[39] This was notwithstanding the US$5 billion aid that Singapore had agreed to provide Indonesia in conjunction with the IMF rescue package. (The real reason for Habibie's anger was Lee Kuan Yew's earlier criticism of the choice of Habibie as Vice-President by Soeharto, which Lee implied would be poorly received by the market and hinder Indonesia's recovery).

The failure of its 'prosper-thy-neighbor' policy has generated a heightened sense of insecurity in Singapore. Although its leaders do not fear a war with its neighbors, they see the need for greater military preparedness to deal with a deteriorating external security environment.[40] George Yeo, a Cabinet Minister in Singapore, recently drew attention to the 'high morale' of the Singapore Armed Forces in preparing for the potential 'evil' consequences of the economic crisis.[41] Bilateral tensions are also contributing to, and are further aggravated by a resurgence of nationalism in SEA, often encouraged by governments for whom external tensions provide a useful way of diverting attention from domestic troubles and failings.

The Asian economic crisis thus demonstrates that the pacific effects of interdependence are less likely to hold if there exist significant economic disparities among states. It also shows that the political gains of interdependence are particularly vulnerable to economic downturns, especially if the impact of the downturn is felt unevenly within a group of states.

Impact on the Military Build-up

The Asian economic crisis has led to significant reductions in national defense budgets and arms acquisitions as well as training activities in SEA. The Thai defense budget was reduced by 12 per cent in October 1997, while in December 1997, the Malaysian government cut its defense budget for 1998 by 10 per cent, with another eight per cent cut under consideration. The Indonesian defense budget has been cut even more drastically, as much as by 50 per cent for 1998 according to conservative estimates.[42] Apart from direct cuts, the devaluation of regional currencies will affect defense purchasing power. As a result of the devaluation of its currency, the Philippines' defense budget was effectively reduced by one-third.[43] On the other hand, Singapore has maintained its level of defense spending, creating some discomfort among its neighbors. In Northeast Asia, Japan carried out its first cut in defense spending since 1954 in 1998, although the cut had already been anticipated as part of a US$8 billion reduction to the 1996-2000 defense program.[44] Japan has also cut back on its support payments for the 43,000 US troops in its territory.[45] China's defense budget, however, has maintained its annual growth rate of about 10 per cent.

The crisis has forced governments in the region to put on hold or cancel major arms procurement programs. Highlights include Malaysia's postponement of programs to acquire attack helicopters (12 Rooivalk from South Africa), a submarine capability, transport aircraft (six CN-235 planes), tanks, armored fighting vehicles (AFVs), and anti-submarine helicopters (Super Lynx from Britain). It has also cut back on its offshore patrol vessel project. Indonesia has cancelled a planned purchase of five surplus German submarines and postponed (with the strong possibility of cancellation) of an order of 12 Su-30K fighters and Mi-17 attack helicopters from Russia. Thailand has cancelled the purchase of eight F/A Hornet fighters, and froze the acquisition of two to three submarines and the upgrade program for its F-5 fighters. The Philippines continues with its comparatively modest programs to acquire fighter aircraft and offshore patrol vessels. Singapore's weapon acquisitions, such as an additional 12 F-16 fighters from the US, submarines from Sweden, and new projects to acquire unmanned aerial vehicles (UAV) and attack helicopters have not been affected by the crisis.

These cutbacks have a mixed impact on regional stability. The uneven reduction in defense spending and arms purchases increases intra-regional military disparities and suspicions. The cutbacks in joint training and exercise activities reduce useful channels for confidence building among the region's armed forces.[46] On the other hand, the cuts lessen the possibility of a regional arms race and dampen the prospect for military conflict, at least in the short-term.[47] Moreover, fiscal constraints are forcing greater caution, transparency and rationality to the process of defense acquisitions. They may also be reducing the role of the military in the defense budget-making processes and its political influence as a whole.

The cutbacks also have a larger implication for regional stability. Prior to the economic crisis, critics used the increases in defense spending and arms buying in the region to refute the view that the pressure of competing in an interdependent global economy would encourage pacifist tendencies in nation states, by forcing them to allocate greater resources to more productive sectors. A counter to this view was that the region's military build-up was a product of increased affluence, rather than enmity. The Asian economic crisis strengthens the latter view.

Impact on Regional Co-operative Institutions

Asia's economic turmoil has cast a shadow over the credibility and effectiveness of regional multilateral institutions that were created with the hope of managing some of the conflict-causing potential of interdependence. Particularly hard hit is ASEAN. Within ASEAN, there was some initial hope that it may engender a greater sense of sub-regionalism, especially solidarity among the troubled economies, prompting them to deepen existing level of cooperation and develop common responses to the crisis. But the crisis has actually diminished ASEAN's international standing, especially in view of the ineffectiveness, indeed, virtual irrelevance, of the collective efforts by ASEAN to manage the crisis. An initial idea explored by ASEAN was to set up a 'co-operative financing arrangement' or a 'stand-by fund' which could be used to deal with future currency shocks and debt crises. The fund could be used only after an IMF package had been put in place; in this sense it was not to be a substitute for global multilateral measures.[48] ASEAN economic ministers have since proposed a regional 'framework' which will allow members to engage in 'mutual surveillance' of each other's economic policies and provide 'early-warning' on impending economic downturns.[49]

But these measures have hardly sufficed. Commenting on ASEAN's response to the crisis, Lee Kuan Yew likened it to the 'solidarity of fellow chicken-flu sufferers'.[50] Apart from exposing the region's dependence on foreign capital and its vulnerability to global market and political forces, the crisis has shown the limits of ASEAN's collective clout to deal with a major regional economic crisis.[51]

ASEAN's limitations inevitably shift attention to larger East Asian regional frameworks. Here too the experience has been disappointing. Japan hastily downplayed its proposal for an Asian Monetary Fund (AMF) to deal with currency crises in the face of US pressure. While the meeting of the East Asian leaders in Kuala Lumpur in December 1998 may be viewed as the continued pursuit of Malaysia's favored notion of an East Asian Economic Caucus, at the outset there was no sign that Japan was ready to lend its support to this idea.

The economic turmoil also threatens the credibility of APEC in several ways. APEC was created at a time of immense optimism and euphoria concerning the region's future. It was meant to celebrate the Asian economic miracle, not to cope with a future economic meltdown. It is, therefore, hardly surprising that APEC was quick to acknowledge its limitations by endorsing the IMF, a global multilateral body dominated by the US, as the chief trouble-shooter for the region's economic crisis. But the crisis threatens APEC's unity and direction. The American opposition to the proposal for an AMF and its open backing for IMF's pressure on the crisis-hit economies to accept further deregulation exacerbated what Higgott has called the 'politics of resentment' within APEC.[52] The crisis creates new doubts about the benign nature of 'open regionalism' that has been the philosophical basis of APEC. Also being challenged is the uncritical acceptance of increased deregulation and capital mobility, that had been encouraged by the advocates of APEC during its initial years. Trade friction resulting from the Asian economic crisis is a further source of intra-APEC friction. This compounds existing tensions between the American (and

Australian) aim of using APEC primarily as a vehicle for trade liberalization versus the Japanese agenda for using it to pursue 'development cooperation' through infrastructure development. All this undermines APEC's ability to foster a positive regional security climate. 'It is now clear', contends Higgott, 'that the euphoric expectation of the 1993-6 period that APEC would provide firm institutional ties to mitigate inter-regional tensions between Asia and the US was wishful thinking of a high order'.[53]

The ARF, as the only multilateral framework for security dialogue, is also affected by the crisis. Preoccupied with their domestic troubles and foreign economic woes, the ASEAN countries risk losing some of their interest in, and capacity for playing a 'leadership' role within the ARF. As a result, the ARF may be driven more by the interests and policies of the major powers, thereby undermining ASEAN's hopes for a more equitable relationship between the region's weaker and stronger states through a cooperative security framework.

Inevitably, the crisis has prompted calls for a review of the purposes and practices of regional institutions. For ASEAN the major debate has been with respect to the doctrine of non-interference. The debate had its origins in a perception that the crisis might have been dealt with more effectively but for the reluctance of fellow ASEAN members to persuade Thailand to attend to its domestic troubles more urgently, a reluctance born out of deference to the doctrine of non-interference. Had ASEAN not been so committed to non-interference, 'friendly criticism' of Thailand might have resulted in more timely Thai action on the economic crisis. But 'any persuasion from fellow ASEAN members to set a new course was so discreet that it was easy to ignore'.[54]

Subsequently, then Thai Foreign Minister, Surin Pitsuan, openly called for ASEAN to review its non-interference doctrine. As he put it, 'it is time that ASEAN's cherished principle of non-intervention is modified to allow it to play a constructive role in preventing or resolving domestic issues with regional implications'.[55] This was an implicit criticism of ASEAN's failure to come up with a collective response to the crisis. To make the grouping more effective, Surin had urged that 'when a matter of domestic concern poses a threat to regional stability, a dose of peer pressure or friendly advice at the right time can be helpful'.[56] But Surin's initiative, dubbed 'flexible engagement', received support from just one other ASEAN member, the Philippines. ASEAN Foreign Ministers, at their annual meeting in Manila in July 1998, decided to stick to the old principle of non-interference.[57] Subsequently, the sacking of Anwar Ibrahim, the proponent of the idea of 'constructive intervention' as a framework for dealing with ASEAN's weaker and less stable members, further weakened the forces advocating more openness in ASEAN.[58]

However, debates within ASEAN regarding greater openness are not likely to fade away. The idea of 'flexible engagement', as one commentary notes, is in 'deep coma...it may well be revived at a more opportune time'.[59] Moreover, this is not the only kind of reform that ASEAN has to come to terms with. The crisis has generated demands for ASEAN to move away from the 'ASEAN Way' and to be more receptive to formal and institutionalized mechanisms for cooperation. Tommy Koh has articulated this need. East Asian leaders, Koh contends, had pursued cooperation by 'building trust, by a process of consultation, mutual accommodation, and consensus' while displaying a 'general reluctance to build institutions and to rely on laws and rules'. But the economic crisis shows the need to supplement the 'ASEAN Way' by institutions.[60] Similarly, the Foreign Secretary of the Philippines raised the possibility of an EU-style ASEAN. ASEAN's economic monitoring agreement, in his view, is already a step 'towards institutionalizing closer co-ordination of national economic policies and performance and fostering rule-based transparency in governance'.[61] Thus, forcing ASEAN to review and restructure itself may be one of the positive consequences of the Asian economic crisis.

The Spillover of Domestic Strife

The economic crisis has been a major factor behind social and political instability, most seriously in Indonesia, but to lesser degrees in Malaysia, South Korea, and Thailand. As in the past, such domestic strife has had implications for inter-state relations. For example, the rise of Islamic political forces in Indonesia following the downfall of Soeharto is rekindling anxieties in Singapore about being a 'Chinese island in a sea of Malays', while the treatment of Anwar Ibrahim has drawn angry protests from the Philippines and Indonesia, thereby creating tensions in their bilateral relationships with Malaysia.

The economic downturn has also aggravated one source of instability, which had been highlighted by the critics of interdependence well before the economic crisis: the issue of migrant labor. The issue is especially serious in Malaysia, which is home to 2.5 million foreign workers; with close to one million of them being illegal workers from Indonesia.[62] By July 1998, Malaysia had already deported 30,000 foreign workers and introduced strict measures to prevent them from working in the service sector.[63] Thailand's one million illegal workers include a vast number (about 80 per cent) from Burma.[64] The problem of illegal immigration, which the Australian Foreign Minister has called 'the people crisis', is likely to be aggravated as countries hit by the crisis experience growing poverty and unemployment resulting in a greater exodus of their citizens overseas.[65] The forced repatriation of illegal workers carried out by Malaysia and Thailand, not only challenges domestic stability (as evident in rioting by Indonesia workers in Malaysia), but also serves as a source of inter-state tension and regional insecurity. Singapore's leaders, for example, are apprehensive that instability in Indonesia would have spillover effects similar to the 1960s transition from Sukarno to Soeharto. Among its concerns are 'problems with illegal immigrants and piracy' as well as the creation of a 'climate of uncertainty and unease affecting the region'.[66]

But domestic strife generated by the Asian economic crisis does have an important silver lining. A classical argument regarding the positive effects of interdependence is that it generates a convergence of values that in turn strengthens the foundations of international peace and stability. Prior to the economic crisis, the proponents of 'Asian values' had challenged this claim. They posited a schism between Western 'individualist' values and Asian 'communitarian' values. But confronted with the prospects for a major regional economic downturn, the very proponents of the Asian values concept have acknowledged its dangers. Lee Kuan Yew warns that nepotism is a Confucian weakness and that networking (Guanxi) is 'not a good Asian value'. Some Asian values were detrimental to development since they were not 'not compatible with the competitive free market'.[67] Musa Hitam has gone even further; arguing that the success attributed to the 'Asian Way' also bred 'arrogance, corruption, dependence, and failures'.[68] By putting the proponents of 'Asian values' on the defensive, the economic crisis might have helped to enhance the cooperative implications of interdependence.

Believers in the pacific effects of interdependence also stand to gain from the domestic political changes resulting from the Asian economic crisis. The Asian economic crisis advances the prospects for democratization in the region in several ways. The first is the outright demise of the Soeharto regime in Indonesia, Asia's third most populous state. The collapse of one of Asia's longest and most repressive regimes should have a demonstration effect. At the very least, it means that the junta in Burma can no longer be able to seek legitimacy by adopting the Indonesian 'model' of civil-military relations. Moreover, Indonesia's new leaders are less likely to condone Burma-style political repression in the Southeast Asian neighborhood. Second, the crisis has challenged political concepts conducive to authoritarianism. This includes not just 'Asian values', but even more importantly, the concept of 'performance legitimacy' which served as a justification of political repression as long as governments were able to deliver high growth rates. The crisis has shown that democratic regimes (as in Korea, Thailand, and Taiwan) may be better able to deal with economic crises than authoritarian ones (as in Indonesia), thereby producing a powerful new conceptual justification for democratization.[69]

Third, the crisis has led to increased pressure from the international community in support of democratization. In the early stages of the Indonesian debacle, the Managing Director of the IMF, Michel Camdessus defined the IMF's task in Asia to include 'dismantling an economic system based on conglomerates, the collusion between the state, banks and business, and the restrictive markets'.[70] But the successful implementation of these measures also requires the dismantling of the political systems in which they had thrived so far. Greater transparency would allow non-elites to have more access to information about growth rates and the state of inequity. An end to the cozy relations between the political elite and big business is likely open up more political space for the middle class and other segments.

Finally, Asian governments are now less willing and able to put forward a culturally-relativist position on democracy and human rights, as they had done in the early 1990s with the so-called 'Asian view on human rights'. With the departure of the Soeharto regime and the further empowerment of democratic forces in Thailand, the Philippines (and quite possibly in Malaysia in the near future), ASEAN would find it hard to excuse authoritarianism in Burma and other countries in the region, even if it does not directly interfere in the internal affairs of such states. This is already reflected not just in demands for 'flexible engagement', but also in the criticism of the sacking of Anwar Ibrahim (seen as a champion of political openness) by the leaders of the Philippines and Indonesia. Moreover, the crisis has empowered social forces in their campaign against political repression and led to growing interactions and cooperation among non-governmental organizations demanding greater democracy not just in their home countries, but also in the neighboring states.

In fostering peace and stability, economic interdependence works best if supported by a shared democratic political framework. Pluralist-democratic political culture and institutions are a key factor in advancing regional economic integration in Europe towards a security community in which intra-mural wars are no longer seen as legitimate or likely. Going by this logic, the Asian crisis advances the pacific effects of interdependence by empowering the forces of democratization. At the very least, it will broaden the social basis of regional cooperation, from being an exclusively state-centric and elite-driven process to one that incorporates a nascent regional civil society. It is difficult to argue that such an outcome will be bad for regional peace and stability.

Conclusion: Rethinking the Nexus

The political and security implications of the Asian economic crisis have inevitably led to a rethinking of globalization and interdependence as tools of development and security. But perspectives have differed among the countries of the Asia Pacific. Consider the views of the leaders of Malaysia and Singapore, the two countries that currently represent the opposite ends of the region's thinking about, and responses to the economic downturn. Malaysia's Mahathir Mohammed has been the most vocal critic of globalization, pointing to its negative impact on sovereignty and security. In June 1998, Mahathir argued:

> We are moving inexorably towards globalization...globalization, liberalization and deregulation are ideas, which originate in the rich countries ostensibly to enrich the world. But so far the advantages seem to accrue only to the rich.

Referring to the political and security turmoil in the region caused by the economic downturn, Mahathir asked:

> In a globalized world, should there be national governments? We have seen that market forces can change governments. What is the need for national elections if the results have to be approved by the market?[71]

Mahathir also warns that the Asian economic crisis, by forcing national economies to submit more closely to the forces of globalization, will produce greater insecurity and violence. Warning of a impending 'war' against globalization in which Asians will fight foreign multinationals controlling their economic destiny, Mahathir notes: 'They [Asians] will regard this as a new war of liberation. Even if they want to avoid violence, violence must come as the new capitalists disregard the signs [of protest among the masses]'.[72]

In contrast, Singapore's leaders continue to affirm the positive impact of globalization on economic well being and security. Its Foreign Minister, S Jayakumar, reminds that 'it was the forces of globalization that gave the developing countries in our region direct access to the financial resources, technology and markets of the developed world...it was also globalization that allowed many developing countries, including those in East Asia, to enjoy decades of sustained economic growth, rapid industrialization and massive improvement in their standards of living, health and education'.[73] A retreat from globalization, warns Deputy Prime Minister Lee Hsien Loong, would undermine not just the prospects for further development, but also security:

> Globalization is an imperative not only for small countries, which need foreign technology and capital, but also for the US. The alternative is not just less competitive industries or lower standards of living, but a world in which countries will be *less secure, and more prone to conflicts* (emphasis added).[74]

But Prime Minister Goh Chok Tong, while reaffirming Singapore's commitment to economic openness and globalization, concedes that a rethinking of the benefits of globalization is bound to occur because the crisis is now perceived to have its origins in the workings of the global economy, rather than in the domestic arena of states:

> In the initial months of the Asian crisis, attention was focused on internal political and economic weaknesses of specific Asian economies that had been overlooked during the boom years. This is still important. But the debate has now widened. As it has become clearer that the problems are global, a more fundamental questioning of free markets and the global economy is emerging.[75]

Because the rethinking of globalization has been prompted by the dramatic political and security impact of the Asian economic crisis, in the future, economic policies in Asia will be much more sensitive to political and security considerations, rather than simply being driven by rational economic calculations. Governments will join academic critics of globalization in reassessing the merits of open economies for domestic politics and national and regional stability.

Amidst the critical responses to globalization, there has also been more questioning of economic interdependence as a force for peace and stability. In the light of the crisis, Ball argues that a 'high degree of inter-dependence can serve as a transmission belt for spreading security problems through the region, and more particularly, if growth falters, or if conflict is introduced into the system, that friction and disputation are likely to quickly permeate the region'.[76] The crisis affects all the areas of linkage between interdependence and security as identified at the outset of this chapter, including competition for markets, prospects for use of force in regional conflicts, allocation of resources to the military, the performance of regional cooperative institutions, and discourses about common values.

By unleashing severe domestic strife in Indonesia, rekindling inter-state disputes in SEA and reshaping perceptions of the regional balance of power, the Asian economic crisis has generated widespread pessimism concerning the impact of globalization on interdependence, growth, and stability. In fact, most commentators on the Asian economic crisis have viewed its political and security implications in starkly negative terms. In the short-term, such pessimism may be justified. The long-term picture, however, is more complex and perhaps, in the light of the analysis presented in this paper, more positive. The regionalization of economic insecurity should be regarded as a blessing if, as likely, it generates a powerful momentum towards democratization, reduces the prospects for a regional arms race, creates a stronger sense of common vulnerabilities of global market forces, and leads to a rethinking of the purposes and practices of regional institutions contributing to demands for their reform and strengthening.

Annex A

Singapore – Malaysia Relations, January – September 1998: The Political Economy of a Bilateral Crisis

January – April 1998: Singapore's Prime Minister, Goh Chok Tong, and Malaysia's Prime Minister, Mahathir Mohammed, meet on five occasions between January and April to discuss bilateral issues. Mahathir assures Goh that Malaysia will continue to supply water to Singapore. In return, Goh offers financial support to Malaysia to help it cope with the economic downturn. But no deal is made (*The Straits Times*, 24 August 1998, p.27). The impasse is apparently due to Singapore's position that its financial aid to Malaysia should be in exchange for a settlement of all outstanding bilateral issues, not just water supply, a position not acceptable to Malaysia. A major deterioration of Singapore-Malaysia relations follows.

August 1998: The bilateral row over the relocation of the railway customs, immigration, and quarantine (CIQ) facilities intensifies. On 1 August, Singapore carries out a planned move of its CIQ facilities from the Tanjong Pagar railway station (inside Singapore territory) to the newly constructed facilities at Woodlands on the Singapore-Malaysian border. Malaysia refuses to follow suit. Both sides had been negotiating the shift since 1989, trying to address an issue resulting from Singapore's separation from Malaysia in 1967. But Malaysia's attitude seemed to have hardened in the wake of the economic crisis and the lack of an agreement on financial assistance from Singapore. Malaysian leaders call Singapore's decision to move its CIQ facilities as 'arrogant and insensitive'. Malaysian Education Minister accuses Singapore of aggravating 'the issue at a time when we are facing economic problems', and warns that it 'can cause big strategic implications' (*The Straits Times*, 3 August 1998, p.21).

August 1998: Singapore's *Straits Times* paraphrases a comment on Singapore's attitude towards the CIQ issue by Malaysia's Education Minister, Najib Tun Rajak: 'the Republic [of Singapore] was too competitive. It always wanted to emerge the winner and did not seem interested in seeking a win-win solution'. 'Singapore Must Think of Long-Term Ties', (*The Straits Times*, 4 August 1998, p.3).

August 1998: While commenting on Malaysia-Singapore relations, Mahathir tells a rally in Johor Baru: 'We don't have a large military to attack others. We have tried to be good neighbors. But don't take us for granted'. (*The Straits Times*, 6 August 1998, p.3). He also criticizes Singapore for not reciprocating the benefits it reaps from entrepot trade with Malaysia. 'A lot of [Malaysian] trade goes through Singapore. We try our best to be good neighbors. We do not report Singapore negatively. But what do we get in return? We are asked to leave Singapore' (*The Straits Times*, 5 August 1998, p.1). The Malaysian government, citing revenue losses and the large amount of money Singapore makes from the use of its port by Malaysian traders, had already begun to use political and financial pressure on the latter with a bid to reduce their use of Singapore's port and make them shift to its own port at Klang.

August 1998: Malaysia pulls out of a joint exercise scheduled in September under the Five Power Defence Arrangements (comprising Singapore, Malaysia, Australia, Britain and New Zealand). Malaysia's Defence Minister cites the economic downturn as the reason for the pull out, but adds: 'Some of the meetings [of the FPDA] were supposed to be held in Singapore. With the current environment, we felt that it was inappropriate' (*The Straits Times*, 29 August 1998, p.3). Later, on 28 August, he denies that the row with Singapore was a factor behind the pull out. Asked whether bilateral tensions between the two countries could result in armed conflict, the Defence Minister replies: 'Armed conflict? Malaysia has never considered such a possibility' (*The Straits Times* 28 August 1998, p.2).

September 1998: Criticizing Singapore's actions in the water and CIQ issues, Mahathir says, 'Singapore has actually prospered by taking advantage of the weaknesses of its neighbors... [Singapore has] no wish whatsoever to assist its neighbors... Whatever businesses [they have] in Singapore, they flourish out of the weaknesses of its neighbors' (*The Straits Times*, 15 September 1998, p.2). Education Minister Najib criticizes Singapore's competitive attitude towards its neighbors, and advises it 'to look at the wider perspective and not just want to win all the time' (*The Straits Times*, 15 September 1998, p.2).

September 1998: On the 16th, Singapore's former Prime Minister, Lee Kuan Yew, releases the first volume of his memoirs, which deals with the circumstances of Singapore's separation from Malaysia in 1967. The youth wing of Malaysia's ruling party, UMNO Youth, joins the chorus of Malaysian condemnation of the book by calling it 'selective in its use of sources and deeply biased in its arguments' (*The Straits Times*, 15 September 1998, p.2). Similar charges had been made against another book published earlier by a Singaporean academic dealing with Singapore's separation from Malaysia. Mahathir condemns the timing of the release of Lee's memoirs, saying that it was designed to take advantage of Malaysia's economic difficulties. Lee responds that the timing had been decided before the crisis really begun to hit Malaysia (*The Straits Times*, 16 September 1998, p.1).

September 1998: A day after the publication of Lee's memoirs, on 17th September, Malaysia rescinds agreements that allowed Singaporean military and rescue planes to over-fly Malaysian territory without prior authorization. The move is seen by some observers as a retaliation against the publication of Lee's memoirs (Joyce Liu, 'Singapore - Malaysia Ties Head Towards New Low', *The Bangkok Post*, 21 September 1998, p.11). Mahathir says that Malaysia would like to 'take back our territory bit by bit' from Singapore (*International Herald Tribune*, 18 September 1998, p.6).

September 1998: In a bid to alleviate concerns of foreign investors regarding the tensions between Singapore and Malaysia, Lee Kuan Yew says that only the 'uninformed' would regard the situation as alarming because the two countries have had a long history of such ups and downs. He argues that the statements and actions by the two countries would provide a release of latent tensions ('to get it out of the system'). Malaysia's actions are likened by Mr Lee to a 'war dance, plumed feathers and so on'. If Singapore is 'to do a similar war dance', says Lee, then there 'may be an accidental clash of plumage', but Singapore is 'not given to such practices' Singapore-KL Problems 'Not Alarming', (*The Straits Times*, 21 September 1998 (*http://ftdasia.ft.com/info-api/sh*).

Notes

1   Scalapino, R. A. (1994), 'Challenges to the Sovereignty of the Modern State', in B. Nagara and K.S. Balakrisnan (eds), *The Making of a Security Community in the Asia-Pacific*, ISIS Malaysia, Kuala Lumpur, Malaysia, pp.50.

2   Montes, M. (1998), *Globalization and Capital Market Development in Southeast Asia*, paper presented at the 'ISEAS 30th Anniversary Conference on Southeast Asia in the 21st century: Challenges of Globalization', Institute of Southeast Asian Studies, Singapore, pp.1.

3   The major reasons for this view are as follows. First, at the initial stages, the crisis was seen as a by-product of the contradictions between the demands of a globalized economy and existing domestic social and political structures in the region with their propensity to corruption, nepotism and lack of transparency. Second, the crisis has subsequently proven not just to be regional in scope, but one with global ramifications, thereby further underscoring its links with globalization of the world economy. Third, the crisis has prompted a rethink on the benefits of globalization, although not everyone is keen to emulate Malaysia's move to roll back the countries' participation in the global economy.
    The Asian economic crisis is thus providing us with an interesting and rich backdrop to understand how the forces of globalization may influence and affect the fruits of economic interdependence, which the region had experienced as a result of decades of impressive economic growth. It necessitates a rethink of the relationship between interdependence, globalization and security.

4   United States Institute of Peace (USIP) (1998), *Beyond the Asian Financial Crisis: Challenges and Opportunities for U. S. Leadership*, Washington, D. C., pp.10.

5   These points are derived from my interviews with regional elites as well as surveys of elite views in the regional media.

6   As Rosecrance, *et al.* (1977, pp.127, 425-45) point out, 'the term interdependence has so many varied meanings that it is no longer fully clear what investigators intend to signify when they use the term', adding that 'interdependence in world politics refers to situations characterized by reciprocal effects among countries or among actors in different countries'. Their definition begins with a 'loose and general' concept of interdependence 'as a state of affairs where what one nation does impinges directly upon other nations'. But they proceed to offer a significant modification of this definition. The new formulation views interdependence as 'direct and positive linkage of the interests of states such that when the position of one state changes, the position of others is affected, *and in the same general direction*'. The significance of these words should not be missed since it assumes that countries gain or lose together in an interdependent situation. It does not allow for the problem of 'relative gain', or the possibility that some countries may gain more from interdependence than others, or even at the expense of others. This definition is blind to the prospect that interdependence may be asymmetric, a point made forcefully by Kenneth Waltz (1983), the leading critic of interdependence theorists. Waltz offers a more straightforward definition; interdependence, in his view, implies a relationship that is 'difficult (costly) to break'. But he also argues such situations are not easily found in the

real world of inter-state relations; the word interdependence 'subtly obscures the inequalities of national capability, pleasingly points to a reciprocal dependence, and strongly suggests that all states are playing the same game'.

7   Keohane, R. and Nye, J. (1977), *Power and Interdependence: World Politics in Transition*, Little Brown, Boston.

8   *Ibid.*, pp.127.

9   The following are some examples of this view. Mittleman (1995) notes that globalization is a 'market-driven' process. Glyn and Sutcliffe (1992) contend that the elements involved in globalization include the interlinking of national economies, increasingly interdependent patterns of production and consumption, highly integrated markets, and a focus on firms instead of on national economies. Campanella (1993) relies on an OECD definition which identifies three aspects to globalization: the emergence of powerful new actors such as multinational corporations, the rapid diffusion of technologies in the areas of information and communication, and the triumph of deregulation policies in OECD countries.

10 The definition by Cox (1997) of globalization falls within this category. According to Cox, globalization involves 'growing connectedness and interdependence on a world scale. It is multidimensional: connectedness in politics and the organization of security, in economics and welfare, in culture, in ecology, in values of all kinds. No area of human activity is isolated; and within each area, no one is untouched by the condition and activities of others'. A similarly broad view is offered by Giddens (1990, p.64) for whom globalization is 'the intensification of world wide social relations which link distant realities in such a way that local happenings are shaped by events occurring many miles away or vice versa'. Other examples of the broad view include Holm and Sorensen (1995): globalization is 'the intensification of economic, political, social, and cultural relations across borders'; and McGrew (1992): globalization is 'the multiplicity of linkages and interconnections between the states and societies which make up the modern world system'.

11 For an excellent review of these arguments, see Levy (1989).

12 Mill, J. S. (1848), *Principles of Political Economy*, London, pp.582, cited in Kagan, D. (1995), *On the Origins of War and the Preservation of Peace*, Doubleday, New York, pp.2.

13 *Ibid.*, pp.2.

14 Gardener, *Sterling-Dollar Diplomacy: The Origins and Prospects of Our International Economic Order*, 1980, pp.7-9.

15 Haas, E. (1987), 'War, Interdependence and Functionalism', in R. Vayrynen (ed.), *The Quest for Peace: Transcending Collective Violence and War among Societies, Cultures and States*, Sage Publications, Beverly Hills, pp.108.

16 Kagan, *On the Origins of War and the Preservation of Peace*, 1995, pp.3.

17 Haas, 'War, Interdependence and Functionalism', 1987, pp.108.

18 This is a point made by Buzan (1984) in his critique of the liberal position.

19 Buzan, B. (1984), 'Economic Structure and International Security: The Limits of the Liberal Case', *International Organization*, vol. 38, no. 4.

20 Waltz, K. (1983), 'The Myth of National Interdependence', in C. Kindleberger and D. Audretsch (eds), *The Multinational Corporation in the 1980s*, MIT Press, Cambridge, Massachusetts.

21 For an analysis of the place of economic issues in the *national security* agenda especially from a realist perspective, see Gilpin (1977), Krasner (1982), Buzan (1994) and Romm (1993).

22 See especially Gilpin (1987, pp.397-401) and 'A Three Region World?', *Far Eastern Economic Review*, 31 January 1991, pp.31-2.

23 Perhaps the leading critic of globalization from a neo-Marxist perspective is Robert Cox (1992).

24 Mittelman, J. (1994), 'The Globalization of Social Conflict', in V. Bornschier and P. Lengyel (eds), *Conflicts and New Departures in World Society,* Transaction Books, New Brunswick; and his article, 'Rethinking the International Division of Labor in the Context of Globalization', *Third World Quarterly,* vol. 16, no. 2.

25 Dibb, P., Hale, D., and Prince, P. (1998), 'The Strategic Implications of Asia's Economic Crisis', *Survival,* vol. 40, no. 2.

26 For an overview of the political and security implications of the crisis, see da Cunha (1998) and Zoellick (1998).

27 The ASEAN countries have acknowledged China's positive role in the economic crisis; as the Malaysian Foreign Minister put it, 'Asean is grateful to China for all its assurance not to devalue the *renminbi* despite pressures upon it to do so'. See 'Abdullah: China Can Help Asean to Rally', *New Straits Times,* 29 July 1998, *http://ftdasia.ft.com/info-api/sh.*

28 'China Improves Ties With ASEAN Through Manila Conference', *China Business Information Network,* 30 July 1998, *http://ftdasia.ft.com/info-api/sh.*

29 Chipman, J. (1998), *Asian Security in the Context of the Asian Economic Situation,* lecture delivered to the 'Yomiuri International Economic Society', Tokyo.

30 USIP, *Beyond the Asian Financial Crisis: Challenges and Opportunities for US Leadership,* pp.15.

31 A casualty of the economic crisis, in so far as Japan's economic leadership of the region is concerned, is the much-vaunted 'flying geese' metaphor. Singapore's Prime Minister revealed a conversation he had with the then Japanese Prime Minister, Ryutaro Hashimoto, at the 1997 ASEAN summit in Malaysia. He had told the Japanese leader: 'The Japanese goose has become too thin and weak. You must nourish it so that it can fly again and lead the other geese to greener pastures'. Responding, the Japanese Prime Minister replied that the Japan is unable to do so because the Japanese goose has refused to eat. *The Straits Times,* 24 August 1998, pp.27.

32 Cronin, R. (1998), *Asian Financial Crisis: An Analysis of US Foreign Policy Interests and Options,* CRS Report for Congress 98-74F, CRS, Washington, D. C.

33 China's current pledge not to devalue its currency is as beneficial as it is burdensome to its economy. It protects Hong Kong's exports and means lower interest payments on its substantial yen-denominated loans. While China has ruled out currency devaluation, this is a promise Beijing may be hard pressed to keep. As its neighbors regain their export competitiveness by taking advantage of their weaker currencies, China faces increasing pressure to devalue its own currency. A devaluation of the Chinese currency will hit the economies of Thailand, Indonesia and the Philippines, which compete with China in products like textiles, shoes and low-level electronics. Malaysia, whose exports comprise largely of high-technology products manufactured by foreign multinationals, will be spared.

34 'Trade Surplus Rises for the 17th Month in a Row', *The Straits Times,* 22 September 1998, *http://straitstimes.asia.1.com.sg/.*

35 Dibb, P. (1997-98), 'The End of the Asian Miracle? Will the Current Economic Crisis Lead to Political and Social Instability', *SDSC Newsletter,* Spring 1997-Summer 1998.

36 *Ibid.,* pp.2.

37 Keynote Address at the '20th Federation of ASEAN Economic Associations (FAEA)' Conference, Singapore, 7 December 1995.

38 Cooper, R. (1968), *The Economics of Interdependence: Economic Policy in the Atlantic,* McGraw Hill, New York.

39 *The Straits Times,* 5 August 1998, pp.16.

40 Asked to comment on the severity of the crisis in Singapore-Indonesia relations, Lee Hsien Loong stated: 'I don't think it will be a military problem. It is not that sort of situation'. *The Straits Times,* 10 October 1998, pp.46.

41 Yeo also commented that 'If at a time like this, our SAF officers are weak-kneed, then we

might as well pack up'. *The Straits Times*, 4 August 1998, pp.21.

42 Ball, D. (1998), *Regional Maritime Security,* paper prepared for a 'Conference on Oceans Governance and Maritime Strategy', Canberra.

43 'Asian Crisis Hits Defence Spending', *The Straits Times*, 14 July 1998 (reproduced from *Strategic Comments,* London, International Institute for Strategic Studies).

44 *Ibid.*

45 Sasser, S. (1997), 'Tigers on the Brink', *The Straits Times,* 9 December.

46 da Cunha, D. (1998), 'Concerns Loom Over Security', *The Sunday Times*, 19 July, pp.44; 'Asian Crisis Hits Defence Spending', *The Straits Times*, 14 July 1998 (reproduced from *Strategic Comments*, London, International Institute for Strategic Studies).

47 USIP, *Beyond the Asian Financial Crisis: Challenges and Opportunities for U. S. Leadership*, pp.11.

48 'Beggars and Choosers', *The Economist*, 6 December 1997, pp.43.

49 *Ibid.*

50 'The Limits of Politeness', *The Economist*, 28 February 1998, pp.43.

51 'Out of Depth', *Far Eastern Economic Review*, 19 February 1998, pp.25.

52 Higgott, R. (1998), *The Asian Economic Crisis: A Study in the Politics of Resentment*, CSGR Working Paper No. 02/98, Centre for the Study of Globalization and Regionalization, The University of Warwick.

53 *Ibid.*, pp.13.

54 'The Limits of Politeness', 1998, pp.43.

55 'Surin Pushes "Peer Pressure" ', *The Bangkok Post*, 13 June 1998, pp.5.

56 *Ibid.*

57 'Thais Retract Call for Asean Intervention', *The Straits Times*, 27 June 1998.

58 'ASEAN Loses Critic Anwar', *Asiaweek*, 18 September 1998, pp.54.

59 'ASEAN Unity Comes First', *The Straits Times*, 5 August 1998, pp.34.

60 'What E. Asia Can Learn from the E.U', *The Straits Times*, 10 July 1998, pp.48.

61 'EU-Style ASEAN Possible', *The Straits Times*, 19 August 1998, pp.21.

62 Mochizuki, M. (1998), 'The East Asian Economic Crisis: Security Implications', *Brookings Review*, 22 June.

63 'In Search of a Better Life: More Workers Likely to Emigrate', *The Bangkok Post*, 22 July 1998, *http://ftdasia.ft.com/info-api/sh.*

64 *Ibid.*

65 'Downer Sees Aggravated Illegal Cross-Border Migrant Flows Around Asia', *AFX News* (Associated Press), 2 August 1998, *http://ftdasia.ft.com/info-api/sh.*

66 Lee Hsien Loong, Deputy Prime Minister, quoted in *The Straits Times*, 10 October 1998, pp.46.

67 Dutta-Ray, S. K. (1998), 'Only Clear Laws Can Stem the Tide', *The Straits Times*, 1 March, pp.4.

68 'Musa: Asia's Dynamic Economic Growth Lulled People into Complacency', *New Straits Times*, 1 June 1998, pp.4.

69 Acharya, A. (1998), 'Is Democracy Best?', *Asiaweek*, 23 October, pp.80.

70 Cited in 'The Right Stuff', *Far Eastern Economic Review*, 18 December 1997, pp.64.

71 Text of Speech at the 'Fifth Symposium of the Institute for International Monetary Affairs', Tokyo Japan, reproduced in the *New Straits Times*, 4 June 1998, pp.12.

72 'Perhaps Mahathir Will Have the Last laugh', *The Sunday Nation*, 14 June 1998, p.A5.

73 'Singapore Urges No retreat From Globalization', *Xinhua News Agency Dispatch*, 3 September 1998 (From Lexis-Nexis).

74 Loong, L. H. (1998), *Whither Globalism—A World In Crisis,* speech at the 'Economic Strategy Conference', Washington, DC, 6 May 1998, cited in Wah, *Globalization and Its*

Challenges to ASEAN Political Participation, 1998, pp.3.
75 Text of Speech at the 'Asia Society', New York, *The Straits Times,* 28 September 1998, pp.38.
76 Ball, *Regional Maritime Security,* 1998, pp.1.

References

Ball, D. (1998), *Regional Maritime Security,* paper prepared for a 'Conference on Oceans Governance and Maritime Strategy', Canberra.

Buzan, B. (1984), 'Economic Structure and International Security: The Limits of the Liberal Case', *International Organization,* vol. 38, no. 4.

Buzan, B. (1994), 'The Interdependence of Security and Economic Issues in the New World Order', in R. Stubbs and G. Underhill (eds), *Political Economy and the Changing Global Order,* McClelland & Stewart, Toronto, pp. 89-100.

Campanella, M. (1993), 'The Effects of Globalization and Turbulence on Policy-Making Processes', *Government and Opposition,* vol. 28, no. 2.

Chipman, J. (1998), *Asian Security in the Context of the Asian Economic Situation,* lecture delivered to the 'Yomiuri International Economic Society', Tokyo.

Cooper, R. (1968), *The Economics of Interdependence: Economic Policy in the Atlantic,* McGraw Hill, New York.

Cox, R. (1992), 'Global Perestroika', in Ralph Miliband and Leo Panich (eds), *Socialist Register,* The Merlin Press, London, pp. 26-41.

Cox, R. (1997), 'The Transformation of Democracy', in A. McGrew (ed), *Global Politics: Globalization and the Nation-State,* Polity Press, London.

Cronin, R. (1998), *Asian Financial Crisis: An Analysis of US Foreign Policy Interests and Options,* CRS Report for Congress 98-74F, CRS, Washington, D. C.

da Cunha, D. (1998), 'Concerns Loom Over Security', *The Sunday Times (Singapore),* 19 July, pp. 44.

Dibb, P. (1997-98), 'The End of the Asian Miracle? Will the Current Economic Crisis Lead to Political and Social Instability', *SDSC Newsletter,* Spring 1997-Summer 1998, pp. 2.

Dibb, P., Hale, D., and Prince, P. (1998), 'The Strategic Implications of Asia's Economic Crisis', *Survival,* vol. 40, no. 2.

Gardener, R. (1980), *Sterling-Dollar Diplomacy: The Origins and Prospects of Our International Economic Order,* Columbia University Press, New York.

Giddens, A. (1990), *The Consequences of Modernity,* Polity Press, Cambridge.

Gilpin, R. (1977), 'Economic Interdependence and National Security in Historical Perspective', in K. Knorr (ed.), *Economic Issues and National Security,* pp. 47-63.

Gilpin, R. (1987), *The Political Economy of International Relations,* Princeton University Press.

Glyn, A. and Sutcliffe, B. (1992), 'Global but Leaderless? The New Capitalist Order', in R. Miliband and L. Panitch (eds), *Socialist Register 1992,* The Merlin Press, London, pp.77-88.

Haas, E. (1987), 'War, Interdependence and Functionalism', in R. Vayrynen (ed.), *The Quest for Peace: Transcending Collective Violence and War among Societies, Cultures and States,* Sage Publications, Beverly Hills.

Henrik-Holm, H. and Sorensen, G. (1995), 'Introduction: What Has Changed?', in H. Henrik-Holm and G. Sorensen (eds), *Whose World Order? Uneven Globalization and the End of the Cold War,* Westview Press, Boulder, CO.

Higgott, R. (1998), *The Asian Economic Crisis: A Study in the Politics of Resentment,* CSGR

Working Paper No. 02/98, Centre for the Study of Globalization and Regionalization, The University of Warwick.

Kagan, D. (1995), *On the Origins of War and the Preservation of Peace,* Doubleday, New York.

Keohane, R. and Nye, J. (1977), *Power and Interdependence: World Politics in Transition,* Little Brown, Boston.

Krasner, S. (1982), 'National Security and Economics', in B. Thomas Trout and J. E. Harf (eds), *National Security Affairs: Theoretical Perspectives and Contemporary Issues,* Transaction Books, New Brunswick, pp. 313-328.

Levy, J. (1989), 'The Causes of War: A Review of Theories and Evidence', in P. E. Tetlock, *et al.* (eds), *Behavior, Society and Nuclear War. Vol. 1,* Oxford University Press, London.

Long, L. H. (1998), *Wither Globalism – A World in Crisis,* speech at the 'Economic Strategy Conference, Washington, DC, 6 May 1998.

McGrew, A. (1992), 'Conceptualizing Global Priorities', in A. McGrew *et al.* (eds), *Global Politics: Globalization and the Nation-State,* Polity Press, Cambridge.

Mittelman, J. (1994a), 'The Globalization of Social Conflict', in V. Bornschier and P. Lengyel (eds), *Conflicts and New Departures in World Society,* Transaction Books, New Brunswick.

Mittelman, J. (1995), 'Rethinking the International Division of Labor in the Context of Globalization', *Third World Quarterly,* vol. 16, no. 2.

Mochizuki, M. (1998), 'The East Asian Economic Crisis: Security Implications', *Brookings Review,* 22 June.

Montes, M. (1998), *Globalization and Capital Market Development in Southeast Asia,* paper presented at the 'ISEAS 30th Anniversary Conference on Southeast Asia in the 21st century: Challenges of Globalization', Institute of Southeast Asian Studies, Singapore.

Romm, J. (1993), *Defining National Security: The Non-Military Aspects,* Council on Foreign Relations Press, New York.

Rosecrance, R., *et al.* (1977), 'Whither Interdependence', *International Organization,* vol. 31, no. 3.

Scalapino, R. (1994), 'Challenges to the Sovereignty of the Modern State', in B. Nagara and K.S. Balakrisnan (eds), *The Making of a Security Community in the Asia-Pacific,* ISIS Malaysia, Kuala Lumpur.

United States Institute of Peace (USIP) (1998), *Beyond the Asian Financial Crisis: Challenges and Opportunities for U. S. Leadership,* Washington, D. C.

Wah, C. K. (1998), *Globalization and Its Challenges to ASEAN Political Participation,* paper presented at the ISEAS 30th Anniversary Conference, 'Southeast Asia in the 21st Century: Challenges of Globalization', Institute of Southeast Asian Studies, Singapore.

Waltz, K. (1983), 'The Myth of National Interdependence', in C. Kindleberger and D. Audretsch (eds), *The Multinational Corporation in the 1980s,* MIT Press, Cambridge, Mass.

Zoellick, R. (1998), 'The Political and Security Implications of the East Asian Crisis'. *National Bureau of Asian Research Analysis,* vol. 9, no. 4.

Chapter 4

Conflict Resolution as Construction of Security: Peace-building, Constructive Intervention, and Human Security in Southeast Asia

Pierre P. Lizée

Peace-building lies at the intersection of international security and development. It poses a challenge for foreign policy and development assistance policy alike: how to address the development needs of societies at risk of violent conflict. Peace-building requires a different mindset, one that cuts across traditional division between development and international security, and focuses on promoting human security.

Foreign Affairs Minister Lloyd Axworthy,
speaking to a peace-building forum in Ottawa.[1]

Democracy and development...are linked because democracy provides the only long-term basis for managing competing ethnic, religious, and cultural interests in the way that minimizes the risk of violent internal conflict...Democracy and development are linked because people's participation in the decision-making processes which affect their lives is a basic tenet of development.

From the United Nations' *Agenda for* Development.[2]

The twin effects of the globalization of economic forces on political dynamics are now part of the jargon of political science. Globalizing trends at once challenge the validity of the traditional sites of political affiliation, especially the state. At the same time, they invite reconstruction of communal identities around forms of political organization that provide a bastion against the homogenization of identity at the global level. Globalization invites new models of politics, and thus fosters dynamics ranging from the rise in ethnic violence to the calls for a kind of politics articulated on local, rather than national realities that underlie the political discourse of many social movements both in Western and non-Western societies.

Globalization, however, can be seen as a factor both in the construction of stable political systems and in the destabilization of these systems. One of the central tenets of the contemporary international order is the economic activity ideals of democracy and the political participation of the individual. The enlargement of markets through globalization also involves the expansion of such political environments.

Peace-building can be seen from that perspective as one of the instruments used by the international community to deal with the issue of promoting peace and political stability of peripheral regions demanded by the dynamics associated with globalization. The publication in mid-1992 of the *Agenda for Peace*, a report from the Secretary-General of the United Nations on the expansion of peacekeeping operations,[3] set out one of the ways in which the international community could attempt to resolve the intractable domestic conflicts that had plagued certain regions of the world for decades. The movement from more traditional peacekeeping (keeping a cease-fire in place) into much more ambitious peace-building operations (where the international community would endeavor to 'identify and support structures which will tend to strengthen and solidify peace in order to avoid a relapse into conflict'),[4] provided the focus of this new effort. It was intended to be a platform for launching international initiatives of economic and social reconstruction meant to provide for the eventual emergence of a complex of political institutions and rights strong enough to allow a non-violent and democratic political order to take hold in societies where it had hitherto been absent or tenuous.

Peace-building operations were, therefore, meant to generate a series of social and institutional developments aimed at putting in place a democratic apparatus able to channel political conflicts. The idea was not to resolve conflict, in the sense of deciding who should be in power in a given society, but to facilitate the emergence of a new social contract allowing the struggle for power to occur in a non-violent form. This approach rested on a gigantic gambit: that the international community and the United Nations could conduct social engineering of very considerable proportions in the short time they could devote to a sustained peace operation; and that they could telescope in a one- or two-year period social and political developments that in other societies have taken decades or centuries to unfold.

Peace-building operations, however, must be seen as standing at the intersection of two contradictory tendencies associated with globalization. They reflect the international consensus on the need to help societies torn by protracted conflict arrive at a new social contract able to foster some measure of justice and democracy. And yet they take place in an environment shaped by global economic forces that often act as obstacles to that goal as they de-legitimize and destabilize the very political structure on which non-violent politics is to be built by the international community.

This chapter is intended to examine the implications of this *problématique* for the Association of Southeast Asian Nations (ASEAN) as it is slowly coming to consider how it should foster political stability and development in cases of protracted violent and near-violent domestic conflicts in Southeast Asia (SEA). This debate was set in motion by the suggestion put forward by Malaysia's Anwar Ibrahim in mid-1997 that the regional community should have engaged in constructive intervention in Cambodia to prevent the relapse into violence signaled by the coup which had just occurred there.[5] The notion echoed to a large degree the logic embodied in the concept of peace-building. Regional economic integration was now proceeding with such a pace and scope that domestic political instability could have region-wide ramifications. For instance, vast movements of refugees or the opening up of spaces where rule of law does not exist would invite further growth in the region of illegal activities linked for instance to the drug trade. The way out, Anwar argued, was for the regional community to strengthen political and social institutions in Cambodia, and to encourage the movement towards revamping the Cambodian political order so that it could become more stable and less prone to violence. It was suggested that international and regional actors should attempt to resolve internal conflicts not so much by imposing or promoting a specific settlement among conflicting groups, but rather by fostering the development of a progressive and democratic political environment where conflicts can be managed in a non-violent fashion.

And certainly the question at stake was the extent to which dynamics of political and regional integration would assist and facilitate, or hinder, this process of social change in Cambodia. Anwar's proposal remained somewhat short on specifics, but certainly did not entail the mounting of large-scale intrusive operations by ASEAN within the territory of some of its members. The idea was rather to benefit from the forces of economic and social integration at play in SEA to foster some dynamics of change in conflict-prone societies, and to guide and sustain these dynamics by broad regional diplomatic initiatives.

Even as a discussion point, Anwar's proposal met with much resistance in ASEAN circles, essentially because of the consequent reconceptualization of the famed 'ASEAN Way'. A second forceful proponent of the concept, Thai Foreign Minister Surin Pitsuwan, tried to give it some impetus in two speeches in June 1998 directed this time at Myanmar and the need for ASEAN of finding more efficient ways of dealing with Rangoon. His ideas also encountered much opposition from many of his counterparts at the following ASEAN foreign ministers' meeting and exposed deep divisions within the Association about the need to change regional diplomatic orthodoxy.[6]

However, ASEAN will most probably have no choice but to contend in the near- to medium-term with at least two prolonged processes of conflict resolution – in Cambodia and in East Timor. These conflicts will undoubtedly force it to engage the set of issues articulated around the concept of constructive intervention. In both cases, a failure to set in motion a coherent and sustained process of conflict resolution could lead to the existence of areas of latent instability, protracted lawlessness, and possible violence. They could have broad ramifications for ASEAN, not only in the irritants they could create between members of the Association, but also as regards the different destabilizing forces and actors they would introduce in regional politics. In both cases, ASEAN will have to contend with a peace process not of its own making. Both the Cambodian and East Timor peace processes were set in motion and framed by the United Nations as exercises in democracy building. As the international community withdraws from both Cambodia and East Timor, the burden of peace efforts shifts towards regional and local actors. These actors will nonetheless have to link peace-building and democracy building if they want the endorsement of the international community. Indeed, as ASEAN envisages different scenarios of post-crisis rebuilding, the ability to settle conflicts democratically in its own backyard will most account to a great extent for the degree of legitimacy it will be able to regain in the international community.

This will not be an easy process. Regional and global dynamics of economic integration might in fact thwart regional attempts at peace-building. For instance, political institutions working for a movement from violent to non-violent politics might lose all legitimacy if they are unable to control economic flows within the national territory that would allow for tangible development in broad segments of the population. Even if Cambodia achieves peace and experiences some economic progress, this development might take place only in the primary sector as a result or regional economic actors orienting their activities in the country essentially around the exploitation of its cheap labor and natural resources. This might prevent political authorities from implementing a development plan that could bring a sustained and broad improvement of living conditions in Cambodia. In turn, it might prevent government from gaining the legitimacy and authority to succeed in marginalizing violent conflict in the country. East Timor might not be a place appealing enough for long-term international investments. This could then lead to a prolonged economic stagnation weighing on government and prevent it from initiating a process of political renewal. Indeed, post-crisis scenarios of regional economic reconstruction might focus on the principal economies of SEA that they might bypass concerns with the economic development of more marginal actors like Cambodia and East Timor.

The two concepts of social capital and human security can provide a framework through which ASEAN can articulate a coherent and effective peace-building doctrine. The concept of social capital supplies a structure through which regional and local actors involved in peace-building can organize and coordinate their actions. Human security can provide a guiding objective on which the peace-building project can be based. This chapter aims to provide not only a demonstration of the validity of the argument, but also to bring to light some of the pragmatics of conflict resolution and peace-building it might entail for ASEAN. It is divided in three parts:

It first outlines how the concept of peace-building framed the intervention of the international community in Cambodia in 1991-93. It presents the difficulties encountered during that operation that have a bearing on the way in which operations of social reconstruction should be conducted, particularly in a context of growing regional and international economic integration.

It then delineates the ways in which the notion of constructive intervention represented an attempt to correct some of the miscalculations of the 1991-93 international intervention in Cambodia viewed from the diplomatic and international culture of SEA. In short accounts of the evolving situation in Cambodian and East Timor, it outlines the nature of the challenges ASEAN is likely to encounter if it indeed confronts issues of peace-building in these two areas.

Finally, a case is made for the need to articulate more clearly the notions of constructive intervention and peace-building with those of social capital and human security. These last remarks clearly lend a prescriptive as much as an analytical aspect to this chapter. They are meant to help demonstrate that constructive intervention can work, and should indeed represent an essential component of the construction of security in SEA.

This chapter might at least provide a useful starting point in deliberations on the best ways for ASEAN to implement and sustain the peace-building process in Cambodia and East Timor. The decision made at the ASEAN Annual Ministerial

Meeting (AMM) in July 1999 to start examining ways of promoting preventive diplomacy in SEA perhaps also indicates a certain measure of enthusiasm in regional circles for a reconceptualization of the Association's role in conflict management and conflict resolution. If this enthusiasm were to permeate discussions on constructive intervention, this chapter would be of some usefulness.

The International Community and Peace-building in Cambodia, 1991-93

The logic of the international intervention in Cambodia during the period extending from late 1991 to the elections held in May 1993 was fixed on a peace proposal put forward by the Australian government in early 1990. The promoter of the peace plan, Australian Foreign Minister Gareth Evans, explained:

> The central concept of the Australian proposal to reinvigorate the [Cambodian] peace process was very simple. So as to sidestep the power-sharing issue ..., we proposed that the United Nations be directly involved in the civil administration of Cambodia during the transitional period [leading to elections]. Along with a UN military presence to monitor the cease-fire and cessation of external military assistance, and a UN role in organizing and conducting elections, UN involvement in the transitional administration arrangements would ensure a neutral political environment conducive to free and fair elections.[7]

The proposal thus parallel the logic of peace-building. The international community would not solve the Cambodian conflict by promoting a certain power-sharing arrangement or endorsing one of the warring parties. It would endeavor, quite differently, to create in Cambodia a 'neutral political environment' where the Cambodians themselves would resolve questions of power and legitimacy through a non-violent competition in the electoral arena.

The central issue then revolved around how best to build this neutral political environment. Essentially, four processes were set in motion by the peace agreement that led to the international operation of 1991-93. Two distinct processes concerned the stabilization of the military situation in Cambodia and the creation of a neutral state apparatus standing above factional rivalries. The peace agreement referred for instance to the establishment of 'military arrangements during the transitional period [intended] to stabilize the security situation and build confidence among the parties to the conflict' through a demobilization process.[8] The process of creating a democratic and neutral state apparatus was enshrined in a section of the agreement stating that:

> All administrative agencies, bodies and offices acting in the field of foreign affairs, national defense, finance, public security and information will be placed under the direct control of the United Nations Transitional Authority in Cambodia (UNTAC), which will exercise it as necessary to ensure strict neutrality.[9]

A third process concerned the protection of human rights in Cambodia and the formation and advancement of groups devoted to the defense of human rights. The agreement stated for example that:

> Cambodia will undertake to ensure respect for and observance of human rights and fundamental freedoms and to support the right of all Cambodian citizens to undertake activities which would promote and protect human rights and fundamental freedoms.[10]

Finally, a fourth process revolved around the need to restart the Cambodian economy and to encourage development once peace was attained. A *Declaration on the Rehabilitation and Reconstruction of Cambodia*, signed in tandem with the peace agreement, enjoined its signatories to launch what was termed an 'international reconstruction plan', which would:

> Promote Cambodian enterpreneurship and make use of the private sector, among other sectors, to help advance self-sustaining economic growth. It would also benefit from regional approaches, involving *inter alia*, institutions such as the Economic and Social Commission for Asia and the Pacific (ESCAP) and the Mekong Committee, and Governments within the region; and from participation from non-governmental organizations (NGOs).[11]

These four processes – achievement of peace in Cambodian society, creation of a neutral bureaucracy, promotion of human rights and economic development – mirrored in fact the dynamics of development that have allowed in many Western societies the emergence of non-violent political frameworks.

The literature on the broad dynamics that allow peaceful societies to emerge in certain political and social contexts is quite substantial,[12] but can be seen to focus on certain themes. The concentration of the means of organized violence within the ambit of state structures is always seen as one of the foremost aspects of these dynamics. This development entails two broad processes. The notion of sovereignty forced states to constitute themselves as politically self-enclosed units able to defend themselves against their neighbors. There is thus a need for the organization of large-scale means of violence at the outer edge, so to speak, of the state. A war machine must be put together to defend against any possible territorial encroachment by other states. A process of the promotion of domestic peace follows, where state elites establish a monopoly of violence by eliminating, physically or through political integration, the groups seen as capable of challenging through violence the political order they are seeking to establish at the domestic level.

A second phenomenon is intertwined with the emergence of the state: the rise of capitalism. The consolidation of the state first allows the elimination of violence from social interaction. It is in that space that a non-violent circulation of goods can occur and in turn permit the development of a capitalist system of exchange. Conversely, the consolidation of a capitalist framework provides the state with the resources necessary to expand and sustain the war machine on which its existence is predicated.

The growth of the *bourgeoisie* associated with these phenomena creates another barrier to the exercise of violence. The *classes bourgeoises* demand that they be integrated in the circles of political power as their economic power increases. They do so through calls for an expansion of the political franchise beyond the confines of the aristocracy, which are articulated in the need to anchor authority and legitimacy on notions of popular representation. In this context, the emphasis on the rights of the individual becomes preeminent. Those rights consequently restrict the violence that can be exercised by the state against the individual.

A third phenomenon, the rise of individual rights, is thus central here. The individual can emerge as a locus of political power in a social universe where the currency of power is not brute force. The *bourgeoisie* then adds to this focus on the individual person in the language of politics by also adopting this vocabulary. It leads to strengthening the framework of individual rights and, by way of consequence, the constraints imposed in society on the use of violence against individuals.

A fundamental tension is thus established. The state controls the means of violence, but it cannot indiscriminately use violence against its citizens. The way power is exercised in these circumstances underscores the importance of a fourth, and last element in the constitution of a non-violent society: the emergence of a bureaucratic order. The power of the state *vis-à-vis* its citizens in a society where strong individual rights prevail cannot involve violence, and must thus be redirected through the elaboration of administrative procedures which allow supervision and control, but in a non-violent way. As Anthony Giddens, the best-known proponent of this notion, argues:

> The consolidation of the internal administrative resources of the state dislocates administrative power from its strong and necessary base in the coercive sanctions of armed force ... In the nation state, ... the claim to effective control of the means of violence is quite basic to state power. But the registering of the more or less complete success of this claim, made possible by the expansion of [administrative] surveillance capabilities and internal pacification, radically lessens the dependence of the state apparatus upon the wielding of military force as the means of its rule.[13]

The process of reconstruction, quite literally, of the Cambodian social and political order was done in a way that it could be expected to conform to these different dynamics.

This process was also to be accompanied by two other parallel developments. New elites were supposed to emerge in Cambodia as the international intervention proceeded. Their power would be tied to the new institutions created and, conversely, they would be expected to endorse and promote the process of social change through which they had gained power. New economic classes were supposed to appear as the economic reconstruction of Cambodia proceeded apace. They were then expected to push this process further because they would in fact benefit from the greater economic activity it would generate. In addition, the growth of a human rights lobby in Cambodia was intended to create a constituency, which would then have a stake in the further unfolding of political pluralism in the country.

A subtler but just as important development was also expected to occur during the international intervention in Cambodia. The very nature of the consensual understanding of politics in Cambodia was to change simultaneously with these two processes.   Politics in Cambodia had traditionally been synonymous with the machinations of the monarchy or with those of the different factional elites that had vied for power in Cambodia over the last decades. This would be changed as new institutions and new elites would bring with them the tangible demonstration that political pluralism could take hold in Cambodia and displace more traditional models of politics. Democracy would appear in this context not only as desirable, but also as plausible.

What happened, in fact, when the time came to implement these different processes? The transformation of Cambodia's political institutions floundered as soon as it started. Demobilization did not occur because the different Cambodian parties either refused to yield, or hid from international observers most of the weapons and troops they were supposed to decommission. While United Nations personnel did take formal control of large segment of the state apparatus, governmental rule remained in the hands of a network of covert organizations. The entire political space in Cambodia remained mired in factional and potentially violent politics, and did not at all move towards the creation of the neutral and non-violent political climate that the UN was trying to build in the country.[14]

The economic reconstruction package also proved quite disastrous, in ways that perhaps indicate most clearly the impact of economic integration on social reconstruction efforts. The capacity for aid absorption in Cambodia was quite weak given the inadequacy of its production infractructure and the lack of competent managerial institutions. International aid mostly found its way to the black market, which thrived because goods could be easily obtained through transborder routes extending principally to Vietnam and Thailand. Most of the private investments that came in went into economic sectors that did not link well with rest of the economy. The typical private investor, for example, would build a hotel with a plan to generate profits over the two years where international personnel would need short-term lodging in Cambodia, and would also most obviously prepare to get out of the country after the international operation there. Arguably, this problem was given an added dimension by the ease with which regional investments flows could move in and out of Cambodia.[15]

In this context, the social process of creating spheres in Cambodian society where human rights would be respected and promoted never had a chance. The inability to disarm the different Cambodian factions and to create neutral and democratic governing structures in Cambodia ensured that politics would still be defined by inter-factional dynamics and the constant threat of violence. In this type of environment, human rights groups had no influence and, indeed, no basis for power. An added impetus to the development of a human rights culture was to be rooted in economic development. Dynamism in the economy would lead to the emergence of new poles of power in Cambodia and to demands for greater pluralism and elite accountability. The breakdown of the plan of economic reconstruction in fact cut short this idea.[16]

Under these conditions, the processes of political renewal and accreditation of democratic ideals, which were supposed to accompany the process of social reconstruction in Cambodia could only falter. The political and social forces that were expected to emerge in Cambodia and endorse a new social contract lacked the basis to gain strength. In the absence of political classes strong enough to push forth alternatives, the political structures also remained unchanged in Cambodia. Immediately after the departure of the international community, governing mechanisms were indeed set by an inter-factional arrangement under the tutelage of the King – the most traditional of political figures in Cambodia.

What lessons can be gained from this experience? Clearly the most striking feature of the events of the 1991-93 period was the degree to which the failure of one aspect of the peace process could lead to the collapse of all the others. Pressures on political leaders to bring about a renewal of the political class, for instance, were futile in a context where dynamics for social change were absent. Conversely, a new social contract in Cambodia could not develop if it was not promoted and sustained by new political and social groupings whose interests would be linked to this movement towards social renewal. This perhaps underscores the necessity of a more holistic approach to the construction of peace in Cambodia. This is one that emphasizes the need for simultaneous and inter-linked efforts aimed at once at the reconstruction of society, the renewal of political classes, and the widespread accreditation of democratic ideals. In contrast, the logic of the 1991-93 intervention rested more on the idea of starting with some of these processes and ending with others. Has this lesson been learned?

The Regional Community and Constructive Intervention

It is the breakup of the inter-factional arrangement fashioned in 1993 after the departure of the United Nations that propelled Cambodia back to the international stage. Hun Sen, the Second Prime Minister, launched in July 1997 a *Coup de force* against the First Prime Minister of the country, Prince Ranariddh, and the members of his party, the Front Uni National pour un Cambodge Independent, Neutre, Pacifique et Cooperatif (FUNCINPEC).[17] While the Prince, who was in exile, called for a condemnation of Hun Sen's action, Ung Huot, a high-ranking member of FUNCINPEC, was named first Prime Minister in his place. The move allowed Hun Sen to claim that the coalition government set up in 1993 was in fact still operating.

The reaction of the international community was swift, if somewhat ambivalent. There seemed to be some consensus around the idea that the coalition arrangement struck in 1993 indeed had to stay in place, and that elections scheduled for 1998 had be held at all cost. There were definite discrepancies, however, in the way international pressures were put forward to ensure that this situation would prevail. The United States (US) represented one pole, marked by the virulence of its attacks on Hun Sen and its insistence on the need to respect democratic procedures in the lead-up to the elections of 1998. The US Senate, for instance, passed resolutions that deemed the events of July 1997 a 'violent military Coup d'etat' and stopped aid to Cambodia to pressure Hun Sen to cease his attacks on members of the FUNCINPEC and abide by the rules of democracy.[18]

Japan was the main exemplar of another pole of opinion. It saw in the situation created by the *coup de force* a possible resolution of the inter-factional tensions at the root of a complete stalemate in Cambodian politics in the preceding years. The new situation, in that view, provided the makings of some stability in Cambodia from which development and peace would perhaps proceed. Tokyo asserted so much when it announced its decision to maintain its aid program to Cambodia, the most important single source of foreign aid given to Phnom Penh, arguing that Hun Sen had respected his commitment to keep in place the coalition arrangement set up in 1993. Australia, another important player on the Cambodian stage, echoed this position.[19]

Two distinct approaches were thus present here. The American position argued that the way to peace in Cambodia must include a series of diplomatic pressures on Hun Sen to open up the structures of power in the country. Another approach, defined by the Japanese position, held that Hun Sen had to be engaged rather than confronted. Peace would result from long-term processes of regional integration and development, which would slowly open Cambodia to the influence of democratic forces. The dichotomy is somewhat puzzling given the remarks made above about the way in which the problem of peace in Cambodia should be approached. The international diplomatic initiatives were still accentuating either dynamics of political renewal or social development without a coherent strategy aimed at linking the two processes in a purposeful fashion. The lessons of the 1991-93 period, in a word, were not being applied.

Against this background, the contribution that the concept of constructive intervention could make to the advancement of peace in Cambodia becomes more apparent. First, the concept linked the evolution of the Cambodian situation to the development of regional security itself. Anwar Ibrahim argued that ASEAN had reached a level of maturity allowing it to go beyond the tenets of non-interference in order to address appropriately the issues of domestic instability that constitutes the core of Southeast Asia's security agenda. This would modify the dynamic of external involvement in the search for peace in Cambodia by setting this involvement in a long-term framework.

The intervention of the international community in 1991-93 had always been considered a finite process. Enormous amounts of resources and political will had been committed to the operation. Precisely for that reason, there was a sense among its sponsors that after its conclusion, Cambodians would very much be left on their own in their search for peace. UNTAC could not be expected to telescope in a matter of months, developments that had occurred over decades, if not centuries, in other societies. Furthermore, the political groupings threatened by the social changes that the international community wanted to bring to Cambodia could simply wait until the international personnel moved out. The Khmer Rouge, for instance, certainly scaled down its activities during the 1991-93 operation, but with the idea that they would resort to violence again once that operation was over. By linking the process of regional political and economic development in SEA to a direct involvement in conflict resolution in Cambodia, the concept of constructive intervention brought forward a logic entailing a sustained engagement in the country on ASEAN's part. Pressures for change in Cambodia, in the event of a regional involvement, would in fact become part of the very process of economic and political development in that country, allowing less leeway for political elites to circumvent them.

By underscoring the linkages between development and political change at both the regional and the domestic levels, the concept of constructive intervention addressed the central failing of the international diplomatic discourse on Cambodia. Rather than confining itself to the dichotomy between political renewal and social development, constructive intervention offered a way to combine and synthesize the two processes. The concept did not bank on the idea that political pressures alone could somehow force Cambodian leaders to democratize their country. Social change was to provide much of the impetus. Conversely, social change was not to be left to proceed on its own in an open-ended way. It was to be guided by the objectives of political pluralism and legitimacy, which would be at the center of the regional engagement *vis-à-vis* Cambodia. From these combined efforts would result a situation where the dynamics of development and of political pluralism would be mutually reinforcing. It is interesting to note, parenthetically, that this new approach was broached first in ASEAN circles. The idea that development and security are coextensive has always been part of the ASEAN discourse, and it was now expanded to address changing conditions, both in Cambodia and at the regional level.

The concept of constructive intervention followed the lead of the Study Group on Cambodia and Laos that, under the *aegis* of Anwar, had published in late 1996 a report that stated:

> ASEAN members, individually and collectively, should engage in the task of 'constructive intervention'. This means that, while non-intervention remains, and should remain, the cardinal principle for the conduct of intra-ASEAN relations, should the countries concerned feel a need for assistance and appeal for it, the ... ASEAN members should be prepared to play 'proactive' roles in removing both the short-term and medium-term constraints on Cambodia's and Laos' development and regional participation.[20]

The actual steps that this process would entail revolved, in Anwar's mind, around four types of activities:

1. assistance in the organization of elections;
2. palpable and expanded commitment to legal and administrative reforms;
3. strengthening of human capital; and
4. strengthening of civil society organizations and of the rule of law.[21]

However, the concept of constructive intervention must be fleshed out in its implementation. How exactly would support for the process of political renewal in Cambodia draw upon domestic forces of broader social change and give them further impetus? How would these processes of social change be encouraged even if progressive political forces were weak, to say the least? And how, indeed, would that process of social reconstruction go beyond the obstacles that dynamics of economic integration has put in its way between 1991 and 1993? Would the risks of social dislocation entailed by the growth of regionalism, in other words, be stronger than regional aspirations for social reconstruction in Cambodia?

These pragmatic questions were never addressed. Diverging political interests stood in the way of concerted action on the part of ASEAN. Vietnam, for instance, was mindful of its historical links with Hun Sen's government when it immediately welcomed the appointment of Ung Huot as First Prime Minister in replacement of Prince Ranariddh.[22] In a movement which again recalled past positions on Cambodian politics, Thailand, Singapore, and the Philippines immediately took harsher positions towards the new government created by Hun Sen.

Second, and perhaps more importantly, ASEAN was reticent to move towards a notion of regional responsibility in domestic conflict that would contradict its long-standing adherence to the principle of non-interference. The only instrument left in the hands of the Association was the power to refuse to admit Cambodia as a full member, as was supposed to happen shortly thereafter. The ASEAN Foreign Ministers did just that a few days after the *coup de force* of July 1997. Stating they would not interfere in Cambodian politics, they nevertheless described the recent use of force in the country as 'unfortunate', and delayed Cambodia's admission in the Association 'until a later date'.[23]

Once this point was reached, ASEAN was left without any mechanism to wield some measure of influence in Cambodia. Three ASEAN foreign ministers – Ali Alatas of Indonesia, Domingo Siazon of the Philippines, and Prachuab Chayasan of Thailand – did attempt to mediate between the government in Phnom Penh and Prince Ranariddh but did not wrest any concession from Hun Sen. ASEAN also expressed satisfaction in September 1997 when, at the beginning of the new session of the United Nations it was decided that the Cambodian seat would remain vacant for the time being. However, this again failed to elicit any movement on Hun Sen's part.[24] At a conference organized in Phnom Penh in early 1998 that assessed Cambodia's situation *vis-à-vis* ASEAN, Hun Sun in fact dashed all hope by reiterating his long-standing position that the Association had no business meddling in Cambodian affairs.[25]

If ASEAN did not manage to achieve any progress towards peace in Cambodia, neither did the other approaches adopted by the international community. The elections held in July 1998 were marred by violence and intimidation, and failed to bring about any movement towards reconciliation. The post-election situation in Cambodia continued to be one where politics simply aimed at bringing about a power-sharing agreement among elites under the somewhat distant tutelage of the King. Under these conditions, Hun Sen managed to form a new coalition government and become Prime Minister.

In the context of the Cambodian elections of July 1998, Surin Pitsuwan attempted to reinvigorate the discussions surrounding the ideas raised earlier by Anwar. The notion of constructive intervention had by that time been watered down to the idea of 'flexible engagement'. The Thai Foreign Minister described the concept in a 'non-paper' circulated at the July 1998 ASEAN Ministerial Meeting as stemming from the 'less clear dividing line between domestic affairs on the one hand and external or trans-national issues on the other', and involving the 'domestic affairs [of some members] having obvious external or trans-national dimensions, adversely affecting neighbors, the region and the region's relations with others'.[26] The proposal was endorsed by the Philippines. Philippine Foreign Secretary Siazon, who also chaired the July 1998 AMM, reiterated some of these ideas in his opening statement. He underscored the need to act on the issues of development and conflict resolution by harnessing the economic and political forces at play in SEA, when he advocated the 'need to think, talk, and act regionally' on such issues.[27] Under much pressure from other ASEAN members, however, the discussions simply led to a final statement about a need for 'enhanced interaction' within ASEAN 'with respect to developments affecting a member-state or ASEAN as a whole'.[28] The repeated refusal of the Association to move beyond the sacrosanct principles of non-interference had won the day.

The return to traditional politics in Cambodia illustrates how little change international diplomacy has been able to effect in the country. Other factors, though, can lead to a more optimistic outlook on Cambodia. The international community has reopened the aid channels and vowed to use its leverage in the country's macroeconomic development to institute more transparency and responsiveness to social needs. The evolving situation regarding possible trials for crimes against humanity involving past Khmer Rouge leaders will also act as a barometer of the government's commitment to the rule of law in the country. Finally, Cambodia's admission into ASEAN and the rise of a vibrant NGO and civil society community in the country should also provide points of entry for regional actors into sustained dynamics of change in Cambodian society.[29] Will ASEAN use these opportunities towards effecting domestic conflict resolution and stability in Cambodia?

It may be in East Timor that ASEAN will have to explore the issue. The question of East Timor will nonetheless entail a long-term process of reconciliation that will undoubtedly compel ASEAN to engage some of its more problematic aspects. Three problems seem to stand out. The economy of East Timor cannot rely on its meager resources to develop in the short- and medium-term. Economic development will therefore have to rely on some form of regional participation and integration. The issue of inter-communal relations and integration will also add a new dimension to the process of peace-building. And finally, the reticence of the Indonesian government and its Army *vis-à-vis* the process engaged by the UN might also create an additional layer of difficulty in the construction of peace and democracy within East Timor.

ASEAN will not be able to ignore the evolving situation in East Timor. Will the dynamics of integration at work in SEA, however, engender a strong and coherent regional stand on conflict resolution? And will the proposals for constructive intervention also find some resonance here, given the additional challenges entailed by the East Timor case? Will ASEAN be able to move closer to the implementation of the principles contained within the notion of constructive intervention? And if ASEAN does in fact move in that direction, the question of pragmatics will remain. What would the practice of constructive intervention actually look like?

Developing Constructive Intervention: Towards Human Security

Dealing with the issue of pragmatics might actually help answer the question of political will. If it can be demonstrated that constructive intervention can serve as an efficient mechanism through which regional permutations of the Cambodian problem can be addressed, a more positive outlook might engage in ASEAN circles. How, then, is it possible to flesh out the concrete procedures through which constructive intervention might proceed?

The study of the 1991-93 period established the fundamental processes at stake in promoting peace and democracy in Cambodia. They include the solidification and pluralization of the state apparatus, the expansion of economic classes that leads to enlargement of the political franchise, and the opening up of spaces where a discourse on human rights can flourish. An obvious area where ASEAN could formulate a more coherent strategy is in the field of private economic development. The approach followed during the international intervention, and indeed the one that has dominated since, has been largely incoherent. Private investors have come and gone as they pleased, provided they had the right connections within the Phnom Penh government. A regional strategy of investment, articulated on the need to prioritize the primary and secondary sectors in Cambodia is something that would be feasible and highly effective.

The field of human rights has been framed in Cambodia since 1993 by the actions of NGOs. Two problems must be attended to. Non-Cambodian NGOs are experiencing great difficulties in attempting to coordinate their actions. And they have also failed to connect their activities with the Cambodian groups working towards the development of a civil society in Cambodia.[30] Here again the formulation of a framework of action by the regional community could have advantageous effects.

This approach would be highly beneficial in helping create a state apparatus whose power is limited and shaped by the rules of democracy. This is the area where the most political resistance has been felt, both in the slow opening up of Cambodian politics, and in ASEAN's reticence to endorse a strategy of direct pressure on political actors in Cambodia. The constructive intervention approach would also have the advantage of creating in Cambodian society autonomous spheres of political pressure on the state able to then draw from local spheres of economic and social development to press demands for good governance upon the state. And perhaps it would also have the added advantage of being politically palatable within regional policy circles. Support for grassroots development would not entail for ASEAN the type of direct political pressure it disdains.

The process of social change is supposed to bring about greater pluralism in Cambodia. As shown earlier, this last element was central in the failure of the 1991-93 operation. UNTAC argued that old models of politics had to be replaced in Cambodia. However, it put forward a substitute model that did not correspond to the nature of the institutions and political practices of the country. It failed to formulate the appropriate principles that should guide Cambodian politics in the transition period. A model of conflict resolution articulated on grassroots dynamics of the type outlined above, precisely because it sees the construction of peace as coextensive with the process of social change, would give such a logical map. It might also provide a platform upon which groups promoting change through the expansion of democracy in Cambodia could base the legitimacy of their actions.[31]

The logic of constructive intervention serves these requirements well since it links processes of political change to broader dynamics of social transformation in a broad overall rationale. However this logic needs to be supplemented by concerns that are perhaps best encapsulated in the notions of social capital and human security. Social capital, defined as the series of norms and acquired sets of knowledge that allow and articulate social action,[32] can provide the conceptual opening through which constructive intervention could be made political palatable to its detractors within ASEAN. It can do so by shifting the onus of the peace-building project to local, rather than regional actors. Social capital presents a core concept through which the expansion of the groups charged with implementing the needed social changes can be organized and legitimized. The construction of peace in Cambodia can be conceptualized as the elaboration of a specific social capital, defined essentially as the sum of the different lessons learned during the 1991-93 period.

The concept of human security meanwhile connects the construction of social capital with the growth of security. It shows how the development of a stable, democratic, and indeed, secure, social environment contributes to the advancement of regional security.[33] Coupling the notions of constructive intervention and human security can thus provide an overall conceptual architecture where the need to support the growth of local peace-building capacities can be linked in the ASEAN discourse with the expansion of regional security. This would then allow local actors, involved in the construction of the social capital associated with peace-building to justify their action on a much broader regional security scale, and to then solicit broader regional support. And Cambodia's membership within ASEAN might actually facilitate this process.

Articulating constructive intervention on notions of social capital and human security could also provide the best defense against the deleterious effects of economic regionalization on peace-building. Creating more autonomous zones of development would make the Cambodian economy less vulnerable to fluctuating regional investment flows. The creation of a set of local actors intent on forcing the Cambodian government to be socially responsive and responsible in its economic policies would dovetail well with the policies of the international donor community requiring more transparency and social responsibility from recipient governments.

This approach would also most surely be beneficial in East Timor. If the situation were to remain unstable after the departure of the United Nations contingent, ASEAN would presumably have to engage the issue in view of its possible repercussions on the stability and international image of the region.[34] Constructive intervention would probably involve convincing Jakarta that regional integration and post-crisis reconstruction should not be impeded by the deterioration of the situation in East Timor and the frictions it would entail between ASEAN and the international community. The argument would build on past ASEAN diplomatic traditions. The idea is not to organize a campaign of regional political pressures on Indonesia. The logic of constructive intervention would be articulated directly on the dynamics bringing together the countries of the area and linking their prospects for development and stability. The idea is to convince the Jakarta government that the situation of interdependence of ASEAN, both internally and *vis-à-vis* the international community leaves it with no choice but to move towards a durable resolution of the conflict in East Timor.

How exactly will these dynamics lead to a precise mechanics of peace in East Timor? Again, the concepts of social capital and human security might make some useful contribution to this regional initiative. Articulating the peace-building project in East Timor on the construction of social capital would again diminish the focus on ASEAN involvement in what would be perceived by Jakarta as an intra-state matter. This approach would help ease relations between the Indonesian government and its ASEAN counterparts. Concentrating the peace-building process on the construction of social capital would also favor the emergence of local actors able to sustain, energize, and direct the peace process with a great degree of autonomy from the vagaries of regional politics. This would not be unimportant in case of Jakarta's equivocations on the East Timor issue.

These actors would endeavor to ensure the East Timor politics can move from a violent to a non-violent setting. NGOs and civil society actors would attempt to reproduce the configurations of state solidification, economic expansion, and human rights development that the Cambodian peace process brought to light. Hopefully, these efforts would move the center of gravity of East Timor politics away from direct inter-communal friction, towards the construction of an institutional framework that would allow peaceful inter-communal relations.

These different elements, in turn, bring to light another advantage related to the concept of social capital. Formulating peace-building in the same conceptual terms would allow an easier transfer of the lessons of the Cambodian case to East Timor. Conceptualizing the construction of peace as learning how to use the social capital developed in one case would in fact encourage and facilitate the development of a greater social capital on the question of peace-building, not only locally in both Cambodia and East Timor, but also within ASEAN diplomatic circles.

This could then bring together the expansion of social capital on conflict resolution and the very idea of greater regional security SEA. There would be a clear conceptual link, in other words, between the construction of a local knowledge on conflict resolution and the attainment of a more secure regional order. As discussed earlier, the problem of peace in East Timor would revolve around the issue of development. The economy of East Timor does not have the resources to sustain itself. Weak economic development could quite swiftly result in political instability and decreased government legitimacy. Perhaps a clear linkage between regional and local development in the cause of peace would allow a greater degree of regional cooperation in ensuring that regional economic integration does not bypass East Timor and thwart its development.

In a word then, the concept of constructive intervention can be seen as marking two quite decisive strides in the formulation of a doctrine on conflict resolution within the ASEAN diplomatic discourse. First, the concept underscores the interconnectedness between domestic conflicts and regional stability, and the need to resolve these conflicts in a democratic manner. Second, the concept suggests that the best way towards some form of democratic resolution of domestic conflict is not only through direct diplomatic pressure on domestic political actors, but also through the judicious use of the dynamics of economic and political integration now at play in SEA. Regional cooperation can promote dynamics of development that in turn can make conflict and violence less likely in many areas of the region where they have been endemic.

The concept of social capital can add a focus on the actual mechanics of peace entailed by such a regional project. First, the concept affixes a local element to the notion of constructive intervention. To a discourse centered on regional initiatives is added the idea that these initiatives should, and would indeed over time, give rise to local actors that would then sustain and develop the peace-building process. This might also make the prospect of constructive intervention more palatable to the detractors of the concept in ASEAN circles. Second, the concept of social capital suggests that the process of peace-building can be learned, and then applied by these local actors. What has been grasped about the construction of peace in Cambodia, for instance, can be tapped in East Timor at present, and in Aceh or Ambon tomorrow, and elsewhere. For ASEAN, social capital underscores how the pragmatics of constructive intervention entail actual interventions in situations of conflict and also, quite simply, cooperation and coordination between the different local actors involved in the resolution of these conflicts.

Moreover, the notion of human security provides the conceptual framework upon which it is possible to connect these different elements in a meaningful way. It does so at two levels. First, it connects local regional stability, and thus demonstrates the need for a sustained regional involvement in local peace-building. Second, precisely because it provides a strong argument for regional involvement in local peace-building, it can serve as a rallying cry for local actors engaged in the peace-building process as they try to gather support and resources within ASEAN diplomatic circles.

Finally, the notions of social capital and human security can also help mitigate the adverse effects of economic regionalism and globalization on the peace-building process. As discussed earlier, these phenomena can bring about a vicious circle. They take away from political and social institutions the legitimacy and efficiency that the peace-building process aims precisely at building. By localizing the economic development entailed by the peace-building process, and by ensuring that political and social institutions remain responsive to local realities and needs during that process, the concepts of social capital and human security can break that circle.

Notes

1   Axworthy, L. (1998), *Remarks for the Second Annual NGO Consultations on Peacebuilding*, Ottawa, 18 February.
2   Boutros-Ghali, B. (1995), *An Agenda for Development*, United Nations, New York, pp.44.
3   Department of Public Information (1992), *An Agenda for Peace: Preventive Diplomacy, Peacemaking and Peacekeeping*, United Nations, New York.
4   Boutros-Ghali, *An Agenda for Peace*, 1995, pp. 11.
5   See Anwar's interview in *Newsweek*, 21 July 1997.
6   See, for instance: Tasker, R. and Hiebert, M. (1998), 'Dysfunctional Family', *Far Eastern Economic Review*, 23 July, pp.20.
7   *Senate Daily Hansard (Australia)*, 6 December 1990. The proposal was entitled: *Cambodia: An Australian Peace Proposal*, Working Papers prepared for the 'Informal

Meeting on Cambodia', Jakarta, 26-28 February 1990. It is contained in Acharya, A., Lizée, P., Peou, S. (eds) (1991), *Cambodia – The 1989 Paris Peace Conference. Background Analysis and Documents*, Kraus International Publication, Millwood, New York.

8   *Agreement on a Comprehensive Political Settlement of the Cambodia Conflict*, October 1991; Part 1 – Arrangements During the Transitional Period; Section V – Cease-fire and Cessation of Outside Military Assistance; Article 11.

9   *Ibid.*, Annex 1, UNTAC Mandate; Section B, Civil Administration; see articles 1, 2, and 3.

10   *Ibid.*, Part III; Article 15.

11   *Ibid.*, Article 12.

12   Some of the best-known texts are: Mann, M. (1988), *States, War and Capitalism. Studies in Political Sociology*, Basil Blackwell, Oxford and New York; Moore, B. Jr. (1966), *Social Origins of Dictatorship and Democracy. Lord and Peasant in the Making of the Modern World*, Beacon Press, Boston; Tilly, C. (1985), 'War Making and State Making as Organized Crime', in P. Evans, D. Rueschmeyer, T. Skocpol (eds), *Bringing the State Back In*, Cambridge University Press, Cambridge; Giddens, A. (1987), *The Nation-State and Violence*, University of California Press, Berkeley and Los Angeles.

13   Giddener, *The Nation-State and Violence*, 1987, pp. 192.

14   On these issues, see: *Progress Report of the Secretary-General (of the United Nations) on UNTAC*, UN Document S/24578, 21 September 1992.

15   One of the best studies of these issues is: Davies, R. (1993), 'UNTAC and the Cambodian Economy: What Impact?', *Phnom Penh Post*, 29 January – 11 February, pp.4-5.

16   See, on these matters, the report prepared at the time by five American specialists: Betts, R., Bresnan, J., Brown, F. Z., Worley, J. W., Zagoria, D. (1992), *Time is Running Out in Cambodia*, East Asian Institute, Columbia University, New York.

17   The acronym stands for Front Uni National Pour Un Cambodge Indépendent, Neutre, Pacifique, et Coopératif.

18   See, for instance: House of Representatives Resolution 195, passed on 28 July 1997.

19   On these points, see: Hiebert, M. (1997), 'ASEAN – All for One', *Far Eastern Economic Review*, 7 August 1997, pp.26. Tony Kevin, the Australian Ambassador to Phnom Penh at the time, expressed his clear support to Hun Sen, whom he dubbed 'a democrat at heart', and argued that the Second Prime Minister was the only person able to bring stability to Cambodia. See: Reuters, 13 July 1997.

20   The report of the Study Group on Cambodia and Laos (SGCL) was presented in November 1996. It is quoted in: Rajaretnam, M. (1999), 'Principles in Crisis: The Need for New Directions', in K. K. Hourn and J. A. Kaplan (eds), *Principles Under Pressure: Cambodia and ASEAN's Non-Interference Policy*, Cambodian Institute for Cooperation and Peace, Phnom Penh, pp.44.

21   *Ibid.*, pp.46.

22   Reuters, 17 July 1997.

23   *Statement on Cambodia (From the ASEAN Foreign Ministers)*, 10 July 1997.

24   Agence France-Presse, 24 September 1997.

25   Speech by His Excellency Hun Sen, Second Prime Minister at the conference 'Cambodia's Future in ASEAN: Dynamo or Dynamite?', Phnom Penh, 20 February 1998.

26   Pitsuwan, S. (1998), *Thailand's Non-Paper on the Flexible Engagement Approach*, 27 July, quoted in Thayer, C. A. (1999), 'Southeast Asia: Challenges to Unity and Regime Legitimacy', *Southeast Asian Affairs 1999*, pp.4.

27   Statement of H.E. Domingo L. Siazon, Jr., Secretary of Foreign Affairs of the Philippines and Chairman of the 31st ASEAN Standing Committee, at the Opening of the 31st ASEAN Ministerial Meeting, 24 July 1998.

28 See Statement of Rodolfo C. Severino, ASEAN Secretary-General, at the final press conference of the meeting.
29 See Lizée, P. P. (1999), 'Testing the Limits of Change: Cambodia's Politics After the July 1998 Elections', *Southeast Asian Affairs 1999*, pp.79-91.
30 Yonekura, Y. (1997), 'The Emergence of Civil Society in Cambodia', *Cambodia Report* vol.3, no.1, May-June, pp.10-17.
31 On the links between these different issues, see Hourn, K. K. (1999), *Emerging Civil Society in Cambodia: Opportunities and Challenges*, CICP Conference Working Paper Series No. 2, Cambodian Institute for Cooperation and Peace (CICP), Phnom Penh, pp.32.
32 Some central writings on the issue are Coleman, J. (1988), 'Social Capital in the Creation of Human Capital', *American Journal of Sociology*, supplement, pp.95-120; Putnam, R. (1993), *Making Democracy Work*, Princeton University Press, Princeton; Wilson, P. (1997), 'Building Social Capital: A Learning Agenda for the Twenty-First Century', *Urban Studies*, vol.34, no.5, pp.745-760.
33 Among the many pronouncements of the Canadian government on the issue, see: Notes for an Address by the Honorable Lloyd Axworthy, Minister of Foreign Affairs, to the Société des Relations Internationales de Québec, 'Human Security and Canada's Security Council Agenda', Department of Foreign Affairs and International Trade, Statement No. 99/13, 25 February 1999.
34 On the long-term risks for instability in East Timor after the departure of the UN, see, for instance, McBeth, J. (1999), 'Living Dangerously. Violence and Uncertainly Fuel Worries About the Forthcoming Timor Poll', *Far Eastern Economic Review*, 15 July, pp.16-17.

References

Acharya, A., Lizée, P., Peou, S. (eds) (1991), *Cambodia – The 1989 Paris Peace Conference. Background Analysis and Documents*, Kraus International Publication, Millwood, New York.

Axworthy, L. (1998), *Remarks for the Second Annual NGO Consultations on Peacebuilding*, Ottawa, 18 February.

Betts, R., Bresnan, J., Brown, F. Z., Worley, J. W., Zagoria, D. (1992), *Time is Running Out in Cambodia*, East Asian Institute, Columbia University, New York.

Boutros-Ghali, B. (1995), *An Agenda for Development*, United Nations, New York, pp. 44.

Coleman, J. (1988), 'Social Capital in the Creation of Human Capital', *American Journal of Sociology*, supplement, pp. 95-120.

Davies, R. (1993), 'UNTAC and the Cambodian Economy: What Impact?', *Phnom Penh Post*, 29 January – 11 February, pp. 4-5.

Department of Public Information (1992), *An Agenda for Peace: Preventive Diplomacy, Peacemaking and Peacekeeping*, United Nations, New York.

Giddens, A. (1987), *The Nation-State and Violence*, University of California Press, Berkeley and Los Angeles.

Hiebert, M. (1997), 'ASEAN – All for One', *Far Eastern Economic Review*, 7 August 1997, pp. 26.

Hourn, K. K. (1999), *Emerging Civil Society in Cambodia: Opportunities and Challenges*, CICP Conference Working Paper Series No. 2, Cambodian Institute for Cooperation and Peace (CICP), Phnom Penh, pp. 32.

Lizée, P. P. (1999), 'Testing the Limits of Change: Cambodia's Politics After the July 1998 Elections', *Southeast Asian Affairs 1999*, pp. 79-91.

Mann, M. (1988), *States, War and Capitalism. Studies in Political Sociology*, Basil Blackwell, Oxford and New York.

McBeth, J. (1999), 'Living Dangerously. Violence and Uncertainty Fuel Worries About the Forthcoming Timor Poll', *Far Eastern Economic Review*, 15 July 1999, pp. 16-17.

Moore, B. Jr. (1966), *Social Origins of Dictatorship and Democracy. Lord and Peasant in the Making of the Modern World*, Beacon Press, Boston.

Pitsuwan, S. (1998), *Thailand's Non-Paper on the Flexible Engagement Approach*, 27 July.

Progress Report of the Secretary-General [of the United Nations] on UNTAC, UN Document S/24578, 21 September 1992.

Putnam, R. (1993), *Making Democracy Work*, Princeton University Press, Princeton.

Rajaretnam, M. (1999), 'Principles in Crisis: The Need for New Directions', in K. K. Hourn and J. A. Kaplan (eds), *Principles Under Pressure: Cambodia and ASEAN's Non-Interference Policy*, Cambodian Institute for Cooperation and Peace, Phnom Penh, pp. 44.

Thayer, C. A. (1999), 'Southeast Asia: Challenges to Unity and Regime Legitimacy', *Southeast Asian Affairs 1999*, pp. 4.

Tasker, R. and Hiebert, M. (1998), 'Dysfunctional Family', *Far Eastern Economic Review*, 23 July, pp. 20.

Tilly, C. (1985), 'War Making and State Making as Organized Crime', in P. Evans, D. Rueschmeyer, T. Skocpol (eds), *Bringing the State Back In*, Cambridge University Press, Cambridge.

Wilson, P. (1997), 'Building Social Capital: A Learning Agenda for the Twenty-First Century', *Urban Studies*, vol. 34, no. 5, pp. 745-760.

Yonekura, Y. (1997), 'The Emergence of Civil Society in Cambodia', *Cambodia Report* vol. 3, no. 1, May-June, pp. 10-17.

Chapter 5

Globalization, Norms, and Sovereignty: ASEAN's Changing Identity and its Implications for Development and Security

David Capie

Introduction

For the past thirty years, the Association of Southeast Asian Nations (ASEAN) has played a central role in the promotion of economic development and security cooperation in Southeast Asia (SEA). Since its inception in 1967, it has gradually deepened economic linkages, forged political ties, and created an incipient sense of regional identity among its members. ASEAN has also been at the forefront of moves to create wider economic and political-security dialogues, through Asia Pacific Economic Cooperation (APEC), the ASEAN Regional Forum (ARF), the Asia-Europe Meeting (ASEM) and the ASEAN+3 meeting with China, Japan and South Korea. Until 1997, ASEAN was widely lauded as an exceptionally successful regional institution, perhaps the only one of its kind in the developing world.

ASEAN's leaders have historically attributed much of its success to the 'ASEAN Way' of cooperation based on the principles of consensus, informality, and non-interference. Malaysian Prime Minister Mahathir Mohammad has described the ASEAN way as a 'winning formula' which 'more than anything else has held ASEAN together'.[1] ASEAN leaders have vociferously rejected Western, liberal, Cartesian models of institutionalism as inappropriate—both too formal and too confrontational —for the circumstances of the Asia Pacific region. This has even led some commentators to suggest that a uniquely Asia Pacific way of institution-building might be evolving.[2]

Until recently there was little debate about the utility and legitimacy of ASEAN's institutional norms. However, the organization's 30th anniversary in 1997 signaled a decisive turning point. The violent overthrow of the government in Cambodia; a serious, seemingly irresolvable environmental disaster known locally as 'the haze', and the onset of an unprecedented economic crisis cast a pall on the ASEAN leaders as they gathered in Kuala Lumpur to celebrate the grouping's first 30 years. Perceptions of ASEAN paralysis in the face of turmoil—whether fair or not —

prompted stern criticism. In the allocation of blame that followed, many believed 'the ASEAN Way got in ASEAN's way', as a Malaysian analyst quipped.[3] For the first time, influential figures within ASEAN publicly called for a more formal, rules-based approach to regional cooperation.[4] There were demands for the organization to abandon its fundamental norm of non-interference and for the establishment of a quasi supra-national authority to monitor economic performance.

This chapter examines the interaction between globalization, development, and security in SEA. Its focus is on ASEAN's institutional norms, where it argues the political and economic forces set loose by globalization have collided with local ideas about how best to manage security and development. It assesses how ASEAN's established model of sovereignty-enhancing regionalism has been affected by globalization, focusing on recent fractious debates within the organization. The first section explains some of the key terms used here, setting out the conceptual relationship between security and development in SEA and defining what is meant by 'the ASEAN Way' and globalization. The second section provides an account of three of the most significant debates about ASEAN's norms that have arisen since 1997. It examines the constructive intervention/flexible engagement controversy in detail, and considers the various reactions to calls for deeper economic integration and the arrest of the former Malaysian Deputy Prime Minister, Anwar Ibrahim. The final section looks ahead, asking what the recent divisions tell us about the prospects for ASEAN's model of facilitating regional development and security.

Development, Security, and Sovereignty

Much has been made of the preference in SEA to conceptualize security in broad, inclusive terms.[5] Typically, this implies that 'security goes beyond (but does not exclude) the military to include the political, the economic, and sociocultural dimensions'.[6] As Muthiah Alagappa notes, 'security through development' is a widely accepted principle in many Asian states.[7] It has underpinned ASEAN's approach to regional security since its creation. At the 1976 ASEAN Summit in Bali, Lee Kuan Yew argued that ASEAN's basic challenge was 'how to ensure continuing stability by stimulating economic development to resolve social and political problems'. Thai Prime Minister Kukrit Pramoj said 'national stability is primarily based on economic and social development'.[8] More recently, Prime Minister Mahathir has been quoted as saying that 'national security is inseparable from political stability, economic success, and social harmony. Without these all the guns in the world cannot prevent a country from being overcome by its enemies, whose ambitions can sometimes be fulfilled without firing a single shot'.[9]

In an attempt to operationalize this inclusive approach to security, a number of Southeast Asian countries have come up with specific comprehensive security policies or doctrines. Malaysian Deputy Prime Minister Musa Hittam set out 'Malaysia's Doctrine of Comprehensive Security' in a speech in Singapore in March 1984.[10] Indonesia used the notion of *ketahanan nasional* or 'national resilience' as part of its national defense planning since the early 1970s;[11] Singaporean defense policy refers to 'total security' (describing economic growth and development as a 'core value'), and ASEAN as a whole has recognized the concepts of 'regional resilience' and 'comprehensive' and 'cooperative' security.[12] But while the substantive content of the security agenda in SEA is traditionally defined in broad and inclusive terms, the primary referent object of the security (and the developmental) discourse is the state. The state, says Alagappa, 'remains the most valued form of political organization in Asia'.[13] This reflects the fact that the states of SEA are all relatively young, with most able to date their independence to the period of decolonization since World War II. The priority of elites in the region has been nation building, sustaining internal unity and cohesion while preventing meddling by neighbors and great powers alike. Not surprisingly, Southeast Asian leaders since independence have all been extraordinarily jealous of their hard won sovereignty.

The legacy of colonialism has had a pronounced effect on the history of integration and regional projects in SEA. As Roger Irvine has noted, 'Southeast Asian attempts at regional cooperation prior to the 1960s were hindered by the preoccupation of most countries with the pressing post-independence tasks of adapting to the severance of colonial links, establishing and consolidating indigenous political and economic institutions and achieving national integration'.[14] It has also meant that since the creation of a lasting regional group in 1967, regionalism in SEA has taken a different path from integrationist projects elsewhere in the world. Unlike Europe, for example, where states have made significant concessions of their sovereignty to supranational institutions such as the European Commission, the European Central Bank, the Court of Justice and, increasingly, the European Parliament, Southeast Asian regionalism has traditionally been *sovereignty-enhancing*. Regional cooperation has been taken up with the goal of strengthening, not weakening the capacity of the state and 'supranationalism is specifically guarded against'.[15] The only exception is in the area of economic cooperation. But even here, initiatives 'have only been undertaken in the belief that they will aid in industrialization and modernization and thus strengthen the state, not weaken it'.[16]

Here is an important conceptual meeting point between security and developmental policies in SEA. Both have the objective of preserving and increasing state autonomy and sovereignty. This is the case, somewhat paradoxically, even when the means for pursuing these objectives is a *regional* community, such as ASEAN. A central concern of Southeast Asian elites therefore has always been safeguarding their freedom of action and autonomy within a regional framework. To facilitate this, ASEAN's member states have adopted over time an informal set of norms, which emphasize the importance of their sovereignty and prevent the regional project from outpacing the desires of any individual member. This cluster of norms is commonly called the 'ASEAN Way'.

The ASEAN Way

According to Filipino scholar Estrella Solidum, ASEAN's norms can be traced to its institutional predecessor, the Association of Southeast Asia (ASA).[17] In 1961 the founders of the ASA declared that problems in the region should be resolved using

'Asian solutions that contain Asian values'. Solidum says the most important of these values was the use of 'very low-key diplomacy [which] avoids fanfare before an agreement is reached'.[18] She stresses the importance of 'invisible ground rules' shared by ASEAN elites. Among the most important of these was the norm of non-interference in the domestic affairs of others.

Non-interference is obviously not a uniquely Southeast Asian norm. Together with the principle of state sovereignty, it is at the very heart of the Westphalian system and is enshrined in the UN Charter. However, non-interference does have an especially powerful resonance in SEA. When ASEAN was created, its founders clearly remembered colonialism and wartime occupation by Japan. Their determination to avoid repeating that experience was reinforced as the cold war became more competitive and divisive in Asia during the 1960s. As a result, when they met in Bangkok in 1967 they declared their determination 'to ensure their stability and security from external interference in any form or manifestation in order to preserve their national identities in accordance with the ideals and aspirations of their peoples'.[19] While the Bangkok Declaration's language stressed 'external interference', this did not just mean extra-regional powers. The injunction on interference applied equally to meddling by other ASEAN member states. The principle laid down in the Bangkok Declaration was repeated in the drawing up of the plan for a Zone of Peace, Freedom and Neutrality (ZOPFAN) in 1971, and in 1976, ASEAN moved to institutionalize the principle further when it adopted the Treaty of Amity and Cooperation (TAC) and the Declaration of ASEAN Concord.[20]

More recently, however, discussion of the norm of non-intervention has centered on the questions of human rights and democratization, in particular ASEAN's policies towards Myanmar (Burma), Cambodia, and East Timor. Despite international criticism of the military regime in Yangon, ASEAN has consistently refused to get involved in Burma's domestic politics, declaring them to be an 'internal affair'. For most of this past decade, it has described its stance on Myanmar as one of 'constructive engagement', meaning a preference for the use of quiet diplomacy, gentle persuasion, and economic ties to encourage change rather than open criticism and sanctions.[21] The latter, ASEAN has argued, not only would breach its norm of non-intervention, but would also be ineffective.[22] In support of this position some ASEAN elites have cited the UN Charter and invoked non-intervention and sovereignty as 'global' norms. This highlights what Brian Job calls ASEAN's 'selective rendering of international norms'.[23] ASEAN elites have historically accepted those norms that 'promote sovereignty preservation and preserve state autonomy in their narrower senses' but have refused to recognize other principles of contemporary international society such as human rights and humanitarian intervention.

The second central element of the ASEAN Way is its use of consensus decision-making processes. At the regional level, this principally means working to avoid the discussion of contentious or controversial matters. In José Almonte's words, 'divisive issues are simply passed over for later resolution—or until they have been made either irrelevant or innocuous by time and events'.[24] Noordin Sopiee has said ASEAN's idea of consensus means 'agreeing to disagree without being disagreeable'.[25] It is, however, important not to confuse ASEAN's notion of consensus with an absolute requirement for unanimity. ASEAN has traditionally shown some flexibility when faced with economic proposals that not all members agree to. Where there is broad support for a particular economic measure, the objections of a dissenting participant can be put aside, provided the proposal does not threaten their most fundamental national interests. This habit is sometimes called the n-X formula or 'flexible consensus'. However, flexible consensus is only acceptable when dealing with a difference of opinion on some economic issues. When divisive *political* matters emerge, the consensus rule is applied much more strictly.

The third of ASEAN's norms is a 'preference for informality and the related avoidance of excessive institutionalization'.[26] Singaporean Foreign Minister Shanmugam Jayakumar has described this as a predilection for 'organizational minimalism'.[27] Robert Scalapino calls it 'soft regionalism' or 'soft dialogue'.[28] According to Khong Yuen Foong 'ASEAN officials have contrasted their approach to [those] that emphasize legal contracts, formal declarations, majoritarian rules and confrontational negotiating tactics'.[29] Officials prefer to stress process and achieving of a level of comfort, rather than the outcome of meetings.[30] The importance of personal ties between ASEAN leaders is another example of this informality. ASEAN leaders prefer what Tun Abdul Razak called 'sports-shirt diplomacy' over Western 'business shirt diplomacy'.[31] Discussions over breakfast or on the golf course are preferred to sitting down to debate a policy in a meeting and bilateral meetings, especially face to face meetings between leaders, are especially important as trust-building measures.

Together the norms that make up the ASEAN Way have had the effect of preserving the sovereignty of members by giving each considerable influence over the pace and shape of Southeast Asian regionalism. Power in ASEAN has remained decentralized, with the most important decisions in the Association still being made in the respective national capitals. The ASEAN Secretariat in Jakarta is comparatively weak, despite the cautious expansion of its powers in recent years. Unacceptable policy initiatives usually either never make it to the bargaining table or are quietly set aside once opposition is raised. And while the norm of non-interference has often been honored in the breach, it has at the very least served to keep contentious bilateral issues from encumbering the ASEAN agenda.[32] Until 1997, few concerns were raised about the efficacy of this approach to regional cooperation. In the past few years, however, ASEAN's model of regionalism has increasingly come into question, strained by the demands of a wider membership and challenged by the political and economic forces of globalization.

Globalization and SEA

Globalization is a slippery and contested term. It has no single meaning and it is often used in ambiguous, confusing, and contradictory ways. As Richard Higgott and Simon Reich note, 'globalization is rapidly replacing the 'cold war' as the most overused and under-specified explanation for a variety of events in international relations'.[33] One commonly used definition of globalization is economic. It refers to a particular stage in the history of advanced capitalism; an era that has seen the break-up of the Bretton Woods system, the end of the Polanyian compromise between capital and labor, and the development of a genuinely global economy.[34] Descriptions of the new global economy typically cite the rapid mobility of financial capital across international borders, the increasingly transnational nature of production, and the removal of barriers to international trade and services.[35] Globalization is also facilitated by the development of 'transnational economic diplomacy' through bodies like the World Trading Organization (WTO), the G7 and the European Union, and by liberalization-promoting institutions like the North American Free Trade Area (NAFTA) and APEC.[36]

Taken in this sense, the pressures of globalization have been strongly felt in SEA since at least the middle of the 1980s. ASEAN states have increasingly opened their economies to foreign investment and generally adopted policies of market liberalization. While the degree of openness has always varied greatly between members, economic liberalization received the blessing of the institution as a whole in 1992 with the launch of the ASEAN Free Trade Area (AFTA) at the Fourth ASEAN Summit in Singapore. AFTA was in large part a response to a perceived external threat, the possibility of 'blocism' emerging following the signing of NAFTA and the deeper integration of the European Union. The pressures of globalization have been even more pronounced in the wake of the economic crisis that hit the region in 1997. Not only has ASEAN been forced to bring forward its liberalization schedule under AFTA. It has also launched a number of other initiatives, that are discussed in greater detail below. ASEAN's members can no longer shrug off questions about transparency, accountability, and good governance by pointing to indicators of impressive economic performance. These topics have been raised, and even used as lending conditionalities by dialogue partners and international financial institutions like the World Bank (WB) and the International Monetary Fund (IMF).

A less economistic understanding of globalization is also widely used in international relations literature. In this view, globalization is more than just a dense pattern of global economic relations, but also includes the mass transmission of Western values, culture, and norms. Anthony Giddens has described an 'intensification of world wide social relations which link distant realities in such a way that local happenings are shaped by events occurring many miles away or vice versa'.[37] In James Mittelman's words, 'globalization compresses the time and space aspects of social relations'.[38] Arguing from a Gramscian perspective, Robert Cox refers to a 'growing interconnectedness and interdependence on a world scale...[a] connectedness in politics and the organization of security, in economics and welfare, in culture, in ecology, in values of all kinds'. Similarly, William Robinson identifies what he calls a global 'social structure of accumulation', an unprecedented 'set of mutually reinforcing social, economic and political institutions and cultural and ideological norms'.[39] Ben Rosamond is even more specific, saying 'globalization may be seen as ...a process involving the world-wide export of the ideologies of free market capitalism and liberal democratic governance'.[40] On the basis of extensive interviews conducted in the region, this chapter argues that the second, broader definition most closely resembles the way the term is most commonly used and understood by Southeast Asian elites. Foreign policy and security analysts, both in and out of government, typically take globalization to mean not only the dominant economic ideology of market neo-liberalism, but also the growing challenge posed by values such as universal human rights, good governance, and liberal democracy.[41]

ASEAN's norms, as was noted in the previous section, have traditionally been based on a common Southeast Asian experience with a special emphasis given to state sovereignty. But as Chin Kin Wah notes, 'for the ASEAN states, regional cooperation today has to take much greater cognizance of [the] intensification of world wide relationships, aided by the revolution in information technology, which have impacted upon and complicated their domestic and regional political agendas'.[42] As ASEAN's members are increasingly forced to interact with extra-regional actors and issues, they are encountering 'global' norms that are often at odds with their own. Since the end of the cold war, governments and NGOs in the West have criticized many ASEAN member states for human rights violations and a lack of democratic governance. The Association itself has been assailed for its relationship with the regime in Yangon and ASEAN has found that its dialogues with important partners like the European Union and the United States (US) have been seriously complicated by the admission of Myanmar.[43] ASEAN members have also found themselves troubled and divided by the North Atlantic Treaty Organization (NATO) and UN-led interventions in Bosnia, Kosovo, and East Timor.

In addition to pressure from the 'top down' from Western governments, financial markets, and international lending institutions, the case for the adoption of 'global' norms like human rights, democracy, and good governance is also increasingly being made from the 'bottom up'. In recent years, SEA has acquired a sophisticated NGO network on human rights, aided by formal institutions like the Human Rights Commissions established in the Philippines, Indonesia, Malaysia, and Thailand. A legion of single-issue NGOs have been empowered by the proliferation of information technologies and the decline of cold war *realpolitik* foreign policy.[44] The result is that, in some countries at least, elites have been caught in a squeeze between supra- and sub-state actors. Nowhere is this more obvious than in the region's democracies, the Philippines and Thailand, where electorates are increasingly pressing for foreign policies that better reflect their national values. Relations with ASEAN have not escaped this pressure. As the next section illustrates, in the past few years this squeeze has led to open divisions within ASEAN and serious challenges to its traditional model of regional cooperation. It examines three examples of these divisions: first, the constructive intervention/flexible engagement debate; second, the fallout from the arrest of Anwar Ibrahim; and third, issues arising from ASEAN's ambitious economic agenda.

ASEAN's *Annus Horibilis* and the Rise of Dissent

The year 1997 was an *annus horibilis* for ASEAN. The coup in Cambodia, the onset of the haze, and the crippling economic crisis led to questions being asked about ASEAN's function and relevance.[45] The first signs of serious discontent came in July in the wake of the coup in Cambodia. In an essay in *Newsweek* magazine, then

Malaysian deputy prime minister Anwar Ibrahim castigated ASEAN for its failure to be more involved in the reconstruction of Cambodia, saying:

> Our non-involvement...contributed to the deterioration and final collapse of national reconciliation. We should have nursed the baby, at least through its teething period...ASEAN must move from being a largely reactive organization to one that is proactive.[46]

He proposed that ASEAN revisit its policy of non-intervention and replace it with what he called 'constructive interventions' or 'constructive involvement'.[47] Anwar added that such an approach need not simply apply to Cambodia, Myanmar might also benefit from greater ASEAN attention. Anwar's remarks attracted some critical comment as well as some praise within the region, but the idea was not given any additional substance by either the Deputy Prime Minister himself, or the Malaysian government.

While discussions in non-governmental circles produced numerous suggestions for change,[48] at the official level 'constructive intervention' laid dormant for almost a year. It was not until June 1998 that the gauntlet of change was again picked up, this time by the newly elected Democrat Party government in Thailand. The Democrats had come to power promising a foreign policy committed to the promotion of human rights and democracy and Thailand had already provoked some resentment with its pursuit of an 'open society' for ASEAN leading up to the Kuala Lumpur Summit in December 1997.[49] The proposal, though vaguely worded, was included eventually in the ASEAN Vision 2020 Statement that came out of the Summit, despite opposition from Indonesia, Laos, Myanmar, and Vietnam.[50] In May, the Chuan government called for the development of a permanent ASEAN Human Rights Commission, an idea endorsed by the 1993 ASEAN Summit, but never acted upon.[51]

In June, the Thai Foreign Minister, Surin Pitsuwan, turned his attention to constructive intervention. Speaking in unusually frank terms at the Asia Pacific Roundtable in Kuala Lumpur, Foreign Minister Surin said the economic crisis offered the region a unique opportunity to rebuild its economic and political foundations. In particular, he suggested that the new members of ASEAN might find this an 'opportune moment to reassess their respective processes of economic and political development in the face of rapid and far-reaching changes in the global arena'. Addressing the wider ASEAN audience, he asked 'whether the time has come for ASEAN to rethink its decades-old policy of non-interference in the internal affairs of member States'.[52] He cautioned that:

> ASEAN members can perhaps no longer afford to adopt a non-committal stance and avoid passing judgment on events in a member country, simply on the grounds of 'non-interference'. To be sure, ASEAN's respect for the sovereignty of fellow members is one reason why the grouping has come this far and enjoyed such longevity. However, if domestic events in one member's territory impact adversely on another member's internal affairs, not to mention peace and prosperity, much can be said in favor of ASEAN members playing a more proactive role.[53]

Surin continued his personal championing of constructive intervention in a speech twelve days later at his alma mater, Bangkok's Thammasat University. This time he related the issue to the need for institutional reform in Thailand in the wake of the economic crisis. He noted that 'the danger lies in the fact that while reform is by and large a domestic process, delays or setbacks in one country can affect the recovery of the region as a whole'. He seemed to suggest that whatever economic and institutional reforms might be made in Thailand, the recovery of the Thai economy was in large part tied to the fate of the region. The image SEA presented to international investors had not been helped by the events of 1997. Surin reiterated his call for a review of the non-intervention principle, noting that he was 'not the first to say this' but 'when a matter of domestic concerns poses a threat to regional stability, a dose of peer pressure or friendly advice at the right time can be helpful'.[54] If things were to improve then ASEAN had 'to play a constructive role in preventing or resolving domestic issues with regional implications'.

By the end of June, the language being used to describe Surin's proposal began to change. After a meeting with senior officials on 26 June it was decided the term constructive intervention sounded 'too radical' and the more palatable 'flexible engagement' was coined.[55] This was apparently a concession to concerns raised by ASEAN ambassadors in Bangkok and after Thai diplomats in Yangon and Vientiane were called in and quizzed about the apparent policy shift.[56] But while some regional press coverage framed the re-naming as a 'retraction' and a 'back down', little actually changed in terms of the proposal's substance.[57] Indeed, the debate about flexible engagement began to heat up as it became apparent to other ASEAN governments that Thailand was determined to bring the matter to the annual ASEAN Ministerial Meeting in Manila at the end of July.

Showdown in Manila

The 31st ASEAN Ministerial Meeting (AMM) in Manila did not intend to have flexible engagement as an issue for discussion and on the official agenda. Therefore, in a typical ASEAN fashion, some of the more intense discussions on the subject took place informally before the meeting began. There is no on-the-record account of those discussions, but according to one ASEAN official the key event was the foreign ministers' working dinner on 23 July 1998. This represented the first time the nine ministers had come together to discuss the issue. The tone was set early. Shortly before the dinner, Indonesian Foreign Minister Ali Alatas gave a briefing to the press, telling them that if the proposal was accepted 'we will be back to when ASEAN was not formed, when SEA was full of tension [and] mutual suspicion'.[58] Malaysian Foreign Minister Badawi, who had just emerged from lengthy bilateral discussions with Surin, similarly rejected the proposal, saying:

The success of Asean's cooperation is that we have to feel comfortable, any feelings that you will be criticized or pointed at, you will not be comfortable. We all have similar cultures. In our culture, we cannot embarrass our friends in public. We must have confidence in our culture.[59]

At the dinner itself Malaysia and Singapore 'moved to kill the idea', while Thailand and the Philippines spoke in favor of it.[60] A solution to the impasse was put forward by Alatas, who, while strongly opposed to any change in the principle of non-interference, suggested that the compromise wording 'enhanced interaction' might be acceptable.[61] According to one ASEAN official, the gist of Alatas's intervention was 'You [Thailand and the Philippines] can do this if you want, can talk more, engage more, you can do it already within ASEAN...we will just do more of it'.[62] However, the formal injunction on interference was to remain.

As a result of the compromise, the issue was brought up during the Ministerial Meeting. Its first mention came not from Surin or the Philippines Foreign Minister Domingo Siazon, but from newly elected Filipino president, Joseph Estrada, whose address opened the meeting. In a speech replete with heady rhetoric and lofty goals, Estrada said ASEAN could only create a true regional community if it moved towards 'greater total convergence, in our economic life and beyond. It is happening in Europe, it can also happen in our part of the world'. To achieve this, he said:

> Let us be open to one another and freely and candidly exchange our views no matter how controversial the issue. Only by being open can we truly appreciate what unites or divides us. Only by talking freely and candidly can we rise and build and prosper together.

As a practical measure, Estrada called for the strengthening of ASEAN's institutions, including the Secretariat. 'By reposing our trust in the institutions we build, we make permanent the ties that bind us. The European Union (EU) – arguably the world's most successful union of erstwhile bitter enemies – did so and triumphed. We too can succeed'. The President concluded with some thoughts for the future, saying 'bigger dreams can beckon. One market. One currency. One community'.[63]

Surin's opening address was somewhat less ambitious than Estrada's and marked a notable softening from his earlier statements. Without referring to either flexible engagement or constructive intervention by name, he couched his call for change in the face of challenges to ASEAN that were not only daunting in their magnitude but also of an 'entirely different nature from those that we have encountered in the past'. He claimed, somewhat disingenuously, that 'the principle of non-interference is not the issue and has never been the issue'. The issue is 'dealing with the new challenges of a new millennium'. He said:

> Like it or not, the issues of democracy and human rights are those that we will have to increasingly deal with in our engagement with the outside world. How are we going to put ourselves on the offensive rather than always being on the receiving end?

He went on:

> In today's globalized world, the issues have become so complex and multi-dimensional that a new vision is needed ... It is not a matter of interfering in the affairs of another country. Rather, it is a matter of being more open with one another on issues that impact on the

region. It is rather a matter of taking more pro-active concern about one another and being supportive of one another whenever needed. It is a matter of enhancing our interactions for the benefit of all.[64]

The Philippines' Foreign Minister Domingo Siazon's opening statement echoed the same theme of open and frank exchange, but in a slightly more low-key fashion. He emphasized the importance of the 'moral, human dimension' in a regional community, and said ASEAN could achieve greater feats:

If we can cooperate among ourselves in the spirit of more openness. We should be able to speak more freely on issues occurring in one member country that affect others, with a view to building more solid ground for regional action. For a stronger ASEAN, we need to think, talk and act regionally, even and particularly on thorny issues.[65]

Although Surin and Siazon had dropped the use of the terms flexible engagement and constructive intervention and framed their proposals in less confrontational terms, strong opposition was still voiced at the Ministerial Meeting. Malaysian Foreign Minister Badawi devoted almost his entire address to the issue, arguing that calls for change were mistaken. 'To abandon the consensus principle', he said 'would be to usher in a divided and fractious ASEAN and consequently, an enfeebled ASEAN in regional and international affairs'. He warned that 'to abandon this time-tested principle would set us on the path towards eventual disintegration'.

But Badawi's address also clarified ASEAN's policy about commenting on the affairs of other member states. He denied that the principle of non-intervention had prevented governments in the past from commenting on the actions of others. He said:

We have not only commented and criticized, we have even expressed reservations when necessary. But we do all of this quietly, befitting a community of friends bonded in cooperation and ever mindful of the fact that fractious relations undermine the capacity of ASEAN to work together on issues critical to our collective well being. We do it this quiet way because criticizing loudly, posturing adversarially and grandstanding bring less results and does more harm than good. Problems existing between two states are best settled at the bilateral level. There is no need to transform such problems to become an ASEAN issue (sic).[66]

Badawi argued that the solution was not 'ditching the principle of non-intervention' but more cooperation and collaboration between ASEAN members. He insinuated that civil society and NGOs could best air some of the more delicate issues: 'Let us leave it to them to do some of the things they are uniquely suited for'. Finally, he restated his confidence in the ASEAN Way, concluding in an intriguing linguistic twist, that 'Malaysia believes that the imperatives for *constructive interactions* are most persuasive and compelling for making changes among us'.[67] Badawi's choice of words were perhaps designed to strike a balance between the concept previously used by his own Deputy Prime Minister, and the compromise agreed upon over dinner the night before.

Singaporean Foreign Minister Shanmugam Jayakumar also dwelled on the question of ASEAN's traditional principles. Discarding the ASEAN Way, he warned, 'may imperil ASEAN's future'. While 'non-intervention does not mean indifference to each other's well being...internal political developments will remain a particularly sensitive area with the potential to set up centrifugal forces that can pull ASEAN apart'. Interestingly, however, even Jayakumar seemed to leave open the possibility that ASEAN might modify its rules in the future. He noted that 'in applying the principles we will have to take into account both regional and global changes as well as the growing maturity of ASEAN as an institution'.[68]

Various degrees of opposition were also voiced by Vietnam and Myanmar. In his opening address the Vietnamese Foreign Minister, Nguyen Manh Cam, simply noted the sections of the Treaty of Amity and Cooperation that prohibited interference, but offered no elaboration. According to one journalist who has discussed the matter privately with Vietnamese foreign ministry officials, this low-key response was in part because Vietnam is less worried by the issue than their Malaysian and Singaporean counterparts.[69] That claim notwithstanding, Vietnamese officials had opposed the proposal in forthright terms before the meeting. Their less assertive stance in Manila could also be explained by a desire, as a relatively new member, not to seem too reactionary within ASEAN.

Myanmar's Foreign Minister, Ohn Gyaw, merely restated the principles set out in the Treaty of Amity and Cooperation (TAC), saving his strongest statements on the Thai proposal for outside the official meeting.[70] In an interview with *Asiaweek* magazine, he derided the idea as 'very poor', saying the call for change was 'unrealistic'. In his address, the Lao Foreign Minister, Somsavat Lengsavad made no reference to the issue of non-intervention, perhaps not wanting openly to confront Thailand, on whom Laos is heavily dependent for investment and trade. According to diplomats in Vientiane, however, Laos was strongly opposed to the proposal and privately its officials were 'delighted' at the lack of support for the idea. They regarded Thailand as having 'embarrassed itself' in Manila.[71] Like Vietnam, however, Laos was happy to defer to more senior ASEAN neighbors when it came to opposing the proposals for change – a respect for seniority entirely consistent with the principles of the ASEAN Way.

For advocates of the status quo, the fact that only Thailand and the Philippines spoke in favor of change showed that they had miscalculated and had failed to unseat ASEAN tradition. However, for proponents of change – in particular the Thais – the meeting's decision to address the question of intervention was a victory in itself. On 25 July, Surin told reporters that he was 'very satisfied' with the outcome of the debate: 'From now on, I feel confident I can raise any issue without cause for being misunderstood or accused of interfering'. Asked about the meaning of the compromise, 'enhanced interaction', Surin said:

What's the difference? To me, we have made our point. We have made our suggestion. Our colleagues understand the rationality behind it...Asean has been rejuvenated and we have probably heightened the awareness of the need to be more open.[72]

Three days later, he displayed his new found confidence. Citing the hundreds of thousands of Karen refugees along the Thai-Myanmar border, Surin described their presence 'as a form of interference' and said that Myanmar's military government could expect no let up in criticism from Bangkok until it satisfactorily resolved problems with cross-border repercussions.[73] He placed the blame for the refugee problem squarely on the lack of political reform in Myanmar.

Indeed, while the Ministerial Meeting laid to rest hopes of any *formal* shift in ASEAN policy, at least for the time being, there was no immediate reduction in the number of calls for more open and frank exchanges within ASEAN. President Estrada repeated the message he delivered to the Ministerial Meeting in a speech to the ASEAN Economic Ministers in Manila in early October 1998. ASEAN Secretary General Rodolfo Severino has also repeated calls for greater openness and dialogue. Speaking at a conference in Bangkok, Thai Deputy Foreign Minister Sukhumbhand Paribatra warned that ASEAN could 'not cling to old values. It needed to restructure itself to face new challenges in the age of globalization'. He argued that more openness was the answer and called for the inclusion of human rights on the regional agenda.[74]

Flexible engagement's profile peaked at the Manila Ministerial Meeting. The formal proposal that ASEAN should adopt a more open and flexible attitude towards sovereignty and the norm of non-interference was soundly defeated. But if advocates of the status quo thought that the touchy subject of intervention was now dead and buried, they were in for a shock. Before the end of 1998, two other divisive issues within ASEAN would raise questions about the golden rule of non-interference. In order to be able to assess the prospects for ASEAN's traditional model of regional security and development we also need to be familiar with these.

Testing Enhanced Interaction: The Anwar Affair

On 3 September 1998, Malaysia's popular Deputy Prime Minister, Anwar Ibrahim, was sacked as Finance Minister and stripped of his position as Vice-President of the United Malays National Organization (UMNO). His sacking came after a long, often bitter power struggle with his former mentor, Prime Minister Mahathir. Their differences had grown more pronounced in the wake of the economic crisis with Anwar largely favoring the adoption of the policies of liberalization recommended by the US, the IMF, and the WB, while Mahathir supported currency controls and raged against what he saw as an international conspiracy.

Rather than differences over economic policy, however, the reason given for Anwar's dismissal was that he was 'morally unfit' to lead the country. On 20 September after weeks of growing tension and protests in Kuala Lumpur, Anwar was arrested and detained under Malaysia's Internal Security Act (ISA). He was eventually charged with five counts of corruption and five counts of sodomy; charges that many considered to be fabricated. While in custody and awaiting trial, he was beaten unconscious by police. His subsequent appearance outside a Kuala Lumpur court sporting bruises and a black eye provoked an outraged reaction within Malaysia as well as from human rights groups and Western leaders. The incident also prompted some unusually frank exchanges between ASEAN leaders, exchanges that again called into question the organization's traditional norms.

On 1 October 1998, Filipino President Estrada announced he was thinking of not attending the November APEC leaders meeting in Kuala Lumpur because of the detention of his 'good friend' Anwar.[75] While his statement was initially justified by his press secretary as a 'personal remark and not for public consumption', Estrada went on to make several additional references to the need for 'due process' for Anwar, including one at an international conference in Singapore.[76] He announced that he planned to discuss the affair with Mahathir when the two leaders met at the APEC meeting. He also received Anwar's daughter, Nurul Izzah Anwar, to accept her thanks for his public support for her father. The Philippines' Congress Committee on Foreign Affairs supported Estrada and at one point planned to dispatch a team of 13 congress people to observe Anwar's trial.[77]

Estrada's concerns were echoed by the then Indonesian President, B.J. Habibie. In an interview with *The Nation* on 5 October, he said he was 'very concerned how my friend Anwar Ibrahim has been treated'.[78] He said the arrest 'was not good' and his foreign affairs adviser, Dewi Fortuna Anwar, warned that the incident was likely to 'cloud relations' between Malaysia and Indonesia.[79] While claiming to support the principle of non-interference, Habibie nevertheless went ahead and postponed a scheduled meeting with Mahathir, citing work pressures.[80] Like Estrada, he also received Nuzul Izzah Anwar, although it was made clear that this meeting was in his 'private' and not presidential capacity. Habibie remained silent as to whether or not he would attend the APEC meeting in Kuala Lumpur, saying only that he would first have to consult the Indonesian parliament.[81]

Despite their criticism, both leaders did attend the November APEC meeting in Kuala Lumpur and there is no evidence that the subject of Anwar's ill treatment was raised in their bilateral meetings with Mahathir. Nevertheless, the very fact that they made such forthright comments was striking. Unlike the overthrow of the government in Cambodia, the haze, or even the perennially sensitive issue of refugees along the Thai-Myanmar border, there was no obvious transnational aspect to Anwar's arrest or his 'ill treatment'. The fact that two ASEAN leaders still saw fit to criticize the actions of the Mahathir government so publicly, suggested that events unfolding in Malaysia might represent the greatest challenge yet to ASEAN's traditional norms.

The reaction of the Thais to the Anwar affair is perhaps more indicative of the immediate prospects of alternatives to the ASEAN Way. While the Philippines and Indonesia were quick to condemn Anwar's detention and beating, Thailand—the original advocate of the concept of flexible engagement—adopted a much lower profile on the issue. Prime Minister Chuan Leekpai went out of his way to discourage the Thai media from sensationalizing the issue 'in order to avoid misunderstandings among friendly nations'. His government also agreed to cooperate with Kuala Lumpur to prevent fugitive Malaysian opposition figures from crossing the border into Thailand. Deputy Foreign Minister Sukhumbhand Paribatra called Anwar's wife to express his concern and to assure her that as a friend he was ready to help her family, but he added 'as a deputy foreign minister I could do nothing, because the government considers the ongoing Malaysian political problems should be tackled internally'.[82]

While a Malay language newspaper assailed Surin, describing him as the 'new puppeteer attempting to intervene' in Malaysia, and accusing him of using the Anwar affair to advance his political agenda in ASEAN, his comments were notably mild.[83] In what was the first real test for enhanced interaction since the Manila Ministerial Meeting, Thailand fell back on tradition. Its response was a textbook example of established ASEAN diplomacy.

The Challenge of Deeper Economic Integration

While flexible engagement and the Anwar affair have received the most attention in discussions about efforts to implement change in the ASEAN Way, it is important to understand that these political events did not take place in a vacuum. Over the ensuing months, ASEAN has also inaugurated a number of economic projects that will also, in the medium term, confront its traditional preference for sovereignty enhancing regionalism. Some examples can be seen in the recommendations of the Hanoi Plan of Action (HPA) launched at the December 1998 ASEAN Summit.

The Hanoi Plan of Action sets outs ASEAN's goals for the period 1999-2004. Among other things, it commits members to adopt and implement: 'international sets of sound financial practices and standards', 'to adopt and implement existing standards of disclosure and dissemination of economic and financial information', 'to study the feasibility of establishing an ASEAN currency and exchange rate mechanism', and 'to harmonize accounting and financial reporting standards'.[84] If the HPA is to be more than just impressive rhetoric, these goals will require a much greater degree of openness, integration, and institutionalization than currently exists in ASEAN. Their implementation would certainly raise more questions about the ability of informal processes constrained by absolute notions of sovereignty to facilitate cooperation. As former Thai Foreign Minister Kasem Kasemsri has noted:

> By creating economic interdependence, Asean has achieved peace and stability. Peace and stability has brought about prosperity. Prosperity was brought about by integration. Further integration requires more transparency which means sharing accurate information which hinges upon sovereignty.[85]

Whether the political will exists to push these various proposals to completion remains to be seen. But in spite of the hoopla surrounding the launch of high profile initiatives like ASEAN's 'Bold Measures' and the HPA, there is some cause for pessimism. Disagreements about the creation of an ASEAN economic surveillance process reveal the deep suspicions some members still harbor about the political consequences of closer economic integration.

The plan for an ASEAN Surveillance Process was hatched at a meeting of Central Bankers in Manila in November 1997 and subsequently reaffirmed by ASEAN Finance Ministers at meetings in Kuala Lumpur, Jakarta, and Yangon. The Ministers agreed that preventing a repeat of the economic crisis, especially given the risk of 'contagion' endemic to the global financial system, required greater cooperation between ASEAN members. The proposal stressed the importance of 'sharing timely and comprehensive information and the need for frank and candid exchanges of views on issues and challenges facing ASEAN'.[86] But while there was unanimity about the plan at the initial meetings, by the time of the Manila Ministerial Meeting in July 1998, another divide within ASEAN had become apparent.

What is noteworthy about the disagreement over the ASEAN Surveillance Process is that the organization split along different lines compared to the flexible engagement impasse.[87] In particular, Singapore, a fierce opponent of flexible engagement and franker political exchanges within ASEAN, has emerged as one of the strongest proponents of greater economic transparency in the region. Indeed, an editorial in the pro-government newspaper *The Straits Times* in September 1998 called for the creation of an institution *'empowered with the capacity to enforce the adoption of prudential structures in individual countries,* and issue warnings to the markets when they are not'.[88] It is difficult to imagine how such an organization would be compatible with the traditional, strict interpretation of the principle of non-intervention.

The strongest opposition to greater transparency and closer cooperation on economic surveillance issues has come from ASEAN's new members, particularly Myanmar and Vietnam. They rejected the proposal as 'intrusive' and refused to divulge what they deemed to be 'private' economic information.[89] The surveillance mechanism, set up under the auspices of the Asian Development Bank (ADB), therefore had to scale back its ambitions. Unlike the original 'Manila Framework' concept approved in principle in November 1997, the surveillance 'process' (the term 'mechanism' is no longer used) approved by the Hanoi Summit relies on 'an informal system of peer review', and on the willingness of member countries to share economic date and information on fiscal policies. According to ASEAN Deputy-Secretary General Suthad Setboonsarng, 'No pressure will be exerted...submission of data will not be mandatory'.[90]

While it could be argued that the very acceptance of a surveillance system hints at some flexibility regarding the notion of interference (at least in the economic realm), the informal, voluntary, peer review formula to be used by the ASEAN Surveillance Process offers no threat to state sovereignty. It has more in common with APEC's requirements for voluntary sectoral liberalization or concerted unilateralism, than it does with AFTA's more formal legalisms. Decisions about the submission of information continue to be made in national capitals and the institution managing the 'process', the ADB acts as a simple repository of information without real enforcement powers. This is clearly another triumph for the ASEAN Way as traditionally conceived.

This, of course, raises the question of whether ASEAN's core members would be prepared to adopt an equally flexible stance on projects like AFTA or the adoption of common financial and economic reporting standards, if the new members found compliance intrusive. Myanmar, Laos, and Vietnam may be able to plead privacy or an inability to comply with an economic monitoring mechanism. Would they be given similar leeway with the development projects at the heart of ASEAN such as AFTA and the newly inaugurated ASEAN Investment Area (AIA)? Until recently, the answer might have been expected to be a blunt 'no'. As Hadi Soesastro has noted, in the past ASEAN has shown real determination not to allow a wider membership to compromise its economic agenda, arguing 'the 7-X or the 10-X principle does not apply to AFTA'.[91] But even AFTA, ASEAN's most cherished and formally structured cooperative venture, has come under threat in the wake of the economic crisis. Despite agreeing to bring forward plans for the elimination of all import duties, some members are finding it difficult even to meet existing obligations.[92] In November 1999, Malaysia announced it was withdrawing automotive products from its AFTA tariff cut basket, despite earlier assurances to the contrary, in an attempt to protect its domestic vehicle manufacturing sector. This immediately prompted the Thai and Filipino governments to consider withdrawing palm oil and petrochemicals from their respective tariff reduction schedules. While they ultimately decided against taking such action, Malaysia's backsliding did not bode well for AFTA's future. It also speaks volumes about the comparative strength of states and regional institutions in SEA.

Potentially more troubling still is the challenge ASEAN's new members face to meet their AFTA obligations on time. In interviews in 1998, ASEAN Secretariat officials were optimistic about Myanmar and Laos's progress on AFTA, insisting there will be 'no surprises'.[93] But many regional diplomats and analysts were more pessimistic.[94] Laos and Myanmar have been harder hit by the economic crisis than anyone in ASEAN, save perhaps Indonesia, and according to diplomats AFTA compliance is effectively 'on hold' in both countries.[95] Indeed, Myanmar recently expanded its range of restrictions on exports and special taxes on imports, leading Singaporean investors to complain to visiting Deputy Prime Minister Lee Hsien Loong.[96] Similar questions must be raised about the ability of the Cambodian government to comply with AFTA, especially given its historical dependence on tariffs as a source of revenue.[97]

The problems are not simply a triumph for protectionist sentiment or a lack of political will. They also reflect a real lack of capacity. For example, according to Jayant Menon, current customs procedures in the new ASEAN members are not good enough even to perform the basic tasks AFTA membership requires, such as measuring rules of origin.[98] It seems reasonable to expect that the new members will only find it more difficult to meet their obligations—even with staggered introductory time frames—under the much more ambitious and demanding HPA.

If these gaps in capacity are to be overcome, then the new members will need much greater levels of technical and financial assistance than they have received before.[99] The need for help has been recognized since enlargement was first contemplated, but as former ASEAN Secretary General Ajit Singh has complained 'nothing is being done for them'.[100] By tightening belts around the region, the economic crisis has made assistance from within ASEAN even less likely, at least for now. While technical and financial help from outside the region—most notably Japan—is arriving, it is quite possible that a growing divide will emerge between those ASEAN states that are able and anxious to push ahead with economic liberalization, and those that prefer a more cautious path.

Conclusion: Whither the ASEAN Way?

What, then, do these three debates tell us about the future of ASEAN and its traditional model of promoting development and security in SEA? They have shown that ASEAN's institutional norms are neither sacrosanct nor immutable. Pressure to adopt norms such as a more flexible notion of state sovereignty, less opaque institutional structures, and human rights, is increasingly being manifested at the inter-state and sub-state level in SEA. Arguably, there has been some gradual evolution in regional attitudes towards non-intervention, at least with respect to economic issues. But claims of an apparent 'change of paradigm' away from the ASEAN Way are highly exaggerated.[101] Despite recent divisions, the ASEAN Way as it has been traditionally understood, complete with its central norm of non-interference, will remain important to ASEAN for some time to come. The debates over flexible engagement, the treatment of Anwar Ibrahim, and ASEAN's ambitious economic agenda for the region illustrate the increasingly diverse nature of the Southeast Asian political community. However, the economic and political forces unleashed by globalization have not yet overturned ASEAN's traditional *modus operandi* or shaken its members' deep attachment to national sovereignty. Indeed, if anything, the debates actually emphasize the continued resilience of the ASEAN Way.

Despite a lot of impressive rhetoric from Thailand and the Philippines, both have been careful not to push too hard with their calls for a more open institution and a relaxation of the non-interference policy. Thailand was noticeably quieter than some of its neighbors when the Anwar controversy began to unfold in Malaysia. Despite the close personal ties between Surin, Sukumbhand, and Anwar, the Chuan government was not prepared to be more critical at the risk of damaging an important bilateral relationship with its southern neighbor. Similarly, after initially criticizing the Mahathir government, both Filipino President Estrada and his Indonesian counterpart, B.J. Habibie, attended the APEC Leaders' Meeting in November 1998,and have toned down their comments since. Notably, only Thai Prime Minister Chuan Leekpai endorsed 'enhanced interaction' at the December ASEAN Summit in Hanoi and the issue of non-intervention was not raised in any of the substantive sessions at the 1999 ASEAN Ministerial Meeting in Singapore.[102]

If the non-intervention principle looked anachronistic and vulnerable in the middle of 1998, then the deterioration of the bilateral relationship between Malaysia and Singapore later in the year may have served to remind some ASEAN leaders just what the norm was originally designed to achieve. Following acrimonious exchanges over issues that included passages in Lee Kuan Yew's memoirs, Singapore's access to drinking water, and the location of an immigration control point, Malaysia announced it was withdrawing from a scheduled Five Power Defense Arrangements (FPDA) exercise which included Singapore. Malaysia also withdrew permission for Singaporean military aircraft and ships to use its airspace and waters. Diplomatic ties were not severed nor ambassadors recalled, but heated rhetoric flew from both sides of the Causeway and it was generally acknowledged that relations had reached a low not seen for many years.

The seriousness of disputes between Singapore and Malaysia (and to a lesser extent between Malaysia and the Philippines) and the speed with which they blew up was a timely reminder that despite ASEAN's achievements in building confidence over the past three decades, significant levels of distrust still remain between neighbors in the region. It hinted at the dangers that might lie in pushing ahead with proposals to try to dramatically change the Association. However much foreign policymakers in Thailand and the Philippines would like to see a more liberal and democratic ASEAN, they clearly prefer a flawed ASEAN to no ASEAN at all.

While the ASEAN Way will remain relevant for some time to come, conflict over the Association's norms will also persist. This is for two reasons. First, as was discussed above, important constituencies in the region's two established democracies will continue to press for foreign policies that support the ideals they cherish at home. Indeed, now that Thailand and the Philippines have been joined by a young democracy in Indonesia, it is likely that there will be even greater pressure for change.

The other likely cause of conflict is the Association's ambitious economic agenda. In the wake of the economic crisis, ASEAN has moved to reaffirm its commitment to greater economic cooperation and increased liberalization. It has agreed to accelerate the timetable for AFTA, and begun to discuss a range of ambitious projects, including a single currency and a broader East Asian economic community.[103] If these proposals are any guide, ASEAN has hitched its wagon to deeper integration, recognizing that this is the only way it will be able to sustain influence in groups like APEC, and the only way it can maintain leverage and competitiveness against the EU and NAFTA. However, if this development strategy is to be effective, it will require all of ASEAN's members to be committed to a common identity and united behind an agreed set of institutional norms. In particular, the various proposals will require all of ASEAN's members to be economically more open and more transparent.

If ASEAN is serious about its commitment to deeper integration, then it will eventually have to confront the limits imposed by its institutional culture. The line currently drawn between economic liberalization (something which is generally acceptable to most members) and political liberalization (not acceptable to most members) is unsustainable. Too many of the projects underpinning the Hanoi Plan of Action and the ASEAN Vision 2020 will require real transparency, clear rules, and strong, autonomous institutions to enforce them. Such a prospect raises real fears for ASEAN's new members. Writing about the analogous situation in Europe, *The Economist* perfectly captures the kind of concerns the new members have about the logic of deeper regionalism in SEA:

> Create a single market and you find you need a single currency to make it work properly. Create a single currency and you find you need a single economic policy to make the currency work properly. Create the political institutions needed to make a single economic policy work properly and they will start doing all sorts of other, unforeseeable things as well.[104]

So far, ASEAN's more conservative members have succeeded in blocking proposals for stronger institutions and franker political exchanges, while allowing the institution to move forward (albeit haltingly) towards deeper economic integration. However, at some point the line between economic openness and political openness will begin to blur. ASEAN's ambitious economic agenda is simply not compatible with the narrow kind of sovereignty-enhancing regionalism that has sustained the grouping since 1967. When that point is reached, the reactions of Myanmar, Vietnam, Cambodia, and Laos will be crucial. Opposing a more 'progressive' regional political agenda is one thing. However, if they impede progress in the economic realm, ASEAN's entire raison d'être will come into question.

How long ASEAN can postpone the inevitable, or just when will the political consequences of economic integration become too much for some members to bear is difficult to predict. The grouping has little appetite for tackling contentious issues even at the best of times. And as it tries to present a united front to international investors in the wake of the economic crisis, these are certainly not the best of times. Consequently, ASEAN will probably try and muddle through, at least for the short term. But if economic stagnation continues in Myanmar and Indochina, and AFTA deadlines continue to be missed, ASEAN will be confronted with a challenge to its very existence—a challenge that will be difficult to simply wish away with compromise terminology.

Notes

1   Quoted in 'Future Ambitions: Is the community of Southeast Asian nations ready for the 21st century?', *Asiaweek*, 12 December 1997.
2   Evans, P. M. (1994), 'The Dialogue Process on Asia Pacific Security Issues: Inventory and Analysis', in P. M. Evans (ed.), *Studying Asia Pacific Security*, University of Toronto-York University Joint Centre for Asia Pacific Studies and Centre for Strategic and International Studies Jakarta, pp.303.
3   Interview with Abdul Rajak Baginda, Director, Malaysian Strategic Research Centre, Kuala Lumpur, 14 July 1998.
4   See for example, Koh, T. (1998), 'East Asians Should Learn from Western Europe', *International Herald Tribune*, 10 July.
5   The literature on broad notions of security in the Asia Pacific is extensive. For the best general discussion see Dewitt, D. (1994), 'Common, Comprehensive and Cooperative Security', *The Pacific Review*, vol.7, no.1, pp.1-15. Other works include, Alagappa, M. (1987), 'Comprehensive Security: Interpretations in ASEAN Countries', in R. A. Scalapino, S. Satao, J. Wanandi and S. Han (eds), *Asian Security Issues: Regional and Global*, Research Papers and Policy Studies No. 26, Institute of East Asian Studies, University of California, Berkeley; Sopiee, N. (no date), 'Malaysia's Doctrine of Comprehensive Security', *The Journal of Asiatic Studies*, vol.XXVII, no.2, pp.259-265; Clements, K. (1989), 'Common Security in the Asia-Pacific: Problems and Prospects', *Alternatives*, vol.XIV, pp.49-76. Papers presented at two CSCAP conferences on comprehensive security are republished in David Dickens (ed.) (1997), *No Better Alternative: Towards Comprehensive and Cooperative Security in the Asia-Pacific*, Centre for Strategic Studies, Wellington; Rolfe, J. (ed.) (1995), *Unresolved Futures: Comprehensive Security in the Asia-Pacific*, Centre for Strategic Studies, Wellington.
6   Alagappa, M. (1998), 'Asian Practice of Security: Key Features and Explanations', in M. Alagappa, (ed.) *Asian Security Practice: Material and Ideational Influences*, Stanford University Press, Stanford, pp.624.
7   *Ibid*, pp.626.

8   Quoted in Irvine, D. (1982), 'Making Haste Less Slowly: ASEAN from 1975', in A. Broinowski, (ed.), *Understanding ASEAN*, Hong Kong, Macmillan, pp.47-48.

9   Speech by Mahathir at the 'First ISIS National Conference on National Security', Kuala Lumpur, 15 July 1986, cited in Dewitt, 'Common, Comprehensive, and Cooperative Security', 1994, pp.4.

10 Sopiee, 'Malaysia's Doctrine of Comprehensive Security', (no date).

11 Alagappa, 'Comprehensive Security: Interpretations', *op.cit.,* pp.57-58.

12 Defence Policy Statement, Republic of Singapore, prepared for the 'Third ASEAN Regional Senior Officials Meeting (SOM)', Yogyakarta, Indonesia, 10-11 May 1996; Ganesan, N. (1998), 'Singapore: Realist cum Trading State', in M. Alagappa (ed.), *Asian Security Practice: Material and Ideational Influences*, pp. 579-607; 588-590.

13 Alagappa, *Asian Security Practice: Material and Ideational Influences*, 1998, pp.613.

14 Irvine, R. (1982), 'The Formative Years of ASEAN: 1967-1975', in A. Broinowski (ed.), *Understanding ASEAN*, pp.9.

15 *Ibid.*

16 *Ibid.*

17 Solidum, E. (1981), 'The Role of Certain Sectors in Shaping and Articulating the ASEAN Way', in R.P. Anand and P. V. Quisumbing (eds.), *ASEAN Identity, Development and Culture,* University of the Philippines Law Center, Manila and the East-West Center, Honolulu, pp.130-148, 136.

18 *Ibid.*

19 Preamble to the ASEAN Declaration, Bangkok, 8 August 1967 in ASEAN Secretariat (1998), *Towards Peace, Freedom and Prosperity: An Introduction to ASEAN Agreements,* Jakarta.

20 Preamble, Zone of Peace, Freedom and Neutrality Declaration (Kuala Lumpur Declaration) 27 November 1971, Kuala Lumpur, reproduced in ASEAN Secretariat (1998), *Handbook on Selected ASEAN Political Documents*, Jakarta, pp.8.

21 For an excellent discussion of the origins and meaning of constructive engagement, see Acharya, A. (1995), *Human Rights in Southeast Asia: Dilemmas for Foreign Policy,* Eastern Asia Policy Papers No. 11, University of Toronto-York University Joint Centre for Asia Pacific Studies.

22 See for example the comments of an ASEAN official quoted in Jacob, P., Choo, T. L., Kassim, I. and Chan, R. (1992), 'ASEAN Prefers Soft Talk to Threats in Dealing with Yangon', *The Straits Times*, 26 August, pp.27.

23 Job, B. L. (1999), *ASEAN Stalled: Dilemmas and Tensions Over Conflicting Norms*, paper presented at the 'Annual Meeting of the American Political Science Association (APSA)', Atlanta, 2-5 September, pp.10.

24 Almonte, J. (1997-98), 'Ensuring Security the 'ASEAN way'', *Survival*, vol.39, no.4, Winter, pp.80-92.

25 Quoted in Richardson, M. (1997), 'Alliance prefers informal consensus', *The Globe and Mail*, 7 June, pp.A19.

26 Acharya, A. (1997), 'Sovereignty, Non-Intervention and Regionalism', *CANCAPS Papier No. 15*, Toronto, York University, October, pp.3.

27 Chew, L. K. (1998), 'Don't discard fundamentals', *The Straits Times*, 25 July.

28 Cited in Stone, D. (1997), *Networks, Second Track Diplomacy and Regional Cooperation: The Role of Southeast Asian Think Tanks,* paper presented at the '38th Annual Meeting of the International Studies Association (ISA)', Toronto, 16-22 March, pp.20.

29 Yuen, K. F. (1998), *ASEAN's Collective Identity: Sources, Shifts and Security Consequences*, paper presented at the '94th Annual Meeting of the American Political Science Association', Boston, 3-6 September, pp.10.

30 ASEAN was slow to add formal projects to the loose framework for dialogue established following the signing of the Bangkok Declaration in 1967. Leaders summits were rare in the organization's first 25 years; even the Senior Officials Meeting (SOM) structure was not created until four years after the Bangkok meeting. Real interest in closer cooperation did not begin until after the fall of Saigon in 1975 and even then, initial attempts to forge closer economic relations were not particularly successful. The first treaty to be signed between the ASEAN members was not concluded until 1976. Until that time, the organization showed a preference for less formal 'statements of principle', or declarations, rather than legalistic formulae, a preference it continues to hold today. ASEAN officials have also stressed their inclination towards informality in region-wide meetings like APEC and the ARF, pointedly preferring to describe the latter as 'dialogue forum' rather than an institution.

31 Quoted in Haas, M. (1973), 'The Asian Way to Peace', *Pacific Community*, no.4, pp.504.

32 For a discussion of such examples see Acharya, A. (1997), 'Sovereignty, Non-intervention and Regionalism', *CANCAPS Papier No.15*, Centre for International and Security Studies, York University, Toronto.

33 Higgott, R. and Reich, S. (1998), *Globalization and Sites of Conflict: Towards Definition and Taxonomy*, Centre for the Study of Globalization and Regionalization Working Paper 01/98, March, Warwick University.

34 Amin, A. and Thrift, N. (1994), 'Living in the Global', in A. Amin and N. Thrift (eds), *Globalization, Institutions and Regional Development in Europe*, Oxford University Press, Oxford, pp.2.

35 See for example, Bernard, M. (1994), 'Post-Fordism, Transnational Production, and the Changing Global Political Economy', in R. Stubbs and G. Underhill (eds), *Political Economy and the Changing Global Order*, London, Macmillan.

36 Amin and Thrift, 'Living in the Global', 1994, pp.4.

37 Giddens, A. (1990), *The Consequences of Modernity*, Cambridge, Polity Press, pp.64.

38 Mittelman, J. H. (1996), *Globalization: Critical Reflections*, Lynne Rienner, Boulder, pp.3.

39 Robinson, W. I. (1996), *Promoting Polyarchy: Globalization, US Intervention and Hegemony*, Cambridge, Cambridge University Press, pp.32.

40 Rosamond, B. (1997), *Reflexive Regionalism? Global Life and the Construction of European Identities,* paper prepared for the 'Annual Convention of the International Studies Association', Toronto, 18-22 March, pp.4.

41 For an excellent survey of the literature on globalization and the region, see the bibliography prepared for the Institute for Southeast Asian Studies' (ISEAS) 30th Anniversary Conference, 'The Challenges of Globalization', ISEAS, Singapore, 1998. My claim that a broad notion of globalization is widely used by Southeast Asian elites is based on interviews with politicians, foreign ministry officials, analysts from various political and economic think tanks, NGO representatives, journalists, academics and diplomats in eight of the ten ASEAN states between April 1997 and May 1999. A similar conclusion is drawn by Soesastro, H. (1999), 'Domestic Adjustments in Four ASEAN Economies', in C. E. Morrison and H. Soesastro (eds), *Domestic Adjustments to Globalization*, Japan Center for International Exchange, Tokyo, pp.24-36.

42 Wah, C. K. (1998), *Globalization and its Challenges to ASEAN Political Cooperation*, paper presented at the 'Southeast Asia in the 21st Century: Challenges of Globalization' Conference, Institute for Southeast Asian Studies, Singapore, 30 July- 1 August 1998, pp.4.

43 See for example, Agence France Presse, 'ASEAN under fire over Burma talks', *The Nation* (Regional Edition), 13 April 1999, pp.1.

44 'Soeharto used decrees to enrich family and friends, says group', *The Straits Times*, 18 October 1998; Richardson, M. (1998), 'Applying the Brakes to 'Crony Capitalism'', *The Straits Times*, 1 July; Dore, R. (1998), 'Crisis Stills Apologists for Corruption', *International Herald Tribune*, February.

45 For a particularly scathing example, see 'Asean inaction wreaking havoc throughout Asia', *Hong Kong Standard*, 6 October 1997.

46 It is perhaps noteworthy that, at the time of the interview, Anwar was Acting Prime Minister while Dr. Mahathir was out of the country on an extended trip. See, Ibrahim, A. (1997), 'Crisis Prevention', *Newsweek*, 21 July, pp.13.

47 *Ibid.*

48 Lertcharoenchok, Y. (1997), 'Asean urged to rethink policy on intervention', *The Nation*, 22 August. Occasional references to the need to 'adjust' or 'reinterpret' ASEAN's prohibition on interference were made by some officials, including from the then Thai Foreign Minister Prachaub Chaiasan. See Chongkittavorn, K. (1997), 'Changing roles for the old players', *The Nation*, 25 July.

49 'Chuan to put 'open society' idea to ASEAN', *The Nation*, 12 December 1997.

50 'Open and just society to be proposed for region', *Bangkok Post*, 12 December 1997. For a text of the ASEAN Vision 2020 statement see *Handbook on Selected ASEAN Political Documents*, 1998, pp.71, Indonesia apparently argued that the term 'progressive society' should be used instead. A compromise was reached when Singapore suggested that the phrase 'consistent with respective national identities' be added. See Chongkittavorn, K. (1997), 'ASEAN accepts 'open society' concept', *The Nation*, 14 December.

51 'Thailand backs ASEAN commission on rights', *The Nation*, 27 May 1998. The 1992 ASEAN Ministerial Meeting had stated that 'ASEAN should coordinate a common approach to human rights and actively participate and contribute to the application, promotion and protection of human rights'. It had also agreed to 'consider the establishment of an appropriate regional mechanism on human rights'. See, Joint Communiqué of the 26th ASEAN Ministerial Meeting, Singapore, 23-24 July 1993, pp.7.

52 H.E. Surin Pitsuwan, *Currency Turmoil in Southeast Asia: The Strategic Impact,* speech at the '12th Asia Pacific Roundtable', Kuala Lumpur, Malaysia, 1 June 1998.

53 *Ibid.*

54 H.E. Surin Pitsuwan, *Thailand's Foreign Policy During the Economic and Social Crises*, keynote address at the 'Seminar in Commemoration of the 49th Anniversary of the Faculty of Political Science', Thammasat University, Bangkok, 12 June 1998.

55 Interview with Kobsak Chutikul, Spokesman, Foreign Ministry of Thailand, 20 September 1998; 'Thais retract call for Asean intervention', *The Straits Times*, 27 June 1998, pp.44.

56 Chongkittavorn, K. (1998), 'Good ideas need discreet lobbying', *The Nation*, 29 June, pp.A4.

57 'Thais retract call for ASEAN intervention', *The Straits Times*, 27 June 1998, pp.44.

58 Quoted in Patiyasevi, R. (1998), 'Ministers reaffirm ASEAN's non-intervention principle', *The Nation*, 24 July, pp.A1.

59 *Ibid.*

60 Interview, Kobsak Chutikul.

61 'Enhanced interaction', while used for the first time in ASEAN at the 1998 Ministerial, was pondered by the former Thai government. Commenting on the need for a new policy to replace 'constructive engagement' once Myanmar was admitted to ASEAN, Foreign Minister Prachaub Chaiyasan said that the new policy would be to 'enhance cooperation and comprehensive' relations. See, Uerpaiojkit, R. (1997), 'ASEAN may scrap policy on Burma', *Thailand Times*, 4 July.

62 Interview, Kobsak Chutikul.

63　H.E. Joseph Estrada, *Towards a True ASEAN Community,* keynote address at the 'Opening Ceremonies of the 31st ASEAN Ministerial Meeting', Manila, 24 July 1998.

64　Opening Statement by H.E. Surin Pitsuwan, Minister of Foreign Affairs of Thailand, at the 31st ASEAN Ministerial Meeting, Manila, 24 July 1998.

65　H.E. Domingo Siazon, Jr., *Winning the Challenges of the 21st Century,* Address of the Chairman at the 'Opening of the 31st ASEAN Ministerial Meeting', Manila, 24 July 1998.

66　Opening Statement of H. E. Dato' Seri Abdullah Badawi, Minister of Foreign Affairs of Malaysia at the 31st ASEAN Ministerial Meeting, Manila, 24 July 1998.

67　*Ibid.* (emphasis added).

68　H. E. S Jayakumar, *Stick to Basic,* Opening Statement of the Foreign Minister and Minister for Law of the Republic of Singapore at the '31st ASEAN Ministerial Meeting', Manila, 24 July 1998.

69　Interview with Peter Eng, Associated Press journalist, Bangkok, 14 September 1998.

70　The fact that the new members took a similar approach in their speeches opposing the proposal was cited by the Thai foreign ministry's spokesman in support of a claim that Singapore had prepared 'talking points' for opponents of the Thai plan. While it was well known that the new members opposed Surin's proposal, the talking points were apparently designed to help them frame their opposition in terms of ASEAN's traditions and history. I have not been able to find any evidence either supporting or refuting this claim, but the fact that the Lao foreign minister did not mention the issue in his address, shows that any talking points that may have been produced were not always used. Interview, Kobsak Chutikul, Bangkok, 20 September 1998.

71　Off the record interviews with diplomats, Vientiane, 28 August 1998 and 31 August 1998.

72　'Thailand satisfied with debate', *The Straits Times,* 26 July 1998.

73　'Thai minister defends his govt's vocal criticism of Myanmar', *The Straits Times,* 30 July 1998.

74　'ASEAN urged to adjust in new world', *The Nation,* 19 August 1998.

75　'Estrada protests arrest of Mahathir's deputy', *The Philippine Daily Inquirer,* 2 October 1998; 'Breaking a taboo', *The Philippine Daily Inquirer,* 4 October 1998.

76　Cañares, C. (1998), 'Erap a hit in open forum', *The Philippine Daily Inquirer,* 14 October; 'Estrada-Mahathir face-off set', *The Philippine Daily Inquirer,* 23 October 1998.

77　*Ibid.*

78　'Habibie unveils grand I'nesia vision', *The Nation,* 6 October 1998.

79　Pereira, D. (1998), 'KL-Jakarta Ties 'may be affected'', *The Straits Times,* 4 October.

80　Jacob, P. (1998), 'Estrada and Habibie to discuss APEC, ASEAN issues', *The Straits Times,* 14 October.

81　Tang, E. (1998), 'Habibie concerned about Anwar's well being', *The Straits Times,* 5 October, pp.25.

82　Quoted in 'ASEAN caught on the horns of a dilemma', *The Nation,* 26 October 1998.

83　'Malay daily blasts Surin', *The Nation,* 7 November 1998.

84　*Hanoi Plan of Action,* paras I.2.1, I.2.4, I.4.1, available on-line at *http://www.aseansec.org /summit/6th/prg_hpoa.htm.*

85　Quoted in 'Towards a common market', *The Nation,* 24 October 1997.

86　Joint Press Statement, Special ASEAN Finance Ministers Meeting, Kuala Lumpur, 1 December 1997, para. 11.

87　'The game goes on: changing views in ASEAN', *The Economist,* 1 August 1998.

88　'Whither globalization?', *The Straits Times,* 22 September 1998 (emphasis added).

89　'ASEAN delays its surveillance system: Official', *The Jakarta Post,* 28 July 1998.

90　'Plan to set up regional crisis warning system', *The Straits Times,* 8 October 1998.

91　Soesastro, H. (1997a), 'Challenges to AFTA in the 21st Century', in Soesastro, *One Southeast Asia in a New Regional and International Setting,* CSIS, Jakarta, pp.87.

92 Baguioro, L. (1999), 'ASEAN to push free-trade plan as part of recovery', *The Straits Times*, 29 November.

93 Interviews with officials from the AFTA Bureau, ASEAN Secretariat, Jakarta, 2 October 1998; and from the Indonesian ASEAN National Secretariat, Ministry of Foreign Affairs, Jakarta, 1 October 1998.

94 Interviews with Thomas Crampton, International Herald Tribune correspondent, Bangkok, 19 September 1998; Kavi Chongkittavorn, Bangkok; Off the record interviews with diplomats in Kuala Lumpur in July; Bangkok, Singapore and Vientiane, September 1998; Jakarta, October 1998.

95 *Ibid.*

96 'Investors hit hard', *The Straits Times*, 2 April 1999.

97 In 1997 the Cambodian government derived 60 per cent of its total revenue from import duties. See, Ashayagachat, A. (1997), 'Relaxed deadlines discussion for new recruits', *The Bangkok Post*, 2 May.

98 Menon, J. (1998), 'The Expansion of AFTA: Widening and Deepening?' *Asia Pacific Economic Literature*, vol.12, no.2, November, pp.10-22, 20.

99 Soesastro, *One Southeast Asia In a New Regional and International Setting*, pp.89.

100 Interview with Dato' Ajit Singh, Hyatt Saujarna Hotel (Regency Club), Subang, Malaysia, 16 July 1998.

101 Möller, K. (1998), 'Cambodia and Burma: The ASEAN Way Ends Here', *Asian Survey*, vol. XXXVIII, no.12, December, pp.1088.

102 Pathan, D. (1999a), 'ASEAN to soul search in Singapore', *The Nation*, 20 July 1999; Pathan, D, (1999b), 'ASEAN ministers stick to non-interference policy', *The Nation*, 24 July 1999.

103 Jacob, P. and Baguioro, L. (1999), 'Stronger ASEAN ties with East Asia', *The Straits Times*, 29 November; Na Thalang, J. (1999), 'EAEC launch set for Nov 28', *The Nation*, 26 November; Joint Press Statement of the Thirtieth ASEAN Economic Ministers Meeting, 7-8 October 1998, Makati City, Philippines.

104 'Love it, like it, hate it, adore it', *The Economist*, 15 May 1999, Review of Books and Multimedia, p.10.

References

Acharya, A. (1995), *Human Rights in Southeast Asia: Dilemmas for Foreign Policy*, Eastern Asia Policy Papers No. 11, University of Toronto-York University Joint Centre for Asia Pacific Studies.

Acharya, A. (1997), 'Sovereignty, Non-intervention and Regionalism', *CANCAPS Papier No.15*, Centre for International and Security Studies, York University, Toronto.

Agence France Presse (1999), 'ASEAN under fire over Burma talks', *The Nation* (Regional Edition), 13 April, pp. 1.

Alagappa, M. (1987), 'Comprehensive Security: Interpretations in ASEAN Countries', in R. A. Scalapino, S. Satao, J. Wanandi and S. Han (eds), *Asian Security Issues: Regional and Global*, Research Papers and Policy Studies No. 26, Institute of East Asian Studies, University of California, Berkeley.

Alagappa, M. (1998), 'Asian Practice of Security: Key Features and Explanations', in M. Alagappa, (ed.) *Asian Security Practice: Material and Ideational Influences*, Stanford University Press, Stanford, pp. 624.

112   *Development and Security in Southeast Asia*

Almonte, J. (1997), 'Ensuring Security the 'ASEAN way'', *Survival*, vol. 39, no. 4, Winter 1997-1998, pp. 80-92.
Amin, A. and Thrift, N. (1994), 'Living in the Global', in A. Amin and N. Thrift (eds), *Globalization, Institutions and Regional Development in Europe*, Oxford University Press, Oxford, pp. 2.
'ASEAN inaction wreaking havoc throughout Asia', *Hong Kong Standard*, 6 October 1997.
'ASEAN urged to adjust in new world', *The Nation*, 19 August 1998.
'ASEAN caught on the horns of a dilemma', *The Nation*, 26 October 1998.
'ASEAN delays its surveillance system: Official', *The Jakarta Post*, 28 July 1998.
ASEAN Secretariat (1998a) *Handbook on Selected ASEAN Political Documents*, Jakarta, pp. 8.
ASEAN Secretariat (1998b), *Towards Peace, Freedom and Prosperity: An Introduction to ASEAN Agreements*, Jakarta.
Ashayagachat, A. (1997), 'Relaxed deadlines discussion for new recruits', *The Bangkok Post*, 2 May.
Baguioro, L. (1999), 'ASEAN to push free-trade plan as part of recovery', *The Straits Times*, 29 November.
Bernard, M. (1994), 'Post-Fordism, Transnational Production, and the Changing Global Political Economy', in R. Stubbs and G. Underhill (eds), *Political Economy and the Changing Global Order*, London, Macmillan.
'Breaking a taboo', *The Philippine Daily Inquirer*, 4 October 1998.
Cañares, C. (1998), 'Erap a hit in open forum', *The Philippine Daily Inquirer*, 14 October.
Chew, L. K. (1998), 'Don't discard fundamentals', *The Straits Times*, 25 July.
Chongkittavorn, K. (1997a), 'Changing roles for the old players', *The Nation*, 25 July.
Chongkittavorn, K. (1997b), 'ASEAN accepts 'open society' concept', *The Nation*, 14 December.
Chongkittavorn, K. (1998), 'Good ideas need discreet lobbying', *The Nation*, 29 June, pp. A4.
'Chuan to put 'open society' idea to ASEAN', *The Nation*, 12 December 1997.
Clements, K. (1989), 'Common Security in the Asia-Pacific: Problems and Prospects', *Alternatives*, vol. XIV, pp. 49-76.
Dewitt, D. (1994), 'Common, Comprehensive and Cooperative Security', *The Pacific Review*, vol. 7, no. 1, pp. 1-15.
Dickens, D. (ed.) (1997), *No Better Alternative: Towards Comprehensive and Cooperative Security in the Asia-Pacific*, Centre for Strategic Studies, Wellington.
Dore, R. (1998), 'Crisis Stills Apologists for Corruption', *International Herald Tribune*, February 1998.
'Estrada protests arrest of Mahathir's deputy', *The Philippine Daily Inquirer*, 2 October 1998.
'Estrada-Mahathir face-off set', *The Philippine Daily Inquirer*, 23 October 1998.
Evans, P. M. (1994), 'The Dialogue Process on Asia Pacific Security Issues: Inventory and Analysis', in P. M. Evans (ed.), *Studying Asia Pacific Security*, University of Toronto-York University Joint Centre for Asia Pacific Studies and Centre for Strategic and International Studies Jakarta, pp. 303.
'Future Ambitions: Is the community of Southeast Asian nations ready for the 21st century?', *Asiaweek*, 12 December 1997.
Ganesan, N. (1998), 'Singapore: Realist cum Trading State', in M. Alagappa (ed.), *Asian Security Practice: Material and Ideational Influences*, Stanford University Press, Stanford, pp. 579-607.
Giddens, A. (1990), *The Consequences of Modernity*, Cambridge, Polity Press, pp. 64.
Haas, M. (1973), 'The Asian Way to Peace', *Pacific Community*, no. 4, pp. 504.
'Habibie unveils grand I'nesia vision', *The Nation*, 6 October 1998.

Higgott, R. and Reich, S. (1998), *Globalization and Sites of Conflict: Towards Definition and Taxonomy*, Centre for the Study of Globalization and Regionalization Working Paper 01/98, March, Warwick University.

Ibrahim, A. (1997), 'Crisis Prevention', *Newsweek*, 21 July, pp.13.

Irvine, D. (1982), 'Making Haste Less Slowly: ASEAN from 1975', in Alison Broinowski, (ed.), *Understanding ASEAN*, Hong Kong, Macmillan, pp. 47-48.

Irvine, R. (1982), 'The Formative Years of ASEAN: 1967-1975', in A. Broinowski (ed.), *Understanding ASEAN*, Hong Kong, Macmillan, pp. 9.

'Investors hit hard', *The Straits Times*, 2 April 1999.

Jacob, P. (1998), 'Estrada and Habibie to discuss APEC, ASEAN issues', *The Straits Times*, 14 October.

Jacob, P. and Baguioro, L. (1999), 'Stronger Asean ties with East Asia', *The Straits Times*, 29 November.

Jacob, P., Choo, T. L., Kassim, I. and Chan, R. (1992), 'ASEAN Prefers Soft Talk to Threats in Dealing with Yangon', *The Straits Times*, 26 August, pp. 27.

Job, B. L. (1999), *ASEAN Stalled: Dilemmas and Tensions Over Conflicting Norms*, paper presented at the 'Annual Meeting of the American Political Science Association (APSA)', Atlanta, 2-5 September, pp. 10.

Koh, T. (1998), 'East Asians Should Learn from Western Europe', *International Herald Tribune*, 10 July.

Lertcharoenchok, Y. (1997), 'ASEAN urged to rethink policy on intervention', *The Nation*, 22 August.

'Love it, like it, hate it, adore it', *The Economist*, 15 May 1999.

'Malay daily blasts Surin', *The Nation*, 7 November 1998.

Menon, J. (1998), 'The Expansion of AFTA: Widening and Deepening?' *Asia Pacific Economic Literature*, vol. 12, no. 2, November, pp. 10-22, 20.

Mittelman, J. H. (1996), *Globalization: Critical Reflections*, Lynne Rienner, Boulder, pp. 3.

Möller, K. (1998), 'Cambodia and Burma: The ASEAN Way Ends Here', *Asian Survey*, vol. XXXVIII, no.12, December, pp.1088.

Na Thalang, J. (1999), 'EAEC launch set for Nov 28', *The Nation*, 26 November.

'Open and just society to be proposed for region', *Bangkok Post*, 12 December 1997.

Pathan, D. (1999a), 'ASEAN to soul search in Singapore', *The Nation*, 20 July 1999.

Pathan, D. (1999b), 'ASEAN ministers stick to non-interference policy', *The Nation*, 24 July.

Patiyasevi, R. (1998), 'Ministers reaffirm ASEAN's non-intervention principle', *The Nation*, 24 July, pp. A1.

Pereira, D. (1998), 'KL-Jakarta Ties "may be affected" ', *The Straits Times*, 4 October.

'Plan to set up regional crisis warning system', *The Straits Times*, 8 October 1998.

Rosamond, B. (1997), *Reflexive Regionalism? Global Life and the Construction of European Identities*, paper prepared for the 'Annual Convention of the International Studies Association', Toronto, 18-22 March, pp. 4.

Richardson, M. (1997), 'Alliance prefers informal consensus', *The Globe and Mail*, 7 June, pp. A19.

Richardson, M. (1998), 'Applying the Brakes to "Crony Capitalism" ', *The Straits Times*, 1 July.

Robinson, W. I. (1996), *Promoting Polyarchy: Globalization, US Intervention and Hegemony*, Cambridge, Cambridge University Press, pp. 32.

Rolfe, J. (ed.) (1995), *Unresolved Futures: Comprehensive Security in the Asia-Pacific*, Centre for Strategic Studies, Wellington.

'Soeharto used decrees to enrich family and friends, says group', *The Straits Times*, 18 October 1998.

Soesastro, H. (1997b), 'Challenges to AFTA in the 21st Century', in Soesastro, *One Southeast Asia In a New Regional and International Setting*, CSIS, Jakarta, pp. 87.

Soesastro, H. (1999), 'Domestic Adjustments in Four ASEAN Economies', in C. E. Morrison and H. Soesastro (eds), *Domestic Adjustments to Globalization*, Japan Center for International Exchange, Tokyo, Japan, pp. 24-36.

Solidum, E. (1981), 'The Role of Certain Sectors in Shaping and Articulating the ASEAN Way', in R.P. Anand and P. V. Quisumbung (eds.), *ASEAN Identity, Development and Culture*, University of the Philippines Law Center, Manila and the East-West Center, Honolulu, pp. 130-148, 136.

Sopiee, N. (no date), 'Malaysia's Doctrine of Comprehensive Security', *The Journal of Asiatic Studies*, vol. XXVII, no. 2, pp. 259-265.

Stone, D. (1997), *Networks, Second Track Diplomacy and Regional Cooperation: The Role of Southeast Asian Think Tanks*, paper presented at the '38th Annual Meeting of the International Studies Association (ISA)', Toronto, 16-22 March, pp. 20.

Tang, E. (1998), 'Habibie concerned about Anwar's well being', *The Straits Times*, 5 October, pp. 25.

'Thai minister defends his govt's vocal criticism of Myanmar', *The Straits Times*, 30 July 1998.

'Thailand satisfied with debate', *The Straits Times*, 26 July 1998.

'Thais retract call for Asean intervention', *The Straits Times*, 27 June 1998, pp. 44.

'The game goes on: changing views in ASEAN', *The Economist*, 1 August 1998.

'Towards a common market', *The Nation*, 24 October 1997.

Uerpaiojkit, R. (1997), 'ASEAN may scrap policy on Burma', *Thailand Times*, 4 July.

Wah, C. K. (1998), *Globalization and its Challenges to ASEAN Political Cooperation*, paper presented at the 'Southeast Asia in the 21st Century: Challenges of Globalization Conference', Institute for Southeast Asian Studies, Singapore, 30 July- 1 August 1998, pp. 4.

'Whither globalization?', *The Straits Times*, 22 September 1998.

Yuen, K. F. (1998), *ASEAN's Collective Identity: Sources, Shifts and Security Consequences*, paper presented to the '94th Annual Meeting of the American Political Science Association', Boston, 3-6 September, pp. 10.

Chapter 6

Human Rights, Security, and Development in Southeast Asia: An Overview

Herman Joseph S. Kraft

Introduction

The issue of human rights has been an ongoing debate within Southeast Asia (SEA) involving policymakers, scholars, and political activists. Much of the debate has focused on the issue of democratization and its implications for development. At the same time, however, an important aspect of the debate is concerned with the way that this issue has become linked with the ideology of state security and, consequently, has become a justification against political democratization in a Western liberal sense. The nature, however, of that linkage has been left largely unexplained even as a number of Southeast Asian governments have taken it for granted.

This chapter presents an overview of human rights as an issue in SEA. It outlines the broad context wherein human rights and the forces that work and impact on it have become a nexus for security and development for countries in the region. Of particular importance is how this nexus operates in a world and regional order increasingly shaped by global forces. In a region where the leading role played by the state in economic development has largely legitimized the authoritarian regimes in a number of countries, globalization has brought about the emergence of social forces that strain existing structures and relations of power. It is in the interplay between these social forces and corresponding but differential state responses that political space for advancing human rights in SEA can be created. The cases of Indonesia and the Philippines illustrate the different approaches that states have taken towards this issue. More importantly, it also shows how the political space that was created has affected state policy towards human rights.

Human Rights and National Security

Human rights have been defined as the rights held by all human beings by virtue of their being human, 'irrespective of any rights or duties one may (or may not) have as citizens, members of families, workers, or parts of any public or private organization or association'.[1] The 1948 Universal Declaration of Human Rights of the United

Nations, the International Human Rights Covenant on Civil and Political Rights, and the International Human Rights Covenant on Economic, Social, and Cultural Rights provide the juridical base for this claim, and list the specific rights that are covered. The claim that the rights listed in the covenants have universal application in and of itself, determines the complex conditions confronting states that have to guarantee and ensure those rights.

The post-colonial states that emerged in SEA after the Second World War largely considered human rights as a non-issue. The priority was on nation building and state-formation, processes that stressed the preservation of post-colonial political structures. The eventual establishment of the Association of Southeast Asian Nations (ASEAN) in 1967 was predicated on this concern for the security of those structures.[2]

The ASEAN states generally consider security to encompass more than purely military or defense issues. They have accepted (in varying degrees of formality) the idea of comprehensive security that recognizes the importance of ensuring the political, economic, and social well being of society and the state within both a domestic and international context. Comprehensive security is officially the security doctrine of Indonesia, Malaysia, and Singapore, and both the Philippines and Thailand have security doctrines that denote a comprehensive approach to the concept.[3]

The adoption of a comprehensive conception of security has been shown to be a sound strategy for post-colonial states embarking on the process of nation building, and whose principal security concerns were largely non-military in nature. It opened the way for building popular consensus around the priorities set by the state in the establishment of societal order. At the same time, however, it had the effect of providing a rationale for strengthening state institutions, and consequently the dominant position of the regime in power, *vis-a-vis* other political forces in society. The situation facing Southeast Asian states at the end of the colonial era was one they shared, and continue to share, with other post-colonial states. The main goal was the establishment of political support for the regime in power. While not all developing states had adopted a comprehensive security doctrine, most took a course that strengthened state institutions and centralized power in those institutions. In the face of multi-faceted challenges, coercion and violence were generously administered by regimes seeking to ensure compliance with its rule. It is in this context that security and human rights have become the key foci of debates involving developing states. Yezid Sayigh described this issue as:

> Reflected in the vulnerability and 'penetrability' of most developing societies and economies, which is exacerbated by the fact that many states in the developing world are suffering from crises of self-definition and from problems of political and historical legitimacy. While the concept of nation-state may be superseded in the developed world, the position in the Third World of a political entity, which is neither nation nor state is at best uncertain and insecure. Arguably, the linkage between the various components of domestic stability is the more important manifestation of the security dynamic in most developing countries. For reasons of political history, social composition and economic reality, there is a strong link between the various domestic and external contributors to security and insecurity. The result is to complicate immensely the task that faces ruling elites seeking to manage security (at all levels) while striving simultaneously to achieve the goals of development and state-building.[4]

The stress on nation building and state-formation focused attention on domestic threats to the well being of the state. Mohammed Ayoob compared this situation to the process of state making in Europe between the 14th and 19th centuries, albeit concentrated within a much shorter time frame.[5] The context of time, however, operates at a different level as well. The historical time period within which the process of state making in Europe took place had a social context different from that facing the developing states of the post-colonial era. European state building was relatively insulated from political complications created by demands for greater political participation and social justice by the masses. Indeed, the consolidation of state power in Europe was characterized by violence, coercion, and political repression. This comparison paves the way for Ayoob's argument that the use of violence by regimes in power to impose order is not necessarily 'morally indefensible'. If seen in the backdrop of the 'failed states', he points out that political repression may be a necessary condition to ensure the survival of states.[6]

The significance of Ayoob's contention is in the way that it provides a rationalization for human rights violations across the developing world. To his credit, he indicates an awareness of the problem and points out that he is not making 'an apologia for authoritarian regimes in the Third World that emphasize order at the expense of both justice and political participation'.[7] Whatever the intention, however, the argument has precisely this kind of effect. State survival and regime security is only separated by a very fine line.[8] Even if a moral distinction between acts of state violence with the purpose of preserving the state and those intended to silence political opposition can be made, the tide of repression often washes out the line in the sand. Acts of state violence have always been rationalized in terms of ending a threat to state security. In many developing countries, regimes in power have equated their survival with the security of the state. The relationship between human rights and state security in this context takes on a zero-sum quality, with human rights mostly on the zero end of the pole.

There is, however, something false about this dichotomy. Human rights merely constitute the juridical aspect of human security. While the security of the community may have greater resonance to the collective community than the security of its individual members, they are not mutually exclusive. Indeed, guaranteeing the human rights (that is, human security) of its citizens could only enhance the security of the state. The adoption of a comprehensive concept of security allows Southeast Asian states to go beyond the traditional context of security. However, they remain rooted to the idea of the state as the object of security and are more than willing to subordinate human rights to the exigencies of state security (that is, regime security).

The human rights-security configuration is complicated further by the legitimacy that regimes in power acquired regardless of their human rights record. The adoption of economic development strategies that led to greater economic prosperity and the successful representation of themselves as the protector of national and cultural identity have allowed authoritarian political regimes in SEA to prosper despite their disregard for fundamental human rights. Their example broadens the context of the human rights and security dichotomy, and incorporates development and cultural identity into the calculation.

Human Rights, Development, and the Asian Values Debate

The attention given to human rights in SEA in recent years is largely a by product of international trends that emerged in the post-cold war period. The international community has become less tolerant of authoritarianism and state repression. Pressure has been brought to bear on countries whose governments were for the most part seen to be authoritarian. The governments of Indonesia, Myanmar and, to a much lesser extent, Malaysia and Singapore have been among those receiving the brunt of international scrutiny since the collapse of the Berlin Wall.

The response from these Southeast Asian states has ranged from simple denial of the existence of human rights abuses within their countries to a more sophisticated redefinition of the human rights discourse. The latter has in fact become one of the most important attempts to engage the complex issues surrounding the increasing internationalization of human rights and the tacit rebuff of traditional ideas on state sovereignty it implies. They have presented arguments that essentially question the universality of human rights as defined in the UN Declaration and the Human Rights Covenants. These arguments focused on two fundamental points. The first is the idea that primacy must be given to economic development within the particular historical context of nation building that developing states faced. The second and more well publicized aspect of the debate involves the idea of taking in the cultural context that must determine human rights norms in any society. As one analyst pointed out, the challenge that these arguments present to international human rights norms has gained 'a unique force' in international fora because of the tacit support that the rest of the members of ASEAN have given them.[9]

The linking of the human rights debate with economic development proceeds from the question of the state's role in the economy, an issue that highlights the experience of the East Asian newly industrialized economies (NIEs). Despite claims to the contrary, a closer examination of this experience showed that the strategies used by the NIEs did not exemplify a laissez-faire approach to economic policy making. The export oriented industrialization (EOI) strategy they adopted did not prevent these states from simultaneously undertaking import substitution policies in selected areas. More than a simple question of strategy, this also emphasized the role of the state in the four 'Asian tigers' as the initiator and director of industrial growth, in contrast to the neo-liberal framework which emphasized minimal state involvement in the economy.[10] Even reflective neo-classical economic analysts who eventually conceded this fact saw the role of the state largely in terms of facilitating the proper operation of the market. As recently as 1997, this argument was still being presented in a book, which continued to look for lessons from the East Asian experience for the rest of the developing world. Leipzinger and Thomas argued that one of the key ingredients in the success story of the NIEs in that region was 'active government' which 'supported markets in helping unleash entrepreneurship'.[11] They pointed out that this required an approach which combined good economic policies with political organization and technocratic decision making.

In this context, the issue focuses on the question of 'state autonomy'. Alain Lipietz has pointed out that state autonomy has three principal elements: freedom from foreign domination, autonomy from ruling classes associated with earlier regimes of accumulation, and autonomy from the popular masses.[12] The developmental state, an activist state largely free of the shackles of factional interests and able to muster the necessary political will to adopt unpopular but correct economic policies, is seen as the model responsible for the development of the East Asian NIEs.[13] The focus, however, on state autonomy *per se* ignores the historical conditions that made possible the institutionalization of the social relations, which allowed the emergence of a developmental state. It likewise glosses over the significance of the relationship that the state has with important players in the private sector that facilitated its developmentalist policies. More importantly, it disregards the political implications for human rights in the region. Deepak Lal aptly observed that the NIE experience showed that 'courageous, ruthless and possibly undemocratic governments' are needed to push the necessary policies for development to take place in Third World countries.[14] This argument clears the way for legitimization of authoritarian rule in a number of Southeast Asian states. The strong performance of their economies allowed these same states to resist international pressure for closer adherence to the letter of the UN human rights covenants, especially on civil and political rights. A number of Southeast Asian political and social leaders, and scholars have argued that human rights cannot be meaningfully enforced by governments without economic prosperity.[15] Therefore, governments must give prior attention and effort to economic development.

This argument is important. It clearly illustrates the dichotomy of principles that had led to separation of the UN Covenant on Human Rights into two documents, one dealing with civil and political rights and the other with cultural, economic, and social rights. It again raises the idea that greater political rights and freedom for individuals can only be provided at the risk of endangering the stability of society. Instability in turn endangers a country's prospects for economic growth. The International Covenant on Cultural, Economic, and Social Rights, however, presumes more than just good macroeconomic performance. It includes the provision of a modicum of distributive justice. What had given authoritarian states such as Indonesia, Malaysia, and Singapore a significant degree of legitimacy are their efforts to limit income inequality.[16] Prior to 1997, the Indonesian government has been able to lessen the disparities between rich and poor because of the country's economic performance. In this context, notable comparison can be made with the Philippines under President Ferdinand Marcos.

A more significant aspect of this argument is the implication that human rights have a historical context, that they are an outcome of a particular level of social development. This means that the societal values supportive of human rights would eventually emerge when developing societies reach a particular level of political, social, and economic development maturity. The crucial question concerns the precise level of development that can sustain human rights. More importantly, who will determine it? This question gains importance if considered with statements of eminent statesmen and political leaders in the region who have long argued that economic prosperity and societal development, and political democratization constitute an 'either-or' proposition.[17] For many of these leaders, the debate on human rights has become symbolic of the struggle for cultural equality with the industrialized West.

The cultural argument attempts to engage the important differences regarding the nature of human rights between the industrialized countries (particularly the members of the Organization for Economic Cooperation and Development (OECD)) and the developing countries in Asia.[18] This has become widely referred to as the 'Asian values' debate. There are several points of contention that define this debate. The most important ones revolve around: (1) the question of cultural relativism against universalism; (2) individual rights as opposed to communitarian rights, and the related issue of rights versus duties and obligations; and (3) the primacy of economic development over civil and political rights.[19] These issues clearly have significant implications for the long-term relationship between the ASEAN states and its Western partners.

The ASEAN countries' stance on this debate takes off from the position that international pressure on human rights comes predominantly from the industrialized West. Hence, the norms Westerners cite are framed within a liberal philosophy grounded on a conception of natural law and the idea of inalienable rights to life, liberty and property.[20] A point of contention is the claim that these norms have universal application and that no government can deny citizens these rights under any circumstance. Asian governments led by some of the ASEAN states have challenged these claims, arguing that human rights are shaped by each society's historical experiences and unique cultural development. They pointed out that the entitlements of individuals are defined by the specific laws of society and, therefore, vary and are not uniform. This argument is not only expressed by political elites in many Asian societies but actually enjoy popular support among significant sectors of the citizenry.

This difference in perspective, however, has a significant consequence on the policy choices states make within a changing international environment. The increasing emphasis on the international character of human rights raises the accountability of all states to the international community for their enforcement. The concern over international accountability was the reason why many East Asian states have refused to sign the different international human rights conventions. They generally believe that human rights concerns are domestic in nature, and the notion of international accountability diminishes state authority and national sovereignty.

The more substantive aspect of the debate, however, involves the concern with which Asian governments view the emphasis given by Western societies to individual rights. They believe that such emphasis is detrimental to social unity and stability that in turn affects economic growth and development. To a number of the political elites in the region, the premium given to individual rights accounts for what they believe to be the moral decay of Western societies. Prime Minister Mahathir Mohamed of Malaysia has warned that developing societies cannot afford to be complacent, and a balance between individual rights and social responsibility must be reached to prevent anarchy and ensure sustained economic development.[21]

The more than fifteen years of sustained economic growth in Indonesia, Malaysia, Singapore, and Thailand boosted the confidence of the ASEAN states. In 1992, they proposed to establish a Commission for a New Asia, which to an important extent was a response to Western pressure over the issue of human rights. The proposed commission was an initiative of the Institute for Strategic and International Studies (ISIS) in Malaysia. The first meeting was held on 19-21 December 1992, and a working draft entitled 'Towards a New Asia' was presented outlining 'a vision for a NEW ASIA over the next generation that is relevant and meaningful for most of the peoples of this vast continent'.[22] The draft accorded the highest priorities to: (1) 'the development of a *sustainable* and *productive* system of representative democracy rooted in our finest values and subservient to our highest ideals'; and (2) 'the establishment of societies where legitimate individual, group and communitarian political and civil *human rights* are protected and nourished and where the justified individual, group and communitarian political and civil *responsibilities* are exercised'. These declarations represent ideals that are at the core of disagreements between ASEAN states and the West.

One of the supporting appendices of the draft stated that democracy will eventually prosper in Asia. However, it cautions that democracy will only grow strong and permanent roots in Asian societies if democratic institutions fit well with the framework of Asian values and mores. The argument is that democracy must develop along consensual and communitarian lines in order to insure societal stability. The concern given to societal stability is an outgrowth of the multi-ethnic nature of most Southeast Asian societies and their ensuing vulnerability to internal strife. However, it made the concept of the rights of the individual against the state alien to many Asian societies. This is encouraged further by the general view that unfettered democracy only invites anarchy and internal conflict, which for most Asian societies is the principal threat to their security.[23]

The report of the Commission for a New Asia can be contrasted with that of the Commission on Global Governance which came out in 1995. Entitled 'Our Global Neighborhood', it described the problems that people and states would encounter in an increasingly globalized world, and how these can be best addressed. It also stressed that while sovereign powers of states are the cornerstone of the international system, they must be exercised so that the rights of states are balanced with the rights of people.[24] On this point, there seems to be no discrepancy between the aspirations of Asian states (as expressed in the vision of the Commission for a New Asia) and the principles enunciated by the Commission on Global Governance. Determining where the balance must be tipped creates the ground for political friction between East Asian states and the West.

The differences in principle on democracy and human rights between the ASEAN states and the West could have remained just a difference in principle. However, it became a point of contention when Western countries began to attach principles of 'good governance', a euphemism for the implementation of international human rights covenants, as a pre-condition for access to overseas development assistance (ODA). The ASEAN states particularly argued that this approach would hurt ordinary people who are the intended beneficiaries of development assistance. Similarly, ASEAN opposed the inclusion of the social clause (which is supposed to protect children and women against forced labor) in the World Trade Organization (WTO), as well as the resolution passed by the European Parliament to include the social clause in the system of multilateral trading and the Generalized System of Preferences (GSP).

According to them, linking international trade and human rights does not deal with the problem of improving labor conditions in the developing world. Some sectors in ASEAN have even argued that the inclusion of human rights and democracy as conditionality is an attempt of some Western countries to regain their international economic competitiveness. Certainly, this approach has been decried by a number of ASEAN leaders and opinion makers as a form of trade protectionism.

ASEAN states have collectively taken a wary position on human rights norms that are supposedly based on Western values. These norms are also seen as inimical to Asian countries' international economic competitiveness. It is believed that the multi-ethnic societies of many Asian states are too fragile and require different social and political arrangements. Accordingly, Asian societies prioritized economic development and growth over political and civil rights because considerations for the community's needs, rights, and security are of paramount importance.[25] More emphatic is Bilahari Kausikan who said that the popular clamor in East and SEA is for 'good government: effective, efficient, and honest administration able to provide security and basic needs with good opportunities for an improved standard of living'.[26] Clearly, the development and cultural arguments not only recast the human rights debate along lines that argue for the legitimacy of Southeast Asian authoritarianism. They also fully represent a variation on the national security rationale discussed earlier. The state, as the guarantor of economic prosperity and the protector of the nation's culture and identity, must be made secure against domestic political challenges. Hence, the need to keep the state's right to put constraints on individual freedom.

The claim to this right is fraught with difficulties. One can question whether there is a particular set of values unique to Asians which is authoritarian in nature.[27] Of greater importance is the sustainability of the 'Asian miracle' of the past twenty years. Legitimacy based on performance is largely contingent. In the long-term, it is an unreliable basis for maintaining state authority.[28]

Human Rights and Globalization

Globalization is a multi-faceted process whose principal aspect is the emergence of a homogeneous capitalist market. For the most part, its effects are seen in greater interpenetration and interdependence of the world economy since the collapse of state socialism.[29] The effect of globalization on traditional conceptions of state authority has become one of the most important concerns of post-cold war international relations.

The link between human rights and globalization stems directly from the question of the legitimacy of the state and the homogenizing tendencies of globalization. In SEA, however, the latter has become more of a sub-text of the former. Expectations over state performance have gone beyond the traditional base of economic development. However, states are increasingly more hard pressed to guarantee good economic performance within an increasingly globalized world economy. The most successful development strategy pursued by many Southeast Asian states has necessarily integrated them further into the global economy. In turn, this development created conditions where the ruling regime increasingly faces challenges, which it can only respond to with more violence and state oppression. In these areas (especially on questions of economic prosperity and cultural identity), states have found their efforts constrained by global forces.

Globalization has highlighted the classic dilemma of capitalist states—how to protect the interests of their citizens while participating in an international economic system that demands greater adherence to market principles. Polanyi described this dilemma in terms of what he has referred to as the 'double movement'. Since the 19th century, capitalist societies have been subject to the action of two organizing principles: (1) economic liberalism, which aims at the establishment of a self-regulating market, relying on the support of the trading classes, and using largely laissez-faire and free trade as its methods; and (2) social protection, which aims at the conservation of man and nature as well as productive organizations, relying on the varying support of those most immediately affected by the deleterious action of the market—primarily but not exclusively, the working and the landed classes—and using protective legislation, restrictive associations, and other instruments of intervention as its methods.[30] Their co-existence in society determines social harmony; as long as the market system functions without great stress and strain, societal peace and order is maintained. Society is threatened when the market is no longer able to maintain tensions between social groups at a moderate level. It falls upon the state to make sure that market forces, especially regarding production, labor, and land, will continue to remain in equilibrium. Put another way, a strong national authority is needed to offset 'market forces that tend to concentrate wealth, economic activity, and power in the core'.[31]

Issues confronting states range from questions of equity in economic rewards to environmental protection and human rights. The ability of states to address these issues is increasingly challenged by international trade agreements and regimes. States are forced to make hard choices about undertaking meaningful intervention within their sovereign boundaries that become more porous in a liberal global economy. The global spread of neo-liberal economic norms has had a critical effect on the condition of people of different cultural, ethnic, gender, and social class backgrounds. States, caught up in the global drive for greater growth have become more concerned with restive members of society that have become disenchanted with traditional political mechanisms. There is a growing perception of the inability of these mechanisms to protect their interests from the adverse effects of an increasingly globalized economy. This problem is particularly important in the case of Southeast Asian states whose legitimacy is built largely on the promise of economic prosperity.

Muthiah Alagappa has referred to the perpetual 'performance dilemma' that authoritarian regimes of SEA must face. They face the imperative of having to constantly improve on past levels of performance in order to meet rising expectations. In the face of globalization, however, economic performance is no longer fully within the control of governments in power. Alagappa points out that:

Growing internationalization and the dependent character of the economies of nearly all developing countries imply that while governments have the power to mismanage their economies, good performance depends on the state of the global economy as well. Legitimation, to the extent that it can be based on economic performance, then becomes a function of the global economy. As this relationship is imperfectly understood by the lay public, opposition groups may manipulate the situation to contest the legitimacy of the incumbent government.[32]

One must note that the 'Asian values' debate is predicated on the claim that authoritarian regimes in East Asia are products of the culture shared by most of the people in the region. The Asian state is seen as the defender of indigenous values and culture, of the national identity that society is built around. The pressures towards homogenization that comes with globalization, however, can erode this regional consensus. Robert Cox has noted that the 'changes taking place in state roles in the globalizing economy give new opportunity for self-expression by nationalities that have no state of their own, in movements for separation or autonomy; and the same tendencies encourage ethnicities and religiously defined groups that straddle state boundaries to express their identities in global politics'.[33]

Indonesia, Malaysia, and Thailand largely followed the East Asian NIE model and posted impressive gross national product (GNP) and gross domestic product (GDP) growth rates between 1980 and 1996.[34] This performance did not only affirm the infallibility of the development model; it also established the claim to legitimacy of the authoritarian political model. Success generated confidence (even smugness) among East Asian political leaders in the efficacy of the 'Asian way'. Consequently, the financial crisis and the speed with which it spread in mid-1997 came as a very unpleasant surprise.

In June 1997, the Bank of Thailand tried to protect the *baht* against financial speculation initially brought about by rising interest rates in Tokyo. The ensuing financial crisis in Thailand quickly spread to its Southeast Asian neighbors and to South Korea. Most of the affected countries asked the International Monetary Fund (IMF) to cobble bail out packages for their economies. These packages necessarily came with IMF conditionalities that demanded structural economic reforms.

The East Asian financial crisis is a stark illustration of the downside of globalization. The liberalization of Asian financial markets has facilitated the easy movement of capital across international borders in a way that has had a constraining effect on the economic policies of national governments.[35] Among the capital hungry countries of East Asia, this was a welcome development for huge corporations that had to kowtow to their governments for funds. For governments, meanwhile, this was an unforeseen challenge to their capacity to manage and regulate the national economy. Ultimately, its more important consequence was to burst the bubble of economic prosperity that underpinned the legitimacy of authoritarian states in the region.

Globalization highlighted the inherent contradictions within the authoritarian regimes of SEA. The governments of Indonesia, Malaysia, and Singapore have successfully engaged critics to reflect on the importance of 'strong states' in providing for the economic welfare of their citizens. Posturing as champions of indigenous values and culture has added to their popular appeal. These claims have made the heavy handed treatment of political dissent and the official brushing off of criticisms from the international human rights community, tolerable to most of their citizenry. Globalization, however, has challenged these same claims. The financial crisis caused national economies to fall into disarray. More than raising questions about the implications of the crisis for the prevailing economic development model, it underscores the problems of these states' human rights policies. While a sudden conversion to a universal interpretation of human rights can be ruled out, it will force ASEAN states to pay closer attention to the issue.

Human Rights, Security, and Development: Two Case Studies

It is clear that the issue of human rights has served as a nexus for development and security in SEA. The link between these concerns focuses on the survival of the state, not primarily through the use of force but by enhancing its stature with its citizens. Representing the state as the purveyor of resources, goods, and services that would ensure economic prosperity and social stability was the means by which this was accomplished. However, this can only be made certain by insuring the ruling regime against political challenges both from within and outside its territory. Accordingly, a number of states refused to recognize the universality of human rights and considered adherence to international norms as contingent on the eradication of threats.

This framework raises problems that revolve around two related but distinct points. First is the false dichotomy attached to human rights and the security of ruling regimes. The second issue is the claim to legitimacy made by these regimes. The first issue establishes a centralization of authority that sows the seeds of political dissent. The second creates Alagappa's difficult 'performance dilemma'. The financial crisis highlighted the increasing effects and influence of global forces on national economies. The vulnerabilities of authoritarian states were laid bare and their claims to legitimacy became contestable. It was the decisions made by the ruling regimes that exposed their citizens to the adverse effects of the financial crisis rather than political opposition and dissent. Their pointed disregard of international human rights norms has guaranteed neither lasting security (either for the state or for its citizens) nor sustained development (either in terms of economic prosperity or social identity).

Indonesia and the Philippines are case studies worth looking into regarding these concerns. Indonesia exemplifies the case of an authoritarian regime that had refused to guarantee international human rights norms. It dismissed strong international pressure, particularly regarding East Timor, and relied on its economic strength to maintain its international standing and its domestic legitimacy. In May 1998, however, this came to a head as the Indonesian economy reeled from the effects of the financial crisis. The Philippines, on the other hand, exemplifies exactly the opposite. Save for an authoritarian interlude, it has professed to be a liberal democracy and signed most international treaties and covenants on human rights. While its economy has been badly affected by the financial crisis, the political and social effects have not been as adverse as they have been elsewhere in the region.

Indonesia

On 21 May 1998, popular pressure forced President Soeharto of Indonesia to resign his office. Up until then, his resignation was the most startling consequence of the financial crisis. It ended the thirty two years of Soeharto's *de facto* absolute rule.

The human rights record of Indonesia under Soeharto was never exemplary or tolerable. Prior to 1997, the government was frequently accused of grave human rights violations, particularly arbitrary detentions without trial, disappearances, torture, and extra-judicial killings.[36] These methods have been primarily utilized in regions where armed insurgency and secessionist activities were prevalent.[37] In general, the regime has relied less on coercion than on its 'persuasive resources' to secure its hold on power. This point buttresses the argument that the alleged human rights violations of Indonesia are actually natural acts of self-defense directed against domestic forces that threaten the security of the state.[38] In such instances, human rights norms had to be suspended in pursuit of a 'greater good'.

Indonesia's acceptance of a comprehensive security concept and its contingent attitude towards human rights are of great interest. Indonesia adheres to an official doctrine of *ketahanan nasional* (national resilience) adopted in 1973. Former Indonesian Foreign Affairs Minister Mochtar Kusuma-atmadja indicated the domestic emphasis of comprehensive security when he argued that national resilience can be best enhanced through 'the development of society in the economic, political, social, and cultural sense'.[39] Together with the related concept of regional resilience, national resilience has also been officially adopted by ASEAN as its framework for regional security. As described by Jusuf Wanandi, this framework assumes that 'if each of the member nations (of ASEAN) can accomplish overall national development and overcome internal threats, regional resilience will automatically result much in the same way as a chain derives its overall strength from that of the individual links'.[40]

With this comprehensive approach to security, any form of dissent could be construed as a threat to the state. The government's heavy handedness was applied throughout Indonesia. Certainly, the insurgency infested districts of Aceh, Irian Jaya, and East Timor bore the worst of the regime's coercion. Yet the rest of the country also had to live with Soeharto's intolerance for dissent. The regime imposed stringent limits on the freedoms of speech, press, and assembly.[41] Before Soeharto's abdication, human rights and democratization (more specifically their advocates) were increasingly seen as the most immediate threats to his New Order regime. The challenge they posed to the government's legitimacy undermined the stability of the political system.[42] The political sensitivities involved were such that the Indonesian government found it necessary to regularly lash out at its foreign critics for interference on issues that it considered to be within its sovereign jurisdiction.

The same 'legitimation' rationale has been presented in relation to questions of development and cultural identity. One analyst noted that the Indonesian government tried hard to shake off its hard line image by pointing out that it accepts the universality of international human rights standards. Sensitivity on this point has in fact led to the establishment of an independent national commission on human rights. What is at issue is the observance of human rights. Indonesia has argued that consideration must be given to the cultural and historical differences that exist among states.[43] In this regard, the problem again goes back to the association between human rights and political stability.

The Indonesian government remains convinced that the polity is still in the process of transformation towards the goal of a unitary nation-state. The country supposedly remains vulnerable to domestic forces that threaten its unity. Anything that could disrupt the process of nation building is to be considered a threat. It is this continuing emphasis on political stability that links culture and development to the issue of human rights in Indonesia. A unitary culture has been used to explain the rejection of any imperative to fully respect the rights of individuals. At the Regional Meeting for Asia of the UN World Conference on Human Rights held in March 1993, for example, the Indonesian delegate explained that Asians 'do not hold to an individualistic view of human rights for we cannot disregard the interest of society, State and nation'.[44] The claim to a unitary culture and identity that is distinctively 'Asian' has been shown in previous sections to be problematic. This problem is complicated by the notion of communitarian 'Indonesian' ideals and interests. The secessionist movement in Aceh, East Timor, and Irian Jaya are based on notions of separate ethnicities. Thus, the Indonesian government makes the hypocritical claim of cultural uniqueness as the basis for non-observance of international human rights norms, while denying the same argument as a basis for the self-determination of specific communities.

Economic development concerns have been similarly invoked. Political dissent is seen as potentially disruptive of economic activity. Dewi Fortuna Anwar succinctly describes the effects by pointing out that:

> Political stability and economic development are perceived to be linked together in an endless chain of cause and effect. Threats to political stability from any source would hinder the smooth process of development by distracting the government's attention and resources from development efforts. Conversely, obstacles put in the way of economic development projects are seen as a direct threat to political stability.[45]

Eventually, Soeharto's regime managed an Indonesian economy and pushed the country into the second tier of new industrializing economies in Asia. The government's economic policies resulted in strong economic performance in the last two decades before the 1997 crisis. GDP rose by an average of 6.4 per cent in 1973-85, 6.9 per cent in 1985-90, and 7.7 per cent in 1990-94. A focus on growth and equity has resulted in higher incomes, reduced poverty, and improved health and welfare for Indonesians.[46]

Given these years of growth and prosperity, the collapse of the Indonesian economy proved to be traumatic to the country. It erased the gains achieved in alleviating poverty and reducing income inequality. The forced resignation of Soeharto certainly exemplified the problem for regimes in power of performance based legitimacy. For human rights advocates, the experience shows how tenuous the economic development-political stability-national security argument is. More importantly, the case of Indonesia shows that arguing the fragility of political stability in a state where the regime in power bases its legitimacy on performance does not necessarily create an imperative for the regime to accede to stricter adherence to international human rights norms. The Indonesian state remains wary of these norms and continues to see them as a function of an imposed external order.

The implications for human rights of the Indonesian experience are not at all encouraging. It has been shown that the alleged incompatibility between human rights protection, on one hand, and political stability and economic development, on the other, is flawed. At the same time, it has not necessarily been completely invalidated.

The Philippines

The Philippines is an interesting case in any review of human rights in SEA. Under President Fidel Ramos, it undertook an experiment on the feasibility of industrializing the economy within a formally liberal-democratic political framework in the face of their neighbors' clear skepticism.[47] To the chagrin of other leaders in the region, the experiment seemed on the verge of success until the outbreak of the Asian financial crisis. This was accomplished with the Philippines government being one of the strongest supporters of human rights in the United Nations. As noted before, the Philippines became a signatory to nearly all international treaties and covenants on human rights between 1986 and 1996. In 1986, the precursor of what eventually became an independent commission on human rights was established to look into reported cases of human rights violations committed by both the state's armed forces and insurgent armies.

The 20-year rule of President Ferdinand Marcos turned most Filipinos against authoritarianism. While the Philippines shares with other Southeast Asian countries the colonial experience and the subsequent travails of post-colonial state-building, the strong liberal political outlook that has been largely internalized by most of Philippine society was largely a reaction to the years under strong arm rule. The Philippines under Marcos possessed the same authoritarian characteristics as Indonesia under Soeharto. The Marcos regime sought to justify its politically repressive policies in terms of national security. Dissent was violently suppressed as threats to the stability of the country. Two major armed insurgencies provided the government with the requisite bogeyman to justify its authoritarian rule. At the same time, the government instituted economic reforms intended to spur the economic growth that would legitimize its authority.[48] The inability of the Marcos regime to replicate the success of Indonesia economically and militarily[49] has been instrumental in its failure to establish political legitimacy. At the same time, strong transnational networks that advocated human rights became the nucleus for generating international pressure and effecting the incorporation of human rights norms into the domestic structure. The success of their activities resulted in the gradual de-legitimation of the Marcos regime.[50]

Since the February 1986 revolution, the Philippine state has clearly associated security with human rights. Together with other Southeast Asian countries, political stability and national security has been considered to be intrinsically linked with economic development by the Philippine government.[51] This link, however, was understood in a different manner. In August 1992, the National Security Council of the Philippines presented a definition of national security which stressed the protection and enhancement of the well being of people's lives and welfare, alongside the preservation of the country's territorial integrity and sovereignty.[52] In this sense, human rights, national security, and economic development were seen as mutually reinforcing concerns.

What is noteworthy about the Philippine case is the differential nature of its human rights record compared to Indonesia. While Indonesia has emphasized equity and poverty reduction over political rights and freedom, the reverse has been true of the Philippines. Though human rights abuses continue to be reported against the police and military forces, institutional remedies have already been put into place to address them. It is really in questions of distributive justice that the Philippines lags behind in its human rights obligations.[53] Years of economic stagnation have exacted their toll on the ability of the Philippine government to provide sufficient social safety nets to protect people from periodic macroeconomic shocks. This has clearly become more important with the effects of the Asian financial crisis. Though not as badly affected as other countries in the region, the Philippines has seen serious increases in its unemployment levels even as it had to re-set its growth targets for 1998 to lower levels.

There has been some movement in this area, particularly noticeable in a number of keynote judicial decisions that had implications for economic and social rights in the country. There has been increasing attention in the courts given to the dimension of human rights concerned with incidence of poverty and decent living conditions, and certain cases have become a balancing test between economic development and social reform. These legal developments have shown that there is a gradual enshrining of a more holistic human rights ideology in Philippine society that is increasingly being affirmed by state institutions.[54]

Conclusion

The cases of Indonesia and the Philippines illustrate the linkages that have been established between questions of national security, economic and social development, and human rights. The relationship between these issue areas is quite complex. While arguments have been made by authoritarian regimes to present some form of mutually reinforcing relationship between national security and economic development that requires the maintenance of politically repressive policies, the case of Southeast Asian states has shown this argument to be tenuous at best. Certainly the Indonesian and Philippine cases point to different results.

The picture is further muddied when combined with the impact of globalization. The state-centric argument made by authoritarian regimes on security and development and directed against universal human rights have proven to be vulnerable in the face of pressure from global forces. Regimes in power, whether authoritarian or democratic, have increasingly become the agents of globalization. In so doing, they have relinquished much of their responsibility for and moral authority to claiming the role of the guarantor of the country's security. Considering the effects of globalization, the argument that human rights will have to be sacrificed for a 'greater good' (that is, the country's security and economic development) holds increasingly less value. Indeed, the converse is increasingly becoming truer. The effects of globalization require stronger guarantees that people's welfare will be upheld and that their voices will be heard.

Notes

1 Donnelly, J. (1993), *International Human Rights,* Westview Press, Boulder, Colorado, pp.19.

2 ASEAN was formed in 1967 and originally included Indonesia, Malaysia, the Philippines, Singapore and Thailand. Brunei was accepted in 1984, Vietnam in 1995, and Laos and Myanmar in 1997 and Cambodia.

3 Singapore's concept of total defense originates from the post-independence philosophy which emphasized national identity, internal unity, and economic development, while Malaysia's own concept of comprehensive security derives from the broad policy measures used during the Emergency of 1948-1960. See Alagappa, M. (1988), 'Comprehensive Security: Interpretations in ASEAN Countries', in R. A. Scalapino, *et al.* (eds), *Asian Security Issues: Regional and Global,* Institute of East Asian Studies, Berkeley, pp.50. Thailand's security perspective varies on specific items of concern with each regime. However, there are areas of commonality which show preference for a multidimensional perspective of security (emphasizing political, economic, psycho-social, and military concerns) rather than its narrow military definition. See Alagappa, 'The National Security of Developing States', 1988, pp.38-39.

4 Sayigh, Y. (1990), 'Confronting the 1990s: Security in the Developing Countries', *Adelphi Paper 251,* Summer, pp.3.

5 Ayoob, M. (1995), *The Third World Security Predicament: State Making, Regional Conflicts, and the International System,* Lynne Rienner Publishers, Inc., London, pp.28-32.

6 *Ibid.,* pp.85-86.

7 *Ibid.,* pp.86.

8 The conceptual difference between the two needs to be emphasized here. The state is used here in the context of a political community which has a structure of domination and coordination, a coercive apparatus and the means to administer society and estract resources from it. Regimes on the other hand refer to the formal and informal organization of the center of political power, and its relations with the rest of society. A further elucidation of these definitions can be seen in Alagappa, M. (1994), 'The Bases of Legitimacy', in M. Alagappa (ed.), *Political Legitimacy in Southeast Asia: The Quest for Moral Authority,* Stanford University Press, Stanford, California, pp.26-27.

9 Robinson, G. (1996), 'Human Rights in Southeast Asia: Rhetoric and Reality', in D. Wurfel (ed.), *Southeast Asia in the New World Order: The Political Economy of a Dynamic Region,* Macmillan Press, Ltd., London, pp.92.

10 See different chapters in Leipzinger, D. M. (ed.) (1997), *Lessons from East Asia,* The University of Michigan Press, Ann Arbor; Brown, R. H. and Liu, W. T. (eds) (1992), *Modernization in East Asia: Political, Economic, and Social Perspectives,* Praeger Publishers, Westport and London; Deyo, F. C. (ed.), (1987), *The Political Economy of the New Asian Industrialism,* Cornell University Press, Ithaca and London; Haggard, S. and Kaufman, R. (eds) (1992), *The Politics of Economic Adjustment,* Princeton University Press, Princeton. See also Amsden, A. (1990), 'Third World Industrialization: 'Global Fordism' or a New Model?', *New Left Review,* vol.182; Bienefeld, M. (1988), 'The Significance of the Newly Industrialising Countries for the Development Debate', *Studies*

in Political Economy, vol.25, Spring; Evans, P. (1987), 'Class, State, and Dependence in East Asia: Lessons for Latin Americanists', in F. C. Deyo (ed.), *The Political Economy of the New Asian Industrialism,* Cornell University Press, Ithaca and London.

11 See Leipzinger, D. M. and Thomas, V. (1997), 'An Overview of the East Asian Experience', in D. M. Leipzinger (ed.), *Lessons from East Asia,* The University of Michigan Press, Ann Arbor, pp.4.

12 See Lipietz, A (1987), *Mirages and Miracles: The Crises of Global Fordism,* Translated by David Macey, Verso, London, pp.72.

13 This concept is largely attributed to Chalmers Johnson in his work which showed the role of the Ministry of International Trade and Industry in Japan's own economic miracle in the 1950s and 1960s.

14 Quoted in Bienefeld, 'The Significance of the Newly Industrialising Countries for the Development Debate', 1988, pp.14-15.

15 See Stubbs, R. (1995), *Legitimacy and Economic Growth in Eastern Asia,* University of Toronto - York University Joint Centre for Asia Pacific Studies Eastern Asia Policy Papers No. 10, pp.12-14. See also Alagappa, 'The National Security of Developing States', 1988, pp. 41. The arguments made along this line have placed the Southeast Asian NIEs alongside dubious international allies. The same argument has been made to justify the Chinese government's refusal to open up their political system, a position which was noticeably strengthened by the events at Tiananmen Square in 1989. For a clear elucidation of this position on the Chinese side, See, Cai, P. (1996), 'Human Rights: A Chinese Perspective', in B. Nagara and C. S. Ean (eds), *Managing Security and Peace in the Asia-Pacific,* Institute for Strategic and International Studies, Kuala Lumpur, Malaysia, pp. 541-548.

16 Thompson, M. (1993), 'The limits of democratisation in ASEAN', *Third World Quarterly,* vol.14, no.3, pp.471-473.

17 Robison, R. (1996), 'The Politics of "Asian Values"', *The Pacific Review,* vol.9, no.3, pp.312.

18 The concept of the 'West' is really a vague cultural concept and is very much different from the economic divide of 'North' and 'South', although most of those countries belonging to the 'West' are identified with the 'North'. For purposes of this study, however, it will be utilized basically to refer to Canada, the industrialized, capitalist countries of Western Europe, and the United States. It is still not clear whether Australia and New Zealand are to be considered as part of the 'West' although for all intents and purpose, Asian countries consider them to be so.

19 See Hernandez, C. G. (1995), *ASEAN Perspectives on Human Rights and Democracy in International Relations,* Peace, Conflict Resolution and Human Rights Occasional Papers Series 95-6, December, Center for Integrative and Development Studies and the U.P. Press Quezon City, Philippines, pp.3; and Ghai, Y. (1994), *Human Rights and Governance: The Asia Debate,* Occasional Paper 1, November, The Asia Foundation's Center for Asian Pacific Affairs. Hernandez actually notes that there are several areas of divergence on the issue of human rights between most of the ASEAN countries and their Western partners. In addition to the three presented above, she included: 1) the timing and sequencing of the implementation and observation of human rights; 2) the issue of attaching conditionalities for overseas development assistance to progress in 'good governance'; and 3) the inclusion of the social clause in the General Agreement on Tariffs and Trade and other multilateral trade regulations.

20 *Ibid.,* pp.4.

21 *New Straits Times,* 20 May 1995, pp.10.

22 See Working Skeleton Draft of *Towards a New Asia: A Report to the Commission for a New Asia* presented at the 'First Meeting of the Commission for a New Asia' on 19 December 1992, Kuala Lumpur, Malaysia, pp. 2.
23 Ayoob, *The Third World Security Predicament: State Making, Regional Conflicts, and the International System,* 1995.
24 See 'A Call to Action', a summary of *Our Global Neighborhood,* 1995, the report of the Commission on Global Governance, Commission on Global Governance, Geneva, pp.10.
25 Chew, M. (1994), 'Human Rights in Singapore: Perceptions and Problems', *Asian Survey* vol.XXXIV, no.11, November, pp.934-935.
26 Kausikan, B. (1992), 'Asia's Different Standard', *Foreign Policy,* vol.92, pp.38.
27 An obvious comparison can be made within ASEAN itself. Indonesia, Malaysia and Singapore have articulated views which hew closely to the 'Asian values' interpretation. On the other hand, the Philippines and, increasingly, Thailand have moved away from this interpretation. Both these states have ratified all or nearly all of the more than international instruments dealing with various aspects of human rights. Outside of formal political structures and policies, individuals and groups in many countries in Southeast Asia have advocated views on human rights and democracy which are increasingly at odds with those of their governments and the ruling elites in their respective countries. The philosophical underpinnings for their perspective, however, are generally of native origin rather than Western in orientation. This makes their arguments more palatable to the general population. Interestingly, Indonesia has one of the most active human rights movements which have emerged in recent years in the region. The NGO Declaration on Human Rights made in Bangkok in 1993 by the human rights and democracy NGOs in the region clearly emphasize the differences between official declarations and the sentiments of the people they govern.
28 Alagappa, 'The National Security of Developing States', 1988, pp. 41-43.
29 See 'Editor's Introduction', in Y. Sakamoto (ed.) (1994), *Global Transformation: Challenges to the State System,* United Nations University Press, Tokyo, pp.4.
30 Polanyi, K. (1957), *The Great Transformation: The Political and Economic Origins of Our Time,* Beacon Press, Boston, pp.133.
31 Gilpin, R. (1987), *The Political Economy of International Relations,* Princeton University Press, Princeton, pp.96. Max Weber, with reference to the German state, also argues that 'economic policy -- including the question of whether, and how far, the state should intervene in economic life, and when it should rather untie the economic forces of the nation and tear down the barriers in the way of their free development -- the ultimate and decisive voice should be that of the economic and political interests of our nation's power, and the vehicle of that power, the German national state'. Weber, M. (1980), *The National State and Economic Policy* (Freiburg Address), translated and reprinted in *Economy and Society,* vol.9, no.4, November, pp.438-439.
32 Alagappa, 'The National Security of Developing States', 1988, pp. 41.
33 See Cox, R. (1996), 'Multilateralism and World Order', in R. Cox and T. Sinclair (eds), *Approaches to World Order,* Cambridge University Press, Cambridge, pp.517.
34 The average economic growth rates recorded in the East Asian region for the decade between 1980 and 1990 was 7per cent, despite the poor economic performance of the Philippines and the Indochinese countries. Malaysia and Thailand sustained growth rates of at least 8 per cent for the last four years of the decade of the 1980s and at least 7 per cent until 1996.
35 Gill, S. and Law, D. (1988), *The Global Political Economy: Perspectives, Problems and Policies,* The Johns Hopkins University Press, Baltimore, pp.92.
36 In a presentation made at the 37th Annual Convention of the International Studies Association held at Toronto on 18-22 March 1997, Anja Jetschke noted that the Indonesian

government's record on these indicators of human rights had been consistently bad throughout the Soeharto years.

37 Thompson, 'The limits of democratisation in ASEAN', 1993, pp.470.
38 In a letter to Amnesty International dated July 1991, the Indonesian government asserted that '[a]ccusations of human rights violations in Aceh . . . are pure inventions and are launched with the intention of discrediting the Republic of Indonesia in the eyes of the international community'. Quoted in Robinson, G. (1996), 'Human Rights in Southeast Asia: Rhetoric and Reality', in D. Wurfel (ed.), *Southeast Asia in the New World Order: The Political Economy of a Dynamic Region*, Macmillan Press, Ltd., London, pp.85.
39 Kusuma-atmadja, M. (1993), *Some Thoughts on ASEAN Security Cooperation: An Indonesian's Perspective (Indonesia dan Kerjasama Keamanan Regional)*, Ministry of Foreign Affairs, Jakarta, pp.15.
40 Wanandi, J. (1984), 'ASEAN Perspectives on International Security: an Indonesian View', in D. Hugh McMillen (ed.), *Asian Perspectives on International Security*, St. Martin's Press, New York, pp.41.
41 See Neher, C. and Marlay, R. (1995), *Democracy ad Development in Southeast Asia: The Winds of Change*, Westview Press, Boulder, pp.85-88.
42 Fortuna, D. A. (1998), 'Indonesia: Domestic Priorities Define National Security', in M. Alagappa (ed.), *Asian Security Practice: Material and Ideational Influences*, Stanford University Press, Stanford,Ca, pp.492.
43 Robinson, 'Human Rights in Southeast Asia: Rhetoric and Reality', 1996, pp.87-88.
44 *Ibid.*, pp.86.
45 Fortuna, 'Indonesia: Domestic Priorities Define National Security', pp.492.
46 See Wardhanan, A. (1998), 'Economic Reform in Indonesia: The transition from resource dependence to industrial competitiveness', in H. S. Rowen (ed.), *Behind East Asian Growth: The Political and Social Foundations of Prosperity*, Routledge, London, pp.135-139.
47 In 1992, the former Prime Minister of Singapore, Lee Kuan Yew, gave a speech in the Philippines wherein he explicitly stated that what the Philippines needed was more discipline and less democracy.
48 It is interesting to note that the Philippine economy has yet to match the 7.2 per cent growth rate it recorded in 1973.
49 Both the guerrilla movement conducted by the Communist Party of the Philippines and the secessionist movement started by the Moro National Liberation Front have persisted beyond the administration of President Ramos which ended in 1998. Groups associated with these movements have been engaged in negotiations towards a political settlement of the armed conflict.
50 The significance of these solidarity groups to the eventual ousting of Marcos in 1986 has been instrumental in the proliferation and growth in influence of non-governmental organizations in the Philippines. It was estimated in 1993 that there may have been as many as 60,000 non-governmental organizations and people's organizations in the entire country.
51 When he was still the Secretary for National Defense, Fidel Ramos pointed out that the security of the country could best be ensured by 'maintaining a desirable level and pace of economic development on the one hand, and the public order at the national and local levels on the other'. See Fidel V. Ramos, *Nation Building and National Security*, speech given on the '81st Foundation Day of the Philippine Columbian Association', Plaza Dilao, Paco, Manila on 11December 1988.
52 See section on the Philippines in C. E. Morrison (ed.) (1997), *Asia Pacific Outlook 1997*, East-West Centre, Honolulu, Hawaii, pp.101.

53 The distinction between political and civil rights, and economic and social rights are evident in the way that the Philippine state has approached human rights. The Philippine Commission on Human Rights has focused primarily on the former. This is again one of the residual effects of the Marcos era.

54 This was noted by Sedfrey Candelaria of the Human Rights Center at the Ateneo de Manila University during the 'Fifth ASEAN Colloquium on Human Rights' held in Manila on 14-17 February 1998.

References

Alagappa, M. (1987), 'Comprehensive Security: Interpretations in ASEAN Countries' and The National Security of Developing States', in R. A. Scalapino, *et al.* (eds), *Asian Security Issues: Regional and Global,* Institute of East Asian Studies, Berkeley, pp. 50.

Alagappa, M. (1994), 'The Bases of Legitimacy', in M. Alagappa (ed.), *Political Legitimacy in Southeast Asia: The Quest for Moral Authority,* Stanford University Press.

Amsden, A. (1990), 'Third World Industrialization: 'Global Fordism' or a New Model?', *New Left Review,* vol. 182.

Ayoob, M. (1995), *The Third World Security Predicament: State Making, Regional Conflicts, and the International System,* Lynne Rienner Publishers, Inc., London, pp. 28-32.

Bienefeld, M. (1988), 'The Significance of the Newly Industrialising Countries for the Development Debate', *Studies in Political Economy,* vol. 25, Spring.

Brown, R. H. and Liu, W. T. (eds) (1992), *Modernization in East Asia: Political, Economic, and Social Perspectives,* Praeger Publishers, Westport and London.

Cai, P. (1996), 'Human Rights: A Chinese Perspective', in B. Nagara and C. S. Ean (eds), *Managing Security and Peace in the Asia-Pacific,* Institute for Strategic and International Studies, Kuala Lumpur, Malaysia, pp. 541-548.

Chew, M. (1994), 'Human Rights in Singapore: Perceptions and Problems', *Asian Survey* vol. XXXIV, no. 11, November, pp. 934-935.

Commission on Global Governance (1995), *Our Global Neighborhood,* Commission on Global Governance, Geneva, pp. 10.

Cox, R. (1996), 'Multilateralism and World Order', in R. Cox and T. Sinclair (eds), *Approaches to World Order,* Cambridge University Press, Cambridge, pp. 517.

Deyo, F. C. (ed.), (1987), *The Political Economy of the New Asian Industrialism,* Cornell University Press, Ithaca and London.

Donnelly, J. (1993), *International Human Rights,* Westview Press, Boulder, Colorado, pp. 19.

Evans, P. (1987), 'Class, State, and Dependence in East Asia: Lessons for Latin Americanists', in F. C. Deyo (ed.), *The Political Economy of the New Asian Industrialism,* Cornell University Press, Ithaca and London.

Fortuna, D. A. (1998), 'Indonesia: Domestic Priorities Define National Security', in M. Alagappa (ed.), *Asian Security Practice: Material and Ideational Influences,* Stanford University Press, Stanford, Ca., pp. 492.

Ghai, Y. (1994), *Human Rights and Governance: The Asia Debate,* Occasional Paper 1, November, The Asia Foundation's Center for Asian Pacific Affairs.

Gill, S. and Law, D. (1988), *The Global Political Economy: Perspectives, Problems and Policies,* The Johns Hopkins University Press, Baltimore, pp. 92.

Gilpin, R. (1987), *The Political Economy of International Relations,* Princeton University Press, Princeton, pp. 96.

Haggard, S. and Kaufman, R. (eds) (1992), *The Politics of Economic Adjustment,* Princeton University Press, Princeton.

Hernandez, C. G. (1995), *ASEAN Perspectives on Human Rights and Democracy in International Relations*, Peace, Conflict Resolution and Human Rights Occasional Papers Series 95-6, December, Center for Integrative and Development Studies and the U.P. Press Quezon City, Philippines, pp. 3.

Kausikan, B. (1992), 'Asia's Different Standard', *Foreign Policy*, vol. 92, pp. 38.

Kusuma-atmadja, M. (1993), *Some Thoughts on ASEAN Security Cooperation: An Indonesian's Perspective (Indonesia dan Kerjasama Keamanan Regional)*, Ministry of Foreign Affairs, Jakarta, pp. 15.

Leipzinger, D. M. and Thomas, V. (1997), 'An Overview of the East Asian Experience', in D. M. Leipzinger (ed.), *Lessons from East Asia*, The University of Michigan Press, Ann Arbor, pp. 4.

Lipietz, A (1987), *Mirages and Miracles: The Crises of Global Fordism*, Translated by David Macey, Verso, London, pp. 72.

Morrison, C. E. (ed.) (1997), *Asia Pacific Outlook 1997*, East-West Centre, Honolulu, Hawaii, pp. 101.

Neher, C. and Marlay, R. (1995), *Democracy ad Development in Southeast Asia: The Winds of Change*, Westview Press, Boulder, pp. 85-88.

Robinson, G. (1996), 'Human Rights in Southeast Asia: Rhetoric and Reality', in D. Wurfel (ed.), *Southeast Asia in the New World Order: The Political Economy of a Dynamic Region*, Macmillan Press, Ltd., London, pp. 85.

Robison, R. (1996), 'The Politics of "Asian Values"', *The Pacific Review*, vol. 9, no. 3, pp. 312.

Polanyi, K. (1957), *The Great Transformation: The Political and Economic Origins of Our Time*, Beacon Press, Boston, pp. 133.

Sakamoto, Y. (ed.) (1994), *Global Transformation: Challenges to the State System*, United Nations University Press, Tokyo, pp. 4.

Sayigh, Y. (1990), 'Confronting the 1990s: Security in the Developing Countries', *Adelphi Paper 251*, Summer, pp. 3.

Stubbs, R. (1995), *Legitimacy and Economic Growth in Eastern Asia*, University of Toronto - York University Joint Centre for Asia Pacific Studies Eastern Asia Policy Papers No. 10, pp. 12-14.

Thompson, M. (1993), 'The limits of democratisation in ASEAN', *Third World Quarterly* vol. 14, no. 3, pp. 471-473.

Wanandi, J. (1984), 'ASEAN Perspectives on International Security: an Indonesian View', in D. Hugh McMillen (ed.), *Asian Perspectives on International Security*, St. Martin's Press, New York, pp. 41.

Wardhanan, A. (1998), 'Economic Reform in Indonesia: The transition from resource dependence to industrial competitiveness', in H. S. Rowen (ed.), *Behind East Asian Growth: The Political and Social Foundations of Prosperity*, Routledge, London, pp. 135-139.

Weber, M. (1980), *The National State and Economic Policy* (Freiburg Address), translated and reprinted in *Economy and Society*, vol. 9, no. 4, November, pp. 438-439.

PART III
COUNTRY CASE STUDIES

Chapter 7

The Security Implications of the Liberalization and Globalization of Financial Markets

Maria Socorro Gochoco-Bautista

Introduction

The former Managing Director of the International Monetary Fund (IMF), Michel Camdessus, remarked that the currency crisis that swept Southeast Asia during the late 1990s underscored the new risks and requirements of a globalized economy.[1] He pointed out that what was disturbing about the Thai crisis was that it was foreseen and preventable, yet struck with full force. Evidently, the lesson to be drawn from the currency crisis is not the risks of globalization *per se*, nor the demonization of markets, but the importance of good citizenship and the acceptance of market discipline when tapping global financial markets. Good citizenship in global capital markets requires countries to pursue sound and transparent policies that instill market confidence and to respect the signals provided by the market. He encouraged countries to get their economic fundamentals right first, by ensuring financial sector soundness and strengthening current account positions, 'rather than spurring growth prematurely'. He emphasized the need for the 'orderly liberalization of capital markets' through the removal of controls in a way that is consistent with sustainable macroeconomic policies, strong monetary and financial sectors, and lasting liberalization.

There are several points worth emphasizing with regard to Camdessus' statement. One is the fact that globalization presents countries with new risks as well as new opportunities. In order to reap the benefits of globalization, countries have to abide by certain rules, particularly market rules, and get their economic fundamentals right first. These are not easy tasks and there are tradeoffs to be faced. Getting economic fundamentals right may necessitate the curtailment of politically convenient methods of inducing economic growth, such as expansionary fiscal and monetary policy. One is given pause, however, by the fact that even countries like Malaysia, which had sound economic fundamentals characterized by good monetary and fiscal policy and impressive rates of growth in the last decade, were not spared by the currency turmoil. Furthermore, despite the currency crisis, more rather than less liberalization is needed to foster the orderly liberalization of capital markets. This seems to be a particularly difficult lesson to impart in the face of the turmoil surrounding the crisis. It also turns the basis for the traditional strategy of Asian economic growth on its head. In the past, countries in Asia used a fixed exchange rate policy as an inflation anchor (preferably one which undervalued the domestic currency), controls on the capital account, tight money, and cheap labor, to earn foreign exchange through exports. The question is whether it is possible to return to this traditional strategy, and if not, how to ensure that the new strategy is internally consistent and delivers as good or better results than the traditional one.

While the effects of the globalization of financial markets is a matter of great interest and concern, its security implications have not been given as much attention. This study is an attempt to address this inadequacy.

Globalization is taken to mean the greater openness of economies to each other, the greater mobility of factors of production, including capital, and the resulting greater integration of production networks and capital markets. Financial liberalization is seen as an important catalyst of this process. Globalization is both a condition and a conscious policy choice to participate in the process of achieving greater economic openness.

Security, on the other hand, is a comprehensive concept and can be analyzed at different levels. Traditionally, the level of analysis is the State, with security concerns referring to people, events, or processes that impinge on State sovereignty and legitimacy. However, a broader level of analysis can be considered. Human security is seen as anything that potentially constrains or raises the risks of attaining the individual or collective well being and expectations of people. The pursuit of both human security and State security may not always be compatible. Even when they are, the desire and ability of people, through civil society institutions to challenge the State in a security discourse occurs through the process of building social capital. Social capital implies the facilitation of collective action through social resources founded on norms of trust and cooperation.

Security Implications of the Globalization of Financial Markets

What are the security implications of the globalization of financial markets? The most apparent is the increased role of external forces in the domestic economy and the decreased ability of the State to steer an independent course or to insulate the economy. As an example, with globalization, it is practically impossible to conduct an independent monetary policy in a world in which capital is highly mobile. A policy to keep the exchange rate pegged in the face of capital inflows necessitates that the monetary authorities purchase the incoming foreign currency and in exchange, release pesos into the economy in order to prevent the peso from appreciating and maintain the exchange rate peg. This will, however, increase the domestic money supply automatically, and tend to subject the economy to a higher rate of inflation. If the monetary authorities contract domestic credit in order to meet monetary targets, this will raise domestic interest rates and contract domestic demand, while attracting more capital inflows that tend to appreciate the domestic currency further. Policymakers thus have to choose between controlling the money supply and inflation or targeting the exchange rate. The inability to target both the money supply and the exchange rate in a world in which capital is mobile is referred to as the 'impossible trinity'. Such a policy dilemma does not arise in a world in which financial markets are not highly integrated. Also, the State's powers are circumscribed by national boundaries whereas global financial transactions are not. Financial institutions in a country can engage in financial transactions offshore beyond the reach of national authorities.

The legitimacy of the State is dependent in large part on its ability to deliver certain desirable outcomes, such as a reasonable rate of inflation, economic growth and employment, a socially equitable distribution of income, and macroeconomic stability. At a broader level of human security, there may be threats or constraints to the attainment of economic growth and job security. It is unclear how people can participate in the process by which the State defines and addresses these new challenges that have far reaching effects on society beyond the State's own concerns. In the aftermath of the financial crisis, collective action and capacity-building for building networks among the State, non-governmental organizations (NGOs), donor agencies, and local communities in moderating the vulnerabilities, which have been both a cause and effect of the crisis, is a challenge linking development and security concerns.

There are many reasons why the State's ability to deliver desirable outcomes may be imperiled. The Asian financial crisis has led to downturns in many economies, reducing the ability of the government to raise tax revenues, while raising foreign debt servicing requirements of the government itself. Both of these curtail the ability of government to finance public investments and safety nets for the poor. Policy tradeoffs are more complex. For example, to stabilize exchange rates and insulate the economy from external turmoil can be accomplished at the expense of running down foreign reserves and/or by raising domestic interest rates. Using foreign reserves at the Central Bank to defend the currency is self-defeating as the stock is limited, and could induce forward-looking market participants to speculate that the defense of the currency cannot go on indefinitely. Raising domestic interest rates would worsen recessionary tendencies in the economy and raise the cost of financing the budgetary deficit through borrowing from the public. At the same time, tightening domestic monetary conditions and driving up domestic interest rates have been undermined by the liberalization of the capital account. The latter allows private corporations to more readily sell equity or borrow from abroad. This has led to huge inflows of capital that are difficult for the State to control. Given a sequencing problem in which state capacity to supervise and regulate the financial system lagged behind the pace of liberalization, the domestic financial system has become more vulnerable, as imprudent lending takes place when obtaining funds from abroad becomes easier. Implicit government guarantees (*via* essentially fixed exchange rates, for example) give little incentive for market participants to manage risks adequately.

At the same time that states are seemingly powerless to counter the effects of global forces on the economy, the wisdom of their policies is now subject to the judgment of a wider constituency. Countries which needed IMF bail out packages as a result of the currency crisis are given funds conditional on taking important, but oftentimes difficult, measures to correct and strengthen economic fundamentals. Consequences of incorrect policies, weak economic fundamentals, or ignoring market signals take place quickly, such as a quick reversal of capital flows and attacks on the domestic currency and/or a cut-off of IMF-World Bank (WB) support.[2]

Social tensions arising from the difficult structural and stabilization measures have intensified. In some countries such as Indonesia, these have renewed ethnic conflict and led to a change in the political leadership. The marginalization of the poor has also been heightened, with many becoming unemployed or underemployed. In general, the ongoing social tensions may erode social capital even as it is apparent social capital can help moderate the vulnerabilities brought on by globalization. Apart from official bail out packages to affected countries, ways to 'bail in' the private business sector and the rest of civil society have to be found to help resolve the crisis.

Since the Asian crisis affected the region, the relationship between interdependence and security concerns has also become important. Given the enormity of the problem and the constraints on individual states, they have begun to seriously consider the need for a collective response to economic problems. In part, these may be seen as attempts by national governments to re-assert state legitimacy through regional cooperation to manage globalization.

In the aftermath of the currency crisis that hit Southeast Asian countries, Association of Southeast Asian Nations (ASEAN) countries revived an old currency fund arrangement to help each other out when their currencies are under speculative attack. Yet, it is unclear how useful this fund is when all the currencies are being attacked simultaneously or sequentially. The first instinct is to use one's foreign currency reserves to help shore up one's own currency, rather than to have them available for a neighbor in need. It is difficult to subsume national interests to regional or global ones when these interests are not perceived to coincide. It is not lost on these countries that their goods compete with each other and that they also compete with each other for investments. While they are all simultaneously trying to survive the crisis, they are also individually trying to differentiate themselves from one another by emphasizing their individual economic strengths. Philippine authorities, for example, have been emphasizing the fact that the country is different from the other countries in the region, as it has not been as badly hit. Again, it is possible that such attempts at differentiation and the conflicts between national and regional interests and concerns (including Malaysia's unilateral response of imposing foreign exchange controls) may erode social capital at the regional level.

Other efforts at regional cooperation include a regional surveillance mechanism to monitor developments in the financial systems of the different countries. This endeavor requires the different states to provide data with respect to their financial systems. Unfortunately, this endeavor has hit many snags, as some were reluctant to provide data.

This chapter will examine the security implications of the globalization of financial markets from the perspective of state security and human security.

Theoretical Underpinnings

While the term 'currency crisis' has been used to describe the ongoing regional turmoil, it bears emphasizing that currencies may be subject to speculative pressure that sometimes is unsuccessful. There are at least three generations of economic models that explain why currencies are subject to speculative pressure.

The so-called 'canonical' model, which posits that macroeconomic policies which are inconsistent with the level at which the exchange rate is being maintained gives rise to speculative pressure.[3]   For instance, if the government were to run large budgetary deficits financed by money creation, the latter would tend to undermine the currency peg. The government will be forced to defend the domestic currency by selling foreign exchange from its stock of reserves. Such a stock is fixed and forward-looking market participants know that the defense of the domestic currency cannot go on indefinitely. Hence, they will attack the domestic currency and precipitate a depletion of the government's foreign reserves earlier than would have been necessary. In this type of model, there is logic to the occurrence of a currency crisis. Speculative attacks against the currency can be avoided by pursuing consistent macroeconomic policies.

Second generation models suggest that speculative pressures on a currency can occur even in the absence of inconsistent policies and poor economic fundamentals.[4] These models posit that government policy itself is conjectured on the public's beliefs and expectations. The public, on the other hand, bases its actions on what they expect to happen, rather than on what is actually happening. For example, suppose the public believes that the currency will be attacked. If it expects such an attack to be successful, the public will demand much higher rates of interest on domestic assets, to reflect expected exchange rate losses. This would raise domestic interest rates beyond that implied by expectations of inflation. The cost to the government of defending the peg is higher. The government has to induce slack in the economy in order to suppress the demand for imports and foreign exchange (raising political costs as well), and the interest burden on any outstanding stock of government debt is higher. If the public thinks that the government will simply choose to abandon the peg at some point because the political and economic costs of defense are prohibitive, the result would be a self-fulfilling prophecy. It is of course possible that the expected attack on the currency is unsuccessful, or that no such attacks come to pass, and the peg would be maintained. These second generation models are, therefore, characterized by multiple equilibria or non-uniqueness. The question for policymakers then becomes how to ensure that 'good' rather than 'bad' outcomes occur. It has been recently suggested that to avoid 'bad' outcomes, it is very important to have a strong, transparent, and well-regulated financial sector. Other policy implications are that speculative pressures may be avoided by enhanced credibility of the economy policies taken (and policymakers), the temporary use of capital controls, or allowing the currency to float.

There are also models that posit contagion arising from different modes of transmission. Contagion simply means that the occurrence of a crisis elsewhere significantly raises the probability of a crisis domestically. There are many modes of transmission. Trade links, such as an attack on one currency may affect import prices and the overall price level in the other countries. Perceived similarities in macroeconomic policies and conditions among countries prevent differentiation of countries by investors. Different degrees of risk aversion among countries and the implications of these on the willingness to pursue cooperative policies to stabilize exchange rates in the face of adverse external shocks may also contribute to contagion. Illiquidity in certain financial markets may also induce investors to liquidate their positions in other countries.

It is now a widely-accepted thesis that the Asian crisis started out primarily as a financial crisis and that the usual reasons for balance of payments (BOP) crises alluded to in canonical models, such as overly expansionary monetary and fiscal policies which are incompatible with an exchange rate peg, were not the primary reasons for the crisis. In fact, before the crisis, many countries in Asia had what could be considered as prudent fiscal and monetary policies. Instead, many are alluding to a 'moral hazard' problem, in which the private sector has little or no incentive to minimize risk because of implicit or explicit government guarantees against failure. The risk of moral hazard increased for many reasons. Capital account opening and financial liberalization combined with stable exchange rates to encourage massive borrowing from abroad. Given the distortions in many economies, including overvalued local currencies, there was a bias toward non-tradeable goods, such as real estate, to which these borrowed funds flowed to liberally, creating asset bubbles. At the same time, liberalization of financial markets was not accompanied by the strengthening of bank supervision and regulation. This resulted in a situation in which domestic financial institutions were intermediating large amounts of foreign funds with little regard for currency and maturity mismatches. In part, crony capitalism prevented the authorities from ensuring good governance by the private sector. When capital flows reversed, asset bubbles burst, and banks found themselves in trouble.

The Domestic Context of Economic Reform

Like many developing countries adversely affected by the oil crisis and the worldwide recession in the late 1970s, the Philippines embarked on a program of economic liberalization and reform in the early 1980s. Reforms encompassed many areas of economic policy, with perhaps the most significant reforms occurring in the areas of trade policy and financial markets.

Financial market reforms began in the early 1980s under a WB program, with the lifting of interest rate ceilings on short-term interest rates in 1982. In the next year, ceilings on long-term interest rates were lifted as well. The early 1980s were a very turbulent time in the economic history of the Philippines, particularly in the banking industry which experienced several bank runs and bank failures. The intent of these reforms was to encourage the mobilization of domestic savings and a greater degree of financial intermediation through the banking system, previously repressed by interest rate ceilings. By relying on the market mechanism to allocate capital, resource allocation efficiency would be enhanced.

After interest rate decontrol, the monetary authorities encouraged bank mergers and consolidations on the assumption that bigger banks could lower costs by taking advantage of so-called economies of scale. Toward this end, capital requirements were increased several times, reaching the present level of P4 billion for a universal bank.[5]

Unfortunately, while greater efficiency was the professed goal, the monetary authorities did not act to simultaneously reduce barriers to entry in the banking industry. In fact, high capital requirements, although ordinarily undertaken as a prudential regulatory measure, came to be regarded as a barrier to entry. The result was the development of what some regard as a banking cartel. Casual evidence usually presented to indicate this includes the wide interest rate differentials between bank lending and deposit rates. Ironically, if indeed the development of an imperfectly competitive industry was the result, this could not have led to greater efficiency. It is well known in economic theory that any kind of imperfect competition is more costly and less efficient, in terms of resource use, than a perfectly competitive market structure.

In 1992, the foreign exchange market was liberalized. First and foremost, the monetary authorities declared that, henceforth, market forces would determine the value of the peso. This meant that rather than being officially fixed and/or administratively guided by the Central Bank, the value of the peso would be determined freely in the foreign exchange market called the Philippine Dealing System.[6] The authorities also lifted the surrender requirements on dollar earnings of exporters, eased restrictions on the repatriation of capital and profits, and removed other forms of capital controls. In 1994, ten foreign banks were allowed entry through different modes into the local banking industry.

The opening of the capital account and the relative success that accompanied economic reforms encouraged massive capital inflows, and the Philippines soon found itself in the league of the 'emerging markets'. The government trumpeted this as a sign that the Philippines was no longer the pariah in the international financial community that it was in the previous decade.[7] The Philippines experienced more frequent surges of capital inflows beginning in the fourth quarter of 1989. As a percentage of gross domestic product (GDP), from 1.23 per cent in 1988, capital inflows rose to 3.43 per cent of GDP in 1989, then to 6.85 per cent in 1991. In 1994, these inflows surged once more to 7.4 per cent of GDP and by 1996, to about 10 per cent of GDP before the massive retreat of capital in July of 1997. It is apparent that the capital account was larger and more volatile in the 1990s. Portfolio inflows, in particular, have increased in subsequent periods, exceeding direct investment flows in the third quarter of 1989 for the first time and maintaining this trend, except for the first quarter of 1994. It may be pointed out, however, that the size of capital inflows to the Philippines was smaller than those in countries like Malaysia and Thailand, and also came later.

These capital inflows, however, soon became more of a bane than a boon to economic managers. While these capital flows could be used to finance growth and development, they also had potentially destabilizing effects. Chief among these was the loss of control over certain important economic policy instruments, such as the ability to conduct an independent monetary policy. This, in turn, would have an adverse effect on inflation. The appropriate response to capital inflows became an important policy question.

Central banks typically resorted to sterilization in an attempt to regain some degree of control over monetary policy. This process entails the purchase of the capital inflows and the simultaneous reduction of domestic credit in order to prevent an expansion in the money supply to which the unopposed capital inflows would automatically lead. Reductions in domestic credit raise domestic interest rates and induce slack in the economy. Aside from the obviously adverse political consequences of such a policy, it actually exacerbates the problem by inducing more capital inflows due to the hiked interest rates. Sterilization also entails quasi-fiscal costs and imperils the central bank's institutional viability since in effect, the Central Bank exchanges high-yielding domestic assets for lower-yielding foreign assets. For all these reasons, sterilization cannot be done indefinitely. The currency itself becomes prone to speculation as to when a policy of sterilization will be abandoned.

Even assuming policymakers had appropriate instruments to influence the amount of capital inflows, they also faced the problem of distinguishing desirable from less desirable or outrightly undesirable capital inflows. The distinction is premised on several assumptions. First, it is generally assumed that long-term capital inflows, such as foreign direct investments or FDI, are preferable to short-term portfolio inflows. FDI contributes directly to an economy's productive capacity and economic growth, while portfolio flows are seen as easily reversible and subject the recipient country to a greater degree of systemic risk.

Second, capital inflows in the presence of domestic currency overvaluation tend to favor non-tradeable sectors, which are not subject to competition from abroad, such as real estate and construction, over tradeable sectors, which compete against imports in the domestic market or are exportable. Between 1989 and 1995, the Philippines' composition of capital inflows, in contrast to its Asian neighbors, was biased in favor of consumption over investment. Total consumption as a proportion of GDP averaged 6.1 per cent while total investment to GDP averaged only 1.7 per cent.[8] This increased the risk of asset bubbles developing in the non-traded goods sector. There is a differential impact among sectors, in which exporters are hurt and the competitiveness of domestic industry is reduced, while favoring the non-traded goods sector. This, in turn, can adversely affect the viability and stability of the banking sector and other sectors which have exposures in the non-traded goods sector and/or whose assets, such as loans, are collateralized by real estate. The recent economic turmoil in Thailand dramatically underscores this point.

Initial Conditions

The sudden weakening of the peso began on 11 July 1997, after the Central Bank announced that it would not actively intervene in the foreign exchange market and allow the peso to trade within a wider band. In the previous two years, the peso-dollar exchange rate had been extremely stable. From an average of P26.41 per US$ in 1994, the average peso dollar rate in 1996 was P26.21, and for the first five months of 1997, it was at P26.34 to the US$.[9]

There are various views as to why the peso suddenly weakened.[10] One view is that the country's improved economic growth was superficial and that the overall direction of economic reforms pursued thus far was incorrect. The weakening of the peso, therefore, is to be seen as a vindication of this view and as an argument for reversing the trend of economic policies and reforms. The other view from within government itself states that there is nothing wrong with the previous exchange rate policy, and that the macroeconomic fundamentals of the economy are sound. The weakening of the peso was not due to weak fundamentals, but can be ascribed to the actions of rogue speculators. In contrast with the earlier view, this one calls for a continuation of existing economic policies.

There is of course a more realistic middle ground. While most economic reforms and policies pursued thus far were correct and largely responsible for the country's improved economic experience, there are some key areas of policy in which the existing ones are inadequate, if not downright incorrect. While economic fundamentals are strong in some areas, in some other areas, they are extremely weak and have not been adequately addressed. Initial conditions are important. They portend how well an economy can take advantage of the economic opportunities arising from globalization, and avoid disastrous consequences of external shocks. There is a consensus in the academic literature on the currency crisis that rapid growth in Asia masked inherent weaknesses in the individual economies, like highly leveraged corporations and a large proportion of short-term external debt. As growth began to taper off, these weaknesses then acted as a financial trigger that set off the *baht* devaluation and the ensuing contagion across Asia.[11]

What were the economic fundamentals of the Philippine economy like prior to the crisis?

The Growth Rate of National Income

Real GDP growth rates have increased since 1992, from 0.34 per cent to 5.68 per cent in 1996.[12] In the first semester of 1997, real GDP growth rate stood at five per cent. Despite the improvement in growth rates, it might be pointed out that these growth rates are far lower than those in ASEAN countries, with the exception of the mature Singaporean economy. In 1996, Malaysia's real GDP grew at 8.2 per cent, Indonesia at 7.82 per cent, and Thailand at 6.7 per cent. Equally important is the fact that by 1997, the Philippines had not regained the level of per capita GDP or income of 1981. It should not be surprising, therefore, that even discounting the grossly unequal distribution of income, many people actually feel poorer than they did in the early 1980s.

The relatively lower growth rate of income in the Philippines has several implications for capital flows. Relative to other ASEAN countries, the Philippines may not be as attractive a destination of FDI or even portfolio flows. The lower growth of income indicates a relatively smaller market size and, hence, fewer profit opportunities.[13] Ironically, there is simultaneous causality in a country needing FDI to grow but not easily being able to attract FDI unless it grows. On the other hand, if there are any problems associated with dealing with capital inflows or their possible reversal, inability to attract substantial inflows may not necessarily be inimical to a country's interests, or such inimical effects may be dampened.

Manufacturing Growth

What the positive rate of income growth masks are the sources of that growth. Manufacturing growth, in particular, has fallen from 5.6 per cent between the first quarter of 1995 and the first quarter of 1996, to 3.9 per cent between the first quarter of 1996 and the first quarter of 1997.[14] Note that these declines occurred before the

11 July de facto devaluation of the peso. There were declines in industries such as textiles, garments, rubber, metals and metal products, and transport equipment. Some of these industries, such as garments, are highly labor-intensive. Therefore, they are major concerns of economic policymakers particularly with regard to their effects on unemployment.

Export Performance and Current Account Deficits

Export growth in non-electronic and non-transport equipment started to decline steeply in 1995. The Philippine export base is not sufficiently diversified and relies heavily on a few products, such as electronics and transport equipment. Even these sectors have grown more slowly than total exports since 1991. Unfortunately, these few main exports also have the least number of linkages with the domestic economy, and rely the least on domestic inputs. The share of manufacturing in total output and in total employment has declined relative to a decade ago. This phenomenon is known as 'de-industrialization', and arose in the context of the effects of real currency appreciation caused by capital inflows to Latin America.[15]

Poor export growth performance gives rise to trade and current account imbalances.[16] In 1995 and 1996, the trade deficit as a percentage of GDP of the Philippines was at 12.06 per cent and 13.42 per cent, respectively. In contrast, Thailand had a trade-deficit-to-GDP ratio of 4.84 per cent in 1995 while Malaysia and Indonesia have had trade surpluses in the 1990s. In 1995, Thailand had a large current account deficit as a percentage of GDP, amounting to seven per cent. The Philippines' current-account-to-GDP ratio was a little over four per cent in 1995, while that for Indonesia was at about 3.5 per cent. In terms of adequacy of international reserves at the Central Bank to cover imports, the Philippines only had enough to cover about three months worth of imports from 1995 to the present. In 1995, Malaysia and Indonesia had about four and almost five months worth of import cover, respectively, and Thailand had a little over seven months worth.[17]

A country with current account deficits is a country whose expenditures exceed its income. A country whose aggregate saving from both private and public sources is insufficient to finance its expenditures must necessarily source funds from abroad. It is not surprising that Thailand, with the largest current account deficits in ASEAN, also borrowed the greatest amounts of foreign savings.[18]

Aggregate Savings Rate

It is a fact that the Philippines has a low savings rate. Its 1995 savings-to-GDP ratio was 21.3 per cent, lower than the ratio for 1981 of 26 per cent.[19] This savings ratio is closer to those of countries in Latin America rather than Asia, where the average savings ratios are about 35 per cent.

A low domestic savings rate means that a country is necessarily dependent on foreign savings, unless it can reduce its expenditures and bring these in line with its income. In such a situation, the relative merits of different types of foreign inflows, or even if foreign inflows are desirable or not, is a second-order problem.

Reducing expenditures is always politically difficult. It is far easier for governments to source financing abroad, as the Philippines did in the 1970s through massive public borrowing, and in the 1990s through private capital flows. The Philippines had budgetary deficits in 1990-93, but managed to generate a small surplus equal to 0.94 per cent of GDP in 1994.[20] In 1996, this fell to 0.61 per cent of GDP. In 1992, foreign financing of the deficit grew to P14.39 billion from P6.8 billion in the previous year, to finance a budgetary deficit of P21.8 billion.[21] Only beginning in 1994, when there were small budgetary surpluses amounting to less than one per cent of GDP, did amortizations of foreign loans exceed gross external borrowings. In contrast, the other ASEAN countries had surpluses as a percentage of GDP ranging from 0.61 per cent for Indonesia in 1993, 2.38 per cent for Malaysia in 1994, and 2.86 per cent for Thailand in 1992. In 1998, the government budgetary deficit was projected to reach about P40 billion, plus another P40 billion deficit from government-owned and controlled corporations.[22]

The ability to tap foreign savings more easily in a world of globalized capital markets makes it easier to postpone, or, in the eyes of some, to remove the necessity of painful adjustments to correct structural weakness of the economy. The latter involves bringing expenditures more closely in line with income and raising domestic savings. Easy money may also engender a larger spending binge and put the stability of the financial system at risk, as prudential lending is less likely when sourcing funds is easy and the domestic liabilities of the financial system are implicitly guaranteed by the government.[23]

While the Philippines has made great progress in certain areas of reform, there are several critical areas in which its performance is lacking. Relative to its neighbors, the macroeconomic fundamentals of the Philippines are weaker. An important reason for the current account deficits in these countries, and the poor performance of exports and manufacturing in the Philippines, is the incorrect exchange rate policy and measures to sustain it, both before and after the de facto devaluation of 11 July 1997.

Exchange Rate Policy

The majority of professional economists in the country have long called for a devaluation of the peso to improve the competitiveness of domestic industries, spur exports, and prevent periodic BOPs crisis that have characterized the economic history of the Philippines. Unfortunately, the term 'devaluation' is associated with failed government policy, pain, and suffering. This is largely because devaluations, including the July 1997 episode, have largely been taken as last-ditch defensive measures to prevent BOP crises and the depletion of international reserves at the Central Bank. The periodic BOP crises are, to begin with, themselves the result of unsustainable economic policies.

Reasons for the Inflexibility of the Exchange Rate

A weak central bank with little or no credibility in controlling inflation can have a credible pre-commitment not to inflate, by pegging the domestic currency to a currency such as the US$. This seems to have been at least one of the ideas behind the long-standing policy of pegging the peso to the dollar. This was not an incorrect policy, *per se*, but it also tied the economy's fortunes to the rise and fall of the dollar. Countries which pegged their currencies to the dollar began to experience unwanted, although not necessarily unwarranted appreciations of their currencies and slower export growth when the US$ began to appreciate, particularly in the first half of 1997 while both the yen and the mark depreciated.[24]

For a long time, there has been wide disagreement between academic economists and the country's monetary authorities on the need to allow gradual and periodic devaluations of the currency for domestic industries to remain competitive. Given the relative disadvantages already existing in the Philippines for the competitiveness of domestic industry with regard to costs and productivity, academic economists have long advocated a higher exchange rate, or equivalently, a weaker peso. This will lower the dollar cost of producing in the country, either for export or home consumption, and compensate somewhat for deficiencies in costs and productivity.

However, monetary authorities and other economic managers have not appreciated this or even so-called 'beggar-thy-neighbor' policies.[25] Officials at the Central Bank dispute the idea that the exchange rate has anything to do with exports, pointing to the experience prior to the crisis, in which exports were growing despite an appreciating peso. This is of course weak evidence. First, there are lags in the effects of exchange rate changes on export growth. Furthermore, as pointed out earlier, the export base is very narrow and the main exports, such as electronics, have high import content. They are, therefore, helped by an appreciating peso, aside from being associated with parent companies in countries with even stronger currencies.

Still another reason was the great uncertainty monetary authorities faced as to what would happen to the domestic currency if they let go of it. Prior to large capital inflows, the authorities were convinced that letting go of their defense of the peso would lead to a large depreciation of the peso. This was what they had been trying to avoid throughout because of the negative political implications attached to a weak currency and the fact that it would hurt the protected, highly import-dependent industries, many of which are owned by business elites. It was not lost on the politicians that the first president of the republic to engineer a peso devaluation and import decontrol in the 1960s, Diosdado Macapagal, was defeated in his re-election bid.[26]

With substantial capital inflows, the peso however appreciated against the dollar, in a manner reminiscent of the Southern Cone countries' experience. There were legitimate reasons for the appreciation of the peso. The country risk premium had declined as the country reaped the benefits of reforms undertaken by the Aquino and Ramos governments. The country had overcome the debt crisis, reducing the debt service burden on foreign debt from 36 per cent of total exports of goods and services in 1986, to 17 per cent in 1993.[27] When the capital market was opened up in 1992, foreigners jumped at the chance to purchase initial public offerings (IPOs) of stocks of previously closed companies.

But the extremely tight monetary policy that the Central Bank pursued partly in an attempt to keep the money supply within IMF program limits also meant that domestic interest rates remained higher than foreign interest rates. As interest arbitrage possibilities were maintained, this induced continued capital inflows, giving rise to further appreciation of the peso. Coupled with a stable peso-dollar exchange rate and an open capital account, it was easier to borrow abroad in dollars at lower interest rates. The economic managers took the inflows of capital and the appreciation of the currency to mean that the economic fundamentals of the country were strong, totally ignoring the need to adjust the exchange rate by devaluing the peso in order to prevent a worsening of the overvaluation of the currency.[28]

Currency Overvaluation

What does overvaluation of the currency mean? Simply put, it means that the currency is kept at a level higher than its true market equilibrium value. Were it not for intervention to keep it at this artificial level, the currency would automatically weaken or depreciate. An overvalued currency, meanwhile, adversely affects the competitiveness of domestic industries.

The Real Effective Exchange Rate (REER) can be interpreted as the amount of a typical basket of Philippine goods a dollar can buy.[29] It is measured as the ratio of the nominal exchange rate to a price index. A higher REER value means that a dollar can buy more Philippine goods, and hence, the competitiveness of domestic industries and exports would be enhanced.

Note that with capital inflows, there is a greater demand for peso-denominated assets, both paper assets such as treasury bills, and real assets, such as direct investment in factories. This would tend to raise the value of a peso relative to the dollar. When this happens, as it did with capital flows in the 1990s, the competitiveness of Philippine goods declines. This is why with capital flows, and no dramatic improvements in productivity or costs, it was more imperative for the authorities to engineer a devaluation.[30]

A comparison of REERs calculated for the Philippines, Thailand, Malaysia, and Indonesia using 1990 prices shows that all countries, except China until 1995, had declining REERs.[31] In other words, the goods from all of these countries were becoming less competitive. The Philippines lost the most ground, with its domestic goods being 26 per cent more expensive in 1996 than in 1990. Thailand was next to the Philippines, but the large depreciation of the *baht* in 1997 has restored some of the ground that it lost. Before 1997, currencies of the Philippines, Thailand, Indonesia, and Malaysia had appreciated in real terms. China's currency appreciated the least. It is, therefore, not surprising that the Southeast Asian currencies have come under attack by speculators betting that these currencies would go back to their true equilibrium values and have to weaken.

Sectoral Effects of Exchange Rate Policy

The stability of the exchange rate and the profit opportunities it creates also builds a constituency for maintaining the status quo and rejecting needed exchange rate adjustments. Two sectors come to mind: the traditionally protected big business sector and the banking sector.

Big Business and Small and Medium-sized Exporters   There had been a very strong lobby by protected industrialists not to devalue, as most of their products have high import content. Thus, it worked to their advantage to have high tariff walls protecting them from foreign competition in the domestic market, while a strong peso would subsidize their imported inputs.

In recent years, however, there has been a clamor from many of these big industrialists, apart from the usual groups of small and medium-sized exporters, for a devaluation to keep the peso competitive. This arose because the trade liberalization program of the government, in which the levels and dispersion of tariff rates were reduced weakened their market power in the domestic market. With less tariff protection, they needed a competitive exchange rate to maintain their foothold in the domestic market against imports, and to make some inroads in world markets, especially in view of the fact that their share in the limited domestic market was under threat. It became, therefore, a rational choice on the part of some members of big business to support devaluation.

Meanwhile, small and medium-sized exporters took the high road in the face of increased willingness of the Ramos administration to open up the economy and to deregulate. Their main umbrella organization, PHILEXPORT, funded by a grant from the US Agency for International Development (USAID) pursued a public advocacy campaign to sustain the reforms and brought attention to the need to promote export growth by maintaining a competitive exchange rate level.[32] This was an example of social capital at its best. At the very least, the traditional protectionists would not go unopposed.

The Banking Sector   In the past, banks in the Philippines continued to reap huge profits from a high interest rate regime despite slow loan growth. They could just put their funds in high-yielding, risk-free, government securities rather than make loans, even as the rest of the economy struggled to stay alive. With foreign exchange market liberalization, another window of opportunity opened up to them. The interest rate differential in favor of the Philippines meant they could source funds from abroad at lower rates and re-lend them locally at higher rates. As long as the exchange rate was stable, there would be no currency risk and they could earn large profits by simply lending locally at higher rates the cheaper funds sourced abroad. Of course, this easier sourcing of funds abroad did not contribute to attempts to raise the mobilization of domestic savings.

Financial liberalization changed the business environment. Whereas, big family-owned businesses were traditionally the main clients of banks, they discovered that they could raise needed funds more easily through an IPO of stocks, or floating bonds in the global financial market. By 1994, domestic interest rates had declined somewhat as there was a small budgetary surplus and the country risk premium had declined due to the favorable effects of reforms. With lower interest rates prevailing compared to the past (which made it less profitable to simply place funds in government securities as before), and with their traditional clientele able to borrow funds more easily in global financial markets, banks had to look for new clients. Major banks started to compete for the traditional clients of mid-sized and thrift banks which catered to retail lending such as car financing, housing loans, and credit cards.

As reported by the country's leading daily: 'The industry was getting blinded by their desire to get a big slice of the credit market, naturally scaled down their lending standards to accommodate more borrowers.' [33]

There are obvious reasons for the increase in foreign borrowing. One was the extremely stable exchange rate, at least before 11 July 1997. Another was the high interest rates in the domestic market relative to those in developed countries and even to those in ASEAN countries with the exception of Indonesia. In 1996, for example, the average Treasury bill rate was 12.4 per cent compared with about 6.4 per cent in Malaysia and 0.90 per cent in Singapore for securities of comparable maturities. In the Philippines, the Treasury bill rate is that on the 31-day bill as this is the most actively traded type. At this level, the yield on a 31-day Philippine Treasury bill is much higher than that on long-term US bonds. [34] High interest rates tend to attract foreign capital inflows. With a stable exchange rate, there is practically no exchange rate risk for holding peso-denominated assets, and this further entices foreign capital inflows to take advantage of interest arbitrage opportunities. In 1994, for example, the average exchange rate was 26.41 pesos to the US$. In 1996, it was at 26.34 pesos to the dollar. [35]

In fact, there was an explosion of foreign borrowing. The total foreign exchange liabilities of private domestic banks increased from a paltry US$715 million in 1990 to US$5.031billion in 1996, with the biggest increases occurring in the 1995-96 period. [36] It rose from US$604 million in 1994 to US$1.741billion in 1995 and then almost five-fold to US$5.031 billion in 1996. The total foreign exchange liabilities of private non-bank institutions increased from US$3.23 billion in 1990 to US$9.112 billion in 1996. Non-bank institutions are mostly composed of large private corporations that can issue bonds in international capital markets. The total foreign exchange liabilities of the private sector, both bank and non-bank, added up to US$14.4 billion in 1996.

The increase in net foreign liabilities of the banking system was caused by the large increase in the growth rate of liabilities or payables to head offices, branches, and agencies abroad, from 5.6 per cent in 1994, to 59.4 per cent in 1995, and to 105.1 per cent in 1996. In other words, there was a dramatic increase in borrowing from abroad. The growth rates of foreign currency deposits also increased but not as dramatically, from 18.1 per cent in 1995, a decline from the previous year's 37.4 per cent, to 59.3 per cent in 1996. There was a total of US$10.8 billion in net foreign loans and discounts in 1996. Note that this amount of foreign loans is almost equal to the entire stock of dollar reserves at the Central Bank of about US$12 billion, before the failed attempts at defending the peso in July 1997. It would have been impossible for the Central Bank to repay these debts in the case of defaults.

Net foreign loans and discounts, an asset item of the banking system, increased from 53 per cent in 1995, to 103.1 per cent in 1996. In other words, much of the funds sourced abroad were being re-lent locally. Prudential borrowing and lending behavior seems to have all but disappeared with an easy source of funds abroad. It is not difficult to see why the stability of the banking system would be imperiled if the peso were to weaken against the dollar. It appears that most of these loans were unhedged (not secured) against exchange rate risks. In a study of local banks, dollar loans constituted an average of 30 per cent of a total loan portfolio of US$12 billion, amounting to about US$3.6 billion.[37] Evidently, these are practically all unhedged, as the Central Bank estimated that unhedged loans as of June 1997 amounted to US$3.6 billion.

Much of this cheap money went to the stock market and the real estate sector. In 1993, for example, the Philippine stock market was the best performer among the so-called 'emerging markets'. Asset bubbles began to emerge as asset prices appreciated quickly. Many simple landowners and businessmen became property barons overnight.

The Central Bank has stated that the share of loans to the real estate sector was not over 10 per cent. Even if this were true for the sector as a whole, it is also true that the ratio is significantly larger for some banks, including some large ones.[38] Furthermore, even if banks wanted to lend only to clients engaged in the manufacture of real goods, following some version of the real bills doctrine, it was difficult to know exactly where the funds would eventually end up since money is fungible.[39]

An example is the collapse of low-cost appliance maker Eyco in September 1997. The money it borrowed from its creditor banks, the biggest of which was the Philippine National Bank (PNB), was used for its real estate subsidiary. When property prices collapsed, it had to apply for debt relief. It now appears that friends of the company's owner themselves borrowed from their bank creditors in order to re-lend to the company owner for speculation in real estate. This seems to be the tip of the iceberg and there are fears that more companies will follow suit. The PNB again figured in the news as the RJ Group almost defaulted on interest payments of P300 million on a multi-billion peso-loan it obtained from the bank. PNB shares also took a beating when it was revealed that another borrower, a small real estate company called Eduarosa, was seeking debt relief. Shares of bank stocks, including that of the country's largest bank, Metrobank, also took a beating because of fears of loan defaults.

The collapse of both the exchange rate and the real estate market has hit the banking industry hard. Since November 1997, there has been a dramatic increase in non-performing loans (NPLs) of banks. By the end of 1997, NPLs stood at P72.15 billion or 4.69 per cent of total loan portfolio, a significant increase from the P34.99B or 2.9 per cent of total loan portfolio in 1996.[40] By March 1998, the NPL ratio of commercial banks stood close to 12 per cent. Three thrift banks have already failed and two more were apparently on their way to failure. Meanwhile, 17 banks, excluding the three thrift banks that have been closed, have been placed on a government watch list for serious cash flow problems.[41] The Central Bank's response has been to raise loan loss reserves (which will impact negatively on bank profitability), and an increase in bank capitalization requirements, in an effort encourage more mergers in the banking sector. However, without better supervision and an understanding of the risks involved in a globalized financial environment, these moves will not have enduring stabilizing effects. They may also further imperil an already vulnerable financial system.

Continuing Biases and Enduring Coalitions

Even after the immediate crash of the peso, there continued to be a bias in favor of a strong peso. On 7 October 1997, for example, the peso hit an all-time low of P35.981 to the US$.[42] Trading was suspended twice after a volatility band, adopted by the Bankers Association of the Philippines (BAP) that operates the Philippine Dealing System was breached. Under the volatility band, trading is suspended for half an hour if the peso rises or falls by two per cent from the previous day's weighted average, and suspended again for an hour if it moves a further one per cent. The Central Bank intervened to prevent the further depreciation of the peso, selling US$20 million at rates ranging from P35.40 to P35.70, reversing the trend after two successive trading suspensions.

In contrast, two days later, the peso strengthened against the dollar, breaking through three successive volatility bands. Opening at P35.40 to the US$, intervention from the Central Bank allowed the peso to rebound to P34.129 to the dollar at the end of the trading day. The Central Bank governor, Gabriel Singson, took the appreciation of the peso against the dollar to signify that the economy is strong, saying, 'I don't see why it should go down. Exports are doing well. Inflation is under control. The economy is still growing'.[43] With no doubts as to where the sentiments of the Central Bank Governor lay, BAP broke its own rules. It allowed trading to continue unhampered even though the volatility band it had set had been breached.

The events described above are disturbing. First, they belie the fact that exchange rate policy in this country is market-determined as the Central Bank claims. Anyone who wants to ascribe credibility to the Central Bank would have to discount the fact that it is the largest player in the foreign exchange market. Related to this, the actions of the Central Bank and of the Bankers Association of the Philippines contribute to the formation of one-sided expectations that the peso should not weaken. Whenever the expectations driving a market are one-sided, either very large losses or very large gains can be made, and speculative opportunities are opened up. As long as the currency is driven to appreciation without any productivity or efficiency gains, exports and economic growth will suffer.

Second, it is not difficult to see why both parties would benefit from collusion with one another to obtain the desired results. In recent years, banks have gained from the exchange rate policy (and high interest rate policy) of the Central Bank. Despite the crisis, the net income after tax of the commercial banks amounted to P38.5 billion in 1997, an increase of 4.7 per cent from the previous year while the return on equity of the country's 54 commercial banks weakened slightly to 13.4 per cent in 1997 relative to 1996's 16.2 per cent.[44] It is truly a practically recession-proof industry. If banks had not toed the line on the exchange rate in the past, it would have been difficult for the Central Bank to maintain the exchange rate for as long as it did. This is disturbing because the regulator and the regulated have common interests and such interests may be in conflict with the interests of the larger society.

In fact, so-called 'gentlemen's agreements' between the Central Bank and the banks were not uncommon. On 31 July 1997, for example, a newspaper article reported that: 'Banking sources said a "gentlemen's agreement" between the Central Bank and commercial banks to keep the peso at 28.50 to the dollar had been changed to allow the peso to fall to the new level of 29. Deogracias Vistan, head of the Bankers Association of the Philippines said the Central Bank had advised the group that the allowed foreign exchange holdings of a bank would be halved to five per cent of unimpaired capital, or US$10 million, whichever is lower. He said banks were *comfortable* (emphasis mine) with this limit'.[45] Some bankers blamed the same type of 'gentlemen's agreement' by the BAP not to allow the peso to fall beyond 34.926 for the peso's sharp fall to over 35 to the dollar. This is because it gave rise to an opportunity to test the resolve of the Central Bank not to allow the peso to depreciate further.[46]

When the regulator of an industry has the same interests as the regulated, it cannot function appropriately. The Central Bank closed its eyes to the massive foreign borrowing that both banks and non-bank institutions undertook, especially between 1994 and right before the events of 11 July. It appears that the supervisory abilities of the Central Bank have not kept up with the demands of the times. When queried about how their supervisory function had changed, a Central Bank official merely said that they were training people to be able to recognize and deal with the new types and greater amounts of risk. Yet they themselves admit that many of the banking laws are outdated and the ability to assess the risk exposure of a bank is inadequately served by traditional asset-to-liability ratios. The Central Bank has yet to fully adopt concepts that determine a bank's 'value at risk'.

Central Bank governor Singson previously announced that there would be no devaluation, and that he would resign first before anything of this sort happened. With such a guarantee from the highest official of the Central Bank, it was rational on the part of banks to borrow abroad cheaply and re-lend here either in pesos or dollars. It is also clear that most of these loans were unhedged against exchange rate risk. The Central Bank, together with BAP have joined hands in mapping out options on how to '*cushion the impact of unhedged loans on the exchange rate*' (italics mine).[47]

What is curious about the statement above on the effects of unhedged loans on the exchange rate is that the causality is reversed. It is because the loans were unhedged against exchange rate risk to begin with that the loans became problematic **after** the de facto devaluation of the peso. The amount of these unhedged loans is not known exactly, but unofficial estimates put it at between $2 billion to $3 billion.[48] Unfortunately, the authorities and bankers seem to be more concerned about banks using pesos to retire dollar-denominated debt. If banks were to exchange pesos for dollars to pay off these loans in dollars, this would also put pressure on the peso to depreciate as the demand for dollars would increase. Hence, according to the Central Bank and agreed to by the bankers, there should be 'coordination of scheduled reduction in the portfolio of unhedged loans'.[49] Once again, there is a bias against peso depreciation and moves are choreographed to achieve the desired result. Once again, the interests of the bankers and their regulator, the Central Bank, coincide, but this does not necessarily coincide with the interests of the many.

The Central Bank also studied the option of requiring banks to stagger or roll over for a period of six months the conversion of dollar loans into peso loans. In December 1997, the Central Bank entered into an arrangement with the Bankers Association of the Philippines to institute a hedging facility called 'Non-deliverable Forwards' or NDFs to lower foreign exchange rate risk for corporations.[50] Under the scheme, the

Central Bank would extend forward cover to unhedged dollar exposures of manufacturing companies, which sell to the domestic market; importers with unsettled letters of credit; and companies which have converted their peso loans into dollar loans without any forward cover.[51] The Central Bank would sell NDF contracts to banks while corporate users would avail of this facility and pay a premium over the prevailing market exchange rate, thus removing exchange rate uncertainty. The NDF contracts are non-deliverable, and settlement entails only the difference between the contract price of dollars and the actual price of dollars on the date specified in the forward contract and is paid out in pesos.

The Central Bank and its allies thought they have found a clever way to provide liquidity to the demanders of dollars while both removing exchange rate risk without depleting the Central Bank's stock of dollars. In reality, the Central Bank is bearing all of the exchange rate risks. If, for example, the peso depreciates against the dollar by an amount greater than the premium over the market rate when the contract was entered into, the Central Bank would incur a loss, even if these were just peso losses. In the past, the Central Bank had incurred large losses on forward contracts on dollars given to oil firms.

In other instances, the Central Bank continued a bias in favor of preventing the peso from freely seeking its true value. The Central Bank apparently requested five major banks to accept dollar placements from it and sell these to the public on cue from the Central Bank.[52] The amounts placed by the Central Bank depends on the banks' expected dollar inflows and could be sold by banks in the spot market for dollars. The Central Bank would also provide forward cover to the banks on these dollar sales. This is a roundabout way of providing dollar liquidity to the market and in some ways, is deceitful. The Central Bank can sell dollars directly in the market without coursing them through the banks. Perhaps the Central Bank wants to pretend that these dollar sales are 'market driven', even though the dollars came from it. The scheme also gives rise to the risk of a liquidity mismatch, because banks are selling dollars even without the dollar inflows yet, but rather in anticipation of them.

Inconsistent Policies

The persistence of monetary authorities and policymakers in preventing the exchange rate from adjusting has spawned a variety of inconsistent and non-transparent policies, which themselves contribute to increased risk for the country and for certain sectors in view of their apparent unsustainability.

The official explanation given for the Central Bank's retreat from the foreign exchange market and allowing the peso to move within a wider trading band as of 11July is that monetary officials realized that 'market fundamentals had changed'. Clearly, market fundamentals do not change overnight. In fact, the only clue monetary officials said they had behind the 'changed fundamentals' statement was the fact that the volume of dollars being sold in the Philippine Dealing System dropped below average a few days before 11 July. In any market, however, this is a possible market outcome. It may be due to transitory shocks and does not necessarily indicate a structural change.

In fact, the actions of the Central Bank up to the day before the de facto devaluation would imply that it saw no change in market fundamentals and hence, no justifiable reason for the peso to depreciate against the dollar. On 7 July and for days before 11 July, the Central Bank had been raising its key interest rates to two-year highs after direct sales of dollars failed to stop the decline in the peso's value. Raising interest rates makes it more costly to abandon a peg and can be seen either as a symbol of the government's resolve to maintain the peg no matter how painful it is to do so, or as a desperate but futile attempt to maintain the peg. Many market participants saw the de facto devaluation as a signal that 'Philippine government resolve had crumbled' in the face of dwindling reserves and a continuing onslaught of speculation against the peso.[53] Once again, a de facto devaluation had been taken defensively and not from a position of strength.

In the eyes of some, the de facto devaluation of the peso represents the apparent powerlessness of the State against the global forces of finance. Prime Minister Mahathir went to the extent of blaming 'rogue speculators' such as George Soros, for the continuing currency crisis in Southeast Asia. Governor Singson said 'some fund managers, some hedge funds' were behind the speculative attacks that led to the fall of the peso. 'First they attacked Thailand, then simultaneously they attacked the Philippines and Malaysia, and now Indonesia...but there is no law against that'.[54]

Blaming speculators for the currency woes is a non-issue. First, data from the Central Bank show that domestic residents themselves, not foreigners owned most of the capital that left the country. Second, the economic fundamentals in countries like the Philippines and Thailand were not as strong as alleged. Foreign fund managers, for example, had the following reactions in the aftermath of the devaluation of the *baht* and the ensuing regional currency crisis: 'It is a reaction to, and symptom of, what happened in Thailand. Traders are picking off apparently vulnerable markets. The Philippines has a structural problem that needs to be addressed. It's not as severe as Thailand, which has a problem in the financial system in general, but the Philippines has a current account issue that must be solved'.[55] Third, Soros himself denied that he had been speculating against these currencies since he had 'not made any sales of Malaysian *ringgit* or Thai *baht* over the past two months with the exception of one trade on 16 June when we sold $10 million of Thai *baht*'.[56]

After announcing that the peso would be allowed to trade within a wider exchange rate band, the Central Bank almost immediately pursued policies that were inconsistent with its expressed intention to allow the peso to trade within a wide band. Rather, its actions are consistent with defending the peso from further deprecation.

On 15 July 1997, Singson said that they would maintain higher interest rates to support the decision to float the peso, maintaining a 32 per cent overnight lending rate and five-day borrowing rates at 25 per cent. The Governor was quoted as saying that, 'We are sending strong monetary signals to let the market realize that while the peso will be allowed to float more flexibly, *we also want to see orderly market conditions* (italics mine). We expect the foreign exchange market to calm down and stabilize in the next couple of days'.[57] He also said that the Central Bank would tighten banks' ability to engage in foreign exchange transactions by including forward dollar transactions in calculating whether a bank exceeded limits set on the amounts of dollars it is allowed to buy and sell. Commercial banks were required to submit weekly reports of forward sales and purchases of dollars to the Central Bank.[58] Non-deliverable forward sales of dollars were suspended for three months. At one point, the Central Bank prohibited foreign banks in the Philippines from transacting in the foreign exchange market, the Philippine Dealing System.

A high interest rate policy is inconsistent with allowing the currency to trade within a wider band. The Central Bank deliberately kept interest rates high to induce people who have dollars to exchange them for pesos, thus raising the demand for pesos and preventing the peso from depreciating. Rather than make the peso move within a wider band, this would, in fact, make the peso not move very much at all. The other point to be made about maintaining high interest rates is that by squeezing liquidity, there would also be less money available for speculating against the peso, or equivalently, for buying dollars. The Central Bank likewise reduced the amount of dollars that banks could sell over the counter to a client from $100,000 to $25,000. Again, by setting quantitative ceilings on the volume of transactions in the market, the freer movement of prices, in this case of foreign currency or the exchange rate, is constrained.

In early October 1997, the Central Bank pursued 'mopping up' operations (of liquidity) in earnest as it attempted to meet monetary targets under an IMF program for January to September 1997 and which was up for review that month. The cost of overnight money surged to a year high of 160 per cent, the highest level since January 1992. On 8 October 1997, in view of the end of the IMF test period, the Central Bank announced that it was reopening its previously suspended overnight lending facility at an opening interest rate of 15 per cent. Singson then said that, 'Interest rates should move on a clearly downward trend'.[59] In any case, if interest rates remained high, the Central Bank could always lay the blame on external forces, mainly the IMF.

It is worth noting that Singson would expect interest rates to begin a downward trend when the peso had tumbled to an all-time low of 35.981 to the dollar the day before. This meant that default risk from companies that had carried dollar-denominated loans had dramatically increased, and hence, the banking system itself likewise faced the prospect of huge loan losses. Country risk had also increased. In addition, in view of the very high interest rates, banks were also facing large loan losses due to defaults. According to the Central Bank, the past due loans of commercial banks increased to 4.69 per cent in 1997 from 2.8 per cent in 1996.[60] On these counts, the increased risk premium would be reflected in higher interest rates and there would be no reason to expect interest rates to be on a downward trend.

Two days later, the Central Bank seemed to have had second thoughts about re-opening the overnight lending facility. It released a very difficult set of guidelines for banks to abide by in availing of the said facility. It set a maximum amount of funds that the Central Bank would release in the system, which meant that it could refuse to lend to banks once some internal limit, known only to the Central Bank, was breached. The Central Bank also said that it would not lend to banks that are large buyers of dollars in the Philippine Dealing System as these banks might use the pesos to hoard dollars. It would also not lend to banks that are not lenders in the money market. It would only lend to banks that have deficiencies in meeting reserve requirements set by the Central Bank, but which have 'square' positions—situations wherein a given amount of dollars bought forward or contracted for a future date is offset by the same amount of dollars sold forward. It is apparent that the Central Bank was attempting to use its overnight lending facility to reward banks that 'behave' by not speculating against the peso, by allowing them access to the facility and a cheap source of funds at a time when credit was very tight.

But the Central Bank would not really allow interest rates to decline. In fact on 16 October, it again raised its overnight lending rate to 16.25 per cent as it was afraid that the banks were using liquidity released earlier to speculate against the peso. This move of the Central Bank once again surprised market participants, because it had already announced that it had completed its mopping up operations under the IMF program and in fact had 'over performed' or overachieved its monetary targets. A day earlier, it reduced the liquidity reserve requirement on banks from six per cent to five per cent which would tend to ease liquidity in the market, and announced that this move ought to reduce interest rates. According to a Central Bank official, they noted that during the past few days, most of the transactions at the Philippine Dealing System were 'speculative' rather than driven by real demand.[61] This was apparently the justification for tightening liquidity again.

Non-transparency and Lack of Information

There is a sense of non-transparency and non-accountability, because policy intentions are never clearly stated, or in cases where they are, actions seem to contradict them. It is difficult to imagine any responsible monetary authority behaving in the manner described above. In this country, it is never clear even on a day-to-day basis, whether interest rates will go up or down because monetary instruments are used erratically. This, in turn, raises the volatility of interest rates and of the money supply, and it also obscures the signals that high interest rates are supposed to convey. This increased volatility in money and interest rates increases the degree of uncertainty and risk in the market. When interest rates are high, people are unsure what this means. It could be because the monetary authority is attempting to defend the peso from depreciating, or because it is attempting to attain its monetary targets in order to contain inflation or stay within IMF program limits.

It is not at all clear how certain transactions can be deemed 'speculative' rather than being market-driven, since market participants act on what they perceive to be profitable market opportunities. As a market participant stated, 'I think there are speculative plays but to what extent, who knows. It's difficult to see where the demands are coming from, because one day there's high demand then the next day, there's none'.[62] These profit opportunities are affected in large part by parameters set by policymakers.

There is another example of less disclosure arising from the fallout of currency turmoil and a high interest rate regime. The Securities and Exchange Commission (SEC) issued a policy barring public access to all legal records filed with it in connection with the suspension of debt payments by certain corporations and intra-corporate disputes. This move was supposedly taken because of the fear that information about these companies would adversely affect their creditor banks. Yet it would seem that more, rather than less disclosure is necessary to protect the greater interests of the investing public, and more importantly, to 'bail in' the private sector (in the monitoring of bank and corporate management) to decrease the risk of moral hazard. By adopting this stance, the SEC unwittingly gave credence to the notion that many corporations and their creditor banks were indeed in trouble, thereby spawning more rumors and fears, which the policy was trying to prevent in the first place. It also prolonged the denial stage of policymakers that there was nothing wrong with the way things are going, and therefore, precluded the necessary policies from being adopted.

The Orient Bank Case One major area of potential conflict between the government and the public, and within the government itself, is what to do with troubled banks. While it is true that the dollar loans plaguing the banks are private sector debts, the problem is that a bank is not just like any other firm that can easily be allowed to fail. On the other hand, some government officials say that not allowing this to happen would encourage banks not to rectify their behavior and induce more moral hazard problems. The Central Bank's preferred solution is to merge a failed bank with a strong one, but it also wants to punish the bank owners. In some cases, this makes the bank difficult to sell, as most of the bank's assets are tied up in litigation, having been collateralized by the owners' assets that the prosecutors are after. The depositors of these failed banks, among whom many are small savers who have deposited their lifesavings, are caught in the middle.

In some cases, such as the Orient Bank, these depositors have formed a group to bring their proposals to the authorities. Again, the depositors were acting rationally and were forced by circumstances to coalesce. The Orient Bank depositors have agreed that if a new buyer for the bank were found, they would keep 80 per cent of their deposits in the new bank for at least a year. Unfortunately, this has not proven to be enough of an incentive to prospective buyers of the bank.

The Orient Bank case is amazing for many reasons. Orient Bank was sunk by loans to its own owners amounting to about P7 billion, in violation of the law limiting such loans. It has been said that the Central Bank knew about the situation sometime back, but did not act on it for many possible reasons. One reason was the fear that acknowledging a problem existed in some bank would reflect badly on the supervisory abilities of the Central Bank. Second, the president of Orient Bank was formerly a high official of the Central Bank.[63] This may have made the supervisory authorities reluctant to move against Orient Bank. Even when it was warranted to do so, Orient Bank was not closed for about nine months. It remained 'dormant', which meant that while it had become unable to service depositor claims, it was not officially closed and liquidated. It was put in a state of suspended animation. Prior to this, the Central Bank had given it an emergency loan, the details of which were not publicly available. In any case, one could question the use of public funds to help a bank that is in trouble because of bad loans made by its owners.

The most amazing thing about the Orient Bank experience is that, the depositors themselves have not questioned the wisdom of the moves of the supervisory authorities. In fact, they would rather plead with the same authorities not to foreclose on the option of the bank being rehabilitated. That the episode has not generated a greater degree of interest or rage among the public, who are also affected by the same forces that brought down Orient Bank is also surprising. Perhaps, this is because of the fact that the rich depositors typically bank with the big banks, and not with banks in the same category as Orient Bank. Enhancing social capital, in this case, entails at the very least, a recognition by the public that poor economic governance by the State and the private sector has negative externalities on all. Only then perhaps can the general public see themselves as stakeholders in the process and take to task those responsible for failures in order to prevent their recurrence. It also demands a greater degree of transparency and accountability on the part of bank owners, managers, and the supervisory authorities. Without sufficient disclosure, the public may not be 'bailed in' to monitor the actions of people acting on their behalf.

Reversal Trends in Liberalization Policy

There were disturbing signs of reversals in the government's trade liberalization program. The include the decision of the cabinet-level Tariff and Related Matters Committee to recalibrate tariff rates based on the stage of processing and the domestic supply of imported goods (or up to 50 per cent of local requirement). This followed appeals by local industries to slow down the tariff reform program scheduled for 1998. From eight tariff levels, the Committee agreed to add three more intermediate tariff levels to ease the inflow of imports.[64]

It might be pointed out that among the objectives of the trade liberalization program was the reduction in the dispersion of tariff rates and the lowering of tariff levels in order to afford more sector-neutral protection. Adding more tariff levels contravenes this, as does slowing down the tariff reform program. In fact, these were exactly the same demands of the protected big business interests when trade liberalization was first pursued in earnest. Yet the State is capitulating to these demands because it felt that it must be seen doing something to protect the interests of society, and the currency depreciation, which hurt the highly import-dependent and traditionally protected business sector was being used as leverage.

Even before President Estrada completed his first year in office, six industries, namely, iron and steel, garments and textile, pulp and paper, automotive battery, disposable lighter, and petrochemicals have been given tax relief for one to two years 'to shield them from the ill effects of the regional economic crisis'. It has been said that some of the favored industries 'were backed by some of Mr. Estrada's associates'.[65]

Regional Co-operation and External Aid

The limits on the abilities of states to unilaterally address problems spawned by the globalization of financial markets have led them to consider a variety of regional cooperation schemes. ASEAN, for example, planned to increase its financial reserves in late 1997 to fight currency speculators. In an accord introduced in 1987 and updated in 1992, the five-party arrangement between Singapore, Indonesia, Malaysia, Thailand, and the Philippines allows for a draw down cap of US$80 million, with each signatory providing US$40 million to the fund. Subsequent events have shown that this amount was inadequate.[66] In July 1998, the five countries agreed to extend the accord by renewing a dormant US$200 million swap agreement which allows a country with short-term liquidity financing problems to exchange its local currency for US$ provided by other members.

The problem with these arrangements is that they are never large enough and they are difficult to implement when all countries' currencies are simultaneously or sequentially being attacked. Consider for example the size of the rescue package for Thailand of about US$17.2 billion. The four other ASEAN countries could not afford to extend this amount of help. This means that any country that finds itself in trouble will need assistance from multilateral sources. The Philippines itself negotiated a US$1 billion loan from the IMF even as it prepared to make an exit from long years of IMF programs.

Of course, the increased dependence on external forces can be used productively. It may also perhaps make the needed adjustments put less of a strain on the State's viability by having someone else to blame. The then Philippine finance secretary, Roberto de Ocampo, for example, urged the IMF to take an aggressive role in helping member countries regulate the financial sector to prevent future currency crisis. According to him, both the IMF and the WB 'have critical roles to play in both preventing excesses by filling market information gaps and containing their consequences through speedy assistance. In this respect, the IMF needs to reinvigorate its surveillance functions and improve its data dissemination'.[67] At least, this view recognized the need for greater information and disclosure, as well as more stringent and prudent regulation of financial systems. There is an implicit admission that the IMF and WB can assist in data gathering and in capacity building while many countries do not have the necessary infrastructure to adequately obtain the necessary information.

The president of the *Bundesbank* went one step further saying that while the IMF warned Thailand in fairly good time about the impending crisis, 'the question is how one can increase pressure on countries that have been put on notice to act in time'.[68] He backed enlarging the IMF's role so that it could scrutinize and probe financial and banking systems in the same way that it does with the macroeconomic situation, pointing out that the decisive factor is the establishment of a set of rules that can be accepted by all.

Another reason why a regional fund arrangement is of limited use is that countries see themselves as both competitors and allies. Ensuing events have reinforced these feelings of competition as countries tried to differentiate themselves from each other. For example, at the joint IMF-WB meetings in September 1997, Camdessus assured the Philippine delegation led by Singson that in discussions with the international community, the IMF 'will carefully differentiate the various countries within the region in terms of actual conditions'.[69]

A major concern about such regional arrangements is that they tend to undermine conditionalities set by the IMF. According to WB chief economist, Joseph Stiglitz: 'A regional facility would provide easy funds without addressing economic fundamentals. What is required in any crisis is the restoration of confidence. You cannot have restoration of confidence if you do not address the fundamentals'. Similarly, Stanley Fischer of the IMF said that the creation of a regional fund 'would be an invitation to assume that there is another and better way of doing things. It would cost a great deal of money before we would realize that it was not going to work'.[70]

There is merit to these concerns. This is not because any fund ASEAN could create would ever really be large enough to compete with funds from the IMF and WB. Instead, it tends to be incompatible with people and governments needing to change their ways. It tends to postpone needed adjustments by providing some ammunition to maintain the status quo.

Proposals ranging from a new system of exchange rate pegs and bands up to the possibility of a monetary union were also considered, such as creating an Asian bloc along the lines of the European Monetary Union (EMU). A Thai official was said to have proposed a common policy on ASEAN interest rates to narrow gaps in the region.[71] After freeing up most of their currencies, an Asian bloc would require refixing them, possibly with Japan taking the lead in this cooperative currency agreement.

Stabilizing exchange rates by establishing a new system of pegs, bands, or target zones within which currencies are allowed to fluctuate against each other requires significant compromises of domestic political and economic autonomy.[72] This is because there may be conflicts between domestic and international policies, of which the 'impossible trinity' is the foremost example.

Monetary union is not an easy way out. If the types of shocks that hit a country are similar in nature to those that hit its neighbors, then a country might be willing to give up its monetary policy independence and adopt a common monetary policy. However, even if the shocks are of the same nature and/or magnitude as its neighbors, a country may want to respond differently and adopt an independent policy for various reasons, such as to moderate the adverse impacts on certain sectors in society. Of course, if there were an easy way to make transfers so that those adversely affected can be compensated as in the case of some type of federal system, then this would not be too binding a constraint.

In any case, some believe that the political preconditions for creating a monetary union were not present in Asia.[73] A monetary union requires the pooling of political responsibility, but East Asia does not have a tradition of political integration nor a Jean Monet or Paul Henri Spaak to speak for regional integration. In addition, there are wide ideological differences between China and the market-oriented regimes in the rest of Asia.

Summary and Conclusions

This chapter examined the security implications of the liberalization and globalization of financial markets. It showed that both of these forces have allowed the Philippines to tap global capital markets more easily. This is generally regarded as beneficial to economic growth. Attainment of the benefits of the globalization of capital and the integration of financial markets necessitates preconditions such as strong economic fundamentals and the willingness to be disciplined by market rules. It also requires the recognition that weak aspects of the fundamentals have to be addressed with transparent and consistent policies from government.

Thus far, the experience of the Philippines with regard to globalization of financial markets has been mixed. This study presents evidence to show that incorrect, inconsistent, and non-transparent policies rather than global forces *per se* were in large part responsible for the compromising of economic goals. Policies that attempt to keep the peso at a particular level gave rise to one-sided, myopic, and incorrect expectations. These policies cannot be seen as increasing the individual or collective well being of the people and themselves increased systemic risk. A policy to sterilize capital inflows in an attempt to attain both monetary and exchange rate targets in a world where capital is highly mobile is not sustainable, and by itself leads to speculation as to when the policy will be abandoned. The high interest rate regime adopted after the announcement that the peso would be allowed to trade within a wider band raised credibility questions about such a policy move, and constrained economic growth.

The ability of the country to have easy access to funds from abroad enriched certain sectors, such as banks, that could borrow abroad cheaply and lend locally at high rates. Evidence was presented to show the tremendous growth in the net foreign liabilities of the banking and non-bank institutions in the private sector. Most of these funds were unhedged and went into the non-tradeable sectors. When the peso suddenly depreciated, the asset bubbles that had developed in non-tradeable markets burst. The financial system, which had grown accustomed to earning money the easy and less-than-prudential way, became imperiled.

Easy access to global financial markets postponed needed adjustments by building a constituency for maintaining the exchange rate at an overvalued level, and against economic growth by allowing the peso to adjust in order to maintain domestic industry competitiveness. Some of these sectors against exchange rate adjustment naturally gravitated into alliances with sectors that shared the same interests, and in some cases, these alliances were with their own regulators. Thus, the ability of the regulator to function properly was compromised, and the interests of the larger majority were not served.

The other problem with easy access to global capital is the disposition of the funds. In the case of the Philippines, the majority of capital flows from abroad raised consumption instead of investment, as a proportion of GDP. Easy access to foreign savings was also a disincentive to raising efforts at domestic resource mobilization. Thus, it tended to reinforce negative structural features of the economy.

The study also discusses the reaction of the State's attempt to deliver on its economic goals, by regaining control over aspects of economic policy which globalization seemed to have taken away. Many of these involved the use of state powers rather than market methods. There are disturbing pieces of evidence, such as the government's bowing to the demands of industries for the introduction of more tariff categories and the granting of tax relief to a few industries, which indicate that there were trend reversals as far as liberalization efforts are concerned.

Some other ideas as to what states can do to regain a bigger say in the economic life of countries require regional cooperation schemes, such as a regional currency fund arrangement, which for reasons discussed are largely symbolic and not radical solutions to the problems at hand. In fact, it seems that the globalization of capital markets increases rather than diminishes the influence of multilateral agencies such as the WB and IMF in the lives of developing countries. The sheer size of the bail out package for countries like Thailand almost makes this inevitable. This is not altogether a bad thing, especially given the poor financial infrastructure present in these countries. Lacunae such as information gaps can be filled by these agencies in part, at least temporarily. But we must also insist on greater transparency and disclosure ourselves so market participants can act on the basis of correct information, and allow for the disciplining effect of market forces to work.

The verities arising from the study with important policy implications are:

1. The benefits from globalization depend to a large extent on a firm and credible commitment in keeping the economy open and managing this process of maintaining open markets to the extent possible.
2. Good economic governance is important. While technically sound policies are important, the political development of civil society is extremely important in furthering good economic governance. Social capital must be developed to allow civil society institutions to participate in the security and development discourse.
3. There must be a credible commitment and greater efforts at the regional level to 'enhanced interaction' to maximize the benefits of globalization, moderate its ill-effects, and enhance State legitimacy.

Notes

1   'IMF Chief Says Asia Turbulence Highlights Global Economic Risks', *Philippine Daily Inquirer*, 24 September 1997, pp.B1.
2   In some cases, contagion is possible, in which a currency attack is not based on a country's economic fundamentals. This happened to some countries in Latin America after the Mexican crisis, in which even countries with strong economic fundamentals experienced attacks on their currency. The spillover effects from the Mexican crisis are called the 'tequila effect'.
3   See Krugman (1979).
4   See, for example, Flood and Garber (1984) and Obstfeld (1986).
5   A universal bank is allowed to undertake certain investment activities, such as underwriting securities, aside from the traditional banking role of raising deposits and making loans.
6   It bears emphasizing, however, that the Central Bank was, until recently, the biggest participant in the foreign exchange market, and hence, the value of the peso cannot be regarded as 'market determined' in the usual textbook case. Recently, the Central bank has opted to conserve its dollar reserves and intervene in the exchange market indirectly, by raising interest rates.
7   The 1970s were characterized by the large amounts of public enterprise borrowing from abroad. In contrast, the capital flows in the 1990s are primarily private capital flows. Policymakers had believed that the private nature of the recent capital flows meant that they would not be problematic.
8   World Bank (1997), *Private Capital Flows to Developing Countries: The Road to Financial Integration*, Oxford University Press.
9   Bangko Sentral ng Pilipinas (BSP) (1997), *Selected Philippine Economic Indicators*, BSP, Manila, Table 12.

10 See de Dios, E. S., Diokno, B. E., Fabella, R. V., Medalla, F. M. and Monsod, S. (1997), *Exchange Rate Policy: Recent Failures and Future Tasks*, paper presented before the House Committee on Economic Affairs, 1997. Published in the first issue of *Public Policy*, vol.1, no.1, 1997, pp.15-41.
11 Factors cited for the tapering-off of growth in Asia prior to the *baht* devaluation include the de facto devaluation of the Chinese *yuan* in 1994, the depreciation of the yen to the dollar in 1995, and weak semi-conductor prices. See Moreno, Pasadilla, and Remolona (1998).
12 Bangko Sentral ng Pilipinas, *Selected Philippine Economic Indicators, 1997*, Table 31.
13 The difference between GNP and GDP is net factor income from abroad. The fact that real GNP growth rates exceed by a large amount those of real GDP also points to the possibility that net foreign income from abroad is overstated in the GNP accounts. The sources of the overstatement, such as the possible double-counting of remittances from overseas contract workers in the capital account and the current account, is something that cannot be adequately explained by officials at the Central Bank. Nevertheless, the attractiveness of a country as a destination of FDI is more closely related to GDP, as it measures the value of domestic production. See de Dios et al. (1997) for a fuller discussion.
14 See, de Dios, *et. al., Exchange Rate Policy: Recent Failures and Future Tasks*, 1997, p.3. The latest figure for the growth of manufactured output is a decline of 13 per cent as of May 1998.
15 Corbo, V. and Hernandez, L. (1993), 'Macroeconomic Adjustment to Portfolio Capital Inflows: Rationale and Some Recent Experiences', in S. Claessens and S. Gooptu (eds), *Portfolio Investment in Developing Countries*, World Bank Discussion Paper No. 228.
16 The current account is the sum of the trade account, and services and transfers, the latter two commonly referred to as the 'invisibles' account. See Bangko Sentral ng Pilipinas, *Selected Philippine Economic Indicators, 1997*, Table 31.
17 *Ibid.*
18 This is not a problem, *per se*, except events now show that these funds were largely funneled by finance companies into the real estate sector, which subsequently collapsed. Since banks owned many of the finance companies, the result was a banking crisis.
19 Gochoco-Bautista, M. S. (1997), *Prospects and Adjustment Imperatives for Philippine Capital Markets,* study submitted to the Long-Term Planning, Research and Development Project, National Economic and Development Authority, Manila.
20 BSP, *Selected Philippine Economic Indicators, 1997*, Table 31.
21 *Ibid.*, Table 17.
22 The Ramos administration had earlier announced a small budgetary surplus of P5 billion, which turned out to involve some 'window dressing' as government contractors, who were owed about P14 billion, were simply not paid.
23 The latter is referred to as the 'moral hazard' problem in which financial institutions take on risky ventures because they are assured of government bailouts in bad states of the world.
24 Besides being tied to an appreciating currency, currencies in countries where there were large productivity improvements naturally experienced appreciating domestic currencies. This seems to have been the case for some countries in East Asia.
25 These are policies in which the domestic currency is deliberately kept weak relative to those of trading partners and competitors, in order to spur exports and economic growth. In the trade dispute between the US and Japan, for example, the US had accused Japan of deliberately using a 'cheap' yen policy to spur Japanese exports at the expense of US exports. In 1985, under the so-called Plaza Accord, the Japanese yen was revalued to correct this.
26 Ferdinand Marcos won in the 1965 presidential elections.

27 de Dios, E. (1995), 'On Recent Financial Flows: Causes and Consequences', in R. Fabella and H. Sakai (eds), *Towards Sustained Growth*, Institute for Developing Economies, Tokyo.

28 If anything, the monetary authorities were trumpeting the fact that they were intervening by buying dollars in order to prevent the peso from appreciating. However, by April of 1997, the Central Bank had become a net seller of dollars.

29 This is equivalent to saying that people do not have the 'money illusion', in that purely nominal variables *per se*, such as the nominal exchange rate, are not what concerns them. Instead, they want to know what their money can buy in terms of real goods.

30 In fact, studies such as the one by the Japan External Trade Organization cited in Fabella (1996) point out that in 1995, Philippine wages in dollar terms were higher than those in China and Indonesia; power costs were the highest after Japan; and freight costs were higher than those in South Korea, Taiwan, Hong Kong, Singapore, and Malaysia.

31 de Dios, *et. al.*, *Exchange Rate Policy: Recent Failures and Future Tasks*, 1997.

32 PHILEXPORT commissioned many policy papers written by academics.

33 Cabacungan, G. (1997), 'VMC, Eyco Group: Where Did They Go Wrong?', *Philippine Daily Inquirer*, 22 September, pp.B18.

34 The differential in yields between developing country and developed country government securities usually reflect country and currency risks.

35 BSP, *Selected Philippine Economic Indicators*, 1997, Table 31.

36 *Ibid.*, Table 11.

37 Deutsche Morgan Grenfell, 'Philippine Banks: Turbulence Ahead', March 1998, pp.18.

38 *Ibid.*

39 The real bills doctrine posits that as long as loans are made for productive purposes, such as lending to producers of real goods, there will be no inflationary impact. The logic was that lending for the production of real goods did not involve much risk because in a sense, the real goods can be used as collateral.

40 Dumlao, D. (1998), 'Past Due Loans Rising', *Philippine Daily Inquirer*, 12 March, pp.B1.

41 '17 Banks Placed on Government Watchlist', *Philippine Daily Inquirer*, 9 June 1998, pp.1.

42 'Peso Hits 35.9 vs $1 as Stocks Plummet', *Philippine Daily Inquirer*, 8 October 1997, pp.1. Note also that this story merited front-page attention rather than being put in the business section of the newspaper.

43 'Peso Rallies, Stocks Surge', *Philippine Daily Inquirer*, 10 October 1997, pp.B1.

44 'No Windfall for Banks from Forex Crisis-BSP', *Philippine Daily Inquirer*, 21 March 1998, pp.B1.

45 'BSP to Curb Dollar Hoarding', *Philippine Daily Inquirer*, 31 July 1997, pp.B1.

46 'Peso Hits 35.9 vs $1 as Stocks Plummet', 1997, pp.1.

47 'Gov't Moves to Ease Loan Conversion Woes', *Philippine Daily Inquirer*, 21 October 1997, pp.B1.

48 'BSP to Limit Coverage of Forex Protection', *Philippine Daily Inquirer*, 19 December 1997, pp.B1.

49 *Ibid.*

50 *Ibid.*

51 Forward contracts refer to agreements to buy or sell a good, such as foreign exchange, at a price specified today for delivery and settlement at a future date.

52 Dumlao, D. (1998), '2 Banks Not Joining BSP Plan to Stabilize Peso-Dollar Rate', *Philippine Daily Inquirer*, 3 July, p.B1. However, the Governor of the Central Bank thereafter vehemently denied that there was such a plan to use some banks in order to stabilize the exchange rate.

53 'London Funds Steer Clear of Southeast Asia Foreign Exchange Market', *Philippine Daily Inquirer*, 14 July 1997, pp.B1.

54 'Government Raises Inflation Target, Sees P27:$1 rate by October', *Philippine Daily Inquirer*, 17 July 1997, pp.B1.
55 *Ibid.*
56 'Soros Denies Role in Asian Money Woes', *Philippine Daily Inquirer*, 31 July 1997, pp.B1.
57 'Peso Float Support: High Interest Rates to Stay', *Philippine Daily Inquirer*, 16 July 1997, pp.B1.
58 'BSP Steps Up Drive to Defend Currency', *Philippine Daily Inquirer*, 24 July 1997, pp.B1.
59 'BSP Reopens Lending Facility: Bank Overnight Rate Hits 160 per cent', *Philippine Daily Inquirer*, 8 October 1997, pp.B1.
60 'Bank Profits to Suffer from Reforms', *Philippine Daily Inquirer*, 24 March 1998, pp.B3.
61 'BSP Raises Overnight Rate', *Philippine Daily Inquirer*, 17 October 1997, pp.B1.
62 *Ibid.*
63 Mr. Arnulfo Aurellano is the president of Orient Bank.
64 Cabacungan, G. (1997), 'Government Plans Wider Tariff Range on Goods', *Philippine Daily Inquirer*, 10 October 1997, pp.B13.
65 Cabacungan, G. (1999), 'Six Industries Get Tariff Relief', *Philippine Daily Inquirer*, 19 January 1999, pp.B1.
66 'ASEAN to Hike Fund Against Speculators', *Philippine Daily Inquirer*, 27 August 1997, pp.B1.
67 'RP Urges IMF to Take More Aggressive Role', *Philippine Daily Inquirer*, 25 September 1997, pp.B1.
68 'Need to Monitor Markets Stressed to Avert Crisis', *Philippine Daily Inquirer*, 22 September 1997, pp.B17.
69 'RP Weathers Currency Crisis 'Pretty Well'', *Philippine Daily Inquirer*, 26 September 1997, pp.B1.
70 'ASEAN Presses Regional Fund Despite IMF Fears', *Philippine Daily Inquirer*, 26 September 1997, pp.B5.
71 'Crisis Spurs Talks of Currency Union', *Philippine Daily Inquirer*, 26 September 1997, pp.B5.
72 Eichengreen, B. (1997), 'Is There a Monetary Union in Asia's Future?', *The Brookings Review*, Spring, pp. 33-5.
73 *Ibid.*, p.35

References

'ASEAN Presses Regional Fund Despite IMF Fears', *Philippine Daily Inquirer*, 26 September 1997, pp. B5.
'ASEAN to Hike Fund Against Speculators', *Philippine Daily Inquirer*, 27 August 1997, pp. B1.
Bangko Sentral ng Pilipinas (BSP) (1997), *Selected Philippine Economic Indicators*, BSP, Manila.
'BSP to Curb Dollar Hoarding', *Philippine Daily Inquirer*, 31 July 1997, pp. B1.
'BSP to Limit Coverage of Forex Protection', *Philippine Daily Inquirer*, 19 December 1997, pp. B1.
'BSP Raises Overnight Rate', *Philippine Daily Inquirer*, 17 October 1997, pp. B1.
'BSP Reopens Lending Facility: Bank Overnight Rate Hits 160 per cent', *Philippine Daily Inquirer*, 8 October 1997, pp. B1.
'BSP Steps Up Drive to Defend Currency', *Philippine Daily Inquirer*, 24 July 1997, pp. B1.
'Bank Profits to Suffer from Reforms', *Philippine Daily Inquirer*, 24 March 1998, pp. B3.

170 out of 324

Cabacungan, G. (1997a), 'Government Plans Wider Tariff Range on Goods', *Philippine Daily Inquirer*, 10 October 1997, pp. B13.

Cabacungan, G. (1997b), 'VMC, Eyco Group: Where Did They Go Wrong?', *Philippine Daily Inquirer*, 22 September, pp. B18.

Cabacungan, G. (1999), 'Six Industries Get Tariff Relief', *Philippine Daily Inquirer*, 19 January 1999, pp. B1.

Corbo, V. and Hernandez, L. (1993), 'Macroeconomic Adjustment to Portfolio Capital Inflows: Rationale and Some Recent Experiences', in S. Claessens and S. Gooptu (eds), *Portfolio Investment in Developing Countries*, World Bank Discussion Paper No. 228.

'Crisis Spurs Talks of Currency Union', *Philippine Daily Inquirer*, 26 September 1997, pp. B5.

de Dios, E. (1995), 'On Recent Financial Flows: Causes and Consequences', in R. Fabella and H. Sakai (eds), *Towards Sustained Growth*, Institute for Developing Economies, Tokyo.

de Dios, E., Diokno, B., Fabella, R., Medalla, F., and Monsod, S. (1997), 'Exchange Rate Policy: Recent Failures and Future Tasks', *Public Policy*, vol. 1, no. 1, pp. 15-41.

Dumlao, D. (1998a), 'Past Due Loans Rising', *Philippine Daily Inquirer*, 12 March, pp.B1.

Dumlao, D. (1998b), '2 Banks Not Joining BSP Plan to Stabilize Peso-Dollar Rate', *Philippine Daily Inquirer*, 3 July, p.B1.

Deutsche Morgan Grenfell (1998), *Philippine Banks: Turbulence Ahead*, March, pp.18.

Eichengreen, B. (1997), 'Is There a Monetary Union in Asia's Future?', *The Brookings Review*, Spring, pp. 33-5.

Fabella, R. (1996), 'Features of the Emerging World Economic Order: Implications on Growth Policy', in C. Paderanga, Jr. (ed.), *The Philippines in the Emerging World Environment: Globalization at a Glance*, University of the Philippines Press, Quezon City.

Flood, R. and Garber, P. (1994), 'Collapsing Exchange Rate Regimes: Some Linear Examples', *Journal of International Economics*, no. 17, pp. 1-13.

Gochoco-Bautista, M. S. (1997), *Prospects and Adjustment Imperatives for Philippine Capital Markets,* study submitted to the Long-Term Planning, Research and Development Project, National Economic and Development Authority, Manila.

'Government Raises Inflation Target, Sees P27:$1 rate by October', *Philippine Daily Inquirer*, 17 July 1997, pp. B1.

'Government Moves to Ease Loan Conversion Woes', *Philippine Daily Inquirer*, 21 October 1997, pp. B1.

'IMF Chief Says Asia Turbulence Highlights Global Economic Risks', *Philippine Daily Inquirer*, 24 September 1997, pp. B1.

Krugman, P. (1979), 'A Model of Balance of Payments Crises', *Journal of Money, Credit and Banking*, no. 11, pp. 311-25.

'London Funds Steer Clear of Southeast Asia Foreign Exchange Market', *Philippine Daily Inquirer*, 14 July 1997, pp. B1.

Moreno, R., Pasadilla, G., and Remolona, E. (1998), *Asia's Financial Crisis: Lessons and Policy Responses*, Working Paper No. PB-98-02, Federal Reserve Bank of San Francisco, Center for Pacific Basin Monetary and Economic Studies.

'No Windfall for Banks from Forex Crisis-BSP', *Philippine Daily Inquirer*, 21 March 1998, pp. B1.

Obstfeld, M. (1986), 'Rational and Self-fulfilling Balance of Payments Crises', *American Economic Review*, no. 76, pp. 72-81.

'Peso Hits 35.9 vs $1 as Stocks Plummet', *Philippine Daily Inquirer*, 8 October 1997, pp. 1.

'Peso Float Support: High Interest Rates to Stay', *Philippine Daily Inquirer*, 16 July 1997, pp. B1.

'Peso Rallies, Stocks Surge', *Philippine Daily Inquirer*, 10 October 1997, pp. B1.

'RP Urges IMF to Take More Aggressive Role', *Philippine Daily Inquirer*, 25 September 1997, pp. B1.

'RP Weathers Currency Crisis "Pretty Well"', *Philippine Daily Inquirer*, 26 September 1997, pp. B1.
'17 Banks Placed on Government Watchlist', *Philippine Daily Inquirer*, 9 June 1998, pp. 1.
'Soros Denies Role in Asian Money Woes', *Philippine Daily Inquirer*, 31 July 1997, pp. B1.
World Bank (1997), *Private Capital Flows to Developing Countries: The Road to Financial Integration*, Oxford University Press.

Chapter 8

Globalization and the Human Security of the Poor in the Philippines[1]

Amado M. Mendoza, Jr.

Introduction

Globalization is comprehensively defined as 'the process by which independent states, their economies, societies, and peoples become increasingly integrated into the international economy and society'. This process consequently 'entails the erosion of national sovereignty, the opening up of domestic economies and societies to external influences, the increasing social and physical mobility of peoples, and the consequent economic, social, cultural, and political challenges posed to the nation-state'.[2] Globalization is considered the most important contemporary factor affecting the development of nations.

Greater integration into the global economy has important security implications for nations. To the extent that globalization fosters economic growth and prosperity, enhanced security for states, governments, and peoples may ensue. This could lead to greater 'performance legitimacy of rulers, promote greater national integration as a result of improved communication and transport, and increase the level of human security enjoyed by the society as a whole, including better access to food, housing, and health-care'.[3]

However, as present day globalization is dominated by the market's logic, it may also impinge negatively on security at all levels. While markets are inclusive, they, in operation with other factors such as the prevailing distribution of assets in a given economy, can also exclude, marginalize, and isolate. When the market dominates with its competitive logic, the opportunities and rewards of globalization spread unequally and inequitably—conferring wealth and power to some (persons, firms, and nations) while marginalizing others. While the new information-communication technologies driving contemporary globalization offer great potential for human progress, the privatization and concentration of technology is dividing the world into the connected and the isolated. The poor are pushed to the margins of a proprietary regime that controls the world's knowledge.[4]

On balance, globalization has mixed or contradictory effects on security in the personal, community, domestic, and inter-state levels. It greatly enhances the opportunities available to those who have the skills and mobility to flourish in international markets. It can assist poor countries to escape poverty. On the other hand, globalization exerts downward pressure on the wages of under-skilled workers, exacerbates economic insecurity for those employed in noncompetitive industries and sectors, calls into question accepted social arrangements, and weakens existing social safety systems.

Globalization and Economic Reform in the Philippine Context[5]

Various Philippine governments, including the late Marcos regime (late 1970s up to 1985) have made commitments to economic and structural reform to international multi-lateral financial institutions. These commitments were without fail responses to balance of payments (BOP) crises, which required mediation of international financial institutions (IFIs) such as the International Monetary Fund (IMF) and the World Bank (WB) to keep the flow of foreign exchange going. The essence of these commitments was a rejection of an inward-looking protectionist policy regime and a choice for active engagement in the global economy.

As globalization was accelerated over the past decade by the end of the cold war and the breathtaking advances in information technology, the implementation of these commitments was facilitated during the post-Marcos regimes with substantial breakthroughs achieved by the government of President Fidel V. Ramos. Elite consensus was achieved on key aspects of the economic reform package as evidenced by the relatively easy ratification of the General Agreement on Trade and Tariff-Uruguay Round Treaty (GATT Treaty) in the Philippine Senate and its acceptance even by hitherto protectionist economic interests and groups. In the Philippine context, the government's accession to the GATT Treaty in 1994 represented the first time that the term 'globalization' entered the political lexicon.

The elite consensus behind marketization and further integration into the world economy is not shared by several sectors of Philippine society. From the late 1970s up to the mid-1980s, opposition to so-called IMF-inspired economic austerity *cum* structural adjustment packages was fundamentally tied to the overall democratic struggle against the Marcos dictatorship. The basic critique was that these programs were 'anti-poor', 'anti-people', and provided much-needed financial support to an oppressive regime.

The advent of democracy in 1986 changed the tenor of the opposition to market reform. For one, it provided additional opportunities for the opposition given relative freedom of information and expression. The strength of the opposition was manifested by a general strike against oil price hikes in August 1987, an occasion exploited by military rebels to mount the first serious coup attempt against the government of President Corazon Aquino. Any reform of an existing trade and economic regime will produce winners and losers within the short- and medium-run. For that matter, trade and economic reform had always been a tangle of technical and political considerations. Why is this so? As early as the 13th century, Machiavelli observed: 'the reformer has enemies in all those who profit by the old order and only lukewarm defenders in all those who would profit from the new order'. It is easy to see why

groups (labor, businessmen involved in 'sunset' sectors, others) that will lose from trade and economic reform will
lobby their governments to restrict trade and protect their incomes. However, those who would gain from the reform will not lobby equally strongly on the other side. Trade economists[6] have long recognized that those who gain from economic reform and trade in any particular product are a much less concentrated, informed, and organized group than those who lose. This means that the per capita benefits of trade and economic reform are grossly outweighed by the per capita costs. For instance, the consumer beneficiaries of trade liberalization of sugar products would run to millions and are often unorganized while domestic sugar producers, who might be adversely affected, are obviously fewer, organized, and have the ability to act collectively and make political contributions to help thwart or adulterate trade policy.[7]

Indeed, questions about the allocation of the social and political costs of economic reform have generated bitter argument within both international development circles and within countries struggling with economic adjustment since the 1980s. A number of observers[8] draw our attention to the attendant problems of market reform. These problems are grouped into two: *political support* and *state capacity*.

Political support for structural adjustment programs in the 1980s was sorely lacking all over the developing world. They entailed sacrifices from social groups not generally included in the negotiations. During adjustment, countries that suffer severe income inequality often experienced political polarization. Adjustment programs became contestable on charges of intensifying perceived inequalities. Notwithstanding their intrinsic technical merit, market reforms will be opposed when some groups realize that they will benefit or suffer more than others. Good policies indeed matter but gaining a consensus for reform is a political question. Gloria Macapagal-Arroyo was the most enthusiastic champion for GATT-UR during the 1994 Senate debates. Is it correct to read her topping the 1995 senatorial by-elections, her election as vice president in May 1998, or even her ascension to the presidency as a result of People Power II in early 2001, as a strong popular consensus for free trade?

Equity, therefore, is a major consideration in assessing the political feasibility of market reform. Nelson[9] points out that two distinct equity issues have emerged from out of the economic adjustment and reform processes in the developing world during the 1980s. The first, driven by humanitarian considerations, focused on reducing the impact of adjustment on the very poor, who are mostly rural folk. In most cases, the pressures from external institutions played an important role. The second is largely defined by domestic political pressures, and focused less on the very poor than on the semi-poor and the urban working classes.

These two equity issues pose different political dilemmas. In the first case, while there are very weak domestic political incentives to assist the very poor (who are also relatively powerless and atomized), there were considerable international pressures on their behalf that have developed since the late 1980s, when economic adjustment sought to have a 'human face'.[10] While external agencies provided financial support for pro-poor programs in many countries, most of them had been defeated by opposition from the more vocal political sectors who stood to lose by the reforms.

The second issue seems to be a greater problem in the Philippines and the rest of the developing world. In contrast to the very poor in the rural areas, urban working and 'popular' classes are more organized and politically active and can pressure reforming governments through a variety of weapons—from the general strike up to the ballot box.

Given the above discussion, any reforming government has to weigh the social and political costs of reform. In the Philippines, opposition to economic and trade reform had traditionally emanated from oligopolistic business interests, big landowners, and organized labor. However, oligopolistic business had displayed greater political sophistication since the downfall of Marcos in 1986. Realizing that multilateral funds were necessary to resuscitate the Philippine economy and secure the post-Marcos political regime, they paid lip service to economic reform to secure these funds and fought rear-guard skirmishes and battles since then. In fact, they made use of their positions in the Aquino government to perpetuate protectionist tariff barriers and block other anti-monopoly measures.

Curiously, these monopolists found strange tactical allies in organized labor, peasants, and other left wing forces in the country. Apart from a perception that these measures were foisted by so-called 'imperialist' agencies, the less powerful classes are also aware that they usually bear the costs of economic adjustment. For instance, the import liberalization program of President Aquino spared the 'white-line' appliance industry identified with her trade secretary while certain agricultural sectors (for example, cotton, sunflower seeds, others) were liberalized.

The tactical alliance may seem curious to a technical analyst who would argue that the lower classes (who are also consumers), would benefit in the long run from freer trade even if they may suffer short-run losses especially if they are employed in inefficient industries. The same alliance is intelligible, however, to Robinson[11] who earlier quipped that the invisible hand of the market will always do its work, but it may work by strangulation. In addition, the visible hand of oligarchic interests and rent seekers will inflict further damage to lower class interests.

To dissipate local opposition to the Uruguay Round Treaty, the Philippine Senate cobbled up a multi-billion peso-safety net package especially directed to peasant and rural beneficiaries.[12] In general, a reforming government may have to buy off opposition through such 'bribes'. However, its difficulties are compounded if it is in a financial bind and under an IMF-prescribed austerity program that calls for reduction of public deficits, among others. The question here involves the funding of these 'reform-buying' efforts. The scramble for government funds will obviously have political implications for any reforming regime.

Fundamentalists would argue that the provision of so-called safety nets is contrary to the logic of the market. The technical objective of market reform, they argue, is precisely to eliminate non-competitive firms, industries, and sectors. These observers believe that the provision of safety nets will simply inject new life into these moribund sectors. Others believe that technical considerations should be tempered by political imperatives especially in a country with a substantial peasant and small grower population as well as a burgeoning service (formal and informal) sector.

This brings us back to the financing problem. Some have suggested that multilateral agencies such as the IMF and the WB, pushing for trade and market reforms in the developing economies should likewise provide funds for safety net packages. This track may have to depend a great deal on the improvement of the capacity of many government bureaucracies to prevent the diversion of these resources to rent seekers.

It is quite clear that market reform entails massive overhaul of state capacities in the developing world. The 'orthodox paradox' stipulates that while reform calls for less intervention of the state in the economy, it requires the same state to initiate and sustain these same changes. The absence of state capacity appears to be a more important reason why economic reform could fail. Even when political support exists, it cannot ensure the successful implementation of reform. In institutions where the bureaucracy is known to be corrupt or inept, the adoption of market reforms will not instantly transform them into honest and competent ones. A democratic state's dismal capacity to administer reform will also feed to its political vulnerability. Capacity, politics, and equity considerations are intertwined. The inability of the bureaucracy to successfully fend off demands for continued preferential treatment of powerful vested interests will only fuel charges that reforms benefit some groups at the expense of others.

As it is, economic and trade reform will be a politically and socially contentious process because not everybody gains in both the short and long haul. Furthermore, more powerful interests who cannot stanch the reform process may manage to pass on the costs to less powerful and marginalized social sectors and groups. This is the usual complaint raised by populist critics with economic reform programs. A government committed both to popular empowerment and economic reform must therefore find ways through which the burdens of reform may be borne equitably.

On the other hand, the advent of democracy and the initial results of economic reform have both resulted in diverse responses from the popular opposition. While a section continues its outright opposition to the incumbent regime, other sections have adjusted to market reform and have 'constructively engaged' government to make the reform process a humane, pro-poor one. Other considerations include extracting a commitment from government in favor of sustainable development and gender equity. These sections of the popular movements skillfully used international initiatives on environment, development, population, human rights, and gender (from Rio de Janeiro in 1992 to Beijing in 1995) to obtain these governmental commitments.

Dimensions of Philippine Poverty

Several observers[13] have painted a composite picture of a typical poor Filipino household showing the following attributes:

1. Its size is larger than average. A 1992 survey of families ranking among the poorest 30 per cent of all families showed their average size to be greater than ten

for urban families and greater than eight for rural families. On the whole, families with five or more members account for over three-fourths of total poverty. The extended family system has nothing to do with their poverty. Single families are, on the average, poorer than extended families as they account for about 80 per cent of total poverty.

2. A male heads the household. Poverty incidence among female-headed households is so much less than in male-headed households. Male-headed households account for over 90 per cent of total poverty.

3. The head of the household is younger than fifty years. This is true for more than two-thirds of all poor households.

4. The head of the household has little or no schooling at all. For 72 per cent of all poor households, the highest educational attainment is a primary school education.

5. The family is more economically active than the rest of the population, with substantially higher labor participation rates, especially among the youngest and oldest age groups, but with less access to the formal labor market. Two-thirds of the men and roughly three-fourths of the women are either self-employed or unpaid family workers.

6. It lives in a rural area (two-thirds of all poor households) and its members are engaged simultaneously in as many as four or more income-earning activities. Yet, they are largely underemployed.

7. If living in an urban area, the family derives income mainly from agriculture, construction, and transport. The percentage of poor households engaged in urban agriculture is larger than in those engaged in any other occupation. More urban poor families are engaged in agriculture than in construction and transport combined.[14]

A singular truth stands out from these points. The poor are neither indolent nor jobless. Many of the poor are employed simultaneously in different jobs. They cannot, in fact, afford to be unemployed. Poverty, therefore, is more the lack of jobs that provide sufficient incomes rather than mere unemployment.

In referring to the poor, this chapter makes use of the terms 'informal sector' and 'marginal sector'. We should define these terms and indicate what they mean in the Philippine context. Admittedly, if one reviews the appropriate literature,[15] these concepts are immediately recognized as fuzzy, at best slippery, constructs. In fact, some commentators[16] have suggested that the ambiguity of the terms is largely responsible for wide acceptance and usage. Feige (1990) prefers to use the umbrella concept 'underground economy' which accounts for four types of economic activities: 'illegal', 'unreported', 'unrecorded', and 'informal'; and proposed several specific methods for measuring these underground types.[17]

In Feige's taxonomy, the concept 'informal economy' is largely shaped by the influential work of the Peruvian Hernando de Soto who stressed an essentially legalist conception of informality. Thus, the informal economy comprises those activities 'that circumvent the costs and are excluded from the benefits and rights incorporated in the laws and administrative rules covering property relationships, commercial licensing, labor contracts, torts, financial credit and social security systems'.[18] While de Soto's legalist conception of the informal sector is dominant, it is by no means the only one available. Apart from legal status, informal economic processes have been defined in terms of production technology, non-normal profit rates, and the organization or control of production. Empirical studies typically use firm size as a proxy for the informal sector.

While Kelley's conceptualization of the informal sector is more limited,[19] he offers a number of key features of the informal sector:

1. Informal production is organized around an individual, family, or small group of friends. This means that the direct producer controls the production process and receives the net product. In contrast, formal sector workers earn a wage.
   a) Informal production is more labor-intensive than formal sector production.
   b) Informal enterprises typically violate regulatory statutes and pay negligible taxes.
   c) Incomes earned from informal activity are less than formal sector incomes.
2. While formal and informal output are similar, instances of product differentiation and imperfect substitutability abound. For instance, informal merchants sell goods in smaller quantities, offer different quality goods (inferior packaging), and occupy different locations (street corners) compared to formal retailers.

While the ability to circumvent regulation and taxation results in higher disposable incomes in the short run, higher wages, greater stability of incomes, and superior working conditions make formal sector employment more desirable than informal activity. Due to rapid population growth, economic stagnation, and the capital-intensive nature of formal production, the formal sector cannot employ the entire labor force. Workers who cannot find formal sector employment are forced to develop alternative income sources in the informal sector. In all, belonging to the informal sector connotes subordinate or inferior status *vis-à-vis* the formal sector.

These features of informal employment were validated by initial empirical work in the Philippines. A 1987 study conducted by the University of the Philippines School for Labor and Industrial Relations[20] established that urban informal activity was predominantly vending work concentrated on selling commodities which range from cooked or processed food to non-food items; that those engaged in this sector tended to be dominated by women and child labor; and that informal activity was essentially a coping mechanism in the face of economic adversity. Furthermore, the urban informal sector largely caters to the needs of the urban poor community.

On the other hand, the term 'marginal sector' does not often surface in development literature and appears to be used exclusively in the Philippines. Here, the poor are segmented according to severity of poverty. Extreme poverty is equated to marginalization; and marginalization in turn means either exclusion or inability to participate or compete in markets. Exclusion from the market is largely a function of deficiencies in education, health, and skills.

According to the *Philippine Human Development Report 1994*, those who belong to the marginal sector include 'subsistence producers such as upland farmers, small fisherfolk, landless farm workers, unskilled workers, scavengers in the cities, and others'.[21] The same report therefore locates the marginalized in the so-called 'core' or 'subsistence' poor, to differentiate them from the 'survival' poor, or those who are closer to escaping poverty (measured according to an income threshold). Accordingly, subsistence poverty refers to the 'inability to earn enough income to meet the minimum food requirements of a normal person (that is, 2000 calories per day)'. In 1991, there were 2.42 million Filipino families in subsistence poverty, or about one in every five Filipino households.[22]

Another work[23] divided the poor into three segments: the 'ultra poor'; the 'near ultra poor'; and the 'marginal poor'. The 'ultra poor' are those whose per capita expenditures fall short of the food threshold set by the National Statistical Coordination Board's Technical Working Group on Poverty Determination (NSCB-TWG). The 'near ultra poor' are those whose expenditures are greater than the food threshold but are less than the mean of the food threshold and the poverty threshold (or m). Lastly, the 'marginal poor' are those having expenditures greater than m but less than the poverty threshold. The 'ultra poor' therefore corresponds to the Philippine Human Development Report's (PHDR's) 'core' or subsistence poor while the 'marginal poor' is equivalent to the 'survival' poor.[24]

In effect, if we are interested in the impact of globalization and trade liberalization on the Philippine poor, the heterogeneity of the poor must be recognized from the very start. A distinction between urban poor and the rural poor must be made. While conditions of the urban poor are not exactly laudable, their lot is comparatively better than that of the rural poor. This fact will introduce some policy dilemmas since the urban poor have stronger political clout than the rural poor. As alluded to earlier by Nelson,[25] governments may be more compelled to buy off the opposition of urbanites than attend to the needs of the rural poor.

Impact of Economic Adjustment in the 1980s

By now, it is widely recognized that the 1980s formed an extraordinary and perverse era for Third World countries. In the Philippines, the contraction of the economy during the 1984-85 period represented the worst economic crisis since the Second World War and led to the demise of the Marcos regime in 1986.

Much of the discussion and agitation over economic adjustment during the 1980s had been its impact on the poor. But to be able to generalize on the matter means we have to know who the poor are, the roles they play in the national economy, and the extent of their vulnerability to economic adjustment. In general, this information is not generally available but the need for such knowledge is accentuated by the heterogeneity of the poor. In fact, the impact of economic adjustment on them depends largely on what they do, where they get their incomes, their position in the national economy.

Thus, the urban poor tends to bear many of the short- to medium-term adjustment costs as a result of public sector retrenchments, other frictional unemployment, and possible losses of food subsidies and other welfare services. With respect to the rural poor, much depends upon their access to land; whether those with land are producing cash crops (most likely to benefit from higher export prices) or local foods (whose relative prices may not change). If rural poor are net buyers of food (especially with imported inputs), they may be adversely affected by the reform. Lastly, the more they are integrated into the modern market economy, the more vulnerable would they be to the effects of the adjustment program. Given the poor's heterogeneity, one can make the 'soft' claim that some of the poor will gain and some of them will lose in the process of economic adjustment.

In view of the economic adjustment record in the 1980s, it can be concluded that the urban poor tends to bear many of the short- to medium-term costs of overall economic adjustment. Nevertheless, the rural poor are not invulnerable to adjustment costs. One danger that particularly affects the urban poor is the loss of jobs resulting from the decline of non-competitive manufacturing industries (to the extent that these are concentrated in urban locations). Rural jobs and incomes are also threatened by more competitive agricultural imports.

Another danger arises from the cutbacks in government spending associated with attempts to reduce absorption and public deficits. At first glance, trade liberalization appears to be unconnected to this peril. However, if one associates the lowering or elimination of border taxes on tradable goods with trade openness, then trade policy will certainly affect the level of public revenues and expenditures. The foregone trade revenues may likewise lead to decreased public spending. Government efforts to regain revenues through internal taxation (especially indirect taxes because of administrative considerations) will introduce complications. The comparative tax burdens of these new levies will have to be assessed. On the other hand, to the extent that freer trade could spur economic growth, growth in turn could increase public revenues. Of course, a lot depends upon the government's capacity to actually collect taxes and prevent tax fraud.

Most public spending cuts fall upon the economic services provided by the state and its investments in the economy's infrastructure, and the poor are liable to lose from these reductions. The government may tend to cut back on food subsidies as these often place severe burdens on the budget. This seems to be the case with the National Food Authority (NFA) wherein government financial support has been declining over the years. It is true that general food subsidies are an inefficient way to protect the poor during economic adjustment because those who can afford to pay market prices capture many of the benefits. The subsidies may also have the effect of depressing prices paid to farmers, who themselves are poor. Nonetheless, some of the poor (especially the urban poor) do gain from these subsidies and can be adversely affected by spending cuts.

There is also a serious danger that the quality of social services will be reduced during times of budgetary stringency, even when the share of social spending is protected. Government may hesitate to reduce the number of civil servants because of political considerations. They may instead prune the supporting expenses that make them productive and useful to the poor: medicines for clinics, books for schools, and transport for social workers. To the extent that farm produce prices increase in response to freer international trade, the poor are harmed if these increases will also translate into higher consumer prices for food products. Net food buyers (the urban poor and the subsistence farmers) among the poor will be adversely affected by this development. In other cases, severe land inequality also worsens the prospects of poor people to gain from, or respond to, liberalizing reforms. In particular, it raises the danger that reform will hurt the poor through more expensive food staples. Meanwhile, net food sellers, namely the rural non-poor, reap immediate gains from the food price rises.

The poor may also lose from any slowdown in economic growth that results from economic reform. As it is, any reform means abandonment of old ways and trying out of new ways. In the process, dysfunctions, discontinuities, and the costs of relearning may affect levels of production.

On balance, globalization and its concomitant market liberalization generates new challenges to policy makers especially in the developing world. One main challenge is to use globalization as a lever for local development by helping local firms and workers take advantage of the opportunities opened up by the global economy. This derives from awareness that the development of transnational networks of economic activities generates heightened possibilities for accessing new markets and resources, acquiring new skills and capabilities, and developing international competitive advantage. Another major challenge is to contain the social and economic imbalances resulting from globalization through spreading the costs and benefits of global integration throughout local industries and communities. Policy makers must respond to growing concerns that vigorous global connections might provide an unstable basis for local growth and development, and contribute to divide and fragment local industries and communities by marginalizing those actors that fail to adjust and develop strong global linkages.

The argument has been made that since the Philippines is a net agricultural exporter, it will benefit from GATT-UR agreement on agriculture. The opportunities for unfair trade in agricultural products, by way of developed country production supports and export subsidies will be clipped to the benefit of poorer countries that could not provide the same protection for lack of budgetary resources.

Since the Philippines does not have export subsidies and the level of production supports, such as fertilizer subsidies, credit programs, and the like, is well below the 10 per cent limit, much of the country's commitments under GATT-UR are in the area of market access. Specifically, the tariff reductions promised by the government may adversely affect crops presently protected by quantitative restrictions: rice, corn, sugar, livestock, meat products, coffee, cabbages, onions, and garlic. For this reason, much of the criticism and fears among organized peasants and other sectors were over a possible flood of cheaper and much subsidized agricultural products from the industrial economies and the possible loss of employment in the agricultural sector.[26]

As requested by the Philippine government, rice has been exempted over the next 10 years, although a minimum access requirement (from 1 per cent or about 60,000 metric tons in the first year of implementation to four per cent or about 240,000 metric tons at the end of 10 years) was imposed on the staple. However, the minimum access tariff has been set at 50 per cent, which is much higher than the historical equivalent tariff (at 30 per cent) resulting from the NFA trade monopoly, according to David.[27]

In addition to higher binding tariffs, the agreement still provides for a special safe-guard duty aimed against import surges, which may result in serious injury to domestic agricultural products. This measure, however, is only available to farm products whose non-tariff barriers had been converted to tariffs.

David also argues that large capitalists and farmers dominate the corn, sugar, poultry and livestock sectors and that the costs of trade liberalization will be borne mainly by the relatively high income group of landowners and capitalists.[28] The agricultural wage worker in these sectors may have to weigh the benefits of lower prices of these food products against possible loss of employment.[29] The point to be made is that even in these sectors, the costs of adjustment are not limited to capitalist and landowners alone.

GATT-UR has the potential of opening new markets for some Philippine products like pineapples, bananas, garments, and some electronic products. The gains from increased exports of pineapples and bananas will accrue largely to landowners and capitalist plantations if much of the production is done on large estates. Some of these gains may trickle down to sub-contracted farmers; but these farmers are definitely better off than the landless or agricultural wage worker.

A related fear is raised with respect to long-standing programs trying to promote self-sufficiency in rice and corn as part of the country's overall food security program. These fears were resurrected during the rice crisis in 1995. Several existing laws, including R.A. 7607 or the Magna Carta for Small Farmers, specifically prohibit the importation of agricultural products produced locally in sufficient quantities. In line with the government's GATT commitments, R.A. 8178, was passed on 28 March 1996 to remove all quantitative restrictions such as quotas and import bans on several agricultural products except rice.[30]

Orthodox economic theory argues that free international trade is beneficial to the participating economies and industries notwithstanding the fact that some groups of economic actors, whose incomes come from inefficient or uncompetitive industries may end up as losers. The interests of the poor farmer cannot be immediately determined without taking land ownership patterns into account. This point is best illustrated through an analysis of the stakeholders in the liberalization-of-sugar-imports debate.

Unlike other agricultural products, sugar imports did not face quantitative restrictions in the pre-Uruguay Round tariff regime. Technically, the industry should not have had a difficult time adjusting to tariffication (the transformation of import bans or quantitative restrictions into tariffs) unlike such crops as corn, rice, and coffee. Still, at the time of the Uruguay Round Treaty's ratification, the sugar industry was beset with severe productivity and competitiveness constraints.[31] Local sugar producers and millers—the so-called big players of the sugar industry—fear that these problems will not allow them to hurdle the competitive challenges of trade liberalization. They were the loudest proponents of high tariff protection for the industry. In contrast, sugar end-users like food processors and exporters welcomed the liberalized entry of cheaper imported sugar and the eventual reduction of sugar tariffs. They argued that the long-protected status of sugar meant higher production costs and reduced competitiveness for their products.

How did the small sugar farmers and workers (and their people's organization (PO)-non-governmental organization (NGO) champions) position themselves within the debate? Observers[32] noted the difficulties of this segment of the sugar industry to arrive at a consistent stance. The question was how to protect their interests without coddling the long-protected sugar barons. To the extent that cheaper sugar imports would result in cheaper processed food products (which they also consume), small sugar farmers and workers should be in favor of lower tariffs on sugar. Furthermore, they also understand that the sugar producers and millers have long resisted the redistribution of their sugar estates through agrarian reform. In fact, some advocacy NGOs have urged sugar workers' organizations to allow the accelerated liberalization of sugar imports on the premise that it will be so severe a disincentive that the sugar barons will give up their lands and agree to have them covered by the comprehensive agrarian reform program (CARP).

Peasant and farm worker groups agree that they should be cautious in opposing sugar import liberalization, because their protest will protect mainly big landed interests. However, they also saw the need to temper the drive to radically scale down sugar tariffs—as proposed by food processors—because hundreds of thousands of **their own** jobs and livelihoods dependent on the local sugar industry are also at stake.

The emerging position among the small players in the industry seems to be a balance between the two extremes posited by sugar barons and sugar end-users. The barons batted for as much as 133 per cent tariff on sugar imports, and end-users in turn proposed that present rates on sugar be reduced to 10 per cent. Both these positions are radical departures from the negotiated schedule in the GATT-UR, which has initial bound rates on sugar at 70-100 per cent, to be reduced to 50 per cent at the close of the Treaty's ten-year implementation period, the year 2004. Maintaining this negotiated pace of liberalization, while earnestly pursuing the redistribution of large sugar haciendas gives small sugar farmers and farm workers the breathing space they need so that their livelihoods, as well as their interest for asset reform, are protected under a framework of inevitable liberalization.

The Asian Economic Crisis and the Filipino Poor

The downside of today's globalization was illustrated by the Asian financial crisis. Though it is largely over, the human impact (especially on the poor and marginalized) is severe and likely to persist long after economic recovery. Balisacan observes that not much is known about the profile of population groups most adversely hit by the crisis.[33] Even less is known about the conditions making some population groups more vulnerable than others to a shock. He used the data collected by the 1998 Annual Poverty Indicator Survey (APIS) that included two questions pertaining to the Asian economic crisis. The first question inquires whether or not the household was affected by price increases, loss of jobs, reduced wages, and the El Niño phenomenon. The second question inquires about the responses of households and pertains only to those households affected by the crisis. Among Balisacan's findings regarding differential impact of the crisis on Filipino households include:

1. There were more households coming from the poorer households that were affected by price increases. For instance, 93.5 per cent of the households from lowest expenditure decile (poorest) compared to 84.7 per cent of the households from the highest decile (richest) were affected by price increases. The middle deciles seem to have been more affected by the loss of jobs within the country and by wage reduction.
2. Most households responded to the crisis by changing their eating patterns. However, the proportion decreases as one considers households from the upper spending deciles. For example, 56.7 per cent of the poorest households changed eating patterns while only 33.3 per cent of the richest households behaved similarly. Increasing working hours also seems to be a major response especially for households in the lower deciles. A disturbing trend is the greater proportion of households coming from the poorest decile (12.4 per cent compared to 1.2 per cent of the richest households) who took their children out of school.
3. The proportion of households that received assistance from relatives and friends was more than the proportion that received assistance from government. For instance, 16.5 per cent of the poorest households received assistance from other households while only 10.7 per cent of the households from the same bracket received government assistance. This indicates that crisis safety nets in the Philippines are more readily provided by private rather than by public or institutional sources.
4. The bulk of safety nets are provided by the extended family system but this will generate its own social impact. The increased dependency burden will further drain the resources of many families as laid-off and deprived individuals and families pass on part of their problems to their relatives. The higher dependency burden will add to the plight of the family head (and other income generating members of the family) as reduced real income (because of the crisis) is diminished further by additional dependents. There is also the additional burden placed on the housewife and mother. She has to find ways to accommodate more people on meager resources. She is also vulnerable to pressures to join the formal labor force in order to supplement family income.[34] Pressures on overseas contract workers will equally be great as their family members will increasingly rely on their remittances.

The above results suggest a possible link between a household's pre-crisis living standards and its response to a macroeconomic shock. Regressing responses to the APIS crisis-related questions and household attributes, including location and living-standard variables, Balisacan finds that the probability of households changing their eating patterns, taking children out of school, migrating to other places, and increasing working hours is inversely related with pre-crisis living standards.[35] This means that a macroeconomic shock tends to systematically hit hardest the poorest groups in society. In addition, compared to a household located in Metro Manila, an average household located in any other region (with the exception of some Mindanao regions) has a lower probability of receiving government assistance during a crisis.

The most obvious impact of the crisis on labor is to increase unemployment.[36] It has been argued, however, that the increase in unemployment will always represent an underestimation of the adverse effects of an economic downturn on labor. The increase in unemployment is just one, but most open or obvious of several consequences of the crisis. The additional phenomena of 'quality effect' (the move from higher-quality to lower quality employment), 'added-worker effect' (the forcible entry of students and housewives into the labor market), and 'discouraged-worker effect' (frustrated workers giving up the quest for work) imply that it is difficult to map changes in labor welfare onto changes reflected in labor force statistics. For a more complete assessment, the following should also be considered: increases in open unemployment; changes in labor force participation, both positive (added-worker effect) and negative (discouraged-worker effect); increase in visible and invisible underemployment; and increases in non-formal forms of employment (self-employed and unpaid family workers).[37]

The immediate welfare effect of job losses and shortened working hours is lower productivity and incomes. In addition, one should expect that the course of the crisis since 1998, combined with the effects of the El Niño drought will increase poverty incidence. This assertion is made not on the basis of direct evidence but inferentially from a consideration of aggregate data and econometric evidence. Past experience with crises has shown that severe economic downturns, through fall in jobs and rise in prices cause an increase in absolute poverty. It is estimated that the 2.3 per cent fall in per capita output in 1998 may have increased poverty incidence by at least two per cent.[38]

While nominal minimum wages increased in 1998, these figures declined in real terms. Minimum rates are set per region by regional wage boards; in 13 of the country's 16 regions, the wage hikes were lower than the inflation rates. Only in Southern Tagalog, Bicol, and Ilocos did workers enjoy increases in real minimum wages. Workers in Eastern Visayas and Southern Mindanao fared the worse with their nominal wages unchanged while prices increased by an average 8.3 per cent. The dismal compliance with minimum wage regulations compounds workers' woes. The proportion of firms inspected by the authorities and found to be violating minimum wage requirements increased from 48 per cent to 57 per cent during the 1997-98 period.[39]

One can investigate other direct measures of social welfare such as infant mortality, school enrollment rates that are highly sensitive to aggregate economic variables. In addition, economic downturns will also lead to cut downs on public entitlements by way of social services. In 1997, the central government imposed deep cuts of 25 per cent (termed 'mandatory savings') in the budgets of all agencies, including those involved in the provision of social services—education, nutrition, and health.

Remittances by overseas workers in 1997 showed no sharp declines, contrary to expectations that the crisis would immediately erode employment opportunities and remittances. Total remittances in 1997 rose by 16.6 per cent to US$5.7 billion, from US$4.3 billion in 1996. This increase is largely accounted for by remittances from the United States (U.S.) as remittances from crisis-affected Asia fell by 15 per cent, from $535 million in 1996 to $454 million a year later. However, there is a slight fall of 2.4 per cent for the first seven months of 1998 and a large drop of deployment to some Asian countries affected by the crisis (Hongkong, 22.9 per cent; South Korea, 50.7 per cent; Malaysia, 64.2 per cent; and Singapore, 10.1 per cent). These remittances should be seen as transfers by workers to distressed relatives and not an increase in aggregate welfare because these increased remittances were not due to higher current incomes on the part of their earners.

In terms of industrial relations, 1998 appears to have been characterized by less open worker-capitalist confrontations. As of November 1998, Department of Labor and Employment (DOLE) reported that only 726 new notices of strikes or lockouts were filed involving 179,552 workers. Compared to the previous year, these figures are 14.7 per cent lower in terms of number of notices and 20.8 per cent lower in terms of workers involved. The figures for **actual** strikes and lockouts have also declined relative to 1997 with a 34 per cent decrease in the number of workers involved and a 15 per cent decrease in the number of man-days lost. Apparently, the economic crisis resolved the usual problem of credibility in resolving deadlocks regarding the actual state of firms' finances. One of the important consequences of the crisis has been to compel both owners and workers to work out ways to weather the crisis by negotiating new arrangements. Many owners and managers have devised new ways to cut costs and still save job stability (through freeze-hiring, job rotation, reduction of fringe benefits). On the other hand, organized labor has demonstrated a great deal of flexibility and maturity, that is, wage restraint and even reduction. This *modus vivendi* may be threatened by crass behavior by employers as exemplified by their proposal to scrap the minimum wage law.[40]

Government tried to assist those displaced by the economic downturn. In February 1998, the DOLE initiated a tripartite forum that led to the signing of the 'Social Accord for Industrial Harmony and Stability'. The pact committed employers to exercise restraint in the retrenchment or rotation of workers and required unions to control strikes and other forms of work stoppages. Several smaller pacts were signed mostly in the economic zones, including the export processing zones in Mactan, Clark, Subic, and Bataan, and the Cavite-Laguna-Batangas-Rizal-Quezon (Calabarzon) growth area. The effectiveness of the pact was severely limited since only one major trade union federation—the Trade Union Congress of the Philippines (TUCP)—participated. Firms unilaterally closing shop without consulting the workers or the government and providing for separation benefits are still common (Tuaño, 1999).[41]

Government assistance to displaced workers was either inadequate or limited. As of March 1999, the DOLE has helped at most 55,000 workers only, roughly over a third of those displaced during 1998. Of this total, only about 8,500 workers were provided with jobs while the majority (25,000-30,000 workers) were assisted by way of emergency loans[42] and training-retraining programs.[43] Labor officials themselves admitted that retrenched workers are more interested in getting employed than participating in training programs. In addition, the DOLE was likewise hampered in its efforts by the mandatory 25 per cent budget cuts.

The current crisis laid bare once more the inadequacy—if not absence—of institutionally provided safety nets for labor. In the first place, the system for monitoring the social impact of crisis is virtually absent. Second, the bias of social policy making is revealed by the refusal to grant labor any publicly provided social insurance while there is no shortage of official concern in bailing out distressed firms with public funds. The effects of the crisis on labor have been severe but were mitigated by several factors. The inflationary impact of the crisis has not been great due to wage restraint and trade liberalization. Coping has taken the form of pragmatic acceptance of lower quality jobs or negotiated settlements. And lastly, intra-family transfers from overseas workers have served to sustain consumption and functioned as *de facto* social insurance.

It must be pointed out that labor has had to make painful adjustments to globalization even before the Asian crisis. In response to the stiffer competition engendered by a more liberalized economy, firms have responded with various cost-cutting measures, including internal and external labor flexibility measures.[44] The shift to more flexible working arrangements has resulted in a decline of labor's security of tenure. According to the DOLE, the number of workers under flexible labor contracts has increased both in absolute terms and as a proportion of the total non-agricultural employment. In 1997, some 598,000 workers, or 20.9 per cent of all employed workers were either part-time, casual, or contractual workers, a significant increase over 1989's 13.7 per cent, equivalent to 359,000 workers. Even when economic growth was proceeding robustly between 1992 and 1996, the ratio of non-agricultural workers under flexible contracts grew from 15.6 per cent to 18.4 per cent. Furthermore, the shift of employment growth to the services sector has also meant a fall in labor productivity, and consequently, workers' incomes. The level of workers' compensation has been declining over the past decade. The DOLE compensation index dropped from a high of 125 in 1988 to 108 in 1998. The drop was most pronounced in the manufacturing sector, with the index down from 128 to 74 during the same period.[45]

Lim[46] finds that the crisis seems to have increased labor force participation rates among the very young (15 to 19 years old) for both sexes and for females aged 20 to 24. Females are also moving out of jobs involving unpaid family work. Female labor participation in directly paid jobs may be seen by the family as a coping mechanism in the crisis since they have better employment opportunities in the service sector, especially in sales. Unfortunately, these types of work require the longest working hours among the occupation groups. In October 1998, women spent 51.3 and 50.3 hours on average per week as sales and service workers, respectively, compared to 46.8 and 48.8 hours, respectively for their male counterparts. Both female and male youths and unpaid family workers were increasingly joining the work force as the crisis deepened. At the same time, the crisis increased the unemployment rates and threw off both young and not so young workers. Most adversely affected were young workers, as male youths are severely unemployed in urban areas, while female youths are severely unemployed in the rural areas because of the El Niño phenomenon and the lack of rural development. Actually, unemployment rates have increased for both sexes and for all ages and all levels of educational attainment. But the hardest hit are young males in agriculture, manufacturing, and construction work. Since males benefited more than the females in the earlier growth period (especially in the late 1980s), the sharp contraction now in agriculture, manufacturing, and construction—all male-dominated sectors—reversed the trend and increased male unemployment rates. Females are moving from agriculture to the service sector or to overseas employment. Nonetheless, females are also significantly affected by unemployment, especially in the rural areas.

1. The increased labor force participation rates for young women and men during the crisis is accompanied by data showing significant declines in enrollment rates in high school for SY 1998-99. While these rates were growing by more than two per cent during the good years, there is a decline of 7.68 per cent for females and 6.63 per cent for males. Data also show a small decline in enrolment of female children at the elementary level that is not matched by declines in male enrolment, which in fact increased substantially in SY 1998-99 (though there was a shift from private schools to public schools). This means that many female children were not sent to elementary school. It would be interesting to find out if the decline in elementary school enrolment of female children is related to the need for unpaid family housework as more young adult females join the formal labor force.

2. The crisis had a significant impact on unemployment. In urban areas, male unemployment rates went up from 9.6 per cent in October 1996, to 11 per cent in October 1997 and to 13.1 per cent in October 1998. Correspondingly, female unemployment rates in urban areas went up from 8.9 per cent in October 1996, to 9.9 per cent in October 1997 and to 10.7 per cent in October 1998. Rural unemployment rates also went up from seven per cent to almost nine per cent in October 1998 for females, from 4.5 per cent to 6.6 per cent for males in the same period. While unemployment for both females and males has increased for all age groups, most especially hit are the young, especially youths aged 15 to 19, followed by those aged 20 to 24, and then by those aged 25 to34. Unemployment of males aged 15 to 19 went up from 19.4 per cent in October 1996, to 30.5 per cent in October 1998. Unemployment for females aged 15 to 19 went up from 16.4 per cent in October 1996, to 22.3 per cent in 1998.

3. While male unemployment hit harder in urban areas, female and male unemployment were equally affected in the rural areas by weather disturbances. The male unemployment rate in rural areas went up from 4.5 per cent in October 1997 to 6.6 per cent in October 1998, while female unemployment went up from seven per cent to 8.9 per cent during the same period. Again, the hardest hit were young people aged 15 to 19 and 20 to 24, especially females. The unemployment for young females in rural areas had gone up for those aged 15-19 from 15 per cent in October1997 to 19.4 per cent in October 1998. Those aged 20 to 24 saw their

unemployment rate shoot from 18 per cent in October 1997 to 25.4 per cent in October 1998. It was the pool of unemployed women in rural and urban areas, as well as unemployed males in urban areas, that provided the migrants looking for work abroad or in large urban conglomerates. However, it is clear that weather disturbances have also caused significant work dislocation in the rural and agricultural areas.

Perceptions on Globalization

Given the impact of the Asian financial crisis, it is not surprising that popular opinion in the Philippines has apparently turned against globalization. A rough estimate of the Filipino public's response to globalization may be represented by results of a September 1999 survey of public opinion on possible changes in the Philippine Constitution. To avoid the suspicion that plans to amend the charter were motivated principally by self-serving motives (such as the lifting or extension of term limits for the President and other elective officials), the administration of President Joseph Estrada initiated an amendment drive called Constitutional Correction for Development (or CONCORD). The said plan intends to limit changes to the economic provisions of the charter with the objective of making it more attuned to the challenges of globalization.

Concretely, the Estrada plan intended to amend the charter by lifting the prohibitions on ownership of land by foreigners and 100 per cent foreign ownership of public utilities, mass media, and other strategic industries.

While the September 1999 survey of Pulse Asia indicated that most Filipinos were against amending the Constitution in general, it was precisely the proposed economic amendments that Filipinos found most unacceptable. While 77 per cent of the survey respondents were against extending the term limits of elected national and local officials, a heftier 92 per cent did not want foreigners to own land in the country. In addition, 88 per cent did not want foreigners to own public utilities or mass media companies while 81 per cent registered opposition to a proposal allowing foreigners to own retail companies in the country.[47] The profile of the respondents suggested that these opinions were held strongly by the poorer sectors of society. Majority (at 64 per cent) of the survey respondents rated themselves as poor or very poor, with nearly half of the total (45 per cent) saying their quality of life in the last year deteriorated rather than improved (19 per cent).[48]

The attitude against alien ownership of land appeared to be common across income classes.[49] Of the six per cent of the survey respondents who rated themselves very poor, 94 per cent were not in favor; 92 per cent of those who rated themselves poor (57 per cent of the respondents) agreed with them. The seven per cent who rated themselves well off or wealthy, were of the same opinion. Strong differences in opinion among the income classes were more pronounced with respect to foreign ownership of media and retail companies. While 93 per cent of the very poor did not approve of foreign ownership of media firms (foreign ownership of retail companies), only 84 per cent of the wealthy had the same opinion.

Fieldwork was undertaken in Cebu Province in order to gain insights into the impact of globalization and rapid economic change on the security of local communities. Cebu was chosen based on the following considerations: (1) it has, together with the progressive provinces of Negros Occidental, Iloilo, and Leyte, the greatest numbers of the poorest rural families; and (2) the industrial activity in Cebu City (and its environs) is apparently transforming it as the hub of an emergent sub-national economic zone that encompasses Northern Mindanao and Central Visayas.

Guiding the fieldwork was an initial hypothesis that industrialization was in the main beneficial, or was perceived to be beneficial, to urban poor people and communities in terms of formal and informal jobs generated by industrial activity. In addition, we likewise hypothesized that industrialization was in the main detrimental to the human and community security of marginalized rural folk.

The relationship between globalization and industrialization has first to be spelled out. As we understand it, globalization is principally a process of international economic integration intensified by advances in communications and information technology. Of course, globalization will have repercussions in spheres other than the economy—to include the political, social, and cultural spheres. We argue that globalization in general stimulates all sorts of economic activities, including industrial activity and services, as mobile capital seek higher returns from so-called emerging markets. Where mobile capital goes will depend on the quality and competitiveness of immobile factors peculiar to a particular location. These immobile factors include the **hard** ones—land, roads, and bridges; information and communications systems; and the like; and the **soft** ones such as quality of labor force, governmental institutions, and contract enforcement and public service delivery systems.

The burden of attracting mobile capital falls squarely on immobile factors. The ultimate competitiveness of each location depends upon the attractiveness of the package of immobile factors it offers. In the contemporary globalizing world, competition for mobile capital among and within developing economies has been confined to providing more attractive **hard** immobile factors. Demand for land to site factories, power and other utilities, new roads, ports, and other infrastructure, and service facilities such as high-class residential villages, hotels and golf courses is thus stimulated all over the developing world as capital became more mobile. In countries where the land frontier has been reached, the increased demand for land will consequently stimulate a political contest for occupied land, water, and air quality. In many instances, marginalized communities in either the rural or urban areas would lose tenure over the lands, foreshore lands, hills, and dwellings they occupy as the commercial value of the latter is enhanced by greater economic activity.

The fieldwork was undertaken in the towns of Sibonga, Carcar, and San Fernando in Cebu Province. These towns are locales for either proposed or existing industrial projects. Sibonga is the site of the proposed $300 million Global Cement Inc. (GCI) factory, a joint venture between Taiwanese, Japanese, and Filipino investors. Carcar is the site of existing factories of the A.C. Steel Corporation and the Genu Seaweed Manufacturing Corporation. San Fernando is host to another existing cement factory operated by the Grand Cement Corporation.

Development and Security in Southeast Asia

Interviews with key informants in these areas revealed communities divided by the industrial ventures. The first divide was between the community and the industrial venture itself while the second divide was within the host community. For the existing factories in Carcar and San Fernando, a significant number of local residents expressed the desire for their closure or relocation on the ground that the facilities were polluting (through the emission of cement dust and bad smells) and were therefore harmful to the health of the community folk as well as their produce. They likewise raised suspicions that the factories were operating illegally without the needed Environmental Compliance Certificate (ECC) from the Department of Environment and Natural Resources (DENR). In San Fernando, local residents were circulating a petition for the closure of the cement factory. Apart from pollution, they complained that the quarrying operations of the plant had led to flooding and destruction of their crops.

Some of these fears may be more imagined than real. In an interview with the manager of the A.C. Steel factory in Carcar, he revealed that the factory was not yet fully operational and, therefore, could not have caused the alleged pollution and consequent diseases. He did admit though that in testing their machines and equipment, bad smells were emitted. But he claimed that the bad smell is 'just normal' and that the factory had complied with all anti-pollution regulations and other laws and has been awarded an ECC by government authorities. In addition, local residents employed by the steel factory do not share these concerns.

Nonetheless, the divisions within the affected communities were quite real. This is quite apparent in the town of Sibonga where the cement plant proposed by the GCI has yet to be constructed. The town of Sibonga is a fourth class municipality with an annual budget of only P13 million. The cement factory will be located in Barangay Bahay.[50] Most, if not all of the local officials of Sibonga were in favor of the proposed project because of the potential revenues it could bring to the town's coffers. In fact, the municipal agricultural office certified that the lands in Barangay Bahay were not prime agricultural areas and that their crop yields do not reach the ideal productivity level due to poor soil fertility and inadequate irrigation systems. This certification was necessary to allow the use of the land for non-agricultural purposes. Of course, several farmers disputed the authenticity of this certification.

A great deal of the fears voiced by the local residents regarding the pollution that could come from the cement factory was the result of vicarious experience gained from neighboring Carcar and its own cement factory, in turn believed to be owned by a consortium of which GCI is just a part. Some of these fears were allayed by repeated assurances by the Global management that of the total project cost of $300 million $30 million will be spent for anti-pollution devices.

To implement its project, GCI had to buy land and displace some of the local residents. The land will be used not as site for the factory itself but will also be mined for raw materials. Dispute again attended the land acquisition process. The president of the Sibonga Federation of Peasant Organizations said that a number of affected farmers felt cheated. They heard that GCI agreed to pay as much as P250 per square meter but the brokers offered the farmers only seven to ten pesos per square meter. These same farmers also expressed pessimism over the possibility that the cement factory will eventually employ them. Given the high capitalization of the proposed factory, they believe that the factory owners will not invest money to train them to operate sophisticated machinery. The peasants believed the factory owners would prefer to import skilled workers.

To generate additional support for the industrial venture, GCI executed a deed of undertaking (DOU) with the local government that promised to provide, among other things, free home lots (100 square meters for *bona fide* tenant farmers and 80 square meters for undocumented tenants), electrification of the relocation site, and free medicines for affected residents. The displaced farmers will receive titles to their respective home lots with the cost of titling to be shouldered by GCI. The same document also promised that every relocated household is assured of one job in the factory. As a result, a significant number of the farmers who initially were lukewarm to the project agreed to sell the tenancy rights over the lands needed by the cement factory.

The efforts undertaken by GCI to inform and socially prepare local residents affected by economic change is quite instructive. It may be the most important factor that could explain the difference between the positive reception accorded to it by a sizeable portion of the Sibonga population and the relatively hostile atmosphere endured by the industrial ventures in Carcar and San Fernando. To the knowledge of our key informants, the industrial ventures in these two towns did not mount any similar social preparation campaign. Most likely, these smaller ventures were deterred by the short-run cost considerations.

The efforts undertaken by GCI so far were designed to win the trust of the host community and affected residents. It remains to be seen, however, whether the promises made in the deed of undertaking will be redeemed. Financial costs of the project will definitely increase as these promises are fulfilled. On the other hand, costs of a different nature will be borne if the same promises were not kept. Of particular concern to the affected residents is the promise of employment in the proposed cement factory. Not a few are skeptical that this promise will be made good. They believe that investment in education and training will have to be done so that they, or their offspring may be employable in industry.

Policy Challenges and Issues

The key policy question concerns the most contentious issue in development theory and policy over the past three or four decades: the relationship between trade regimes, growth, and inequality. Globalization could not be stopped; to the extent that it has beneficial effects, it should not be stopped. As the United Nations Development Programme (UNDP) (1999) counsels, the challenge is to find the appropriate rules and institutions applicable at various levels—local, national, global—that could preserve the advantages of world markets and competition as well as ensure that globalization works for people, specially the poor.[51]

If globalization were to benefit the poor in any given society, then it is necessary to provide for ways of increasing their participation in sectors of production that are expected to grow. What resource would the poor have in abundance except their labor power? In effect, any economic change that will utilize more and more of their labor will ultimately improve the lives of poor people. In a globalizing world, mobile capital will be attracted to places where the labor force possesses the appropriate skills and training, among other things. Investment in education and human capital appears to be the key measure. If lessons are to be learned, we should do so from the East Asian economies that have experienced rapid growth over three decades and which have also reduced income inequality. According to Birdsall and associates (1995), policies adopted by the East Asian states that reduced poverty and income inequality, such as emphasizing high quality basic education also stimulated economic growth. Rapid growth and reduced inequality in turn led to higher demand for, and supply of education.[52] In effect, investment in education is key to sustained growth, because it contributes directly through enhanced productivity and because it reduces income inequality.

While not to be ignored, a pronounced bias in favor of the **hard** components of economic development such as roads, bridges, irrigation works, and other public works will only further enable those who are already active participants in the economy. The best way to ensure active economic participation of poor people from both the urban centers and rural areas is to develop their productive capabilities. Central to this capability building process is the state of their health, nutrition, and education. The resources of the state must be allocated towards this direction.

However, a better understanding of the need to utilize both market and asset reform in reducing poverty and stimulating economic growth must be reached. Reformers in favor of redistribution in the past often underestimated the dependence of their proposals on more robust and freer markets. As a result, even if the poor obtained some education or land, the products and incomes from these new resources were restricted by market or price distortions. Conversely, the complementary role of state redistributive reform has been denigrated by market reformers since the 1980s simply because the state has fallen into disfavor. Free market advocates have eschewed redistribution largely because states, which they see as inferior institutions, oversee these efforts. What they overlook is the fact that states are the principal, though not the only agencies that carry out reforms, including market reforms. These market reformers fail to see that people with no proper nutrition, education, employable skills, or land are often unable to capitalize on new market opportunities.

Efforts must be undertaken to develop strong linkages between local institutions such as governments, entrepreneurs, community-based employers' and laborers' associations to reinforce social ties within the local community. Such strong linkages will help generate a local dynamic of continuous learning and innovation that will enable local communities to respond positively to the challenges of globalization. It is believed that these linkages are particularly important at the local level, where globalization pays more, or hits harder, and where consensus about collective interests may be easier to achieve. In this manner, the local community can acquire new knowledge and competencies and at the same time ensure that the gains from learning are distributed on a fair basis among local actors.

Short-term relief for the poor and other adversely affected social groups and economic sectors must be provided in times of crisis. Funds for this purpose could be raised from both private and public sources (domestic and international) and must be administered by multi-stakeholder mechanisms as one way to repair earlier damage to community trust and cohesion.

However, the technical, moral, and political difficulties attendant to any anti-poverty program must not be glossed over. To be effective, these programs need to hurdle technical problems. Cost-effective and efficient targeting of scarce resources to achieve poverty reduction objectives requires sound information about the poor and their circumstances—who they are, where they live, what economic activities they are involved in, what socio-economic conditions, they face, etc. It is technically challenging to study and reach the poor. All governments, in whatever society, find it difficult to reach the poor (more so the ultra-poor) effectively. They exist on the margins of society, are unorganized, poorly educated and fed, and hardly articulate. In addition, they are often suspicious not only of the state and its officials but also of strangers (including researchers). Some of them do not stay put and are frequently mobile. A great number of the poor are NPAs, not insurgents, but people with no permanent addresses. In many cases, their mobility is a function of a strong dislike against being located, observed, and studied. While some of them are criminals, others are running away from the law because they have been victimized by and continue to be vulnerable to predatory agents of the law. For others, their absence within the radarscope of policymakers, do-gooders, developers, and the like is a good thing in that they are left alone and undisturbed.

Thus, even in the presence of a strong political commitment, protecting the poor is difficult. To make things worse, the daunting technical requirements may erode political determination.

This means that only efforts based on careful planning and determined implementation are likely to be effective. Often a starting point is to find out more about the economic and social characteristics of the poor and vulnerable and how they fit into the economy. Only when government can identify the target groups and trace how different policy measures affect them shall it be able to provide effective service and assistance and safeguard against the danger that these same benefits are actually captured by the 'not-so-poor' or even the well-off.

Of course, calls for more research can be used as an excuse to postpone substantive action indefinitely. However, when basic information simply does not exist, it is difficult to see how an effective package of measures to protect the poor can be put in place. The proper approach may be to act on the basis of what is already known while striving to know more so we can improve on the effectiveness of our actions.

However, dilemmas of a non-technical nature must be duly considered. First, the poor are not only materially deprived; they are also weak politically. Furthermore, the heterogeneity of the poor also results in power differentials across the poor classes and groups. For instance, the urban poor, whose lot is generally better than that of the rural poor, are generally more influential than their rural counterparts. Predictably, politicians and other resource allocators may and will prove to be more responsive to urban poor demands. Power differentials across the poor may likewise result in the disposition of resources for the 'not-so-poor' rather than for the 'ultra-poor'.

Any reforming government will have to make a better go at the social marketing of economic reform. One cannot ignore the obvious truth that in most cases the argument for free markets is too intricate to be intelligible or convincing to the general public, not least to those adversely affected by the reform. To be sure, the task is made more difficult in a social situation where mass understanding of economics is poor, where memories of the social costs of earlier economic reform episodes are quite vivid, and where populist politicians can find a ready and appreciative audience.

To be sure, political support for initially unpopular reforms which bear their intended beneficial fruits will materialize after the fact. Reforming governments will have to contend with the Olson syndrome—that the beneficiaries of economic reform are not as inclined to demonstrate their support compared to those who would be adversely affected by change. But reformers need not just accept the existence of this syndrome. Governments may have to actively seek out the sectors benefited by reform, solicit their support, and communicate this support to the rest of society in a credible and sustained manner.   The basic point is, as Montes puts it, **if economic reform meets the opposition of the politically powerful, the political support of the supposed beneficiaries should always be welcome.**[53]

To broaden political support further, democratic governments will have to protect adequately the vulnerable during the adjustment period.   These efforts must be undertaken with the myriad of private organizations (POs, NGOs, volunteer groups) that are currently working within these sectors in order to build trust, strengthen capabilities, and reduce dependence. It may even be argued that government assistance to the marginal groups who have never enjoyed state support before may enjoy greater political returns compared to a strategy of buying off the opposition of groups that will sustain real and permanent losses due to reform and will, therefore, oppose them even if they are compensated. Nevertheless, for this political support to materialize, these same marginal groups must likewise be empowered to participate in the political arena.

Assistance to the poor also introduces other moral and political dilemmas. A government may have to make hard decisions in its pro-poor policy and program mix. It may make sense to target assistance to the near-poor or marginal poor (those who are just below the poverty line) than to the ultra-poor despite moral imperatives. The marginal benefits of the assistance may be more substantial enabling the escape of the former from poverty instead of simply alleviating the conditions of the ultra-poor without decreasing overall poverty. For example, if the poorest are malnourished and sickly (and most of them are), they may not be able to take advantage of increased public expenditure on education. In addition, it also costs more—in terms of resources and administrative time—to reach the poorest and raise them above the poverty line. Furthermore, the near-poor have greater political clout than the ultra-poor. To this end, it will also be easier to mobilize the political support of those groups who were able to escape from poverty through state assistance.

The moral and political conundrum is further complicated if economic reform may bring, even if only in the short-run, previously non-poor groups, such as displaced industrial or public sector workers, close to or below the poverty line. These 'new' poor are obviously more vocal and better organized and will demand for safety nets during reform even if they are less needy. At times, the most politically viable means of reaching the poor may be with programs that simultaneously benefit the 'popular' or middle groups of society, who may be losing more during economic adjustments than the ultra-poor. But then again, governments will have to make sure that enough resources are available to meet this purpose. Apart from accessing external assistance, developing country governments must enhance their capacities to collect internal revenue, to reduce waste, and to spend efficiently.

To carry liberalization further, democracies must build political coalitions for reform as well as improve their governance. State capacities must be improved and reforms must show positive results. Reforming democracies must likewise educate the general public and mobilize newly emergent beneficiaries of freer markets. Democratic methods and enhanced state capacities will enable democracies to sustain market reform in the long run.

The importance of including actors who are formerly excluded from the benefits of economic change to democratization cannot be ignored. The marginalization of the poor in both the economic and political arenas must end for market reforms and democracy to triumph. Then and only then can we claim that human security has been enhanced. When and where the security of the individual is ensured, that of the state and the international community is similarly assured.

Notes

1   Research assistance was provided by Catherine Ramos of the University of the Philippines School of Economics. Of course, the opinions and conclusions as well as the errors contained in this chapter are entirely those of the author.

2   Hernandez, C. (1996), 'Political Reform for Global Competitiveness: The Philippines in the 1990s', in W. S. Thompson and W. Villacorta (eds), *The Philippine Road to NIChood*, De La Salle University and Social Weather Stations, Manila, pp.119.

3   Acharya, A., Soesastro, H., Gochoco-Bautista, M S., and Evans, P. (1995), 'Report of the Task Force on Globalization and Security', *Development and Security in Southeast Asia: Task Force Reports*, Canadian Consortium on Asia Pacific Security (CANCAPS) Reports, Centre for International and Security Studies, York University, North York, Ontario, Canada, pp.1.

4   United Nations Development Programme (UNDP) (1999), *Human Development Report 1999*, Oxford University Press, New York.

5   The discussion in this section takes off from Mendoza (1996).

6   Krugman, Paul and Obstfeld, M. (1988), *International Economics: Theory and Policy*, McGraw Hill, New York.

7   This apparent irrationality is called the Olson syndrome after the economist Mancur Olson, who made the insight that collective or political action is not usually in the interest of any individual belonging to a group even if beneficial to the group as a whole. See Olson (1965) for a fuller discussion.

8   Root, H. (1996), *Small Countries, Big Lessons: Governance and the Rise of East Asia*, Oxford University Press (China) Ltd., Hongkong; Przeworski, A. (1992), 'The Neoliberal Fallacy', *Journal of Democracy*, vol. 3, no. 3, pp. 45-59; Dahl, R. (1992), 'Why Markets are not Enough', *Journal of Democracy*, vol. 3, no. 3, pp. 82-9.

9   Nelson, J. (1992), 'Poverty, Equity, and the Politics of Adjustment', in S. Haggard and R. Kaufman (eds), *The Politics of Economic Adjustment*, Princeton University Press.

10   Cornia, G. A., Jolly, R., and Stewart, F. (eds). (1987), *Adjustment with a Human Face*, Oxford University Press, New York.

11   Robinson, J. (1962), *Economic Philosophy*, Cambridge University Press.

12   A total of P32 billion was allocated in the 1995 budget for GATT-related projects especially in agriculture, the sector believed to be hit the hardest by the Uruguay Round agreements. Some 500,000 irrigated hectares and 10,000 kilometers of farm-to-market roads are targeted over the 1995-1996 period. For more details, see Payumo (1994).

13   Monsod, S. (1998), 'The War Against Poverty: A Status Report', in D. Timberman (ed.), *The Philippines: New Directions in Domestic Policy and Foreign Relations*, ISEAS and The Asia Society, Singapore, pp. 85-110; Balisacan, A. (1999b), *Poverty Profile in the Philippines: An Update and Reexamination of Evidence in the Wake of the Asian Crisis*, University of the Philippines School of Economics (unpublished manuscript).

14   Monsod (1998) explains this seeming anomaly. Areas in the Philippines are classified as urban when population density reaches a certain level, even if activities in the area remain predominantly agricultural. Thus, dependence on subsistence agriculture is the biggest contribution to poverty in both rural and urban areas.

15   Feige, E. (1990), 'Defining and Estimating Underground and Informal Economies: The New Institutional Economics Approach', *World Development*, vol. 18, no. 7, pp. 989-1002; Kelley, B. (1994), 'The Informal Sector and the Macroeconomy: A Computable General Equilibrium Approach for Peru', *World Development*, vol. 22, no. 9, pp. 1393-1411.

16   Peattie, L. (1987), 'An Idea in Good Currency: The Informal Sector', *World Development*, vol. 15, 7, pp. 851-60.

17   Feige, 'Defining and Estimating Underground and Informal Economies: The New Institutional Economics Approach', 1990.

18   Cited in *Ibid.*, pp.993.

19   Kelley (1994) excludes subsistence production, or production from one's own use, from the informal sector. If applied to the Philippine situation, this will most likely exclude a sizable amount of economic activity we would normally classify as part of the informal sector.

20   Gatchalian, J., Gatchalian, M., Almeda, C., and Barranco, N. (1987), *The Nature, Consequences, and Prospects of Underground Employment in the Four Major Cities of Metro Manila*, University of the Philippines School for Labor and Industrial Relations, Quezon City.

21   UNDP, *Philippine Human Development Report 1994*, 1994, pp.2.

22   *Ibid.*

23   Balisacan, A. (1995), 'Targeting Transfers to the Poor: The Case of Food Subsidies', in *Essays in Social Science and Development: A Tribute to Gelia T. Castillo*, Philippine Institute of Development Studies, Makati.

24   *Ibid.*

25   Nelson, 'Poverty, Equity, and the Politics of Adjustment', 1992.

26   A sample of peasant-sector critiques of GATT-UR include Canlas (1994), 'PabiGATT: NGO-PO Statement on the General Agreement on Tariffs and Trade', and Montemayor (1994).

27 David, C. (1995), 'GATT-UR and Philippine Agriculture: Facts and Fallacies', in *Essays in Social Science and Development: A Tribute to Gelia T. Castillo*, Philippine Institute of Development Studies, Makati.

28 *Ibid.*

29 *Ibid.*

30 Aquino, C. Jr. (1998), *When Tariffs Rule: Philippine Smallholder Agriculture under the GATT/WTO Tariff and Trade Liberalization Regime*, Philippine Peasant Institute, Quezon City.

31 Philippine sugar is most expensive in the ASEAN region. In 1995, the going rate was already PhP29 per kilo. In contrast, ASEAN countries sold their sugar at an average of PhP11 per kilo. In addition, ASEAN countries outpaced the Philippines in terms of stability of production and supply (Aquino, 1998).

32 *Ibid.*

33 Balisacan, *Poverty Profile in the Philippines: An Update and Reexamination of Evidence in the Wake of the Asian Crisis*, 1999.

34 Lim, J. (1998), *The Social Impact and Responses to the Current East Asian Economic and Financial Crisis: The Philippine Case*, country paper prepared for the United Nations Development Programme, Regional Bureau for Asia and the Pacific.

35 Balisacan, *Poverty Profile in the Philippines: An Update and Reexamination of Evidence in the Wake of the Asian Crisis*, 1999.

36 de Dios (1999) explains how a financial crisis leads to a general economic crisis or how the money problem becomes a problem for people without money. The first impact of the financial turmoil comes from the large devaluation of the peso. From this, there were two mechanisms that transformed the currency turmoil into a general economic crisis: the financial and the real. Financially, the devaluation of the peso caused liquidity problems for corporations, which borrowed heavily in dollars. These borrowers need debt relief from their bank creditors. However, most banks are now unwilling to lend new money during the crisis. The result then was that credit was rationed, being denied to both distressed and otherwise healthy firms. Credit rationing during a crisis has the bad effect that even potentially good borrowers are penalized. Crises produced uncertainty and banks are constrained to raise their lending rates for everybody regardless of relative creditworthiness. How is the crisis transmitted to the real economy? Credit shortage deprives firms of working capital or confronts them with higher interest rates. This causes firms to reduce output, which leads to a fall in employment. Or the rise of interest rates and credit shortage will lead to a fall in investments and a fall in aggregate demand and total output.

37 *Ibid.*

38 *Ibid.*

39 Tuaño, P. (1999), 'Labor: Bearing the Crisis Cross', *Politik*, vol. 6, no. 1, August.

40 de Dios, E. (1999), *The Economic Crisis and Its Impact on Labor*, Oxfam and the Philippine Center for Policy Studies, Quezon City.

41 Tuaño, 'Labor: Bearing the Crisis Cross', 1999.

42 The low figure is the number of beneficiaries facilitated by the Department of Labor and Employment (DOLE) while the high figure is the actual number of beneficiaries provided loans by the Social Security System (SSS), the agency which actually provided the P200 million funding for the emergency loan program (Conferido, 1999).

43 Details of the various government programs to assist retrenched workers are discussed in Conferido (1999).

44 Internal flexibility refers to measures that afford a more manageable deployment of the firm's regular employees to respond to changing work demands. Among these measures include the use of multi-skilling, job rotation, part-time work, overtime work, flexible shift work, voluntary or forced retirement, compressed work week, and flexible wage systems. External flexibility refers to measures that enable firms to change the number of regular workers during unstable business periods. These include sub-contracting, short-term employment contracts, and agency hiring (Conferido, 1999).
45 Tuaño, 'Labor: Bearing the Crisis Cross', 1999.
46 Lim, J. (1999), *The Effects of Globalization and the East Asian Countries on Employment of Women and Men: The Philippine Case*, University of the Philippines School of Economics (unpublished manuscript).
47 Gonzales, S. O. (1999), 'Majority says no to Cha-cha', *Philippine Daily Inquirer*, 14 October, pp.1 & 20.
48 Jimenez-David, R. (1999), 'It's the economy, Sir', *Philippine Daily Inquirer*, 14 October, pp.9.
49 A noted Manila columnist warns against a simplistic reading of the survey results on this question. He asserts that both the Filipino businessmen and public perceive President Estrada's CONCORD 'as an opening wedge to allow Chinese, domestically and in Asia, to expand their ownership and control of land and the public utilities' rather than an even-handed invitation to all foreigners (Doronilla, A. (1999) 'New currency for the Filipino First Policy', *Philippine Daily Inquirer*, 5 November, pp.9).
50 In the Philippines, local government units are classified according to income class. The barangay is a sub-administrative unit of a municipal government.
51 UNDP, *Human Development Report 1999*, 1999.
52 Birdsall, N., Ross, D., and Sabot, R. (1995), 'Inequality and Growth Reconsidered: Lessons from East Asia', *World Bank Economic Review*, vol. 9, no. 3, pp. 477-508.
53 Montes, M. (1994), 'What is Wrong with Structural Adjustment Programs?', *Issues and Letters*, vol. 3, nos. 4-5, January-February.

References

Acharya, A., Soesastro, H., Gochoco-Bautista, M S., and Evans, P. (1995), 'Report of the Task Force on Globalization and Security', *Development and Security in Southeast Asia: Task Force Reports*, Canadian Consortium on Asia Pacific Security (CANCAPS) Reports, Centre for International and Security Studies, York University, North York, Ontario, Canada, pp. 1-47.
Aquino, C. Jr. (1998), *When Tariffs Rule: Philippine Smallholder Agriculture under the GATT/WTO Tariff and Trade Liberalization Regime*, Philippine Peasant Institute, Quezon City.
Balisacan, A. (1995), 'Targeting Transfers to the Poor: The Case of Food Subsidies', in *Essays in Social Science and Development: A Tribute to Gelia T. Castillo*, Philippine Institute of Development Studies, Makati.
Balisacan, A. (1999), *Poverty Profile in the Philippines: An Update and Reexamination of Evidence in the Wake of the Asian Crisis*, University of the Philippines School of Economics (unpublished manuscript).
Birdsall, N., Ross, D., and Sabot, R. (1995), 'Inequality and Growth Reconsidered: Lessons from East Asia', *World Bank Economic Review*, vol. 9, no. 3, pp. 477-508.
Canlas, C. (1994), 'GATT Issues, Gut Issues', *Kasarinlan*, vol. 9, no. 4, pp. 25-44.

Conferido, R. (1998), 'Human Resource and Social Impacts of the Financial Crisis: The Philippine Experience', *Philippine Labor Review*, vol. 23, no. 1, pp. 27-50.

Cornia, G. A., Jolly, R., and Stewart, F. (eds). (1987), *Adjustment with a Human Face*, Oxford University Press, New York.

Dahl, R. (1992), 'Why Markets are not Enough', *Journal of Democracy*, vol. 3, no. 3, pp. 82-9.

David, C. (1995), 'GATT-UR and Philippine Agriculture: Facts and Fallacies', in *Essays in Social Science and Development: A Tribute to Gelia T. Castillo*, Philippine Institute of Development Studies, Makati.

de Dios, E. (1999), *The Economic Crisis and Its Impact on Labor*, Oxfam and the Philippine Center for Policy Studies, Quezon City.

Feige, E. (1990), 'Defining and Estimating Underground and Informal Economies: The New Institutional Economics Approach', *World Development*, vol. 18, no. 7, pp. 989-1002.

Gatchalian, J., Gatchalian, M., Almeda, C., and Barranco, N. (1987), *The Nature, Consequences, and Prospects of Underground Employment in the Four Major Cities of Metro Manila*, University of the Philippines School for Labor and Industrial Relations, Quezon City.

Hernandez, C. (1996), 'Political Reform for Global Competitiveness: The Philippines in the 1990s', in W. S. Thompson and W. Villacorta (eds), *The Philippine Road to NIChood*, De La Salle University and Social Weather Stations, Manila, pp.118-38.

Kelley, B. (1994), 'The Informal Sector and the Macroeconomy: A Computable General Equilibrium Approach for Peru', *World Development*, vol. 22, no. 9, pp. 1393-1411.

Krugman, Paul and Obstfeld, M. (1988), *International Economics: Theory and Policy*, McGraw Hill, New York.

Lim, J. (1998), *The Social Impact and Responses to the Current East Asian Economic and Financial Crisis: The Philippine Case*, country paper prepared for the United Nations Development Programme, Regional Bureau for Asia and the Pacific.

Lim, J. (1999), *The Effects of Globalization and the East Asian Crisis on Employment of Women and Men: The Philippine Case*, University of the Philippines School of Economics (unpublished manuscript).

Mendoza, A. Jr. (1996), 'Impact on the Informal Sector', in C. Paderanga, Jr. (ed.), *The Philippines in the Emerging World Environment: Globalization at a Glance*, University of the Philippines Press, Quezon City, pp. 193-231.

Montes, M. (1994), 'What is Wrong with Structural Adjustment Programs?', *Issues and Letters*, vol. 3, nos. 4-5, January-February.

Monsod, S. (1998), 'The War Against Poverty: A Status Report', in D. Timberman (ed.), *The Philippines: New Directions in Domestic Policy and Foreign Relations*, ISEAS and The Asia Society, Singapore, pp. 85-110.

Montemayor, L. (1994), 'World Trade under GATT and the Filipino Peasantry', *Kasarinlan*, vol. 9, no. 4, pp. 74-82.

Nelson, J. (1992), 'Poverty, Equity, and the Politics of Adjustment', in S. Haggard and R. Kaufman (eds), *The Politics of Economic Adjustment*, Princeton University Press.

Olson, M., Jr. (1965), *The Logic of Collective Action*, Harvard University Press, Cambridge.

'PabiGATT!: NGO-PO Statement on the General Agreement on Tariffs and Trade', *Kasarinlan*, vol. 9, no. 4, pp. 141-3.

Payumo, F. (1994), 'Year-end Review and Prospects: A View from Congress', *Kasarinlan*, vol. 10, no. 2, pp.25-46.

Peattie, L. (1987), 'An Idea in Good Currency: The Informal Sector', *World Development*, vol. 15, 7, pp. 851-60.

Przeworski, A. (1992), 'The Neoliberal Fallacy', *Journal of Democracy*, vol. 3, no. 3, pp. 45-59.

Robinson, J. (1962), *Economic Philosophy*, Cambridge University Press.

Root, H. (1996), *Small Countries, Big Lessons: Governance and the Rise of East Asia*, Oxford University Press (China) Ltd., Hong Kong.

Tuaño, P. (1999), 'Labor: Bearing the Crisis Cross', *Politik*, vol. 6, no. 1, August.

United Nations Development Programme (UNDP) (1999a), *Human Development Report 1999*, Oxford University Press, New York.

United Nations Development Programme (UNDP) (1994b), *Philippine Human Development Report 1994*, UNDP, Makati.

Chapter 9

Development, Security, and Global Restructuring: The Case of Philippine Export Manufacturing Industries

Leonora C. Angeles[1]

Introduction

This chapter examines the linkages between development and security in the context of global industrial restructuring affecting the export manufacturing sector in the Philippines. Foreign direct investments (FDIs) and global/regional integration of production are most visible in this sector, particularly in the garments and electronics industries. As the most significant contributor to industrial growth in the last two decades, export manufacturing could play a vital role in stimulating production, demand, and technological innovations.

Globalization is understood not only as the spatial and functional integration of markets and economic, political, cultural, and technological activities across the globe.[2] It also refers to activities of firms within a system of interlinking firm networks and world wide production, distribution, and consumption chains. Globalization, as a more complex and advanced form of internationalization, is not only expressed in cross-cultural, regional, and international spaces, but also in local sites. At the industry and firm levels, globalization is expressed in increasing amount of FDIs, a rise in intra-firm trade, the creation of networks, and the use of 'flexible' production strategies such as inter-firm cooperation arrangements in the areas of sourcing, production, distribution, marketing, and research and development.[3]

This study links security and development issues by addressing a number of questions that deal with **the geographic patterns of production, comparative,** and responses of Philippine export manufacturing to global industrial restructuring. Critical questions are addressed. What are the determinants of the international competitiveness of the Philippine garments and electronics industries, their strengths, and vulnerabilities? What is the impact of the economic crisis on industrial restructuring in the export manufacturing sector? How are FDIs in the region, particularly in garments and electronics, responding to the crisis? What are the effects of the crisis and consequent restructuring on the work environments, production requirements, and labor policies that have significant effects on the workers' welfare and industrial peace in the region?

These questions are linked by a common concern to understand how restructuring within the export manufacturing sector affects the long-term security and sustainable development of Southeast Asia (SEA), using the Philippines as a case study. This concern is not only academic, but also has practical and with strategic implications for development policy and planning. It will help us understand how global restructuring trends within export manufacturing affect the chances of developing countries in implementing strategies of self-reliant and sustainable industrialization patterns. It will also point to policy directions and recommendations for Philippine state agencies, domestic entrepreneurs, exporters, and civil society forces to address the challenges of the export manufacturing sector.

Market-oriented strategies in an increasingly competitive environment are important. However, it is also significant to consider the more sustainable path provided by an enabling local environment based on endogenous development that is not only resilient to change but also able to chart its own direction. As the effects of globalization are localized, endogenous development becomes crucial to the formation of social capital within and among civil society forces, particularly in local communities. Endogenous development provides the necessary condition for improving *social capital*, that is, horizontal linkages, and relations of trust and co-operation within communities and between the state and civil society forces.

This chapter analyses primary and secondary literature, and information from Philippine government agencies, particularly the Department of Trade and Industry (DTI), and the Philippine Economic Zone Authority (PEZA) and its administrative offices in four government-owned and operated export processing zones in Baguio City, Mactan in Cebu Province, Mariveles in Bataan Province, and Rosario in Cavite Province. Twenty-five key informant interviews were conducted with administrators and staff of these agencies: managers, floor supervisors, engineers and production workers in one semiconductor multinational company in Baguio Export Processing Zone (EPZ), two electronic firms in Cavite and Bataan, and three garment factories in Baguio, Cavite, and Bataan EPZs; officials from the DTI, Cebu Chamber of Commerce, Garments and Textiles Exporters Board (GTEB), and manager-owners and women workers of three small garments factories in Bulacan Province.

This chapter is divided into five major sections. The first examines how global restructuring has affected operations of the Philippine garments and electronics industries, and the restructuring taking place in these industries in the light of the economic crisis. The second examines the effects of the economic crisis on FDI and the Philippine garments and electronics industries. The third section provides an analytical framework to understand the development and security implications of the globalization of export manufacturing. The fourth and fifth sections conclude by examining some lessons on social capital and good governance from the Philippine export manufacturing sector, and making policy recommendations.

The Philippines' Garments and Electronics Manufacturing Industries

The aggressive export oriented industrialization (EOI) policy that started under the Marcos regime was continued by the post-Marcos governments, leading to the restructuring of the PEZA and the DTI, more investment missions abroad, and more local briefings for prospective investors. In December 1989, the Aquino government created the Investment and Capital Corporation of the Philippines (ICCP) to develop private industrial estates. By February 1998, PEZA has approved 27 new economic zones and industrial estate sites, and the expansion of three others in 1997. These new zones involved the conversion of 8,028.53 hectares of farmland into industrial zones, particularly in provinces closer to Metro Manila, such as the Cavite-Laguna-Batangas-Rizal-Quezon (CALABARZON) area and other regional centers such as Cebu and Davao, where the biggest new industrial projects are located.[4]

To further attract foreign capital, the Philippine government has restructured its incentive package for export companies in the free trade zones, zone developers, and operators of facilities and utilities, and tourism and domestic market enterprises.[5] Total investments in the regular government zones and special industrial estates have increased exponentially since 1986, by as much as 43 per cent in 1986 and 21 per cent in 1991. Likewise, total exports from the export zones increased dramatically beginning in the early 1990s, as more capital poured in from the East Asian newly industrializing countries (NICs). By 1997 exports from the four government EPZs and 19 private industrial estates reached US$10,647 million (against imports of US$6,894 million) for a positive balance of US$3,753 million. The average direct employment for the four government-operated zones was 114,835 employees. The 19 private industrial zones contributed jobs for 183,828 people.[6] Total employment of 298,663 represents jobs for less than one per cent of the working population. Electronics and garments manufacturing firms, owned by foreign and Filipino investors are the biggest contributor of employment in these export-oriented economic zones.

One consequence of globalization-induced growth is the increased diversity of foreign capital participation in Philippine export manufacturing. The profile of foreign participation in these economic zone investments has changed slightly from the traditional American and European sources to East Asian capital. Another effect is the increased capabilities of Filipino-owned corporations to invest in export oriented industries, although they still have impaired capacity in developing outward FDI. There is a significant participation of Filipino investors in the special economic zones in 1996 and 1997, accounting for between 9-11 per cent of new investments. Filipino landed capitalists who belong to powerful political families in the country have also created their own private industrial parks, such as the Ayala and Aboitiz companies, Luisita Industrial Park Corporation, and Fil-Estate Corporation.

The Philippine Garment Industry

The country's garment industry is composed of the export sector and the internal sector for the domestic market.[7] This 'dual structure' and lack of dynamic linkages between the domestic textile and export garment production hamper the development of the industry.[8] This must be understood in light of the industry's origins 'as a basically subcontracting re-exporting industry where raw materials are shipped from abroad for processing (cutting, embroidery, sewing, others) and then re-exported. Part of the production process goes into the factory but the bulk is subcontracted to cottage-type producers in the rural areas'.[9] The garment industry is dominated by large multinational corporations (MNCs) and Filipino-owned export firms, mostly based in government-owned EPZs (Baguio, Bataan, Cavite and Mactan) and privately-operated industrial parks, with an average of 500 to 1,000 predominantly female workers. It is also composed of many small subcontractors, employing an average of 10 women workers. The number of garment firms operating in the country increased from 316 in 1972 to 1,556 in 1988.[10] The total number increased almost ten-fold five years later. The 1993 national survey of manufacturing establishments revealed 15,220 garment firms, of which 13,498 or 89 per cent are small-scale operations, employing less than 10 workers, and 1,722 firms employing 10 or more workers. Of these firms, only 932 or 6.12 per cent are active exporters, which suggest the importance of small subcontractors in satisfying orders of garment importers.[11] In 1996, there were some 1,947 subcontractors, 19,216 indirect workers; 74,252 direct garment workers; and 2,381 home workers, located mostly in Metro Manila, Central Luzon, and Southern Luzon area.[12]

Garment exporters or subcontractors are required by the government through the GTEB to have at least 20 high speed sewing machines. Garment production accounts for almost 30 per cent of total industrial employment in EPZs in the Philippines by the end of the 1980s. This is a relatively low figure compared to 90 per cent in Jamaican and Mauritius EPZs, 80 per cent in Bangladesh, 46 per cent in the Dominican Republic, and 68 per cent in Sri Lanka,[13] suggesting a more diversified manufacturing production in Philippine EPZs. This is due to its pursuit of the EOI policy since the 1970s. The biggest markets for Philippine garments are the United States (US), European Community member countries, and Canada.[14]

Philippine garment exports grew by 195 per cent in 1970 to 1975, and its value increased by 482 per cent in 1985 from its 1975 level.[15] Total sales to the US alone reached $1.8 billion in 1997, experiencing an average annual growth rate of almost 10 per cent in the period 1980-97.[16] Total export sales of the Philippine garment sector reached US$10.4 billion for the period 1993-97.[17] However, the industry's share of total exports have consistently declined since 1992, compared to the electronics industry's sustained growth—see Table 9.1.

The above trends point to the industry's biggest setbacks—its import dependence and cut-throat international competition—that threaten the industry's potentials to contribute to sustainable development. The garments industry is one of the first global industries to utilize outsourcing and flexible specialization as its organizing principle. It relies strongly on subcontracting relations and importation of fabrics, yarns, and fibers. In 1996, 49 per cent of the total value of garment exports was used for such imports, 52 per cent of the same total was manufactured from materials imported on a consignment basis. These are re-exported after adding the labor input of Filipino workers. Such import dependence is due to the inefficient and non-competitive domestic textile industry that supplies only 16 per cent of the local industry's needs, as it provides poor quality textiles at prices higher than better-quality imports.[18]

Table 9.1 Comparative Export Performance: Garments and Electronics 1991-1998

Product Group	Garments		Electronics	
Year	Value in US$	% Share of Total Exports	Value in US$	% Share of Total Exports
1991	1,740,277,599	19.69	2,239,118,609	25.33
1992	2,014,313,916	20.50	2,729,381,848	27.78
1993	2,133,985,187	18.76	3,518,131,544	30.93
1994	2,218,810,539	16.46	4,886,862,693	36.24
1995	2,416,845,339	13.85	7,556,860,712	43.31
1996	2,304,435,642	11.22	10,610,004.470	51.65
1997	2,249,491,393	8.92	14,961,888,340	59.31
1997*	1,855,436,533	8.97	12,181,232,337	58.88
1998*	1,885,090,314	7.73	16,266,320,032	66.70

*Data for January to October period

Source: Department of Trade and Industry, 'Philippine Export Performance, Export Winners', 1991-1998.

Thus, the Philippines lags behind Indonesia, Thailand, and Malaysia in developing backward linkages to domestic textile and other raw material production. The industry also suffers from low labor productivity and faces stiff competition from countries like Indonesia, Thailand, Vietnam, Pakistan, Bangladesh, India, and Sri Lanka that have lower labor costs.[19] The growth of automated production technologies could have disastrous impacts on the Philippines and other countries that consider cheap labor as their main competitive advantage. This will further enhance the competitive position of the US and other Organization for Economic Cooperation and Development (OECD) countries in garments production. On the other hand, it is also possible that developing countries could utilize new technologies to their advantage by producing higher quality garments for the upscale markets.[20] This suggests that the garments industry's contribution to dynamic economic growth hinges upon developing linkages to the domestic textile industry, utilizing more local materials, and tapping export markets directly instead of remaining as subcontractors in the garment production chain.

The Philippine Electronics Industry

The Philippine electronics industry, particularly semiconductors, has grown since US interests in developing countries rapidly expanded during the 1979-80 chip shortage. This has led to new geographic location patterns of semiconductor firms, for example, shifts among the major OECD countries such as US and Japan, shifts from the center to periphery within OECD such as Ireland, Scotland, and Wales, shifts to traditional export countries in East Asia, and then to SEA, South Asia, and the Caribbean. These shifts led to new patterns of specialization between American and Philippine firms, especially in the subcontracting of assembly work.[21] Since 1980s, the majority of semiconductor companies in the Philippines have been wholly or in majority of cases foreign-owned. Their outputs are sold to parent companies or direct clients abroad. There are also Filipino 'merchant manufacturers' or independent subcontractors connected to multinationals like Motorola, Intel, Texas Instruments, Philips, American Micro-electronics, Incorporated, and Fairchild Semiconductors. Many electronics companies, owned largely by American, Japanese, Taiwanese, and Korean capital operate in government-owned EPZs, while others operate within private industrial parks.

Electronics firms comprise almost 30 per cent of all companies based in government-owned EPZs.[22] The industry ranked second biggest non-traditional export product in the 1970s but has surpassed garments since the late 1980s in export value. By 1991, garments' share in total exports stood at 20.51 per cent while electronics was 25.33 per cent. The difference in their export share further widened in 1997, with garments at nine per cent, and electronics increased to 59 per cent.

Although the global electronics industry is seen as the archetype 'sunrise' industry, the sun does not shine evenly throughout the industry. By participating in the spatial division of labor in the semiconductor industry, the Philippines has inserted itself in a rapidly growing market for microchips. Its continued participation, however, is becoming increasingly limited (in its share of the value-added), as the creative and knowledge-intensive stages of design and wafer fabrication remain concentrated in the industrialized OECD countries. The geographic concentration in the international division of labor within the semiconductor industry will continue. The US, Japan, and other OECD countries in Europe remain as the site of critical and creative, knowledge-intensive, and capital-intensive stages in the production of the silicon chip. Due to the capital-intensive nature of wafer fabrication and the complex technological support needed for its operations, only Singapore has been able to develop backward linkages in this stage of semiconductor production.

The Philippine electronics industry, especially semiconductors, has a higher *export propensity*, that is, exports as a percentage of total sales, than other Southeast Asian countries. For example, US firms in electronics and electrical machinery have an export propensity of 46 per cent in Indonesia, 51 per cent in Malaysia, 69 per cent in Thailand, and 82 per cent in the Philippines.[23] This suggests the presence of a narrower domestic market for electronic products and the limited ability of the local electronic firms to utilize the assembled inputs of the semiconductor industry. The dependence on imported raw materials, inadequate services for the local maintenance of imported equipment, and the unavailability of spare parts and tools locally had also been pointed out by Semiconductor Electronics Industry Foundation Incorporated (SEIFI) as the biggest problems of the industry.[24] As we will see below, some of these characteristics common to garments and electronics industries circumscribe their responses to the Asian financial crisis.

Philippine Export Manufacturing and the Asian Crisis

The economic crisis in Asia that started in 1997 could increase FDI inflows in SEA because currency depreciation, lower property prices, and bargain prices offered by indebted and cash-strapped companies have enabled foreign investors to establish and expand production. This scenario could influence the development and security of the Asian countries most affected by the crisis in at least three ways: (1) the increased trend towards mergers and acquisitions of corporations could potentially lead to foreign control over strategic industries and increased concentration of capital that does not lead to new job creation; (2) the decreased trend in outward FDI from the East and Southeast Asian regions could limit the investment potentials of emerging domestic capitalists; and (3) the increased exports of local affiliates of MNCs due to currency devaluation could exacerbate current level of dependence on export markets and ignore the importance of creating domestic markets.

Due to increased global and international integration of production, local affiliates of MNCs are able to compensate for the decline in domestic sales by increasing exports, now made more attractive by currency devaluation. This response to the crisis is stimulated by the increased export propensity of foreign subsidiaries in SEA, especially those owned by Japanese and US companies. In 1995, Japanese MNC affiliates in Indonesia, Malaysia, Thailand, and the Philippines had a combined export propensity of 36 per cent in all industries: 76 per cent in the primary sector; 40 per cent in the manufacturing sector, with electrical machinery registering the highest at 70.7 per cent; and 25.3 per cent in service sector. US affiliates in all industries have an export propensity of 65 per cent in Indonesia, 40 per cent in Malaysia, 27 per cent in the Philippines, and 25 per cent in Thailand.[25] This indicates that the crisis has not only constricted domestic consumer demand, but could potentially raise dependence of SEA on foreign markets.

The Philippine electronics industry appeared not to be affected by the 1997 financial crisis as much as garments, as total export values remained consistently strong, growing by 41 per cent in 1996-97, and by 34 per cent in the first three quarters of 1998 – see Table 9.1. Employment in the semiconductor industry alone quadrupled in the growth period, from 11,253 in 1983 to 40,646 in 1994,[26] posting a 17 per cent annual growth rate in employment and an average of 20 per cent growth in export sales since 1986.[27]

Since the financial crisis started, the Philippine garment industry's share in total export earnings has slightly decreased, although its total export value grew by 1.6 per cent in the January-October 1998 period compared to the first three quarters in 1997.[28] Even before the crisis, 'garments' was one of the three commodities among the top 10 merchandise exports in 1996 that experienced a decrease from an export value of $2.569 billion in 1995 to $2.422 billion in 1996.[29] The Cebu garment industry, for example, experienced a 32 per cent decline, from $95.218 million in 1996 to $64.833 million in 1997, due to the financial crisis, although its share of national sales increased from 3.46 per cent in 1996 to 8.9 per cent by the early part of 1998[30] – see Table 9.2. Similar declines in production and sales were reported in other provinces, especially for EPZ-based garment factories. According to managers of large subcontractor firms in the Baguio and Cavite EPZs and owners of small home-based garment exporters in Bulacan, the financial crisis has resulted in decreased orders from abroad, forcing them to either lay off workers, freeze hiring, reduce the working hours of their employees, or stop operations altogether. A manager of a garment exporting firm in the Cavite EPZ admitted that his company has been operating at less than full capacity and decreased budgets because of currency depreciation and higher costs of their imported inputs such as fabrics, machines, threads, zippers, and buttons.[31]

Table 9.2 Total Garment Exports from the Philippines and Cebu 1993-1997 in US$

Year	Philippines	Cebu	% Share
1993	2,347,356,240	33,447,595	1.42
1994	2,475,734,790	50,302,534	2.03
1995	2,795,169,251	60,579,580	2.17
1996	2,752,955,930	95,218,740	3.46
1997	2,269,475,627	64,833,000	2.85
Total	10,371,216,211	239,548,449	2.30

Source: Department of Trade and Industry, Cebu City.

Women garment workers who were informed by management of the decline in foreign job orders and sales, forcing companies to tighten control over operating budgets and production costs, confirmed the slump. One particularly striking case was shared by a women worker at a Canadian-owned garments and linen factory based in the Baguio EPZ. The factory has been operating at less than full capacity since 1996. Workers like her who have been working for more than 10 years in the company have experienced drastic cuts in their working hours and, consequently, their wages. Many of them have been reduced to working for only three days a week, with no security of tenure, or prospects of a decent severance package in the event that they quit.[32] Stories like this provide credence to claims of exploitation of women garment workers, especially piece-rate workers in firms facing recession. The plight of women garment workers in the Philippines are nurtured by the industry's labor-intensive character, the layers of subcontractors facilitating linkages between village households and foreign clients, and the need for women workers to increase their income by lengthening their work hours or accepting higher volumes of piece-work.

The bigger garment firms are also notorious for paying their workers below the minimum wage, enforcing unrealistic production quotas, hiring contractual workers, using the piece-rate system, delaying wage payment, undermining workers attempts to unionize, dismissing union members, forming management-controlled unions, and neglecting safety and health standards. Workers in EPZs are also prohibited under the law to unionize. Protest actions are a good indication of how workers themselves react to these labor practices. In 1996 alone, only 3.17 per cent of 15,220 garment companies had unions. Of this number, 86 were served notices of strike due to unfair labor practices (74) and bargaining deadlock (12), involving 37,598 workers. Ten actual strikes took place involving 8,903 workers and another 74 preventive mediation cases were filed involving 22,341 workers.[33]

The financial crisis has revealed the vulnerability of import-dependent export firms. For example, Japanese export firms most affected by the crisis have a high import dependence, with imported inputs accounting for 62 per cent of total procurements of their manufacturing affiliates in Indonesia, Malaysia, Thailand, and the Philippines.[34] The ability of export-oriented firms to increase their exports to compensate for decreased domestic demand is determined by their import-dependence. This 'further underlines the importance of integrating foreign affiliates into their host economies: such integration not only contributes to the building up of local capacities; but the more foreign affiliates can draw on backward linkages with local enterprises, the less import-dependent they are'.[35] The crisis may prove to be a blessing if exporting firms respond to the crisis by substituting local materials for imported products. Such move could be aided by national development plans aimed at reducing the import-dependence of export firms by providing incentives to integrate their operations with domestic enterprises, by procuring their supplies from local sources, by helping upgrade the quality of local products, and by improving local technological capabilities and human resources.

Development and Security Links in the Globalization of Export Manufacturing

The global geographic concentration and spatial integration of export manufacturing have serious implications for the security and sustainable development of the Southeast Asian region in general and the Philippines, in particular. FDIs in general, and their location to high-tech 'growth triangles' in the Southeast Asian region serve a positive role in enhancing regional security as they increase the stake of MNCs and major industrialized countries in the stability of region. This security-enhancing contribution of FDIs may however be offset by intra- and inter-state conflicts over uneven distribution of resources and benefits.[36] Export oriented industrialization through FDIs may pose serious security-diminishing impacts because of its enclave nature and lack of strong linkages with the domestic economy.

This section examines seven trends in export manufacturing that have serious effects on the development and security of the Philippines and SEA. This chapter sees the aggressive promotion of industrial manufacturing to have significant effects on the country's long-term development and security, particularly on agro-industrial development and human resource development, on the one hand, and on the resulting distribution of economic benefits, social welfare, and externalities or negative costs like environmental degradation, on the other. Each of these trends and related processes, and their development and security implications are explained below.

First, the aggressive promotion of industrialization is often done at the expense of agriculture, the latter often viewed as a residual sector in a modernizing world. The persistent neglect of agriculture has deprived the sector of needed input subsidies, post-harvest facilities, and other support. Foreign capital in agricultural projects declines because investors and international lending agencies prefer to invest in other sectors.[37] This neglect has been aggravated by poor implementation of the agrarian reform law and aggressive farmland conversion for industrial, commercial, or residential use. Such land conversion, which takes place in the absence of a comprehensive national land use policy threatens national food security and leads to an unbalanced agro-industrial development.[38] The prioritization of industrial growth over agricultural development and the failure of agrarian reform condition the continued stagnation of Philippine industry. A failed agrarian reform program, exacerbated by a regressive taxation system has perpetuated the skewed distribution of land and income in the country. It has led to social and economic inequalities and limits the already narrow tax base, domestic market, and consumer demand.[39] This brings to light the need to examine the wisdom behind the common conflation of 'development' with 'urban-based industrialization', which not only perpetuates the rural-urban spatial division of labor, but also underpins the lack of modernization in agricultural production.[40]

Second, globalization of production has, on the one hand, benefited multinational and domestic capitalists in utilizing the comparative advantage of each country in the region, and on the other, transformed nation-states into 'entrepreneurial' agents that are overly concerned with maintaining a favorable business climate for international capital and curbing the activities of labor unions, particularly those based in female-dominated industries such as garments and electronics. Challenges to state industrial and labor policies (including those that pertain to the labor market supply, wage policies, and labor market segmentation) could lead to the lack of industrial peace and growth of social unrest. Unmet economic demands and social justice expectations could create crises in regime and/or state legitimation and hamper political stability, job creation, and economic growth.

This brings us to the importance of 'an effective state, capable of delivering stable economic policies and a range of public services necessary for development against the pressures of international and domestic interest groups'.[41] In a globalizing era, it is imperative for states to develop their capacity to build institutions and strengthen civil society so they could effectively govern. As debates increasingly focus on the promotion of accountability, cooperation between people and government and efficient use of public resources for market efficiency or 'getting institutions right', civil society forces must push for the recognition of cultural diversity, citizenship rights, and social justice agenda, including gender justice, within good governance and market reform debates. Given that economic growth is generally destructive and disruptive of old institutions and ways, the achievement of social cohesion and political consensus around the objective of 'growth with equity and justice' could be reached when there is a wide distribution of the benefits of that growth and opportunities for poor women and men to participate in development.[42]

The policies on labor unions and labor-management relations in EPZs in the Philippines may in the short-term promote stability, but could in the long-term result in further industrial labor problems. This is especially true in EPZ-based firms that continue to violate labor and other human rights of workers. The government has adopted within EPZs 'a policy of industrial peace and productivity within the ECOZONES through cooperation between labor and management to eliminate necessary conflicts and providing for effective mechanisms in the early settlement of disputes'.[43] In the case of the Cavite EPZ, this policy of industrial peace translates into an effective 'no union, no strike' policy backed by the provincial government. In a published interview, a retired military officer and spokesperson of the government extension office in Cavite EPZ had both recognized the constitutional right of workers to unionize, and precluded workers' right to strike. He interpreted industrial peace as 'the absence of strikes, pickets, and other forms of labor-management disturbances which will upset the harmonious relationship between labor and management'.[44] The subservience of states to foreign capital often leads to policies that prioritize the needs of foreign investors over that of Filipino workers and to company practices that violate legal rights and protection available to workers. A study conducted by a church-based workers' solidarity group on the situation of workers in Cavite EPZ revealed workers' complaints of 'illegal dismissal or suspension, delayed and non-remittance of Social Security System (SSS) premium, violation of minimum wage order, non-payment of overtime work, forced overtime, maltreatment and non-payment of benefits' brought to the attention of the Department of Labor and Employment (DOLE) and the Cavite Export Processing Zone Authority (CEPZA).[45] These unfair labor practices and violations often affect casual and contractual workers who already suffer from depressed wages and job insecurity. The number of contractual, seasonal and part-time workers in the Philippines, many of whom are women and young workers, aged 15 to 24 have been rising,[46] particularly in the aftermath of crisis-related readjustments by manufacturing companies.

Genuine industrial peace through better labor-management cooperation can only take place when working and living standards are improved. Such improvements could begin by ensuring that minimum wages are adequate to cover workers' basic needs. The same CEPZA study cited above showed that the minimum wage received by workers (155 pesos for an eight-hour work day in 1995) barely covers food, housing, tax and other deductions, and other expenses. Due to high food prices in the country, the study showed that workers typically spend 59.6 per cent of their monthly income on food (higher than the national average of 40 per cent), 12.6 per cent on personal items, eight per cent on housing, six per cent on local transportation, six per cent on taxes, 5.8 per cent on pension and medical benefits contributions, 1.1 per cent on cooking fuel, and one per cent on savings.[47] It is estimated that in 1991, more than 44.07 per cent of total families in the Philippines are dependent on wages and salaries, 8.66 per cent in agriculture and a huge 35.41 per cent in the non-agricultural sector.[48] However, while the daily minimum wage in 1995 had been pegged at 155 pesos, the daily cost of living for a family of six that same year had been computed at 278.79 pesos, with a slightly higher figure for those living in the capital region (341.37 pesos) and lower for non-agricultural areas outside the capital.[49] Since wages are too close to the poverty threshold, many workers become heavily indebted to finance the education of family members, and emergency expenses such as hospitalization. The low wages of workers also explains why the Philippines has one of the lowest personal savings rates and highest incidence of poverty in SEA.

There is a need for more national, industry-wide, and local studies on the effects of globalization on labor unions and industrial relations in the Philippines.[50] There is also a need for states to re-examine their policies not just towards labor and trade unions, but also their wage policies and programs on poverty alleviation, especially in light of globalization and the financial crisis. More studies are also needed on the effects of the crisis and globalization on poverty, particularly on the kinds of social safety nets needed to mitigate the effects of the crisis on the most vulnerable groups such as the unemployed, senior citizens, and poor households, particularly those headed by unskilled women and single mothers.

Third, global integration of production and its accompanying trend towards trade liberalization has created jobs and economic growth without reducing the import-dependent character and low productivity of the Philippine manufacturing sector. Poor productivity and import dependence of the export manufacturing sector hamper the success of macro-level approaches to job creation and poverty reduction. The import-dependence of the garments and electronics industries is manifested by the continued reliance on imported inputs due to the relatively cheap cost of inputs and the inefficiency of domestic industries. Import dependence is also aggravated by the concentration of the more strategic phases of integrated circuit production, such as research and development (R & D), wafer design, and wafer fabrication in the advanced industrial countries. It is also exacerbated by the lack of sustained and significant linkages of MNCs to local businesses and their inadequate contribution to physical and social infrastructure building and technology transfer, leading to unbalanced urban and rural development.[51]

Despite some optimism that the localization of production processes under 'flexible specialization' are more conducive to local development than under 'global fordism',[52] core R & D functions of transnational corporations (TNCs) continue to be minimal in host Southeast Asian countries because:

1. The conduct of extensive R & D activities in the host countries by employing local staff would weaken the superiority of TNCs when not properly handled;
2. TNCs do not get any special incentives for conducting R & D activities in the host countries—instead they have to face certain risks;
3. Government support and co-operation with other research establishments which are available in the home countries may not be readily available in the host countries; and
4. The lack of skilled personnel to undertake such responsible and high-risk work for TNCs does not favor conducting major R & D in the host countries. As a

consequence, the nominal R & D activities conducted by TNCs were limited to market research—particularly aimed at the local market.[53]

While some of the highly technical phases of production of silicon chips have already moved to Singapore, most Southeast Asian countries only get the more labor-intensive phases of etching, bonding, and assembly. The overall dependence of these industries on foreign capital and technology reduces domestic entrepreneurs into perpetual subcontractors for large foreign firms. It also discourages them from investing in the design of garments and micro-processors, the improvement of marketing strategies, and development of creative innovations. Hence, limited domestic capability in technological development hampers industrialization efforts and makes domestic manufacturers vulnerable to currency fluctuations, as shown in the 1997 financial crisis.

Unlike Singapore, the Philippine's consumer and industrial electronic industry has not been able to fully exploit the strategy of attracting FDI for the purpose of technological upgrading. A full 92 per cent of direct exports and 80 per cent of value-added output, and capital expenditures and 60 per cent of manufacturing employment and domestic sales were contributed by wholly-owned foreign firms and joint ventures in Singapore in 1990.[54] While the Philippines has a more diversified resource base than Singapore, a comparison of the Association of Southeast Asian Nations (ASEAN) countries' electronics investment profile shows that the Philippines only ranks fourth after Singapore, Malaysia, and Thailand in density and variety of consumer and industrial electronic goods.[55] Since the industry has not been able to maximize its potentials to expand, it has only registered modest growth rates in spite of increasing demand. For example, in the 1992-94 period, semiconductors and electronic circuits have only increased their merchandise exports from 18 billion pesos in 1992, 20.726 billion in 1993, and 23.687 billion in 1994 at constant 1985 prices. These figures were overshadowed by principal merchandise exports and non-traditional exports such as cut flowers and asparagus.[56]

The decision to modernize the manufacturing sector and upgrade the technological content of their operations may ultimately rest on the location-based decisions of individual multinational firms. However, it appears that the Philippines has not fully maximized its potential in providing a well-trained labor force, stable industrial relations, excellent transportation and communication infrastructure, and well-developed industrial parks to investors. Problems like 'inefficient and insufficient energy infrastructure, high cost of energy, water shortage, and inadequate telephone lines' had already been pointed out by SEIFI members in a 1990 report commissioned by the Board of Investments. The report recommended government action in the maintenance of an environment conducive to expansion and entry of new firms; promotion of investment in ancillary or support industries; creation of adequate physical infrastructure, and promotion and maintenance of stable and harmonious relationships between labor and management.[57] These proposals point to the strong linkage between forward and backward integration of the economy and sustainable development, and between industrial peace and security and economic growth.

There is likewise a need to undertake more research on how Philippine firms and industries stand in the productivity-technology game, particularly in design and engineering tools, computers, integrated circuits production, and other. More research is also needed on the macro-economic conditions, economic institutions, and organizational and institutional changes affecting R & D, productivity and technological competitiveness.[58] R & D expenditure and transfer are not enough unless the Philippine manufacturing sector improves both its *technical efficiency*, that is, the shift to 'best practice' from current practice, and *technological progress*, that is, development of new technology, acquisition of new technology, building capacity for reverse engineering, learning-by-doing or imitation. As one analyst puts it: 'The evidence indicates that at best, even if some industries are moving toward 'best practice' according to the industry, the 'best practice' itself is way below the best in international standards'.[59] The development of high-tech regions with a strong R & D component depends on political factors such as the framing of related policies in technology, research, industry, and education. These factors may be steered by policy on technical infrastructure such as transport, research infrastructure, and venture capital, and other factors such as skilled labor pools, networks between R & D-intensive enterprises, access to product markets, and entrepreneurial spirit.[60] The stimulation of these factors requires the central role of governments in attracting the more high-end technology transfers from within and outside SEA.

Fourth, the Philippines' current level of industrialization through export manufacturing has limited potentials in developing the country's human resources through cutting-edge education and training, particularly in science and technology. The labor market created by the export manufacturing sector only requires the development of low-level skills, as those needed in the garment production, or at most, technical skills in the processing or assembly of intermediate inputs, as in the electronics sector. Hence, the minimal R & D activities of MNCs in the Philippines is in part due to the low technical requirements of these industries and the lack of trained graduates produced by the educational system.

The educational system has been suffering from decades of poor administration, uneven distribution of resources, large enrolments, inefficient funding, and lack of visionary leadership to develop and prepare the available human resources for jobs needed in a more technology-driven and competitive economy.[61] The rapid expansion and establishment of many post-secondary educational institutions have sacrificed the quality of university and college education in the country over profits. As a result, many graduates find themselves unemployed because of the poor match between their educational training and the skills required by the job market, especially in high-growth industries.[62] Many college- and university-educated Filipinos have no choice but to migrate as overseas contract workers or as permanent immigrants due to the inability of the domestic economy to absorb new entrants to the labor force.[63]

Fifth, the globalization of export manufacturing has led to the persistence of a regional division of labor and global hierarchy that could further widen disparities between developed and developing countries, among countries in the region, as well as within each country (for example, between investment-poor rural areas and investment-rich EPZs). Such global, regional, and national disparities could worsen national political tensions, conflicts, and cleavages along geographic, class, gender, and ethnic lines. They could also intensify the competition among Southeast Asian countries to attract higher-value FDIs. This calls for more effective mechanisms of region-wide economic cooperation within ASEAN, and the harmonization of such mechanisms within the ASEAN Free Trade Agreement or AFTA.

The combined forces of economic globalization and the productivity-enhancing technologically driven electronics industry perpetuate unequal and unstable economic relations among nations and people. It also shifts control over markets, resources, and technologies away from people and communities to MNCs, transnational financial markets, and other institutions that are beyond the reach of public accountability.[64] The current globalization of industrial manufacturing simply continues the new international division of labor, which the United Nations Industrial Development Organization (UNIDO) itself described in 1979 as a strategy meant to serve the long-term interests of industrialized countries.[65] Under this order, people in the non-industrial world simply serve as consumers of information and assemblers of manufactured goods produced by the information and high-tech industries increasingly concentrated in the hands of world powers. The dismal fate of the United Nations Educational, Scientific, and Cultural Organization's (UNESCO's) call for a 'new international information and communication order' (NIICO) in the 1980s only highlights failed international attempts to counter the adverse effects on security and indigenous cultural development of continued MNC monopoly in integrated microelectronics production and information dissemination.[66]

The Asian crisis has also created ripe opportunities for increased concentration of ownership through mergers and acquisitions (M & As) by global firms. From July 1997 to June 1998 alone, 30 major companies in Indonesia, South Korea, Malaysia, Thailand, and the Philippines were acquired by companies from the US, Germany, Canada, Japan, and Singapore, mostly based in banking, financial services, chemicals, electrical and electronic engineering, and other manufacturing lines.[67] M & As occurring in the aftermath of the crisis may have serious implications on long-term security and development. They could potentially lead to foreign control of large segments of industries or of strategic industries that are critical to national security, such as public utilities, transportation, communications, and defense. Foreign take-over of the film making and broadcast industries, which serve important functions in the preservation of national culture and tradition could potentially lead to loss of identities. Such scenario could lead to a resurgence of nationalist movements, with or without military support, clamoring for the protection of the national heritage, arts, language, and culture that may prove to be politically destabilizing.

Compared to 'greenfield' FDIs or new productive investments, M & As may not lead to new job creation, capital formation, tax base expansion, or structural diversification of the economy. In fact, M & As may lead to job reduction, and reverse resource transfer, especially if the acquiring owners intend to pirate technology and knowledge base from the acquired firm. They also provide less chances of creating new taxable business units, and diversification into new industries that may have linkages with the domestic economy.[68]

Sixth, although the complementary character of Southeast Asian economies could provide them with some collective protection against the 'footloose' nature of multinational investments, there is still no guarantee that foreign capital would not move to countries with comparable cheap labor and other advantages, especially as the economies of China, South Asia, Latin America, and Africa undergo further liberalization and infrastructure development. There is evidence showing that since 1997, more private capital had flowed into China and Latin American countries that had remained relatively insulated from the financial crisis. In this case, Southeast Asian countries have the choice of either ensuring a more stable political climate for foreign investments by addressing domestic security and regime legitimacy issues, or reducing their dependence on foreign capital by ensuring the forward and backward linkages of export industries to the national economy. Either choice in the short-term, could create dislocations in the political economy as their effects may have differential impact on certain sectors and groups. For example, ethnic Chinese business groups in the Philippines and Indonesia are better positioned to take advantage of new domestic opportunities. But their enhanced commercial success at home could revive anti-Chinese sentiments and ethnic conflicts in the case of Indonesia, and exacerbate the already serious problem of kidnapping of Chinese business community members in the Philippines. At the same time, prioritizing short-term political stability over long-range economic development planning could simply postpone the emergence of potential security problems created by unmet economic goals and rising popular expectations.

Seventh, governments and civil society forces must also examine the forms of conflict that might arise directly or indirectly from the feminization of the industrial labor force, and the technical division of labor within garments and microelectronics production. This gendered labor differentiation and segregation are often intersected by ideological and socio-cultural factors that include stereotypes around racial hierarchies and characteristics and cross-cultural differences in sex roles.[69] Potential areas of conflict could operate in the realm of gender, family, and women-state relations, and have differential dynamics in the case of women migrant workers and women who work close to their homes. Despite the popular social construction of women workers, especially working mothers, as merely 'secondary breadwinners', families rely increasingly on their income for survival of poor families and for improved living standards of middle-income families. As more mothers work outside the home by choice or force of circumstance, they have to count on household helpers, older siblings, and extended family members for childcare and other domestic tasks, especially in the absence of accessible and affordable day care in many Southeast Asian countries. In the face of economic hardships caused by economic restructuring, particularly structural adjustments programs, women stretch their labor by working at multiple part-time or informal jobs that are typically unregulated, lowly paid, and with no benefits. Since the sexual division of labor at home remains unchanged even when women join the workforce (a sad fact that feminist movements in Asia and elsewhere have not successfully challenged compared to more visible gains in other spheres), the greater intensification of women's paid work and household responsibilities could have devastating consequences on women's health, well being, and the quality of family life.

Lessons on Social Capital and Good Governance from the Export Manufacturing Industry

The above development and security concerns posed by export-oriented manufacturing, however, should not be entirely attributed to global restructuring trends. In fact, one could argue that globalization and FDI flows in particular, could help further integrate the economies of the SEA and create a complementary regional character that may spare individual nations from suffering a disproportionate share of burdens and dislocations, as in the most recent crisis. The 'we-are-all-in-same-boat' argument bolstered by globalization is certainly not reassuring to the poor, hungry, and unemployed who suffer the costs of structural adjustment and other austerity measures imposed by their governments and international financial institutions. If indeed globalization and regional integration are inevitable and irreversible, then a comprehensive forward-looking strategy requires national policies that could enhance endogenous development and prepare nation-states for readjustments foisted upon them by global forces.

The kinds of national policies that stimulate the location-based decisions of foreign investors, the determinants of FDIs in host countries, and their promotion of technological upgrading processes within their operations have already been identified. These are the policies that relate to the creation of higher skilled labor, better infrastructure, financial support facilities, and easier bureaucratic procedures.[70] Technological upgrading and transfer become critical to multinational firms as surplus labor begins to decline and real wages begin to increase. It also becomes cost-effective to companies when supported by a well-educated and highly skilled population.[71] It may be argued that technological upgrading and transfer through the use of FDIs within the export manufacturing sector could have taken place in the Philippines if not for the predatory crony capitalism under the Marcos regime. For example, subcontracting ventures in semiconductors were taken over by bureaucratic capitalists and other cronies of the Marcos family who funneled surpluses into unproductive uses at a time when rapid technological innovations were taking place within the industry.[72]

It is instructive to realize that the underlying problem in the distribution of benefits in Philippine society is not only due to inequalities in wealth, but also in social capital formation. *Social capital* is defined as the horizontal ties of trust and cooperation among civil society forces, especially within local communities. Social capital may be viewed as a form of 'wealth' created by people's sustained organizing, information-sharing, alliance-building, networking, building of trust, and community self-help efforts.[73] This 'wealth' however, has hitherto been maximized by elites who have been sharing information on the latest business opportunities, political secrets and strategies, critical to their political maneuvering and economic success. This is the kind of social capital exploitation that does not help build communities, but rather is conducive to the manipulation of social ties for personal benefit and selfish ends.

Multinational firms and other corporate entities may utilize various strategies to form and develop social capital for their own profit-oriented goals. There is of course an on-going debate on whether the private business sector, especially MNCs should be analytically considered part of civil society forces.[74] What is often overlooked, however, is how private businesses and MNCs cultivate their own forms of social capital, capitalizing on the same culture of strong 'social ties' within the communities and localities where they operate. This is based not on purely narrow economistic ends for 'wider corporate domination', but rather on the belief that strong communities and civic-minded employees are healthy to corporations' balance sheets. MNCs realize that this serves even their 'bottom line' objectives in an era of increased pressures towards strong business-government-civil society cooperation and greater corporate social responsibility.

One good example in harnessing social capital in local communities is Texas Instruments Philippines Inc. (TIPI) that has a 2,000-strong work force in the Baguio EPZ. In contrast to women workers in garment industries interviewed in Baguio City and elsewhere, the technical staff and assembly line production workers interviewed at TIPI have expressed overall satisfaction with company policies, pay scale, practices, and working environment. The benefit package of staff and senior production workers include profit sharing, on-site dental and medical service, hospitalization insurance, productivity bonus incentives, and high overtime pay rates. This satisfaction is borne out in the low rates of absenteeism and on-site accidents, and the high percentage of workers who have remained with the company for more than 15 years. TIPI consistently garners national and international awards as an exemplary employer and for observing high environmental standards. In fact, it has continuously strived to achieve the highest international standards for quality control such as the ISO 9000 and 14000 certifications.[75]

The company conducts regular seminars on the latest corporate strategies to ensure that its workers are on the cutting-edge of technological and management know-how. They include those on the shift from 'Total Quality Control' to 'Total Quality Culture', and from 'Total Quality Management' to 'Total Productivity Maintenance'. TIPI has emphasized the 'empowerment' of workers within their working teams or cells, which conforms to 'flexible specialization' and 'cross-functionalism' strategies, as well as the creation of 'total quality culture' as a 'personal and corporate commitment and lifestyle' towards a 'customer-centered culture' diffused to suppliers, customers and the workforce. Such efforts are propelled by the desire to make its management staff, production engineers, and workers conform to their strategic plans. TIPI's regular activities, from its early morning rituals to yearly Christmas programs and productivity team awards, are meant to bolster the satisfaction, confidence, and leadership skills of its work force. It provides recognition to its employers who do community volunteer work, and creates working relationships with various city associations and institutions, especially the nearby universities from where it recruits many of its engineers and production workers. While other companies encourage high labor turn over rates, in contrast, TIPI cultivates company loyalty and develops strategies to avoid losing its workers to other companies or to overseas work opportunities. In fact, TIPI assigns its technical and management staff who want to work abroad to its branch plants in the US, Japan, Taiwan or Singapore. Production workers who apply for overseas contract work are encouraged instead to work for TI factories in Taiwan.[76]

These examples illustrate how social capital within the workplace could be used not only for creating a 'company culture' to discipline workers. In an increasingly globalized world, it is even more important to understand the local grounding of global practices, such as the importance of trust, community, and loyalty to make the necessary global-local connections in the strengthening of social capital. This form of social capital that builds on local knowledge and strong community participation may also be used to create locally-specific and culturally-sensitive forms of innovation-related networks within and outside the corporate world. OECD leaders recognize these innovation networks as:

> An outcome of cumulative 'virtuous circles' of knowledge accumulation in local and regional contexts. As illustrated by industry clusters that were established a long time ago, localized networks appear to be more durable than international alliances. In contrast to international networks, *inter-organizational local networks are reinforced by personal and cultural relations in which trust plays an important role.*[77] [emphasis supplied].

Social capital building, therefore, is essential to the *governance question*, that is, the question of how relationships between government and civil society, and between rulers and the ruled can be transformed in ways that lead to more effective institutions, capacity development, and an enabling environment for making sound economic policy choices and better cooperation between government and people. Good governance is more than just governments and increasing their resources and powers to better perform their responsibilities. It also involves allowing more space for peoples' organizations, community and neighborhood associations, non-governmental organizations (NGOs), and the voluntary sector to access resources, make decisions and take action on matters that concern their lives. This entails 'the move from discussing 'what poor people need' to what decision-making powers, access to resources and political influence should low-income people have to allow them to ensure that their needs are met, their rights respected and their priorities addressed'.[78]

Good governance could lead to a better working environment for investors and workers, when workers themselves are given a strong political voice, resource access, and decision-making powers within and outside the workplace. For export manufacturers, good governance means not only public accountability and transparency in government leadership. It is also manifest in government's determination to gain a broad base of support for growth-oriented policies and building its capacity to eliminate corruption, minimize cumbersome bureaucratic procedures, and provide support for small business and local entrepreneurs.

Policy Recommendations

The above discussion points to a number of issues and spaces where interventions may be made by government leaders and policymakers:

1. **A balanced agro-industrial development strategy.**
   This entails the creation of a comprehensive national land use policy and the harmonization of agrarian reform principles and objectives with current national policies on industrial promotion and export-oriented development. This policy could provide specific guidelines on land use and allocation for industrial purposes, while ensuring that farmlands are not converted at a rate that could threaten agricultural productivity and food security. The enactment and implementation of such policy could meet obstacles unless the following issues are addressed: (1) the broadest representation of all affected stakeholder groups in the policy-making body and consultation processes; and (2) the involvement and cooperation of grassroots organizations and local governments in implementing the policy guidelines, especially in view of current weaknesses in the devolution of powers under the 1991 Local Government Code.[79] This policy also promotes ownership of land by cultivators, reaffirming the ownership rights of agrarian reform beneficiaries and tribal minority groups, prioritizing labor-intensive rural industries, modernizing agricultural production, and supporting small- and medium-scale enterprises in the provinces. The idea of a *balanced agro-industrial development strategy*, called BAIDS by international financial agencies, has unfortunately been misconceived as a strategy for strengthening the export capacity of the agricultural sector, resulting in the neglect of the domestic market needs and railroading agrarian reform principles. An alternative strategy to be developed by the state in collaboration with civil society groups would need inputs and support from farmer and fisherfolk organizations, and NGOs especially those promoting community-based natural resource management and agrarian reform. For their part, farmer organizations, advocacy groups, and NGOS need to re-examine the factors behind the splintering of their ranks, their internal ideological differences, and other weaknesses that had led for example to the demise of the Congress for a People's Agrarian Reform (CPAR), which has been an effective legislative lobby group during its short-lived five-year history.[80] Government agencies, particularly the Departments of Agriculture (DA) and Agrarian Reform (DAR), and the National Food Authority (NFA) also need to examine their role in exacerbating such weaknesses in the ranks of farmer organizations, as well as in their overall bureaucratic operations.[81] At the same time, the government must combine agricultural modernization with the dispersion of non-polluting, labor-intensive industries to the rural areas.

2. **Development of a pro-poor social development agenda.**
   In a crisis, the stimulation of consumer demand and enlargement of the domestic market may be achieved through an effective pro-poor social development agenda that will develop local human resources, provide on-the-job training, and engage the poor in the mobilization of local resources through small rural and urban

enterprises, expanded micro-credit, strong cooperatives, and other programs meant to reduce poverty. Although poverty reduction has been declared a 'centerpiece' in the development plans of three administrations after Marcos, successive governments have not made any real achievements. There is a need for well coordinated efforts of all line government agencies in the delivery of social programs to tackle poverty reduction, by moving away from the 'beneficiary model' to the creation of an enabling environment to support programs aimed at developing the capacities and entrepreneurial energies of poor households and communities. The national budget for a pro-poor social development agenda and welfare transfer to some highly vulnerable groups such as poor single mothers, unemployed, and disabled people could come from expanding the tax base, especially through increased direct taxation of wealth and less use of indirect taxes that disadvantage the poor like sales taxes, improving the efficiency of the tax collection system, and a creation of a more progressive taxation system, where the rich get a higher effective tax rate than the middle classes and low-income groups. Low taxation rates of business income, corporate profits, idle agricultural lands, and the wealthy are compounded by severe inefficiency in tax collection. This is the policy area where government is most likely to meet intense opposition from business interest groups, landlord lobby organizations, and other state-connected rent-seekers. Its success requires a strong political will, revamp of the tax collection system, and most importantly, the government's demonstration to these groups that a progressive taxation policy for the purpose of strengthening social development programs would be beneficial to mutual public and business interests by raising overall 'social capability', and its educational, institutional, and organizational components that are essential to productivity enhancement and absorption of new and advanced technologies.[82]

3. **Educational reforms.**

Reforms of the educational system should emphasize locally-specific market and community needs, technological training, and a community economic development orientation so that universities, colleges, and schools could develop their capacity to assist local communities in examining their problems and working collectively towards solving them. Teachers, students, and school administrators could be mobilized to participate in this restructuring that would require the reorientation and development of the curriculum to emphasize analytical, technical, and problem-solving skills, realigning national science and technology policies with educational needs, nation wide programs for teacher training, modernization of educational facilities, especially the use of new computer-aided technologies, reward incentives and salary increases to excellent teachers in order to develop teaching skills, and attract bright students into the teaching profession. Other excellent recommendations identified by the Congressional Commission to Review and Assess Philippine Education (EDCOM) in 1991 also need to be pursued more systematically, particularly those related to curricular relevance to the labor market and improvement of quality of teachers through higher salaries and programs to strengthen their academic qualifications.[83]

4. **Empowerment of labor groups in national and local decision-making bodies.** Political reforms are needed to ensure the stronger representation of labor groups in national and local decision-making bodies, and to encourage the organizing efforts of workers in large and small firms, including agricultural workers and piece-rate home workers. Labor unions, with assistance from government agencies could also give priority to organizing women workers, home-based workers, and raising gender issues within their ranks. The state's commitment to improving workers' welfare could be demonstrated by setting a realistic wage policy commensurate to the current cost of living. More importantly, the state should guarantee the right of workers to form unions and engage in collective action which is a necessary condition required for free competitive market, especially in the face of the susceptibility of the public good properties of labor standards to 'free rider problem' that undermines both legal compliance and the bargaining position of individual workers. This suggests that states and business should have a mutual interest in maintaining well defined negotiation rules and minimum labor standards that enhance the productivity gains induced by stable industrial relations.[84] In other words, since the prescribed conditions of employment usually lack enforceability and are often unilaterally determined by employers, there is a need to review state-labor relations, particularly the current 'industrial peace policy', so that workers' organizations could have a stronger voice in the workplace and become effective proponents of legislative changes on labor and industrial policies and shift their energies from mere advocacy and opposition, to that of pro-active decision-making and action.

The above spaces for policy reforms in the Philippines are not exhaustive. It is important to note that they require further liberalization not only of the economic environment, but also democratization of the political environment to support dynamic grassroots organizing and community development efforts. The challenge, therefore, is for governments to ensure that the demands of the non-governmental, non-corporate members of civil society are not in complete disagreement with their own interests and the interests of the industrial sector. A 'win-win' situation conducive of a secure future and well being for all is possible when governments are able to maneuver through particularistic elite interests, and negotiate spaces and opportunities for the less privileged majority to be heard and given their rightful place and power within the political and economic landscape.

Notes

1   I am grateful to the Development and Security in Southeast Asia (DSSEA) research program of CIDA for the financial support of this research; York University Center for International and Security Studies (YCISS), and Institute for Strategic and Development Studies (ISDS) in the Philippines for providing administrative support; Elsa de los Reyes and Rady Angeles in Baguio, Cynthia Garcia and Hong Soon-Suk in Cavite, Dr. Lilia Garcia and Dr. Bonifacio Separa in Bataan, for facilitating interviews and visits to EPZ

companies; and the research assistance provided by Clare Mochrie, Mona Linus, Jill Poulton, Ranee Veerassamy, and Jojo Santo.

2   Waters, M. (1995), *Globalization*, Routledge, New York.

3   Organization for Economic Cooperation and Development (OECD) (1994), *Globalization and Local and Regional Competitiveness*, no.16, OECD, Paris, pp.7-8.

4   These new biggest projects are the Rancho Montana Ecozone in Tanauan, Batangas (518 hectares, 34.68 billion pesos); Smokey Mountain Development and Reclamation Project in Tondo, Manila (400 hectares, 19.03 billion); Piatco Special Economic Zone in Villamore Air Base in Pasay City (65 hectares, 10.58 billion); Samal Casino Resort in Davao del Norte (215 hectares, 8.53 billion); Cebu South Reclamation Project in Talisay, Cebu City (330 hectares, 3.82 billion); and Rizal Industrial Estate (326 hectares, 3.24 billion). Economic Zones: From Tough Sell to Hot Prospect, *Asiamoney*, February 1998.

5   For list of incentives, see Omnibus Investment Code; see also 'Economic Zones: From Tough Sell to Hot Prospect', 'A Leader in Industrial Park', *Asiamoney*, February 1998.

6   Philippine Economic Zone Authority, *1997 Performance Indicators of Philippine Economic Zones*, 1998.

7   Aldana, C. (1989), 'The garment industry in the Philippines: multinationals, subcontracting, homework and new technology', in *New Labor Relations: International Developments in the Garments Industry and the Consequences for Women Workers*, Seminar Report, Dordrecht, The Netherlands, June, News from International Education Network Europe (IRENE), pp.15.

8   Austria, M. (1994), *Textile and Garment Industries: Impact of Trade Policy Reforms on Performance, Competitiveness and Structure*, Philippine Institute of Development Studies, Makati, pp.7.

9   'The Garment Industry: Growth Potentials and Prospects', *Philippine Trade and Development*, August 1975, pp.26, quoted in Pineda-Ofreneo, R. (1985), 'The Garments Industry: Restructuring for Whom?', *World Bulletin*, vol.1, nos.5-6, Sept-December, pp.93.

10 *Ibid.*, Table 1, pp. 4-5.

11 'Industry Features', *IBON Facts and Figures*, vol.20, nos.9-10, May 1997, pp.4-5, citing National Statistics Office, *Annual Survey of Manufacturing Establishments*, 1993.

12 *Ibid.*, pp.6, citing GTEB data (1996).

13 World Bank and Energy Department (1990), *Garments: Global Subsector Study*, Working Paper, Industry Series Paper No. 19, World Bank, Washington, January, pp.37.

14 Securities and Exchange Commission, based on National Statistics Office data, cited in 'A Foreign Playing Field', *IBON Facts and Figures*, vol.20, nos.9-10, 15 and 30 May 1997, Table 11, pp. 7.

15 'Growth From Without', *IBON*, vol.20, nos.9-10, May 1997, pp.2-3.

16 Figures from 1980 to 1988 were obtained from World and Energy Department, *Garments, Sub-sector Study*, pp.7; 1997 figure was from Department of Trade and Industry, Cebu City, *Garments Industry Profile*, 1998.

17 Data from the Department of Trade and Industry, Cebu City (1998).

18 'Industry's Features', 1997, pp.5-6.

19 Department of Trade and Industry, Cebu City, *Garments Industry Profile*, 1998.

20 World Bank and Energy Department, *Garments, Global Sub-sector Study*, 1990, pp.71.

21 Ernst, D. (1981), 'Recent Developments in the SemiConductor Industry: Implications for International Restructuring and Global Patterns of Technological Dominance and Dependence', based on a chapter of a larger study, *Restructuring World Industry in a Period of Crisis - the Role of Innovation: An Analysis of Recent Developments in the Semiconductor Industry*, UNIDO/IS. 285, 17 December 1981, pp.1-41.

22 Of the 65 companies in Bataan EPZ, there are19 garments firms and 1 electronics firm; in Baguio EPZ, there are 3 garments and 3 electronics out of 13 companies; in Cavite EPZ, 40 garments and 82 electronics out of 213 companies; in Cebu EPZ, 22 garments and 22 electronics out of 129 companies. PEZA administrative offices in Baguio EPZ, Bataan EPZ (data as of May 1998) and Cavite EPZ (data as of December 1997), and Cebu Department of Trade and Industry (1998).

23 United States Department of Commerce, 1998, cited in United Nations Conference on Trade and Development (UNCTAD) (1999), *World Investment Report 1998: Trends and Determinants*, Geneva, UNCTAD, Table VII.3, pp.216.

24 Semiconductor Electronics Industry Foundation, Inc. (SEIFI) and SGV and Co. (1990), *The Semiconductor Industry*, Board of Investments, Makati.

25 UNCTAD, *World Investment Report 1998*, Table VII.3, 1999, pp.216, citing statistics from Japan, Ministry of International Trade and Industry, 1998, and United States, Department of Commerce, 1998.

26 SEIFI and SGV and Co., *The Semiconductor Industry*, 1990.

27 SEIFI, *The Semiconductor Electronics Industry: Facing Up to Global Challenges* (company publication).

28 Garments exports stood at $1.855 billion in Jan-Oct 1997, and slightly increased to $1.885 billion in the same period in 1998, but its share in total export decreased from 8.97 per cent in 1997 to 7.73 per cent in 1998. Data was for the January to December 1997 period stood at $2.249 billion. Data for full Jan-Dec 1998 period was no yet available at the time of research. See Department of Trade and Industry, 'Philippine Export Performance, Export Winners'.

29 The two other merchandise exports that suffered declining growth rates were coconut oil at negative 30.92 per cent and cathodes (metal like lead or copper) at 12.88 per cent. In contrast, electronics and components grew by 40.38 per cent. 'Stripping the Garments Industry', *IBON Facts and Figures* vol.20, nos.9-10, May 1997, pp.3.

30 Department of Trade and Industry, Cebu City, *Garments Industry Profile*, 1998.

31 Interviews C.1 (Manager of a Cavite EPZ garment exporter specializing in men's tuxedo and formal suits), May 1998; B.1 (Manager of a Bataan EPZ garment manufacturer specializing in gloves and leather goods), June 1998; D.1 (owner-manager of a garment subcontractor in Plaridel, Bulacan, specializing in women's wear), April 1998; and D.2 (owner-manager of a garment subcontractor in Pulilan, Bulacan, making sports and winter wear); May 1998.

32 Interview A.5. (Woman garment worker in Baguio EPZ), June 1998.

33 'At Labor's Expense', *IBON Facts and Figures*, vol.20, no.9-10, May 1997, pp.9, citing data from the Department of Labor and Employment.

34 UNCTAD, *World Investment Report 1998*, Box VII.13, 1999, pp.234.

35 *Ibid.*, pp.216.

36 Acharya, A. (1995), 'Transnational Production and Security: Southeast Asia's 'Growth Triangles'', *Contemporary Southeast Asia*, vol.17, no.2, September, pp.172-185.

37 Figures on foreign capital in agricultural projects for 1990 stood at $6.04 million and for 1991 at a low $520,000. See Ferreira, A. J., Batalla, MC. R. and Magallanes, N. (1993), 'Investments and TNCs in the Philippines: Towards a Balanced Local and Regional Development', *Regional Development Dialogue*, vol.14, no.4, Winter, pp.79.

38 Angeles, L. (1998), *Beyond Golf Courses, Memorial Parks, and Prawn Farms: Globalization, Land Conversion and the Politics of Food Security in the Philippines*, paper presented at the 'Rural Sociological Society Meeting', Portland, Oregon, August. See also 'Industrial Estates: A Lure for Development?', *IBON Facts and Figures*, vol.13, no.23, December 1990; 'Land Reform 2000: Gone With the Land' and 'What it Means: Lives and

Livelihood', *IBON Facts and Figures*, vol.16, no.20, October 1993.

39 Angeles, L. (1992), 'Why the Philippines Did Not Become a NIC', *Kasarinlan*, vol.7, nos.3-4.

40 Friedmann, J. (1988), *Life Space and Economic Space*, Transaction Books, New Jersey; and his article, 'Modular Cities: Beyond the Rural-Urban Divide', *Environment and Urbanization*, vol.8, no.1, April, pp.129-131.

41 Garnaut, R. (1996), 'The Asia-Pacific: Role Model and Engine of Growth', *OECD Proceedings, Globalization and Linkages to 2000: Challenges and Opportunities for OECD Countries*, OECD, Paris, pp.22.

42 Goetz, A. (ed.), *Getting Institutions Right for Women in Development*, Zed, London, pp.3-6.

43 PEZA, *Rules and Regulations to Implement the Special Economic Zone Act of 1995*, Section 1, Part IX.

44 Interview with retired Col. Pete Manalo, 7 October 1996, in *Ang Kalagayan ng Mga Manggagawa sa Cavite Export Processing Zone*, Workers' Assistance Center, Rosario, Cavite, December 1996, pp.8.

45 *Ibid.*, pp.14-15.

46 See 'Labor Only Contracting: The Permanence of Contractualization', *IBON Facts and Figures*, vol.19, no.9, 15 May 1996.

47 *Ibid.*, pp.16-17, Figure 1.

48 'Mirrors of the Social Crisis', *IBON Facts and Figures*, vol.19, no.17, 15 September 1996, pp.2.

49 'Of Making Ends Meet', *IBON Facts and Figures*, vol.19, no.24, 31 December 1996, pp.8; computation based on data provided by the National Statistics Office (NSO) and the National Economic Development Authority (NEDA).

50 A good initial study on this topic has been done by professors at the College of Social Work and Community Development on 'Globalization in the Garments Industry: Impact on Women Workers', particularly report by Professor Maureen Pagaduan on 'Women Garment Workers: Losing Out in Union Organizing Work for Women's Empowerment'.

51 Ferreira, *et. al.*, 'Investments and TNCs in the Philippines: Towards a Balanced Local and Regional Development', 1993, pp.75-82.

52 Fujita, K. and Hill, R. C. (1995), 'Global Toyotaism and Local Development', *International Journal of Urban and Regional Research*, vol. 19, no. 1, pp. 19.

53 Kumara, U. A. (1993), 'Investment, Industrialization and TNCs in Selected Asian Countries', *Regional Development Dialogue*, vol. 14, no. 4, Winter, pp. 16.

54 Chia, 'Foreign Direct Investment in ASEAN', pp.90; see also Yue, C. S. (1997), 'Singapore: Advanced Production Base and Smart Hub of the Electronics Industry' in W. Dobson and C. S. Yue (eds), *Multinationals and East Asian Integration*, IDRC and ISEAS, Ottawa and Singapore, pp.32.

55 Montes, M. (1997), 'Direct Foreign Investment and Technology Transfer in ASEAN', *Asian Economic Bulletin*, vol.14, no.2, pp.181-183.

56 'Investing on Exports', *IBON Facts and Figures*, vol.18, nos.1-2, January 1995, pp. 4.

57 SEIFI and SGV and Co., *The Semiconductor Industry*, 1990.

58 Patalinghug, E. (1996), 'Competitiveness, Productivity and Technology', in Paderangan (ed.), *The Philippines in the Emerging World Environment: Globalization at a Glance*, University of the Philippine Press, Quezon City, pp.255-260.

59 *Ibid.*, pp.243.

60 See Sternberg, R. (1996), 'Regional Growth Theories and High-Tech Regions', *International Journal of Urban and Regional Research*, vol.20, no.3, Figure 4, pp.534.

61 Cortes, J. R. and Balmores, N. R. (1992), *State of Philippine Education: Tension Between*

Equity and Quality, Centre for Integrative and Development Studies and University of the Philippines Press, Quezon City.
62 Thomas, M. L. (1991), 'Social Changes and Problems Emanating From Industrialization in the ASEAN Region', *Regional Development Dialogue*, vol.12, no.1, Spring, pp.3.
63 See Tigno and Lusterio in Volume II of this series.
64 Korten, D. (1996), 'Civic Engagement in Creating Future Cities', *Environment and Urbanization*, vol.8, no.1, April, pp.38-39. See also Korten, D. (1995), *When Corporations Rule the World*, Earthscan Publication, London.
65 UNIDO (1979), 'Industry 2000 – New Perspectives', *The UNIDO Joint Study on International Industrial Cooperation*, August, pp.100, cited in Ofreneo, R. (1987), 'Transnationals and Industrial Restructuring: The Tasks Facing the Trade Union Movement in the ASEAN', *World Bulletin*, vol.3, nos.2-3, March-June, pp.72-73.
66 Such monopoly in the early 1980s reached '90 per cent of the accumulated world facts and figures, 54 per cent of computers, 82 per cent of micro-electronic components, 75 per cent and perhaps more of TV programs, 65 per cent of news dissemination, 50 per cent of films, 35 per cent of short wave radio broadcasts, 30 per cent of book editing, and more than 800 satellites, 'most of them of a secret nature and purpose', Manet, E. G. (1985), 'NIIO: Issues and Trends, 1983' *Democratic Journalist*, 7/8/83, cited in Constantino, R. (1985), 'The Transnationalisation of Communications: Implications on Culture and Development'; and Jose, V. R. (1985), 'Towards a New International Information and Communication Order', in R. Pineda-Ofreneo (ed.) (1985), *The New International Information and Communication Order (NIICO): Implications for the Philippines*, International Studies Institute of the Philippines, University of the Philippines Law Complex, Quezon City, pp.8 and 31, respectively.
67 The total value of these M & As reached $9.832 billion, of which $1.230 billion were minority acquisitions involving 8 Asian companies, $1.9 billion were joint ventures involving 4 companies, and the rest were full acquisitions involving 18 companies. UNCTAD, *World Investment Report 1998*, Annex Table A.VII.2, 1999, pp.336-337.
68 *Ibid.*, pp.211-214.
69 Pena, D. and Cardenas, G. (1988), 'The Division of Labor in Microelectronics: A Comparative Analysis of France, Mexico, and the United States', *Studies in Comparative International Development*, Summer, pp.104-105.
70 UNCTAD explains the differences in the determinants of FDI among firms that are resource-seeking, efficiency-seeking and market-seeking, see UNCTAD, *World Investment Report 1998*, 1999.
71 Montes, 'Direct Foreign Investment and Technology Transfer in ASEAN', 1997, pp.188-189.
72 de Dios, E. and Villamil, L. (1990) (eds), *Plans, Markets and Relations: Studies for a Mixed Economy*, Philippine Center for Policy Studies, Manila, pp.187.
73 Angeles, L. (1998), 'Review of Soliman Santos' Papers of Party in the Making and Working Papers, Working Group: NGO-PO Perspectives for the Local Government Code Review', *Pilipinas*, no.30, Spring, pp.109.
74 This lack of definitional clarity has been acknowledged by UNCTAD, although it believes that civil society could include the non-profit business sector and cooperatives. See UNCTAD, *World Investment Report 1998*, Box III.1, 1999, pp.60.
75 Texas Instruments Philippines' national awards include the Outstanding Quality Company for 1990, Countryside Investor of 1990, EPZA's Most Outstanding Enterprise, among others.
76 Interview A.4, Baguio, June 1998 (Production worker at Texas Instruments).
77 OECD, *Globalization and Local and Regional Competitiveness*, 1994, pp.17-18.

78 Editor's Introduction, 'Future Cities and Habitat II', *Environment and Urbanization*, vol.8, no.1, April 1996, pp.4; see also United Nations Centre for Human Settlements (UNCHS) (1996), *An Urbanizing World: Global Report on Human Settlements*, Oxford University Press, Oxford.

79 On problems related to the devolution, see Osteria, T. (1996), 'Implementation of the Local Government Code in the Philippines: Problems and Challenges', in T. Osteria (ed.), *Social Sector Decentralization: Lessons from the Asian Experience*, International Development Research Centre, Ottawa, pp.16-83; and Santos, S. (ed.) (1997), *Working Papers, Working Group: NGO-PO Perspectives for the Local Government Code Review*, Institute of Politics and Government, Quezon City.

80 On CPAR's demise and relationship with the state, see Gono, C. (1997), *Peasant Movement-State Relations in New Democracies: The Case of the Congress for a People's Agrarian Reform (CPAR) in Post-Marcos Philippines*, Institute on Church and Social Issues, Quezon City.

81 While this is not the place to do a systematic institutional analysis of these agriculture departments, it is worthwhile to note the analysis of agricultural economist Cristina David: 'The problem is not so much that [agricultural] expenditures are relatively low. Rather, expenditures are misallocated, programs are of poor quality, and the implementation of programs is very inefficient due to organizational structure of the DA bureaucracy and the relatively low competence of bureaucrats particularly at the upper echelons.... The DA budget for extension and related services in 1995 was only 1.8 billion pesos. On the other hand, the budget for central administration of the agriculture agencies (DA and DAR) was about 15 billion pesos... The budget for R & D is relatively high. But such expenditures are apparently unproductive. Neighboring countries which are outperforming us in agriculture are spending much less on R & D. NFA, which has absolutely nothing to do with productivity, has a budget of 1.6 billion pesos'. David, C. and Balisacan, A. (1996), 'Agriculture and Food Security: Protection versus Liberalization' (a panel discussion), in C. Paderanga (ed.), *The Philippines in the Emerging World Environment: Globalization at a Glance*, University of the Philippines Press, Quezon City, pp.156.

82 Abramovitz, M. (1986), 'Catching Up, Forging Ahead, and Falling Behind', *Journal of Economic History*, vol. 46, pp.385-406.

83 On EDCOM recommendations and analysis of the problems of the Philippine educational system, see Cortes and Balmores, *State of Philippine Education: Tension Between Equity and Quality*, 1992, pp.43-58.

84 Esguerra, E. F. (1996), 'Labor Standards in Open Economies and the Social Clause', C. Paderanga (ed.) *The Philippines in the Emerging World Environment: Globalization at a Glance*, University of the Philippines Press, Quezon City, pp. 173-175.

References

'A Foreign Playing Field', *IBON Facts and Figures*, vol. 20, nos. 9-10, 15 and 30, May 1997, pp. 7.

'A Leader in Industrial Park', *Asiamoney*, February 1998.

Abramovitz, M. (1986), 'Catching Up, Forging Ahead, and Falling Behind', *Journal of Economic History*, vol. 46, pp. 385-406.

Acharya, A. (1995), 'Transnational Production and Security: Southeast Asia's "Growth Triangles"', *Contemporary Southeast Asia*, vol. 17, no. 2, September, pp. 172-185.

Aldana, C. (1989), 'The garment industry in the Philippines: multinationals, subcontracting, homework and new technology', in *New Labor Relations: International Developments in the Garments Industry and the Consequences for Women Workers*, Seminar Report, Dordrecht, The Netherlands, June, News from International Education Network Europe (IRENE), pp. 15.

Ang Kalagayan ng Mga Manggagawa sa Cavite Export Processing Zone, Workers' Assistance Center, Rosario, Cavite, December 1996, pp. 8.

Angeles, L. (1992), 'Why the Philippines Did Not Become a NIC', *Kasarinlan*, vol. 7, nos. 3-4.

Angeles, L. (1998a), *Beyond Golf Courses, Memorial Parks, and Prawn Farms: Globalization, Land Conversion and the Politics of Food Security in the Philippines*, paper presented at the 'Rural Sociological Society Meeting', Portland, Oregon, August.

Angeles, L. (1998b), 'Review of Soliman Santos' Papers of Party in the Making, and Working Papers, Working Group: NGO-PO Perspectives for the Local Government Code Review', *Pilipinas*, no. 30, Spring, pp. 109.

'At Labor's Expense', *IBON Facts and Figures*, vol. 20, no. 9-10, May 1997, pp. 9.

Austria, M. (1994), *Textile and Garment Industries: Impact of Trade Policy Reforms on Performance, Competitiveness and Structure*, Philippine Institute of Development Studies, Makati, pp. 7.

Constantino, R. (1985), 'The Transnationalisation of Communications: Implications on Culture and Development', in R. Pineda-Ofreneo (ed.), *The New International Information and Communication Order (NIICO): Implications for the Philippines*, International Studies Institute of the Philippines, University of the Philippines Law Complex, Quezon City, pp. 8.

Cortes, J. R. and Balmores, N. R. (1992), *State of Philippine Education: Tension Between Equity and Quality*, Centre for Integrative and Development Studies and University of the Philippines Press, Quezon City.

David, C. and Balisacan, A. (1996), 'Agriculture and Food Security: Protection versus Liberalization', in C. Paderanga (ed.), *The Philippines in the Emerging World Environment: Globalization at a Glance*, University of the Philippines Press, Quezon City, pp.156.

de Dios, E. and Villamil, L. (1990) (eds), *Plans, Markets and Relations: Studies for a Mixed Economy*, Philippine Center for Policy Studies, Manila, pp. 187.

Department of Trade and Industry (1998), *Garments Industry Profile*, DTI, Cebu City.

'Economic Zones: From Tough Sell to Hot Prospect', *Asiamoney*, February 1998.

Ernst, D. (1981), 'Recent Developments in the SemiConductor Industry: Implications for International Restructuring and Global Patterns of Technological Dominance and Dependence', based on a chapter of a larger study, *Restructuring World Industry in a Period of Crisis - the Role of Innovation: An Analysis of Recent Developments in the Semiconductor Industry*, UNIDO/IS 285, 17 December 1981), pp. 1-41.

Esguerra, E. F. (1996), 'Labor Standards in Open Economies and the Social Clause', C. Paderanga (ed.) *The Philippines in the Emerging World Environment: Globalization at a Glance*, University of the Philippines Press, Quezon City, pp. 173-175.

Ferreira, A. J., Batalla, MC. R. and Magallanes, N. (1993), 'Investments and TNCs in the Philippines: Towards a Balanced Local and Regional Development', *Regional Development Dialogue*, vol. 14, no. 4, Winter, pp. 79.

Friedmann J. (1996), 'Modular Cities: Beyond the Rural-Urban Divide', *Environment and Urbanization*, vol. 8, no. 1, April, pp. 129-131.

Friedmann, J. (1988), *Life Space and Economic Space*, Transaction Books, New Jersey.

Fujita, K. and Hill, R. C. (1995), 'Global Toyotaism and Local Development', *International*

Journal of Urban and Regional Research, vol. 19, no. 1, pp. 19.

'Future Cities and Habitat II', *Environment and Urbanization,* vol. 8, no. 1, April 1996, pp. 4.

Garnaut, R. (1996), 'The Asia-Pacific: Role Model and Engine of Growth', in *OECD Proceedings, Globalization and Linkages to 2000: Challenges and Opportunities for OECD Countries,* OECD, Paris, pp. 22.

Goetz, A. (ed.), *Getting Institutions Right for Women in Development,* Zed, London, pp. 3-6.

Gono, C. (1997), *Peasant Movement-State Relations in New Democracies: The Case of the Congress for a People's Agrarian Reform (CPAR) in Post-Marcos Philippines,* Institute on Church and Social Issues, Quezon City.

'Growth From Without', *IBON,* vol. 20, nos. 9-10, May 1997, pp. 2-3.

'Industry Features', *IBON Facts and Figures,* vol. 20, nos. 9-10, May 1997, pp. 4-5.

'Industrial Estates: A Lure for Development?', *IBON Facts and Figures,* vol. 13, no. 23, December 1990.

'Investing on Exports', *IBON Facts and Figures,* vol. 18, nos. 1-2, January 1995, pp. 4.

Jose, V. R. (1985), 'Towards a New International Information and Communication Order' in R. Pineda-Ofreneo (ed.), *The New International Information and Communication Order (NIICO): Implications for the Philippines,* International Studies Institute of the Philippines, University of the Philippines Law Complex, Quezon City, pp. 31.

Korten, D. (1995), *When Corporations Rule the World,* Earthscan Publication, London.

Korten, D. (1996), 'Civic Engagement in Creating Future Cities', *Environment and Urbanization,* vol. 8, no. 1, April, pp. 38-39.

Kumara, U. A. (1993), 'Investment, Industrialization and TNCs in Selected Asian Countries', *Regional Development Dialogue,* vol. 14, no. 4, Winter, pp. 16.

'Labor Only Contracting: The Permanence of Contractualization', *IBON Facts and Figures,* vol. 19, no. 9, 15 May 1996.

'Land Reform 2000: Gone With the Land' and 'What it Means: Lives and Livelihood', *IBON Facts and Figures,* vol. 16, no. 20, October 1993.

Manet, E. G. (1985), 'NIIO: Issues and Trends, 1983', *Democratic Journalist,* 8 July 1983.

'Mirrors of the Social Crisis', *IBON Facts and Figures,* vol. 19, no. 17, 15 September 1996.

Montes, M. (1997), 'Direct Foreign Investment and Technology Transfer in ASEAN', *Asian Economic Bulletin,* vol. 14, no. 2, pp. 181-183.

Organization for Economic Cooperation and Development (OECD) (1994), *Globalization and Local and Regional Competitiveness,* no. 16, OECD, Paris, pp. 7-8.

'Of Making Ends Meet', *IBON Facts and Figures,* vol. 19, no. 24, 31 December 1996, pp. 8.

Ofreneo, R. (1987), 'Transnationals and Industrial Restructuring: The Tasks Facing the Trade Union Movement in the ASEAN', *World Bulletin,* vol. 3, nos. 2-3, March-June, pp. 72-73.

Osteria, T. (1996), 'Implementation of the Local Government Code in the Philippines: Problems and Challenges', in T. Osteria (ed.), *Social Sector Decentralization: Lessons from the Asian Experience,* International Development Research Centre, Ottawa, pp. 16-83.

Pena, D. and Cardenas, G. (1988), 'The Division of Labor in Microelectronics: A Comparative Analysis of France, Mexico, and the United States', *Studies in Comparative International Development,* Summer, pp. 104-105.

Pineda-Ofreneo, R. (1985), 'The Garments Industry: Restructuring for Whom?', *World Bulletin,* vol. 1, nos. 5-6, Sept-Dec 1985, pp. 93.

Santos, S. (ed.) (1997), *Working Papers, Working Group: NGO-PO Perspectives for the Local Government Code Review,* Institute of Politics and Government, Quezon City.

SEIFI and SGV and Co. (1990), *The Semiconductor Industry,* Board of Investments, Makati.

Sternberg, R. (1996), 'Regional Growth Theories and High-Tech Regions', *International Journal of Urban and Regional Research,* vol. 20, no. 3, Figure 4, pp. 534.

'Stripping the Garments Industry', *IBON Facts and Figures* vol. 20, nos. 9-10, May 1997, pp. 3.

'The Garment Industry: Growth Potentials and Prospects', *Philippine Trade and Development*, August 1975, pp. 26,

Thomas, M. L. (1991), 'Social Changes and Problems Emanating From Industrialization in the ASEAN Region', *Regional Development Dialogue*, vol. 12, no. 1, Spring, pp. 3.

United Nations Centre for Human Settlement (UNCHS) (1996), *An Urbanizing World: Global Report on Human Settlements*, Oxford University Press, Oxford.

United Nations Conference on Trade and Development (UNCTAD) (1999), *World Investment Report 1998: Trends and Determinants*, Geneva, UNCTAD, pp. 216.

United Nations Industrial Development Organisation (UNIDO) (1979), 'Industry 2000 – New Perspectives', *The UNIDO Joint Study on International Industrial Cooperation*, August, pp. 100.

Waters, M. (1995), *Globalization*, Routledge, New York.

'What it Means: Lives and Livelihood', *IBON Facts and Figures*, vol. 16, no. 20, October 1993.

World Bank and Energy Department (1990), *Garments: Global Subsector Study*, Working Paper, Industry Series Paper No. 19, World Bank, Washington, January, pp. 37.

Yue, C. S. (1997), 'Singapore: Advanced Production Base and Smart Hub of the Electronics Industry' in W. Dobson and C. S. Yue (eds), *Multinationals and East Asian Integration*, IDRC and ISEAS, Ottawa and Singapore, pp. 32.

Chapter 10

The Security Problematique of Globalization and Development: The Case of Indonesia

Rizal Sukma

Introduction

In early 1998, students of Indonesian politics rightly predicted that Indonesia's Soeharto would be re-elected as the Republic's president for the seventh consecutive term. They believed that the foundation of the New Order regime established by Soeharto in 1966 remained invincible. Many confidently argued that after more than three decades of unassailable rule, Soeharto remained powerful as ever. The main reason often cited to support this confident forecast was the fact that Indonesia's Armed Forces (ABRI, now TNI), the most powerful political pillar of New Order's pyramid of power, was still solidly behind Soeharto. Indeed, in March 1998, Soeharto was re-elected by the People's Consultative Assembly (MPR) without any significant challenge from within the ruling circles. Moreover, the fact that the MPR also elected the Minister of Research and Technology, B.J. Habibie, as vice-president and approved a decision to give extraordinary powers to Soeharto clearly suggests that nobody could ever prevent Soeharto from getting what he had wanted.

Given such 'academic' analysis, a number of Indonesian specialists also confidently argued that it was very likely that President Soeharto would once again be able to pull himself out of the worst economic and political crisis the country ever faced in three decades. Even during the critical moments following the May 1998 riots, some analysts still believed in their 'expertise' in understanding Indonesian politics when they predicted that President Soeharto might be able to maintain his power. Therefore, when President Soeharto resigned on 21 May 1998, the news caught them by surprise. None of them would have thought that events in Indonesia could in fact move so fast. From the shooting of four university students on 12 May, immediately followed by the outbreak of the most devastating riots that rocked Jakarta on 13-15 May, to the President's resignation on 21 May, it only took ten days before Soeharto, once the most feared leader in Indonesia, finally realized that he must go.

Indeed, with Soeharto's resignation, Indonesia entered the beginning of a dire period of uncertain democratic transition. Indonesian society is now imbued with a sense of freedom long denied by Soeharto's New Order regime. The apparent results of leadership change are, for the time being, still messy. The departure of Soeharto from power has not meant the complete removal of the political system he had created. Many view the transition government under President Habibie as an extension of Soeharto's government or even as 'Soeharto's regime without Soeharto'.

The fall of Soeharto, and its attendant changes in Indonesia's domestic politics and implications for regional relations present a curious case for understanding how political changes in a developmental-authoritarian regime came about, and what implications those changes might have on regional relations. This chapter argues that recent political changes in Indonesia and their implications for Southeast Asian regional relations can be understood in terms of the security *problematique* of globalization and development faced by a developing state. Such a state is often faced with the burden of its own success in tapping the benefits of the capitalist mode of development brought about by the state's inevitable integration into the globalization process. The main question this chapter seeks to address, therefore, is how Indonesia's encounter with globalization, as the inevitable consequence of its strategy of development, has resulted in intensifying rather than mitigating the security *problematique* posed by globalization and development.

The chapter is divided into four sections. The first section provides a brief discussion of the concepts underpinning the study. The second section examines how globalization is perceived and assessed by both the government (national and local) and society. The third section analyses the impact of globalization on regime stability and legitimacy, how it undermined political stability and development that finally led to regime change, and how that change finally brought the problem of national cohesion, national identity, and regional disparities to the fore. The fourth section discusses how globalization-induced domestic changes might affect intra- Association of Southeast Asian Nations (ASEAN) relations and regional security.

The Security *Problematique* of Globalization and Development

Globalization has become one of the key concepts often used by scholars and practitioners alike to characterize the main feature of the contemporary world. It has become the latest buzzword when efforts are made to explain recent developments in almost all spheres of human life. However, there has been no agreement among scholars as to what globalization really means and how it works. Contemporary scholarly discussions on the concept clearly suggest that globalization means different things to different people. Indeed, it has been asserted that 'students of international relations have been trying to come to grips with the myriad international economic and political changes which appear to characterize globalization, finding that there are perhaps as many meanings as there are analysts'.[1]   Therefore, any attempt to generalize the meaning of globalization at this stage of theoretical development is futile and not desirable.[2]

However, few would dispute that globalization first came in its economic form. The term was first used by Theodore Levitt in 1985 to characterize the vast changes that have taken place in the international economy over the past two decades marked by a rapid diffusion of production, consumption and investment goods, services, capital, and technology around the world.[3] It is then characterized by 'the widening and deepening of international flows of trade, finance and information in a single, integrated global market'.[4] So strong is this process that states and firms—the two main economic actors—are forced to acknowledge the permeability of borders. It has also been argued that 'globalization means the internationalization of the state'. Within this context, it is not surprising that the most common usage of the term 'globalization' refers to the process of opening up of the national economy and its integration into the global economy.

It has often been argued that the state is most affected by the process of globalization. Indeed, one of the crucial aspects of globalization is its implication for the state's role as the dominant actor not only in international relations but also in domestic politics. This, in turn, puts the state in a rather problematic situation. On the one hand, it has been argued that globalization poses a challenge to the sovereignty of state and limits state power.[5] The state no longer serves primarily as a buffer or shield against the rest of the world.[6] The scope for state autonomy is then reduced in the context of economic globalization. However, on the other hand, the state may attempt to regain its central role by seeking material gains from globalization. The state may increasingly facilitate globalization, acting as an agent in the process.[7]

Within the context of the developing world, the attempt to seek material gains from globalization may help the state retain its role as a principal agent of development. This role is indeed crucial for the state since it serves as a primary factor that sustains security of the incumbent regime. It is also imperative for the government to welcome the positive impact of globalization on economic development because it encourages growth and brings about new economic opportunities. However, on the other hand, economic growth driven by states' integration into the economic globalization process may also bring about political consequences, primarily through the free flow of information, new ideas and cultural values, made possible by the revolution in information technology. Such political consequences, among others, manifest themselves in the rise of new groups in society that demand greater participation in politics, and the absorption of new ideas and demands (such as democracy, human rights, and social justice). Under such circumstances, the autonomy-eroding impact of globalization is more apparent in developing states. Many governments in the developing world, especially those that rely on the capitalist mode of development may expect the rise of challenges to regime legitimacy/governance and the changing state-society relations as two attendant effects of globalization. For such states, globalization poses a delicate question of how to reap the economic benefits of globalization without having to submit to its unexpected political consequences. In other words, states face the formidable task of managing the security *problematique* of globalization and development. As the following discussion demonstrates, Indonesia during Soeharto's New Order was faced precisely with such a *problematique*. In the end, its inability to understand and manage the forces of globalization led to economic and political turbulence.

Elite's Perceptions of Globalization: Opportunities and Threats

The term '*globalisasi*' (globalization) entered the Indonesian vocabulary approximately in the late 1980s or early 1990s. As in other parts of the world, globalization was initially conceived of also in terms of economic processes. Globalization was debated largely in terms of its implications for Indonesia's economy. The main thrust of the debate revolved around two major themes. Firstly, there were concerns over what economic globalization really meant for Indonesia, especially regarding challenges it brought for the country. Secondly, the debate addressed the question of strategies and responses that Indonesia should take in order to meet these challenges. For Indonesians, therefore, economic globalization was both a description and a prescription.

Not surprisingly, economists spearheaded the initial debate over globalization. The primary concerns over challenges posed by economic globalization to Indonesia focused on questions regarding Indonesia's 'economic sovereignty' (*kedaulatan ekonomi*) amid the globalization process. One question often raised was whether Indonesia still had sovereignty over its economy at the time when 'the world economy is becoming more integrated' and 'the world is moving rapidly towards an economic globalization'.[8] In this regard, there were at least two opposing views among economists regarding the meaning and impacts of economic globalization on Indonesia and how to respond to it.

The first view maintained that globalization was an inevitable process. Dorojatun Kuntjoro-Jakti, for example, argued that the growing interdependence among states in the economic process makes it difficult for Indonesia to isolate itself from external developments. Another leading economist, Anwar Nasution, also conveyed the same impression when he stated that 'we cannot swim against the tide when we formulate our economic policies. Without looking at what is happening around us, we may become like Burma which isolates itself from other countries'. In order to cope with economic globalization, both Kuntjoro-Jakti and Nasution stressed the need for Indonesia to adjust itself to the growing trend of globalization.[9]

On the other hand, there was also a group of scholars that tended to view globalization in a more cautious way. This group maintained that economic globalization was not neutral, but can be a means of economic domination. The foremost concern was not to let economic globalization serve as a gateway for strong economies like the United States (US) and Japan to control and dominate Indonesia's economy. One scholar, for example, argued 'we [Indonesia] have to try to make the process [of globalization] take interdependence as its main form so that we will not be trapped into economic domination by foreign powers'. The policy prescription offered by this kind of analysis was usually inward looking in nature. According to the scholar cited above, the globalization trap could be avoided if Indonesia better understood the importance of economic sovereignty.[10]

As the debate evolved, the first view seemed to have gained much support both within and outside governmental circles. There were at least four significant aspects of economic globalization that received greater attention from Indonesia's elites. Firstly, globalization was seen as an inevitable development in the contemporary international economy that leaves states with limited choices, namely resistance or participation. This has been acknowledged by a number of Indonesia's leaders.[11]

Secondly, globalization was also seen as a powerful force intensifying competition among states. In this regard, former President Soeharto believed that 'economic globalization....will result in increased competition [among nations]'.[12] He also maintained that 'globalization will become the main characteristic of the world in the coming years....In facing such a world, we have to improve the quality of our human resources and the competitive advantage of our economy'.[13] Another member of the ruling elite also stated that it was imperative for Indonesia to develop export-oriented industries in order to compete with other states in the globalization process.[14] Indeed, the theme of competition was widely seen by the Indonesian elite as the main aspect of globalization to which Indonesia was obliged to respond.

Thirdly, globalization was perceived as the result of dramatic developments in science and technology, especially in information and communications technology (ICT). It has been acknowledged by former President Soeharto that 'rapid progress in science and technology has accelerated the on-going process of globalization'.[15] More specifically, globalization in this context is often perceived and interpreted as the opening up of the state to all kinds of information from outside. It has been asserted, for example, that globalization has made it impossible for government institutions to prevent the flow of information from entering Indonesia.[16] The same interpretation was also offered by leaders of the TNI who maintained that Indonesia was facing challenges posed by 'the global environment which becomes more transparent due to rapid progress in communication and information technology'.[17]

Finally, globalization was also regarded as an attempt by developed countries, especially the West to dominate the whole world. According to this view, globalization is no longer a 'natural process', but it has been 'engineered' by certain developed countries by using science and technological advancements, especially ICT. For example, it has been argued that a developed country 'uses the rapid globalization process as an offensive and anticipatory measure in order to assure that the progress achieved by developing countries will not threaten the superior position and status of developed countries'.[18] Within this view, globalization is also seen as a new form of imperialism. Former Speaker of the House, retired General Amir Machmud, for example, defined globalization in terms of a global struggle 'among developing countries for the benefits of the developed world which still adheres to imperialism-colonialism ideology'. He also maintained that 'globalization is a super new-imperialism [which presents]its many faces in a sophisticated way'.[19]

It seems that the value of globalization for Indonesia, as perceived by its leaders, is closely related to and influenced by the aspects of globalization described above. There is a tendency among Indonesia's elite to assess the value of globalization in terms of its contribution to and consequences for national development in general. This approach is noticeable especially among governmental leaders. Such a view, for instance, was expressed by Soeharto in early April 1991 when he stated that it was impossible for Indonesia to isolate itself from the globalization process.[20] He reiterated this standpoint again in October 1997. In his view, despite some of its implications which may not benefit the nation, globalization should not be resisted.[21]

Therefore, he maintained that Indonesia's government would continue to make use of the positive elements of globalization for the benefit of development, but it would remain vigilant of the negative elements that might hamper the process of development.[22]

Soeharto's view clearly suggests that Indonesia's New Order government recognized both the positive and the negative impacts of globalization for the Republic. In this regard, as clearly suggested by his view above, the attitude of the Indonesia's government towards globalization was mixed. On the one hand, it was eager to tap the fruits of globalization for the benefits of national development as defined by the regime. On the other hand, Soeharto's New Order government was particularly aware of the attendant political impact of globalization on the domestic order it has built. Minister of Information Harmoko, for example, stated that 'the globalization of information carries with it positive as well as negative impacts'.[23] Indeed, for Indonesia's New Order, globalization posed a delicate problem of maximizing benefits on the one hand and minimizing, if not eliminating losses on the other.

What then are the positive contributions of globalization to Indonesia as perceived by Indonesia's elite? There is general agreement among Indonesia's political elite that globalization has much to offer in terms of economic benefits. For example, Soeharto acknowledged that globalization 'provides a greater opportunity for improving national development in order to achieve national prosperity'.[24] However, despite the general tendency to welcome globalization for the economic benefit it brings, note that the New Order government also claimed that it had some concerns over a number of economic implications of globalization. For example, economic globalization was seen to have brought about a number of unexpected effects such as consumerism, materialism, and unemployment. Former Minister for Food Affairs, Ibrahim Hasan, saw globalization as a force that 'encourages a materialistic and hedonistic life, but it failed to give meaningful hopes for the human soul'.[25] Former Minister of Labor, Abdul Latief, also maintained that 'globalization will create a condition not beneficial to unskilled labor' which might create high rates of unemployment.

The New Order government also believed that globalization posed a number of challenges, if not threats, to Indonesia's domestic order, whether ideological, political, or social and cultural. There are at least three negative effects of globalization often emphasized by government officials and political elite.

Firstly, and most importantly, it was often emphasized that globalization may pose a potential threat to the state's ideology of *Pancasila*. According to former President Soeharto, for example, 'it is not unlikely that the opening up of the society due to the globalization process will change our attitude towards national ideology, but we should not let this happen'. He also stated that 'if our faith in *Pancasila* fades away, this will certainly have unexpected results, namely, enormous negative impacts on our life as a nation'. If this is allowed to happen, Indonesia 'will be a weak nation and pushed around by the strong currents of globalization'.[26] Such a threat, as identified by former Coordinating Minister for People's Welfare, retired General Surono, can also stem from 'a friction between the value system of *Pancasila* and new value systems'.[27]

Secondly, there was a recurrent reference to the impact of globalization on Indonesia's national identity and cultural values. There are worries among Indonesia's leaders that the process may threaten social and cultural values in the society. Former Commander of Indonesia's Armed Forces, General Try Soetrisno, stated that even though the globalization process cannot be avoided, it is imperative for Indonesia 'to maintain its... identity as a nation which adheres to *Pancasila* philosophy'.[28] He also warned that 'globalization...may have negative impacts on Indonesia's culture'.[29] It has also been stated that 'growing contacts among nations in an era of globalization can change the attitude and outlook of a nation, so that it will weaken the nation's identity'.[30] Surono also believes that globalization might bring about 'post-industrial cultural pressures and the penetration of foreign culture due to international relations, progress in communication technology, and the relative ease in getting foreign publications'.[31] The same view was also expressed by Minister of Justice, Oetoyo Oesman, when he stated that globalization characterized by clash of cultures, may 'remove us from our own cultural values'.[32]

Thirdly, globalization was seen to have the potential to threaten Indonesia's national unity and regime security. As former Minister of Home Affairs, retired General Rudini, has put it, 'globalization can strengthen the influence of liberalism which foster individualism, and deteriorate our nationalism, which, in turn, can encourage ethnic separatism to the effect of undermining the authority of the government'.[33] Soeharto also warned that in an era of global integration, Indonesia may experience national disintegration if it does not prepare itself with a strong national identity. According to him, 'foreign values which enter Indonesia through the process of the globalization of information, or through the process of economic globalization, can weaken national values and national outlook (*wawasan kebangsaan*)'.[34]

What are the recipes offered by the New Order government to cope with the negative influences of globalization? In general, Indonesian officials seemed to emphasize normative values as an instrument to cope with the adverse effects of globalization. Such negative impacts can be overcome by strengthening people's understanding of the state's ideology of *Pancasila* and the Constitution of 1945 (UUD 45). Soeharto, for example, maintained that '*Pancasila* is important for the survival of the Indonesian nation, because the process of globalization is now penetrating every aspect of the nation's life'.[35] He also stated that the nature of Indonesia's political system has not been understood by certain segments of Indonesia's society, and this is one manifestation of the negative impacts of globalization, that 'can be overcome by giving them a real understanding of what *Pancasila* and UUD 45 really mean'.[36]

Cultural, historical, and religious values were also invoked as a means to cope with the unexpected impact of globalization. Surono stated that in order to overcome the negative impacts of globalization, it was imperative for Indonesians 'to study... the soul and the spirit of 45 values'.[37] There have also been some suggestions that the negative effects of globalization can also be prevented by improving, strengthening, and implementing religious values in daily life. 'Our answer to the challenges of globalization', General Soetrisno maintained, 'is to strengthen national resilience (*ketahanan nasional*) in the field of religion'.[38] Finally, globalization should be embraced by upholding tightly Indonesia's cultural values. Minister of Information, Harmoko, stated that 'we accept globalization, but our mentality and culture should be based on Indonesian-ness'.[39]

To sum up, it can be said that there are at least two main aspects in Indonesia's elite's perceptions of globalization. Firstly, globalization is generally welcome provided it contributes positively to economic development in Indonesia. Secondly, it is also realized that globalization brings with it non-economic consequences that need to be dealt with cautiously. It can be said that growing concerns over the non-economic effects of globalization has marked the elite discourse on globalization in Indonesia. In other words, Indonesia's political elite and leaders see globalization as an economic process with political consequences. By May 1998, the unanticipated and contradictory consequences of globalization caught them by surprise when Soeharto's New Order was brought to a tragic end.

Crisis, the End of Soeharto's Rule, and Domestic Uncertainties: The Impact of Globalization?

It was noted earlier that Soeharto's New Order government perceived globalization in the main, as a favorable force that encouraged the development of Indonesia's economy. Moreover, Soeharto's New Order was also aware of the negative impacts of globalization on the ideological, political, and socio-cultural aspects of Indonesia's life. Many Indonesian leaders expected that these negative aspects could be overcome by maintaining and enforcing ideological and political values inherent in the New Order's political system. Therefore, the New Order government tended to subscribe to the view that on balance, globalization would be beneficial.

However, it was the relative success of the New Order in exploiting the opportunities presented by economic globalization that resulted in social and political transformations in Indonesia. Indeed, it has been observed that 'globalization and the process of uneven capitalist development bring with them formidable challenges to Soeharto's New Order. When capitalist development is often seen as the key to political and social stability, historically it has also been central to social diversification and the generation of conflict. The very success of capitalist development under the New Order is central to the crisis and political decline of Soeharto's regime since the second half of the 1980s'.[40] One aspect of that political decline was the failure of Soeharto's New Order to acknowledge and accommodate social diversification and conflict brought about by the unresolved tension between the state and the society.

Globalization at the Margin: The Transformation of New Order's Society and Global Forces

The economic progress achieved by Soeharto's New Order, made possible by the state's integration into the global economic system did pose a dilemma to the regime. On the one hand, three decades of New Order rule had resulted in a steady improvement of Indonesia's economy. The dramatic process of industrialization transformed the economy. The economy grew at an average of seven per cent annually. Gross national product (GNP) per capita rose from US$70 in 1970 to around US$1000 in 1996. The incidence of poverty has dropped sharply from 60 per cent in 1970 to around 15 per cent in 1990.[41] Education, literacy, and health indicators were all in the upswing. The internal structure of the economy has also undergone impressive changes. The contribution of oil and gas to national revenue from export earnings, which in the early 1980s accounted for more than 80 per cent, dropped sharply to only 20 per cent in the mid-1990s.[42] In 1991, the share of agriculture in the gross domestic product (GDP) declined to 19.5 per cent, compared to 53.9 per cent in 1960. Meanwhile, the share of manufacturing increased from 8.4 per cent to 21.3 per cent over the same period.[43] It is important to note, however, that such progress was attained by strengthening the authority and the dominance of the state over society that gave the New Order regime considerable power to implement its program of economic development.

On the other hand, the success of economic development also resulted in a number of significant changes in Indonesia's social and political structures that begun to unfold during the late 1980s. There were three major developments that had significant bearing on the nature of state-society relations in the late New Order period.[44] The first was the strengthening of large private-sector firms and of the capitalist class in general, including the rise of a sizeable *pribumi* (indigenous) capitalist class. A sharp decline in government revenues due to the drop in oil prices since 1982 had led to the restructuring and greater liberalization of the economy with the objective of promoting non-oil and gas exports, especially manufacturing-based products and goods. This policy has led to the increasing role of the private sector in the national economy.

The second development was the entry of what Robison and Goodman have called 'the New Rich' into the national stage. Thirty years of New Order's economic development have bred a new urban population with skills, jobs, and income comparable to those of their counterparts in most developed countries. Accompanying this group was the rise of critical, educated groups in society. There were those who were involved in, and channeled their political and social concerns through non-governmental organizations (NGOs). The number of NGOs increased sharply in the last twenty years to approximately around 10,000 with more than one third located in Jakarta. This group also represented a new generation of Indonesians, born after the inception of the New Order in 1966, with outspoken voices expressing their societal and political concerns. The other group consisted of critical intellectuals, both within the state bureaucracies (such as the Indonesian Institute of Sciences and private and state-owned universities) and without (such as in mass organizations and private think tanks). Upon the emergence of these groups, many commentators and analysts speculated whether they already constitute the seeds of a civil society in Indonesia.[45]

The third development is the spread of labor activism. According to official sources, there were 190 strikes in 1992, an increase from 130 in 1991 and 60 in 1990. Almost all of these strikes were considered illegal. Indonesian workers were obliged to pass through a series of arbitration tribunals and to secure permission from the

Ministry of Manpower before they can call a strike. Aware that such regulations constrained the articulation of their interests, more and more workers ignored the required procedures and engaged in wildcat strikes instead.[46] In addition, two independent labor unions emerged since 1990 despite government regulations which permitted the existence of only one labor union, the All Indonesia Workers Union (SPSI). More importantly, the spread of labor activism has put the New Order's policy towards labor movements into close international scrutiny, especially from the US.[47]

The emergence of these new groups clearly constituted a major transformation of Indonesia's society. These new groups and their political agendas and values have brought about a number of discernible impacts on state-society relations. Indeed, they constitute the catalysts for change in both the core political values and the style of governance of the New Order government. In this regard, it is important to understand that the rise of new forces in Indonesia as discussed earlier means at least two things. First, it signifies greater pluralism in Indonesia's society. New actors in the society began to assert their rights to participate in national politics, an area that has long been dominated by the state. Secondly, it indicates the weakening of the state's domination over the society. These two conditions resulted primarily from the imbalance between economic developments on the one hand and political reforms on the other. Rapid economic transformation has not been followed by a corresponding development in the political field.

Such a gap serves as a source of tension between the state and society. On the one hand, the government continues to invoke the significance and continuous relevance of the existing political values upon which the country's political process has been based. Consequently, there have only been little changes in the style of governance that reflects the patrimonial nature of the New Order state. On the other hand, some social forces began to press for change by demanding the government to incorporate new values—such as greater democracy, transparency in decision-making process, and respect for human rights—which are seen as imperatives for a modern state. These demands posed a challenge both to the legitimacy of the regime and the state's dominant position over society.

The growing challenges to regime legitimacy were in fact reinforced by two other conditions that had developed as a result of the New Order's economic development strategy and governing style. Firstly, there has been a widening economic gap in society. Economic development was seen to have benefited only a small stratum, primarily those close to the regime. Secondly, there has been a growing disillusionment with the nature of Soeharto's New Order. The New Order state had increasingly become more authoritarian and personalized. Given these two negative qualities, pro-democracy forces began to argue that the New Order government could no longer meet contemporary challenges facing Indonesia. By implication, the society increasingly saw the need for a regime change.

The transformation of the New Order's society was also matched by a parallel development in the international environment hospitable to demands for democratization. During the first two decades of the New Order, the global economic structure was said to be unfavorable for democracy in Indonesia because 'as long as Indonesia adapts to its role in the international capitalist system and implements policies favorable to international capital, the regime will enjoy widespread international support despite the lack of democracy and respect for human rights'.[48] However, with the end of the cold war, this favorable external factor for continued authoritarianism in Indonesia began to disappear. A number of leading Western countries, especially the US and members of the European Community, began to put democratization and human rights high on their foreign policy agendas. These countries were increasingly less inclined to support an authoritarian regime.

The rise of pro-democracy movement within Indonesia cannot be separated from the fact that globalization has provided the space for pro-democracy forces to gain leverage. It has been mentioned earlier that globalization made state boundaries irrelevant for the flow of ideas. Globalization also reduced state power and control over the flow of communication and interactions among private citizens and non-state actors of various countries. In the Indonesian context pro-democracy groups were able to develop links with counterparts abroad. In many cases, these groups also secured financial assistance from foreign foundations in order to support their activities. No less important was the fact that the revolution in information technology has made it easier for pro-democracy forces to find inspiration from the democratic struggles in other countries, make use of large amounts of information available on the Internet, and at the same time, use this facility to communicate and spread their ideas.

The ruling elite failed to recognize the dynamic changes in society and how the forces of globalization were reinforcing these changes. In this regard, the government's perception of negative elements of globalization colored its response towards challenges from society, especially the demands for greater democracy. While welcoming the impact of globalization on economic growth in Indonesia, the New Order government also repeatedly warns of its 'negative' impact on Indonesia's cultural identity and way of conducting politics. In other words, the New Order government was fully aware of the implications of such developments for its longevity.

The government thus sought to prevent 'foreign elements' from exacerbating domestic tensions. Such attempts were made, among others, by contrasting the suitability of Indonesia's own political values for Indonesia's political process with those of other 'foreign' values, which originated from the West. Excesses of the experiment with parliamentary democracy during the 1950s were often cited as evidence of the unsuitability of such a system for the country.[49] Such thinking clearly reflected the New Order's perception of globalization as a form of competition between the developed West and the developing East. It maintained that developed countries have used globalization as an instrument to pressure developing countries. There have also been 'warnings' by government officials that the West, by riding on the globalization process, tries to impose inappropriate political and cultural values on others, including Indonesia.[50]

This perception also explains the New Order's strong reaction to any attempt by Western countries to use issues like human rights, democratization, labor rights, and environment as underlying parameters of their policies towards Indonesia. While some elements in the government recognized the need for gradual change, there was deep suspicion among ruling circles that domestic opposition forces can use these same issues easily. It is not surprising, therefore, that political leaders stepped up their dismissal of the Western notion of democracy as inappropriate for Indonesia. For example, Minister of Research and Technology (later President), Habibie, condemned voting as a manifestation of a 'conflict-prone democracy' suitable only for a society with a culture of conflict.[51] Liberal democracy has also been criticized as a democracy based on individualism, excessive obsession with personal rights, interests, and individual freedom as opposed to the common interests of the whole society.

In short, it is clear that in its response to the global democratization wave following the end of the cold war, the New Order continued to stress that *Pancasila* democracy, with its roots in Indonesia's cultural values was the most suitable form of democracy for the country. Government's response to demands for greater democracy remained vague. It continued to claim that the need to maintain stability, social order, and development should be the defining framework for greater freedom in the society. However great was government's resistance to change, the pillars of regime legitimacy—stability and economic development—finally collapsed in May 1998.

Crisis and the Breakdown of Regime Legitimacy

During the early years of its rule until the early 1980s, the New Order government relied heavily on the values of 'stability-for-development' as the prime foundation of its legitimacy. By the mid-1980s, the very success of economic development had itself become the most important source of regime legitimacy. However, as a consequence of the rapid pace and expanded scale of economic development, the New Order government was faced with new economic, social, and political problems to include the increasing demands for democracy and respect for human rights.

These challenges became more evident since the early 1990s when criticisms against distorted economic policies of the New Order were increasingly voiced by almost all segments of the society—intellectuals, activists, artists, religious leaders, ordinary citizens, and some officials of the regime itself. The criticisms focused on three major issues. The first was the problem of nepotism. The development strategy of the New Order government was criticized because it only benefited Soeharto's family and its cronies. Secondly, the increasingly personalized character of the New Order's political system was seen as the source for increasing practices of collusion between state officials and crony businessmen. The third issue was the level of corruption that has become so rampant. As the attention of the society turned to these fundamental issues, demands for comprehensive political reform grew.

Challenges to regime legitimacy gained more impetus with the outbreak of the economic crisis in 1997. When the currency turmoil swept Thailand in July 1997, many in Indonesia believed that the danger would not severely affect the country. Such confidence seemed to have some basis at the time. During the first six months of 1997, it was estimated that Indonesia's economy grew around 6.4 per cent.[52] Until July 1997, exports had grown by 9.2 per cent, while inflation reached only 5.1 per cent, a marked decrease from 7.5 per cent during the same the period in 1996.[53] Due to such a promising start, it was predicted that Indonesia's economy in 1997 would grow by more than 7.8 per cent but less than 8.2 per cent.[54]

By September 1997, however, such optimism slowly faded when it became clear that following the Thai *baht*, the Indonesian *rupiah* began to tumble. By early September the *rupiah* lost about 20 per cent of its value against the dollar,[55] and about 39 per cent by the end of the month.[56] After spending US$1.5 billion defending the *rupiah* in August, the Indonesian Central Bank announced that it would allow the currency to float. The government was likewise forced to seek help from the International Monetary Fund (IMF), which agreed in October to provide US$18 billion for a three-year recovery program. However, the move did not help much to strengthen the currency's value. To restructure the financial sector, the government was forced to liquidate 16 private banks in November. In the same month, the government also introduced a new deregulation package. However, these measures similarly failed to improve the economy.

The overall situation moved very quickly from bad to worse when acute political problems, long swept under the carpet by the apparent harmony and stability of the New Order regime surfaced as news broke out that Soeharto was seriously ill. It started with the government's announcement that he needed time to rest for ten days after his long trip abroad to attend the APEC Summit in Vancouver, Canada. Rumors about Soeharto's deteriorating health grew stronger when he cancelled a trip to Kuala Lumpur for the Second ASEAN Informal Summit. Consequently, the value of the *rupiah* continued to fluctuate. By the end of 1997, the currency fell sharply and lost its value further against the dollar.[57]

As the economy continued to decline, criticisms against the government began to gain more momentum in the form of debates on the causes and the nature of the crisis. While conceding that the contagion effect may have played a part in Indonesia's crisis, many argued that the economic crisis had more to do with politics rather than economics. A leading Muslim intellectual, Nurchalis Madjid, described it as a systemic crisis in political life. A leading businessman, Sofjan Wanandi, shared this view. He saw that political uncertainties have affected the confidence of foreign investors. Muslim leader Amien Rais blamed the lack of transparency and inconsistency among government officials as contributing factors that worsened the situation. A group of New Order critics, the Petition-50, stated that the current monetary crisis was only an accumulation of a number of other crises in social, political, cultural, and economic life potentially ingrained in Indonesia's New Order.[58]

Many believed that the crisis was a reflection of a growing crisis of confidence within Indonesian society. Economist Hadi Soesastro wrote that the 'monetary crisis in Indonesia has turned to a crisis of confidence... Many feel that the government is unable to take the necessary measures to cope with the crisis because too many interests block [such measures]'.[59] The extent to which both society and the markets can be easily affected by rumors clearly reflect such a crisis of confidence. Therefore, many argued that to solve the economic turbulence and to prevent it from occurring again in the future, confidence must be restored. Moreover, that task can only be fulfilled effectively by balancing economic and political reforms.

The transformation of the financial crisis into a crisis of confidence on Soeharto's leadership did not deter the ruling elite from re-electing Soeharto as President in March 1998. However, forces in the society became more restive when it was clear that Soeharto did not seem to understand the extent and seriousness of the crisis. As expected, criticisms and anti-government movements became stronger. Student demonstrations, which were initially initiated within university campuses began to take a bolder stance. Unlike the previous months when criticisms were primarily directed at 'the system' rather than at the government, by April 1998 Soeharto himself became the direct target of student criticisms. For weeks, students and security authorities were on the brink of physical clashes as the former tried to broaden the protests by taking to the streets. The kidnapping of political activists, the fatal shooting of four students on 12 May, followed by the most devastating riot that shocked Jakarta on 13-15 May clearly demonstrated the breakdown of regime legitimacy. Soeharto was finally forced to step down on 21 May 1998 and Vice-President B.J. Habibie assumed power as the country's third president. The resignation of Soeharto, however, did not mark the beginning of a new regime. The New Order system created by Soeharto remained in place.

Turbulent Domestic Transition and the Breakdown of Security

The main problem facing Habibie's New Order regime was how to manage the process of democratic transition. With Soeharto's fall, many expected that the transition to democracy and the installation of a democratic government would proceed apace. While optimism for democratic transition was not unwarranted, the country was actually gripped with uncertainty. What was observed in post-Soeharto's Indonesia was a process of delicate 'negotiation' among various contending political forces, which could either result in a return to authoritarianism or an advance towards democratic consolidation.

The first, and arguably the most significant challenge that faced the Habibie regime was the controversy surrounding its legitimacy. Habibie's rise owed much to his being hand picked by Soeharto himself as vice-president in March 1998. Though many circles, including significant segments in the military challenged his nomination, no one dared challenge Soeharto directly. Parliament then had to endorse Soeharto's choice. After Soeharto's abrupt resignation, his replacement by Habibie sparked controversy. Those who supported Habibie argued that the transfer of power was done in accordance with the 1945 Constitution. Those who opposed Habibie, on the other hand, argued that Habibie's presidency was not legitimate because the process of Soeharto's departure from power itself was not legitimate.

The legitimacy debate was reinforced by doubts over Habibie's ability to lead the country. First, he had a track record of being a big spender, a quality deemed inappropriate for a country in deep economic crisis. Secondly, Habibie was seen as a figure that promoted sectarianism. He was involved with the Association of Indonesian Muslim Intellectuals (ICMI). In the eyes of many, this sectarian image made him unsuitable to lead a country as diverse as Indonesia. Thirdly, Habibie was seen as a leader given to the practices of corruption, collusion, and nepotism. Fourthly, Habibie was regarded no more than an extension of the Soeharto's regime. There were strong doubts whether he could bring Soeharto (and his family) to justice for all the wrongdoings during his tenure.

Due to its unique position in Indonesia's politics, there is no doubt that TNI constituted a significant player in the transition process. It played an important role not only in setting the pace of political bargaining but also in influencing the direction of democratic transition. Both military and civilian forces sought to advance their particular views and conceptions of politics in post-Soeharto Indonesia. Under the circumstances, however, the political arrangements cannot be shaped solely by civilian forces by asking the military to simply go 'back to the barracks'. Similarly, it was increasingly difficult for the military to re-dominate the whole process without facing strong resistance from the resurgence of civilian politics. Both parties had to negotiate their respective agendas in determining where Indonesia should be heading, what kind of polity and political system should be created, and what type of political arrangements should be formed.

Promoting democracy and dealing with the rise of civil society posed another challenge to Habibie's regime. The measures taken by his government sent mixed signals. On the one hand, certain steps contributed to the efforts towards greater democratization. The release of a number of political prisoners, the holding of general elections, the introduction of new political laws, greater openness, and more political freedom are often cited as positive steps. On the other hand, it was clear that Habibie's regime continued to employ Soeharto's governance style. To cite a few examples, Habibie introduced new restrictions to freedom of expression, proposed 'recalling'[60] of a number of members of parliament who were critical of his rule, and continued the practice of nepotism.

An equally difficult challenge that confronted the post-Soeharto regime was in the economic field. When Habibie took over, Indonesia's economy was in a very bad shape. The result of the monetary crisis has been devastating. Economic growth, which was earlier expected to reach more than seven per cent, fell to less than five per cent in 1997. Then the economy contracted by four per cent in 1998 while the inflation rate reached 77 per cent. By the middle of 1999, external debt increased to US$150 billion. The government had to postpone a number of projects. Thousands of business, especially in the property sector became bankrupt due to the tight money policy pursued by the government since August 1998. It was also estimated that approximately two million people lost their jobs.[61] Things were made worse by the sharp increase in prices, especially those of basic foodstuff. To complete this dismal picture, Indonesia also experienced the longest drought in 1997 that adversely affected the agricultural sector. Most threatening to the recovery was the total collapse of the banking sector and the difficulty of restructuring the huge corporate debt.

The fall of Soeharto's New Order also brought to the fore a number of sensitive issues that had been contained for more than three decades by the regime's complete domination over political discourse. During Soeharto's rule, there were clear limits on what issues could be discussed publicly. The New Order's strong emphasis on the imperative of maintaining stability, harmony, and unity had succeeded in suppressing potential sources of differences and conflicts. Differences and conflicts had been dealt with only in normative and symbolic ways backed by the use of force. In other words, Soeharto's New Order tried to manage potential conflicts without addressing the sources of the problems themselves. Such strategy was also pursued in the attempt to deal with the implications of globalization and economic development on the state of national cohesion, the question of national identity, and the problem of regional disparities.

Among the economic and political problems mounting in post-Soeharto's Indonesia, the most critical was the potential for disintegration. Excessive concentration of power in the hands of the central government during Soeharto's rule has led to an unbalanced relationship not only between the center and the region but also between Java and the outer islands. Growing regional dissatisfaction with this feature of the New Order had been felt long before the fall of Soeharto. There have been continued attempts in the East Timor, Aceh, and Irian Jaya provinces to secede from the Republic. However, harsh reactions from the military managed to suppress these secessionist movements, especially against those that resorted to armed struggle. With the regime change at the center, regional aspirations towards either gaining greater regional autonomy or achieving outright independence have been voiced more openly not only by these regions but by other regions as well.

The potential for disintegration was not only felt in the case of center-region relationships but also in inter-ethnic relations. As the May 1998 riots demonstrated, the long-standing tension between indigenous Indonesians and the ethnic Chinese community remained unresolved. The dominant role of the ethnic Chinese in economic activities has been a major reason for this tension. Many indigenous Indonesians maintained that economic globalization has benefited only big businesses that are mainly owned and run by ethnic Chinese.[62] There were fears that inter-ethnic conflicts could mar communal relations in a number of areas, such as between Dayak and Madurese in Kalimantan, between Bugis and East Timorese in East Timor, and even between Javanese and non-Javanese in many parts of the country.

A debate also started on the question whether Indonesia should be defined solely in terms of ideological uniformity (*Pancasila* as the sole ideology) or to allow other ideological beliefs such as Islam be used as the organizing framework for social and political activities. Some Muslim groups have already formed political parties with Islam as their organizing principle. These groups consequently demanded that the government abolish *Pancasila* as the sole ideology. On another front, the debate on the nature of Indonesia as a unitary state also ensued as the result of a suggestion by the Chairman of the newly formed National Mandate Party (PAN), Amien Rais, to open up public discourse on the merits of a federal state system.

By way of conclusion, it can be said that Indonesia has failed in its struggle to cope with the globalization process. Considering the Indonesian case, one might be tempted to argue that the global economy divides 'every society into conflicting economic interests. It undermines every nation's ability to maintain cohesion. It mocks the assumption of shared political values that supposedly unite people in the nation-state'.[63] However, it has also been observed that 'if the current financial crisis in the region has resulted in severe socio-economic turbulence in some countries, that is made explicable not so much in terms of the effects of globalization *per se* but rather in terms of their conjunction with local macro-economic mismanagement, lack of supervision and discipline, bad economic fundamentals, corruption, crony-capitalism and ossification of political institutions'.[64] Indeed, the case of Indonesia demonstrates the presence of all these problems and the state's failure to address them.

Soeharto's New Order failed to understand that only by addressing these problems could the positive effects of globalization be attained.

Implications for ASEAN: Intra-ASEAN Relations and Regional Security

Dramatic changes in Indonesia also had important implications for regional relations. What happened in Indonesia was not an isolated process. As mentioned earlier, Indonesia served as an illustrative example where the security *problematique* of globalization and development was strongly felt. Its inability to manage the social and political consequences of economic globalization that required domestic political adjustments has resulted in the weakening of regime legitimacy, the collapse of political order, and the breakdown of security at all levels. Indeed, these political processes took place in an environment where changes at the global level penetrated traditional state boundaries. Change constituted a consequence of 'the intensification of world wide social relations which link distant realities in such a way that local happenings are shaped by events occurring many miles away or vice versa'.[65]

ASEAN cooperation must be placed in the context of the same security *problematique,* which all member states, once they embraced globalization, were bound to face. Chin Kin Wah observed that 'for the ASEAN states, regional cooperation today has to take much greater cognizance of this intensification of world wide relationship, aided by the revolution in information technology, which have impacted upon and complicated their domestic and regional agenda'.[66] Within such an interdependent environment, changes in an ASEAN member state were bound to have effects not only on another member state, but also on the region as whole. In this regard, intra-ASEAN relations and wider regional security constitute two main areas where the implications of domestic economic and political changes for member states will be increasingly felt.

With regard to intra-ASEAN relations, the effects of globalization on domestic changes in Indonesia and in a number of other ASEAN countries such as Thailand and the Philippines elicit a number of implications. Firstly, it raises questions on the efficacy of regional cooperation, which is still centered on the role of state-actors. ASEAN remained an inter-governmental form of cooperation that puts strict emphasis on the centrality of state sovereignty. However, the emergence of new, powerful non-state actors such as NGOs whose activities are not confined within traditional territorial boundaries serves as a reminder that states were no longer the only actors on the regional stage. While national sovereignty does matter, a strictly government-focused approach to regional cooperation has become irrelevant to today's reality. Therefore, the main problem facing ASEAN in coping with the impact of globalization is to strike a balance. It must transform itself into an organization short of a supra-national institution but more than just an inter-governmental form of cooperation.

Secondly, the rise of powerful non-state actors such as NGOs has also transformed the domestic context within which national policies on ASEAN cooperation has been formulated. As suggested earlier, the importance of these new actors in regional relations can no longer be ignored. Moreover, there has been a widening gap between the state and the NGOs regarding their respective agendas, interests, and aspirations. The economic crisis in Southeast Asia (SEA) and its attendant domestic political consequences have put ASEAN in an entirely new domestic and regional political context. The increased importance of non-state actors poses a challenge not only to the privileged position of the state as the author of what constitutes the agenda of regional undertakings but also to the very nature of ASEAN as a form of inter-governmental cooperation.

It is likely that if the current trend towards democratic transition and consolidation continues, one may expect the rise of contending views and expectations between the state and society over ASEAN's future agenda, role, and functions. Already, there is evidence suggesting that elite conceptions on the value and functions of regional cooperation and how it should be conducted may no longer correspond with those held by the rest of society. The debate that arose after the crisis on whether or not ASEAN should stick to its traditional principles of non-interference is illustrative in this regard. Therefore, the growing role played by civil society in shaping regional relations can no longer be overlooked.

Thirdly, it has also questioned the relevance of existing principles, norms, values, and *modus operandi*—the so-called 'ASEAN Way'—upon which ASEAN cooperation has been based for more than three decades. In this context, pressures have been building up for ASEAN to redefine 'the ASEAN Way'. Some, especially within the non-official 'second track' organizations, have argued that this redefinition is imperative to make ASEAN cooperation more effective, especially with the increasingly more complex issues and challenges facing the regional organization. For example, cooperation in dealing with trans-boundary pollution, such as the haze problem, is often hampered by the principle of non-interference as understood in its conventional terms by some member states. On this question, attempts by Thailand and the Philippines urging ASEAN to reconsider its traditional position on the principle of non-interference clearly demonstrate that pressures for change have come not only from non-state actors in the society but also from those member states where the previous antagonistic state-society relations has been transformed by globalization.

Finally, globalization-induced changes in some member states have also raised concerns over the possibility of ASEAN developing into a two-tier structure: one consisting of more democratic members and the other consisting of authoritarian states. Such a division could create a polarizing attitude between the two sub-groupings. On the one hand, the more democratic member states such as Thailand, the Philippines, and possibly Indonesia will increasingly find themselves at odds with the rest. On the other hand, less democratic states might also find themselves pressured by growing concerns on issues like democracy and human rights in the more democratic member states.

The regional security implications of domestic changes have been self-evident in the rise of new challenges to ASEAN's security agenda. In this regard, regional security will be affected by the nature of the government's response to such challenges. In coping with such a challenge, the government will be faced with two options: accommodation and resistance. It can be argued that differences in responding to attendant effects of globalization may set the context for new conflicts to arise not only within ASEAN but also between ASEAN and democratic members of the international community. Differences between less democratic ASEAN countries and Western powers over the question of democracy and human rights would also create difficulties for ASEAN as a whole. The case of Myanmar and its impact on ASEAN's relations with the West, for example, illustrates this point.

Secondly, there is also the challenge of uneven growth. Few would disagree that economic globalization is not always a benign process which brings benefits to all. Instead, many agree that globalization, largely a market-driven process, opens up space for competition, and competition is bound to produce losers and winners. Not all countries are well equipped to tap the many benefits offered by economic globalization. Some are quick in resorting to domestic adjustments, while others are constrained by concerns over possible damages such adjustment might bring to, say, vested interests. Consequently, states will grow at different rates, and the end result would be a widening gap between the rich and the marginalized, both within and between states. And, as noted by Zoellick, 'throughout history, adjustments in comparative wealth and power have posed risks to peace'.[67] The sensitivity of a weak and vulnerable country within an uneven regional distribution of wealth may exacerbate feelings of insecurity from which conflict often arises. In other words, deepening economic integration unmatched by an even pattern of development creates the potential for instability and conflict in the region.

Thirdly, intra-ASEAN security might also be affected by increased competition over resources and markets. The improved capacity of ASEAN states to move up the ladder of value-added production could serve as one source of heightened competition for markets. As a result, states will increasingly challenge one another. Malaysia's determination to develop Port Klang, for example, has been cited as one example of increased competition with Singapore.[68] Moreover, the relative success of economic development in the region also has disturbing implications for resources. Oil and gas, for example, stand prominently in the *problematique* of development and security. Overlapping territorial claims in the South China Sea among some ASEAN countries seem to be motivated by the need to secure vital resources. Unfortunately, as noted by Zoellick, 'the drive for security in resources has made many nations unwilling to rely on others'.[69] The slow progress in finding an acceptable formula for joint exploration in the South China Sea is a testimony to this problem.

Fourthly, regional security has also been affected by new sources of conflict stemming from potential (if not actual) spillover effects of domestic crises on non-conventional security areas. For example, economic hardship might increase illegal movement of labor across national borders. Warnings have been raised that 'bilateral friction between Indonesia and its neighbors could also increase in the years ahead if domestic economic and social conditions continue to deteriorate and massive numbers of Indonesians pour particularly into Malaysia and strong preventive measures are not taken'.[70] Other issues, such as increased transnational crime and piracy will also add to the non-conventional security threats facing ASEAN.

Fifthly, the projection of domestic ideas onto the regional domain, either by governments or NGOs might open up new sources of bilateral conflicts. The push for democratization and respect for human rights initiated by NGOs has moved across national borders. Some NGOs based in Thailand, the Philippines, Indonesia, and Malaysia have begun to exert pressures on the Myanmar government over democratization and human rights issues. The stable relationship between Malaysia and Indonesia has also been affected by growing concerns on the part of Indonesian NGOs over the fate of former Deputy Prime Minister Anwar Ibrahim. As the democratization process in a number of ASEAN countries gets consolidated, it will increasingly become more difficult for governments of those countries to prevent 'intrusion into domestic affairs' by NGOs. This trend will consequently increase the possibility of more friction among ASEAN member states.

Finally, economic globalization also poses a number of common security problems for ASEAN as a whole. Firstly, since the development strategy of ASEAN countries stressed export-oriented manufacturing industries, the volatile international markets will continue to be important. Dependence on international markets increases strategic dependence since it also increases the vulnerability of trading nations to pressure from other states in economic or strategic terms.[71] In this context, the actions of individual countries will matter, as demonstrated by the turmoil in Southeast Asian financial and currency markets.[72] Secondly, vulnerability to external shocks may exacerbate domestic problems. And protracted economic crisis could lead to national instability that in turn can affect regional security. Thirdly, the growing role of international financial institutions in an interdependent capitalist world may spark domestic and regional debates on state autonomy, sovereignty, and independence. Dependence on financial assistance from foreign institutions would also bring about consequences that do not always correspond to the domestic interests of the ruling elite. Such dependence will also undermine ASEAN's aspiration that regional countries alone solve regional problems.

Taken together, all these security implications pose a delicate challenge for ASEAN's role as a manager of regional order in the wider Asia Pacific region. ASEAN's credibility as a regional organization had been based on the achievements made by core member states in economic development. In the aftermath of the regional crisis of the late 1990s, that credibility has also been questioned. The restoration of ASEAN's credibility will largely depend on how far the Association is able to address the challenges discussed earlier. For example, ASEAN's image as an association capable of maintaining its relevance will depend on the ability to refine its principles, norms, and values and make them more aligned with a new post-cold war world. Moreover, the efficacy of ASEAN cooperation will also depend on how far its member states are prepared to recognize the inevitable impact of globalization on governance and adjust themselves accordingly.

Conclusion

This chapter has addressed the security *problematique* of globalization and development in Indonesia and how the failure to address that *problematique* reduces security at the local, national, and regional levels. Based on the above discussion, a number of conclusions can be drawn from the Indonesian experience.

Firstly, globalization is indeed an inevitable process for states with open economies. In the Indonesian case, globalization was generally welcomed provided it contributed positively to economic development. There was an understanding that the globalization process served as an important driving force for sustained economic growth. It was also realized that globalization had non-economic consequences that must be dealt with cautiously. In fact, it çan be said that growing concerns over the non-economic impact of globalization marked the national discourse on globalization during Soeharto's New Order era. In other words, Indonesia's political elite and leaders saw globalization as an economic process with political consequences.

Secondly, the economic globalization process also brought about non-economic implications for state-society relations in Indonesia. A consequence of the increased integration of Indonesia into the global economy was a greater exposure to ideas and values from abroad. Democracy and human rights were the most attractive ideas that came together with globalization. As new social forces grew stronger as a result of economic development, growing demands for broader participation in politics and policy-making ensued. The strengthening of new social groups, in turn reduced state's control over society.

Thirdly, the economic advantages brought about by globalization will be difficult to sustain without the state's willingness to accommodate demands for more transparency, wider political participation, and improvement in governance. The lack of transparency, corruption, and other negative practices of the state are not compatible with globalization. The Indonesian state's resistance to this imperative of globalization resulted in growing tensions between the state and the rest of society. In the end, it led to the corrosion of state legitimacy. When social challenges to state control are met with stubborn and unimaginative resistance, the breakdown of security becomes almost inevitable. And the negative effects on security will be felt not only at the individual, societal, and national level but also at the regional sphere.

However, it is important to note that Indonesia's encounter with the dilemma of globalization and development does not suggest that globalization is bound to produce devastating effects on the nation-state. Indonesia's participation in the globalization process, especially in economic terms, has initially resulted in some positive results. The Indonesian case has also demonstrated that problems occurred only when the state failed to undertake the necessary domestic adjustments in coping with the non-economic challenges of globalization. The Indonesian state's attempts to resist new demands for good governance and for a more democratic political arrangement led to the negation of previous achievements in the economic front. The positive effects of globalization can only be attained and sustained by addressing the political and structural weaknesses of a given social order.

Notes

1   Sjolander, C. T. (1996), 'The Rhetoric of Globalization: What's in a Wor(l)d?', *International Journal*, vol. LI, no. 4, Autumn, pp.603.

2 Rosenau, J. N. (1996), 'The Dynamics of Globalization: Toward an Operational Formulation'. *Security Dialogue*, vol.27, no.3, September, pp.249.

3 Levitt, T. (1985), 'The Globalization of Markets', in A.M. Kantrow, (ed.), *SunriseSunset: Challenging the Myth of Industrial Obsolescence*, John Wiley & Son, New York, cited in Raghavan, C. (1995), *What Is Globalization?*, paper presented at the University of Lausanne, reprinted in *Third World Network, http://www.twnside.org.sg/souths/twn/title/what-cn.htm*. See also, Supratikno, H. (1991), 'Globalisasi Ekonomi Dunia, Peluang dan Strategi' (The Globalization of World Economy, Opportunities and Strategies), *Kompas*, 3 August.

4 United Nations Development Programme (UNDP) (1997), *Human Development Report 1997*, Oxford University Press, Oxford, pp.82.

5 Mittelman, J. H. (1994), 'The Globalization Challenge: Surviving at the Margin', *Third World Quarterly*, vol.15, no.3, September, pp.432.

6 *Ibid.*, pp.431.

7 *Ibid.*

8 'Perekonomian Indonesia: Harus Bisa Berselancar di Atas Ombak Globalisasi' (Indonesia's Economy: The Ability to Surf on the Wave of Globalization is Crucial), *Angkatan Bersenjata*, 16 August 1990.

9 Both Kuntjoro-Jakti and Nasution gave their views in *ibid.*

10 *Ibid.* However, two years later, Swasono revised his view. He began to stress the important for Indonesia to join the globalization process and take an active part in it. See, *KOMPAS*, 17 February 1992.

11 See, for example, *Suara Karya*, 4 April 1991 and *Suara Karya*, 8 September 1997.

12 President Soeharto, speech before the '13th Congress of All Indonesian Workers Union', Jakarta, 26 November 1990 in *Himpunan Pidato Presiden Republik Indonesia (A Collection of Speeches of the President of the Republic of Indonesia)*, Fourth Quarter, State Secretariat, Jakarta, pp.688.

13 President Soeharto, speech before the '6th Congress of Indonesian Association of Accountants', Jakarta, 22 September 1990 in *Himpunan Pidato Presiden Republik Indonesia (A Collection of Speeches of the President of the Republic of Indonesia)*, Third Quarter, State Secretariat, Jakarta, pp.568.

14 See, *Suara Pembaruan*, 15 May 1991.

15 *Angkatan Bersenjata*, 1 April 1991.

16 Comments made by Minister of Defence, General L.B. Moerdani, *Merdeka*, 29 May 1991.

17 *Angkatan Bersenjata*, 22 May 1991.

18 See, statement by ABRI Commader-in-Chief, General Try Soetrisno, in *Angkatan Bersenjata*, 8 February 1993.

19 *Pelita*, 25 May 1993. See also, Sutan Ali Asli (1993), 'Remember, Globalism is also Imperialism, *Merdeka*, 29 May.

20 *Suara Karya*, 4 April 1991.

21 *Media Indonesia*, 3 October 1997.

22 *Ibid.*

23 *Antara*, 3 December 1992.

24 *Suara Karya*, 12 March 1997.

25 *Suara Karya*, 8 September 1997.

26 *Media Indonesia*, 3 October 1997.

27 *Angkatan Bersenjata*, 18 January 1992.

28 *Suara Karya*, 9 February 1991.

29 *Bisnis Indonesia*, 15 August 1997.

30 *Antara*, 20 November 1992.

31 *Angkatan Bersenjata*, 18 January 1992.

32 *Suara Karya*, 16 March 1991.
33 *Angkatan Bersenjata*, 25 September 1992.
34 *Suara Karya*, 12 March 1997.
35 *Media Indonesia*, 3 October 1997.
36 *Suara Karya*, 12 March 1997.
37 *Angkatan Bersenjata*, 18 January 1992.
38 *Angkatan Bersenjata*, 15 January 1993.
39 *Antara*, 3 December 1992.
40 Berger, M. T. (1997), 'Old State and New Empire in Indonesia: Debating the Rise and Decline of Soeharto's New Order', *Third World Quarterly*, vol.18, no.2, June, pp.346.
41 Schwarz, A. (1994), *A Nation in Waiting: Indonesia in the 1990s*, Allen & Unwin, St. Leonards, N.S.W., pp.58.
42 See, Schwarz, A. (1997), 'Indonesia After Soeharto', *Foreign Affairs*, vol.76, no.4, July-August, pp.125.
43 Robison, R. (1996), 'The Middle Class and the Bourgeoisie in Indonesia', in R. Robison and D. S. G. Goodman (eds), *The New Rich in Asia: Mobile Phones, McDonalds and Middle Class Revolution*, Routledge, London:, pp.79.
44 This section is drawn from Sukma, R. (1997), *Values, Governance, and Indonesia's Foreign Policy*, a paper presented at the Conference on 'Values, Governance and International Relations', Tokyo, December.
45 For a more comprehensive study on NGOs in Indonesia and their political aspirations, see Eldridge, P. J. (1995), *Non-Governmental Organization and Democratic Participation in Indonesia*, Oxford University Press, Kuala Lumpur.
46 Schwarz, *A Nation in Waiting: Indonesia in the 1990s*, 1994, pp.259-260.
47 Suryadinata, *Indonesia's Foreign Policy*, pp.142.
48 See, Uhlin, A. (1997), *Indonesia and the 'Third Wave of Democratization': The Indonesian Pro-Democracy Movement in a Changing World*, Curzon Press, Surrey, pp.167-168.
49 Liddle, *Leadership and Culture*, pp.184-185.
50 See, for example, speech by Indonesia's Foreign Minister Ali Alatas at the 'Inaugural Meeting of the Indonesian Council on World Affairs (ICWA)', Jakarta, 2 December 1997, p.14.
51 *Republika*, 19 January 1994.
52 *Kompas*, 26 December 1997.
53 Ikhsan, M. and Tuwoi, L. D. (1997), 'Tinjauan Triwulanan Perekonomian Indonesia' (A Quarterly Assessment of Indonesia's Economy), *Ekonomi dan Keuangan Indonesia*, vol.XLV, no.2, June, pp.195.
54 *Ibid.*, pp.181.
55 *Asiaweek*, 12 September 1997.
56 Rafinus, B. H. and Suryabrata, W. A. (1997), 'Tinjauan Triwulanan Perekonomian Indonesia' (A Quarterly Assessment of Indonesia's Economy), *Ekonomi dan Keuangan Indonesia*, vol.XLV, no.3, September, pp.373.
57 *Kompas*, 6 January 1998.
58 Their views are reported in *ibid.*
59 Soesastro, H. (1997), 'Harus Diupayakan Krisis Rupiah Berakhir' (The Rupiah Crisis Should be Ended), *Kompas*, 23 December.
60 In the system created by Soeharto, political parties have the right to withdraw its members in the Parliament.
61 *Tiras*, 29 December 1997.
62 This view is voiced often enough by respondents interviewed for this study either in Jakarta or in Ujung Pandang, the capital of South Sulawesi province in northen Indonesia

(September 1998), and in Banda Aceh, the capital of Aceh Province in western Indonesia (in February 1998).

63	Graider, W. (1997), *One World, Ready or Not: The Manic Logic of Global Capitalism* Simon and Shuster, New York, pp.18, quoted in Wah, C. K. (1998), *'Globalization and Its Challenges to ASEAN Political Cooperation'*, paper presented at 'ISEAS 30th Anniversary Conference on Southeast Asia in the 21st Century: Challenges of Globalization', Singapore, 30 July – 1 August, pp.2.

64	*Ibid.*, pp.3-4.

65	Giddens, A. (1990), *The Consequences of Modernity*, Polity Press, Cambridge, pp.64, quoted in *ibid.*, pp. 4.

66	*Ibid.*

67	Zoellick, R. B. (1997-98), 'Economic and Security in the Changing Asia-Pacific', *Survival*, vol.39, no.4, Winter 1997-1998, pp.36.

68	*Ibid.*, pp.40.

69	*Ibid.*

70	Hassan, M. J. (1998), *Impact of Globalization on Political Change in Southeast Asia*, paper presented at 'ISEAS 30th Anniversary Conference on Southeast Asia in the 21st Century: Challenges of Globalization', Singapore, 30 July – 1 August 1998, pp.7.

71	Harris, S. (1995), 'The Economic Aspects of Security in the Asia/Pacific region', *The Journal of Strategic Studies*, vol.18, no.3, September, pp.39.

72	Zoellick, 'Economic and Security in the Changing Asia-Pacific', 1997-98, pp. 31-32.

References

Berger, M. T. (1997), 'Old State and New Empire in Indonesia: Debating the Rise and Decline of Soeharto's New Order', *Third World Quarterly*, vol. 18, no. 2, June, pp. 346.

Eldridge, P. J. (1995), *Non-Governmental Organization and Democratic Participation in Indonesia*, Oxford University Press, Kuala Lumpur.

Giddens, A. (1990), *The Consequences of Modernity*, Polity Press, Cambridge, pp. 64.

Graider, W. (1997), *One World, Ready or Not: The Manic Logic of Global Capitalism* Simon and Shuster, New York, pp. 18.

Harris, S. (1995), 'The Economic Aspects of Security in the Asia/Pacific region', *The Journal of Strategic Studies*, vol. 18, no. 3, September, pp. 39.

Hassan, M. J. (1998), *Impact of Globalization on Political Change in Southeast Asia*, paper presented at 'ISEAS 30th Anniversary Conference on Southeast Asia in the 21st Century: Challenges of Globalization', Singapore, 30 July – 1 August, pp. 7.

Ikhsan, M. and Tuwoi, L. D. (1997), 'Tinjauan Triwulanan Perekonomian Indonesia' (A Quarterly Assessment of Indonesia's Economy), *Ekonomi dan Keuangan Indonesia*, vol. XLV, no. 2, June 1997, pp. 195.

Levitt, T. (1985), 'The Globalization of Markets', in A.M. Kantrow, (ed.), *SunriseSunset: Challenging the Myth of Industrial Obsolescence*, John Wiley & Son, New York.

Mittelman, J. H. (1994), 'The Globalization Challenge: Surviving at the Margin', *Third World Quarterly*, vol. 15, no. 3, September, pp. 432.

'Perekonomian Indonesia: Harus Bisa Berselancar di Atas Ombak Globalisasi' (Indonesia's Economy: The Ability to Surf on the Wave of Globalization is Crucial), *Angkatan Bersenjata*, 16 August 1990.

Rafinus, B. H. and Suryabrata, W. A. (1997), 'Tinjauan Triwulanan Perekonomian Indonesia' (A Quarterly Assessment of Indonesia's Economy), *Ekonomi dan Keuangan Indonesia*, vol. XLV, no. 3, September, pp. 373.

Raghavan, C. (1995), *What Is Globalization?*, paper presented at the University of Lausanne, reprinted in Third World Network, *http://www.twnside.org.sg/souths/twn/title/what-cn.htm*.

Robison, R. (1996), 'The Middle Class and the Bourgeoisie in Indonesia', in R. Robison and D.S. G. Goodman (eds), *The New Rich in Asia: Mobile Phones, McDonalds and Middle Class Revolution*, Routledge, London:, pp. 79.

Rosenau, J. N. (1996), 'The Dynamics of Globalization: Toward an Operational Formulation', *Security Dialogue*, vol. 27, no. 3, September, pp. 249.

Schwarz, A. (1994), *A Nation in Waiting: Indonesia in the 1990s*, Allen & Unwin, St. Leonards, N.S.W., pp. 125, 259-260.

Schwarz, A. (1997), 'Indonesia After Soeharto', *Foreign Affairs*, vol. 76, no. 4, July-August, pp. 125.

Sjolander, C. T. (1996), 'The Rhetoric of Globalization: What's in a Wor(l)d?', *International Journal*, vol. LI, no. 4, Autumn, pp. 603.

Soesastro, H. (1997), 'Harus Diupayakan Krisis Rupiah Berakhir' (The Rupiah Crisis Should be Ended), *Kompas*, 23 December.

Sukma, R. (1997), 'Values, Governance, and Indonesia's Foreign Policy', a paper presented at the Conference on *Values, Governance and International Relations*, Tokyo, December.

State Secretariat (1991), *Himpunan Pidato Presiden Republik Indonesia (A Collection of Speeches of the President of the Republic of Indonesia)*, Fourth Quarter, Jakarta.

Supratikno, H. (1991), 'Globalisasi Ekonomi Dunia, Peluang dan Strategi' (The Globalization of World Economy, Opportunities and Strategies), *Kompas*, 3 August.

Uhlin, A. (1997), *Indonesia and the 'Third Wave of Democratization': The Indonesian Pro-Democracy Movement in a Changing World*, Curzon Press, Surrey, pp. 167-168.

UNDP (1997), *Human Development Report 1997*, Oxford University Press, Oxford, pp. 82.

Wah, C. K. (1998), *Globalization and Its Challenges to ASEAN Political Cooperation*, paper presented at 'ISEAS 30th Anniversary Conference on Southeast Asia in the 21st Century: Challenges of Globalization', Singapore, 30 July – 1 August 1998, pp. 2.

Zoellick, R. B. (1997-98), 'Economic and Security in the Changing Asia-Pacific', *Survival*, vol. 39, no. 4, Winter 1997-1998, pp. 36.

Chapter 11

Globalization and the Military in Indonesia

Kusnanto Anggoro

Introduction

A number of seminars, workshops, and conferences within Indonesian military circles during 1999 intensely discussed wide ranging issues, especially on threat assessment and the role of the armed forces in new circumstances at the domestic as well as international levels.[1] In the blueprint of military reform published by the Department of Defense and Security, it was acknowledged that global issues of democratization, environment, and human rights will continue to be contentious issues in international relations.[2] The blueprint and other statements made by high-ranking military leaders suggest that global issues were being taken seriously. A great deal is being said about 'democracy and civil society', 'peacekeeping missions', and other issues that are considered relevant to the new roles of the military. Yet what the Indonesian military considers as the 'new paradigm' appears to be preoccupied mainly with internal military matters and reforms within the state machinery. However, the military has yet to come up with an official policy on how to respond to the challenges of globalization.

Enormous stresses and strains have rocked militaries throughout the world in the aftermath of the cold war. The pressures of globalization have affected the military as well. This chapter examines the military's perception of and response to globalization. In Indonesia, globalization has posed the compelling issue of how the military will adapt to the changing environment. In the global arena, public pressures for civilian supremacy, refocused enmities, international and regional transformation, revolution in military affairs (RMA), and fragmenting polities have all challenged the very foundation of military politics. In addition to its response to globalization, the military's views on security interdependence, state security, and matters related to their own survival and progress as an institution will also be discussed in this chapter. Furthermore, the tension between the strong current of global turbulence and the commitment of the military to its established role in Indonesian politics will also be examined.

In Indonesia the military has been part of the elite who, along with their civilian counterparts has played and will continue to play an important role in the affairs of the state.[3] The Indonesian experience is somewhat distinct, compared to that in Latin

American and African countries. Indonesia's historical background and national security doctrine, for example, have provided the Indonesian military with the justification for political involvement. Indonesian soldiers and officers see themselves as the guardian of the institutions and machinery of the state. They are *securocrats*. As unconditional legitimacy has always been problematic in Indonesia, security issues are prone to politicization. This tends to make the military no more than an apparatus of an autocratic state or government. The dynamics of the military's response to the changing environment could be an illuminating case that could show how globalization presents challenges not only for the state but also for particular groups within it.

The Military's Perception of Globalization

The closing years of the 20th century have been marked by phenomenal developments that have transformed the concept of security. Security is now understood more broadly than before. It extends beyond the security of the state to the security of groups and individuals in society as well as to the international system and to the shared global environment. Contemporary definitions of security encompass not only military defense but also the conditions for peace, which includes sustainable development, economic and social equity, and protection of human rights. More than ever before, security is seen as affecting, and is affected by the exploitation of natural resources, environmental degradation, population dynamics, and gender identities. The Balkans, the Middle East, and the Korean Peninsula remain the global hotspots, but security analysts are becoming increasingly interested in the causes of protracted violent conflicts. Development has become more relevant to long-term and genuine security. If security remains to be considered as a prerequisite for the development of states and non-states actors to enhance their ability to survive, the link between security and development should accordingly be obvious.

Another hallmark of the century is the remarkably intensifying process of globalization, which is now an indispensable part of the discourse in political science, sociology, economics, and international relations. Globalization should be understood as a multifaceted dynamic with many different meanings. The word 'global' has at least three meanings: (1) spherical; (2) total/universal; and (3) worldwide. Assuming that the third meaning is the most relevant, one can conclude that the capacity to erode boundaries is the common denominator inherently attributed to the phenomenon of globalization. States are becoming geographically vulnerable and politically susceptible to external intrusions, a phenomenon commonly believed to have serious national security implications.

Such structural definition of globalization is necessary to describe present social interactions. Globalization can produce an enormous degree of improvement in human well being in countries that have taken advantage of the opportunities it provides. The opposite is also true. Not only has globalization undermined the Soviet empire; it may also bring about similar effects in China. Therefore, it is imperative to specify the realms wherein globalization takes place. In the economic realm, for example, globalization could be described as increased mobility of capital, liberalization of exchange, and flexible responsiveness to global norms. In a similar vein, political globalization is a multiple process that involves three *loci* of development: the transcendence of 'state-centric' value commitments, the advancement of liberal democracy, and the decentralization of state powers. Cultural globalization may be described as the widening de-territorialized identity, global distribution of images, and homogenization of global culture. In international relations, globalization could simply mean the diminishing of state sovereignty and the increasing focus on the global-local nexus.

The perception of a particular group in society of any phenomenon relates very closely to its identity. The Indonesian military is unique due to its multiple identities. The question is whether its members have a common perception of and response to globalization. One aim of this chapter is to examine whether there are significant differences within the Indonesian military elites: between those that are part of the government bureaucracy and those in the chain of military command. Also, whether a retired officer would provide similar answers as those in active service. It is also important to examine whether there are significantly different perceptions and responses among the different services—the army, the navy, and the air force—in view not only of their varying political clout but also their different exposure or vulnerability to global issues.

In the Western tradition of liberal democracy, the military is subject to civilian control. In Indonesia, at least until very recently, there is strong support for the notion of the military not only as a professional entity but also as a political elite. Thus, the military is a professional entity that has a distinct responsibility for defending the state's interest. Like its Western counterparts,[4] the Indonesian military is skeptical towards globalization. Conservatism toward change and things foreign appears to be a character of most military establishments. This seems more so in Indonesia, where the military is responsible not only for external security but also for internal security. The Indonesian military is overly concerned about the growth of international interdependence, believed to have made the nation-state increasingly vulnerable to external forces with all its attendant security implications.

The military may be the most cohesive group within Indonesian society. As in other countries, the hierarchical chain of command is undoubtedly very strong in the Indonesian military. Yet, this does not necessarily mean that there are no differing perceptions on particular subjects. A new generation of young officers is coming to the ranks. The military elite of the future Indonesia could have different perceptions from their predecessors due to greater international exposure and different interpretations of social reality. Even within a peer group, the different benefits enjoyed from the *dwifungsi* (dual function of the military) or the different skills among the services cannot be ignored. However subtle these differences may be, it is possible to identify the diversity of opinions among them by means of recognizing generational changes, hierarchy of command, closeness to authorities, or intra-service specialization. Other relevant variables include political affiliation, educational background, and sectional interests.

To better understand the Indonesian military's perception of globalization, the latter must be specified further. Globalization may be too broad an issue for professionally restricted institutions as the military to fully comprehend. It will be irrelevant to understand military perceptions of globalization in terms of its general characteristics. It could also be misleading to limit globalization to just economic liberalization. To the military, globalization could simply refer to a 'global phenomenon'. The relevant issue here is national governance on security affairs.

The military of Indonesia is both a political and a professional entity. In authoritarian Indonesia, perhaps there was no need to discern the different opinions held by the military and by the civilian elite. Indeed, their perceptions of and responses to globalization may not be significantly different after all. The mentality of 'stability first' and other authoritarian biases could well be found stronger within the military than in the civilian elite. This certainly does not mean that the military is more conservative than its civilian counterpart. Rather, it may be a product of its own distinct morale and norms derived from its history, doctrine, and non-qualified support for Soeharto's authoritarian regime.

It is useful to examine this issue at three different levels: the individual, societal (group), and national (state) level. At the individual level, the challenges of globalization are seen in the form of the revolution in military matters and the concept of war. Even in the West, these two impulses created enormous pressure for the military to downsize its forces, to adapt to the need for greater transparency in security policy, and to redefine military doctrine and strategy to be more suitable for modern warfare. The individual perceptions of officers and soldiers will eventually determine their concerns over challenges to the military as a corporate group or to society as a whole.

The main concern at the societal or group level is undoubtedly 'the erosion of military legitimacy and authority' as the consequence of political, economic and cultural globalization. The liberal ideas regarding civil society and multi-party systems are seen as posing a challenge to the established bureaucratic authoritarian regime of Indonesia. They deal with issues of security that presents challenges to regime legitimacy and authority. Participatory democracy is a stark counterpoint to the centralized system of political governance. Allegiance to state enterprises and a pessimistic assessment of privatization suggest the reluctance to accept democratization in the economic sphere. An emphasis on 'Indonesia-ness' could be seen as a rejection of sub-national rights and identities. The devolution of power from the center is also a global tendency. The reform that is taking place in the Indonesian military in many ways reflects this development. However strong the domestic impulses are, the reform is also influenced by global tendencies of the dissolution of corporate culture. Globalization could influence the military in the direction of a greater acceptance and recognition of 'others'.

Of relevance to the national or state level is the notion of globalization as a boundary-eroding phenomenon. One of the key features of the international system is the principle of state sovereignty. In particular, the state has the absolute right to autonomously determine and control its internal affairs. In the contemporary period, the capacity of nation-states to act unilaterally has increasingly been challenged by globalization. The idea of intervention in the domestic affairs of others has gained currency in recent years and has presented serious challenges to the political authority of national states.

The military's perceptions of globalization can be observed in terms of its understanding and degree of acceptance of international norms and conduct, transparency in defense and security affairs, and soft regional security arrangements. The Indonesian military as a part of the national leadership plays a role at two different levels. The first is on the international level. Here, the military would identify itself with the state. At this level, it is concerned with protecting the national interest. At the second level, namely the military as a corporate entity, it plays the role of balancing between the globalizing and localizing tendencies in the world today.[5]

Globalization as a Threat?

Having no clearly identifiable external [conventional] threats, internal threats to unity and socio-political order have figured prominently in the military's strategic and security calculations. Nation building and state building have become the most important values the military are committed to defend. Thus, it is natural that national integrity, state authority, and government legitimacy have been very important in military thinking on national security. The military perceives the threat to national security as a spectrum of dangers, beginning with the subtle ones and progressing to brutal and direct threats to national survival. With regard to ideological threats, the traditional left and right extremists (communist and Islamic fundamentalists) are considered as the principal internal enemies. While these forces continue to be considered as threats, new ones have emerged. These include the so-called 'global interactions'.

The first Defense White Paper of Indonesia issued in 1997 acknowledged that globalization has become a factor in the country's strategic calculations. However, the Paper did not directly and explicitly address the problems of globalization. It suggested that globalization should be understood as a structural dynamic and process of interaction. The military elite perceived globalization as a cluster of forces that is affecting the entirety of human activities. Globalization was also seen as a process of increasingly interdependent relationships.

More importantly, the military saw globalization as an external dynamic that influences domestic politics. As a result of dramatic developments in information technology, communication, and transportation, globalization is often perceived and interpreted as the dynamo that opens up the state and society to all kinds of information from outside. In the military's view, 'globalization has made domestic and external affairs almost inseparable'.[6] No institution, including government, would be able to prevent the flows of information from entering Indonesia.[7] The military elites seem to believe that the adoption of global values or culture would eventually influence the political foundation of the country.

It is difficult to say whether this perception is widespread within the Indonesian military. In the interviews conducted for this study, the arguments presented remained vague. An active military officer mentioned that liberal ideas could bring about a fragmentation of the nation-state as they accommodate allegiances to sub-national entities, such as ethnic groupings. Another officer pointed to the impact of globalization on national ideology: 'if it weakens the ideology of *Pancasila*, this will certainly have a negative impact on our life as a nation'.[8] The fundamental concern of the military is that globalization might strengthen the influence of liberalism and foster individualism.[9] Globalization has the potential to erode the fundamental values of the nation that is the glue for national unity;[10] and that 'becoming a member of the global community may threaten the social and cultural values of the society and in turn potentially threaten national security'. Perhaps the military's main concern is reflected in the view that 'deteriorating nationalism will in turn encourage ethnic separatism'.[11] In 1994, the Chief of the State Intelligence Coordinating Agency, Lt. Gen. Sudibyo, went as far as claiming that the state ideology *Pancasila* 'is being besieged from inside and outside Indonesia by proponents of liberal democratic ideology',[12] echoing an earlier statement against western liberalism by President Soeharto.

Cultural influences are seen to have a greater effect on political stability than economic liberalization. As an intellectual in the military puts it, 'culture is a repository of symbolic forms and social as well as individual experiences. It is the medium for personal, interpersonal and group exchange, expression and reception of ideas... and globalization required more explanation other than a mere political economic explanation'.[13] This particular view was widely shared in the military.

In the economic realm, globalization is seen as a challenge rather than a threat. The military has argued that globalization can be beneficial to economic development as it helps promote external trade and attract foreign investment. Economic interdependence is viewed as something that has brought about 'a shift of emphasis in international relations from ideology to economic interest'.[14] A middle-ranking officer at the Department of Home Affairs said that 'if the government conducts the correct policy, then Indonesia can benefit from economic globalization'.[15]

This attitude may have changed somewhat as a result of the 1997 economic crisis. The skeptics have grown stronger. They argued that the process of market-oriented economic development *cum* globalization does not ensure that the gains would be distributed equitably within Indonesia, creating stresses on social and political stability. Some began to argue that 'free trade is not necessarily beneficial, especially for less developed countries. Opening up a country to free trade can undermine the local economy, and a region that becomes too dependent upon a few products in the world market is very vulnerable to shifts in prices as well as to technological changes'.[16] This was the argument posed by an active military officer with an Master of Business Administration (MBA) degree. There is clearly a disappointment that faster growth has failed to reduce poverty and to raise living standards as quickly as many had hoped. Yet there seems to be a greater concern as the same officer has argued that the risk of pursuing economic globalization 'will be the increased demand for greater freedom of political expression and participation'.

The common perception about globalization in the military is that it entails cultural and economic processes that have serious political consequences.[17] It should be noted, however, that the military also believes globalization could not be avoided and should not be resisted, and that Indonesia cannot possibly isolate itself from that process.[18] The challenge is how national development can benefit from globalization. Realizing that Indonesia will not be able to avoid globalization, the military's positive response to globalization is 'to prepare ourselves to be able to join the process consciously and creatively'.[19] However, there is as yet no clear recommendation for coping with the negative effects of globalization. Many in the military expect that these negative aspects can simply be overcome by maintaining and strengthening ideological and political values inherent in Indonesia's political system, namely the state ideology of *Pancasila* and the 1945 Constitution.[20] Cultural, historical, and religious values are also invoked as the means to cope with globalization.[21] Conservative civilian leaders have made similar suggestions. However, they cannot provide any operational guidance on how the country and the nation should deal with the more practical aspects of globalization. If, indeed, globalization is perceived as a threat, the military is at a total loss on how to respond to this kind of threat.

Sovereignty and Globalization

Many have argued that globalization has not only broadened the concept of security to include non-military dimensions, but also changed the character of inter-state relations. The global phenomenon of multilateralism is most clearly evident in the security realm. Security cooperation among states tends to become more elaborate, cross regional, and inclusive. It includes not only traditional political and security questions but also economic security and new concerns regarding non-traditional threats. Since the early 1990s, the Indonesian military has become supportive of certain forms of multilateral security arrangements. The Defense Ministry and Military Headquarters have viewed positively the utility of the Association of Southeast Asian Nations (ASEAN) and the ASEAN Regional Forum (ARF) in maintaining regional security. However, they continue to believe in the concept of regional resilience, wherein the security of Southeast Asia (SEA) could be served primarily by the domestic security of countries in the region. They also believe that the unilateral use of force has become irrelevant. Instead, diplomacy and involvement in regional processes have gained greater importance. Perhaps, regional cooperation is seen as a devise to create a political buffer against external forces.

It remains unclear, however, how far the military is prepared to surrender sovereignty in forging regional cooperation. As far as security cooperation is concerned, this is still opposed by the military. On this issue, there are no significant differences of opinion between active officers and retired ones. On the issue of whether security cooperation should be enlarged to include closer cooperation in defense policy, however, there exist remarkable differences within the rank and file. The older generation seems to favor less coordinated cooperation and prefers to manage ASEAN in the usual manner. The reluctance of the Defense Ministry to accept the proposal of establishing a Regional Peacekeeping Training Center is a case in point. A similar reluctance has been shown on the issue of greater transparency in defense policy. The two Defense White Papers published for the first time in 1995 and subsequently in 1997, are indicative of how far the military is willing to go.

There will always be limits to cross-border cooperation. Future military leaders may or may not become more receptive to the idea of deeper security cooperation.[22] The nationalist hold is still strong in the military culture. On the issue of transparency, for example, a fairly representative group of the military contends that 'we have nothing to declare. It is almost impossible to report to them [United Nations Register on Conventional Arms] on an annual basis. We did not buy anything significant this year [1997]... we have no increase in defense budget, it was similar to that of last year... we bought weapons from Western countries where they could easily be traced'.[23] There is also the belief that deterrence depends more on credibility than on capability. As a middle ranking commander argued: 'We are militarily a weak country... and, as our history of guerrilla war against the Dutch has shown, the weaker side could only survive in a prolonged war if they manage to hide something.'[24]

The sense of nationalism and the prevailing professional culture tend to limit how far the military is prepared to deepen its defense cooperation. There is widespread support for regional confidence building measures (CBMs). There are no problems in undertaking joint exercises and receiving foreign officers at national military education and training institutions. However, the more elaborate measures of transparency, for example in defense procurement, are still opposed. Transparency can help reduce the fears of aggressive arms acquisition or intent, and thus help promote regional and global peace, security, and stability. Self-restraint or transparency in military procurement can also discourage diversion of resources from social and economic goals. Nevertheless, it may have a different impact on militarily weak countries or those with a 'defensive military posture' than on militarily strong countries or those with an 'offensive military posture.'[25]

It is quite possible that in the future, the Indonesian army will be more and more prepared to cooperate with other militaries. The Indonesian military is aware of the increasing importance of international trade, the large potentials of offshore resources, and the porous nature of an archipelago's territorial boundaries. These have led to a greater recognition of the value of regional cooperation. As a retired general formerly charged with military planning, argues: 'We simply have no capacity to compensate for our military security deficit with military options. In fact, we have nothing else but to join the larger power to balance our potential enemy and to support the ASEAN Regional Forum to engage China by political process.'[26]

The Indonesian military sees in regional cooperation both 'boundary strengthening' and 'boundary eroding' elements. It perceives the issue of greater transparency as surrendering the state's autonomy and power to decide on its own survival. In a world where there is intensified competition among states, developing countries will be left with even more limited choices. Such anxiety about the loss of autonomy is also felt by the military in other areas, in particular with regard to political conditionality that could be attached to bilateral and multilateral assistance. It is a common perception in the military that 'developed countries use globalization to prevent developing countries from threatening the superior (economic) position and status of developed countries. Non-tariff and tariff barriers, for example, are no more than Western instruments to prevent developing countries from becoming a challenger.'[27] Transfer of technology, international property rights, eco-labeling, and human rights issues are Western offensive measures that are insensitive to the need of developing countries. However strong the nationalist sentiments are, the military realizes it will have to recognize the utility of regional and global cooperation. Although the military favors an evolutionary approach in the development of the ARF, it has begun to argue that 'it may be necessary to develop a wide and full range of partnership as possible at all levels of society in order to strengthen a network of direct links'.[28]

The Indonesian military has long been involved in economic and business activities.[29] These activities may be negatively affected by economic globalization. There is concern that this perceived danger may reinforce the military's tendencies towards nationalistic policies. However, the military has not been able to articulate its concerns in this field. On the other hand, the military may also perceive that economic globalization could be beneficial to its involvement in business activities.[30] This research was unable to conclude about the impact of the military's involvement in business activities on its perceptions about globalization. It should be noted, however, that most military business activities are undertaken on a personal rather than institutional basis. At best, the attitude to opening up the economy to foreign investment and free markets is ambivalent.

Civil-Military Relations

Within the construct of a state, the dynamics of globalization are manifested in the interdependent relations among political and social groups in a national polity. Democratization is now taking place in Indonesia and in many other parts of the region. The question is whether the military will be prepared to subordinate itself to civilian authority. Equally important is the view of the military about the role of civil society and human rights in national development. In most plural societies, state institutions are to function as instruments for *nation-craft*, including the interrelationships among elements required in the formation of the state—constitution, government, political society, as well as civil society. Discussions about the relations between the nation and the state often assume that it is always the nation that seeks to create itself within a state. In order to remain viable, states seek to create a feeling of belonging among its citizens. This is an important theme in the history of Indonesia. To maintain the integrity of the state in a democratic setting, society must forge a collective identity. Nation building is as important as state building, and democracy is not simply a matter of statecraft but also nation-craft.

The question of military politics is problematic since the military establishment is constitutionally bound to support what Buzan called 'institutions of the state' and 'physical base of the state': constitutions, the authority of a legitimate government, a functioning state bureaucracy, and national—population and territorial—integrity.[31] These aspects have created a security predicament for the military.[32] In this particular context, it is critical where the military locates itself. Most frequently, especially in an authoritarian setting, it aligns itself with the executive branch of the state. It sees itself as a part of a regime and tends to serve the regime's own security. In a democratic polity, the military is put in a more difficult predicament. It has to strike a balance between supporting the authority of the state and protecting the interest of the populace. This becomes more complicated in a democratizing polity, especially where the military has a legacy of supporting an authoritarian regime. In the absence of national cohesion and state legitimacy, the military may be compelled to use force against the people. Students of civil-military relations have shown the extremely precarious experience in the post-military politics of some African and Latin American countries. Indonesia might prove to be an even more difficult case.

It is the belief of the Indonesian military elite that the complexity of globalization alone is sufficiently great to weaken central authority. Since the late 1980s, domestic pressures have built up such that government had to adapt to the changing nature and culture of politics. In part, this resulted from the rapid economic development during the Soeharto administration that led to great changes within Indonesian society. As is happening anywhere else, development is a material process that brings with it consequences for state and/or regime security. A remarkably sustained high economic growth has created demands for greater political participation. The years of economic liberalization may not have produced radical changes in the structure of income at the national level. But it is indisputable that there has been a substantial growth of the urban middle class. The structure of employment has also changed in the urban areas. The private and informal sectors have accounted for the bulk of employment opportunities. This is politically significant as they are relatively independent of the Indonesian state.

There is an unavoidable need for the military to strike a precarious balance between regime security and popular demands. It must have recognized that its own survival in the Indonesian polity is at risk and would very much depend on how it could array adequate responses to this challenge. Today, civilian supremacy is a given and democratizing civil-military relations is the answer. This will require a rereading of Indonesian history, a redefinition of the security doctrine, and a reorientation of the military's perception of politics.

However, it is unlikely that the military will easily give up the *dwifungsi* concept in the near future. The concept has some durability, being embodied in Indonesian politics. The country's struggle for independence in 1945 has legitimized the inseparability of the military from public life. The doctrine of the People's Total Defense requires an intense relationship between the military and the populace. The concept of *dwifungsi* is embedded in the Indonesian military's political culture. It is seen as a manifestation of the military as 'citizen, fighter, and soldier with the responsibility for the maintenance of national security and the realization of a just and prosperous society, materially and spiritually, on the basis of *Pancasila* and the 1945 Constitution'.[33] Regional unrest in the 1950s and the aborted communist coup in 1965 have all strengthened the military's role in nation-craft. It has put down separatist movements in South Sulawesi and Ambon in the 1950s as well as defeated the communist *putsch* in 1965.

The military argues that it has a role to play not only during times of war but also in times of peace, and in non-military matters. This tendency is still as strong today as it was in the past amid increasing people's rejection of *dwifungsi*. Needless to say, Soeharto's long reign has deepened the military role as an inherent part of statecraft. Soeharto was very successful in entrenching the *dwifungsi* concept in a series of legislative acts. General Soeharto was able to convince the military that its strong role in the government and political affairs had provided the stable atmosphere necessary for economic development. As supreme leader, Soeharto had also successfully asserted his personal rule, relying as much on his seniority in the military as on his powerful presidential post.

Within the military, there is a strong anti-liberal tradition and a sense of supremacy, both affecting civil-military relations. Military officers regard the liberal ideology of the mid-1950s as the main source of political instability. However, applying this view in contemporary Indonesia is erroneous. The parliamentary system of the 1950s is different from the current presidential system. It also has problems adhering to the concept of civilian supremacy as the military views itself as a partner of or participant in civilian politics and the most organized social force in Indonesian society. In practice, it was quite common for the military elite during the era of Soeharto to assert military supremacy on the bases of discipline, readiness, spirit of serving the people, and to set *an example* in carrying out *Pancasila* Democracy.[34] Most believed that a democratic polity should only be established if 'the society already matures and is able to behave in an appropriate manner ...so that they are able to apply consciously the distinction between the function of state and that of society'.[35]

It will not be easy under such circumstances to accommodate the global trend of civilianizing military politics, which is to transform military dominance into civilian supremacy. It would need a gigantic jump before the military would eventually accept a genuine democracy. This is not at all impossible. Soldiers and officers are not habit-cast. They also are susceptible to learning and change as their skills expand and their opportunities change. Less than a year after the downfall of Soeharto in May 1998, the Indonesian military has committed itself to a number of key structural reforms aimed at reducing the military's role in the state, including withdrawing support for the single ruling political party (*Golkar*) and pledging neutrality in the June 1999 election, separating the police from the military command, requiring military personnel who accept jobs as civilian administrators to resign from the military service, and eliminating the position of Chief of Staff for Social and Political Affairs—the very embodiment of the military's political role.

It remains to be seen how far this reform will go further as 'negotiations' between civilian and military elites are taking place. The Department of Defense and Security has published a blueprint for military reform entitled 'Redefinition, Reposition, and Redefinition of the Armed Forces in National Development'.[36] The blueprint no longer refers to the military as the 'dynamizers and stabilizers' of [political and social] development, as often done in the past and as mandated by Regulation No. 2/1982. It further reduced the military's official presence in governmental posts, legislative branches, and state bureaucracy. Organizational changes are also taking place, along with a reassessment of the military doctrine and the rewriting the curricula of the army's college.

Nevertheless, vestiges of the old thinking are still strong,[37] given the substantial number of military representatives in legislative bodies and in the cabinet and state bureaucracies. It is not yet clear how far they would go. Discussions in military circles are apparently aimed at setting the time frame of 15 years before military officers surrender their political privileges.

Further military reforms could be hampered by the contemporary politics of nation-craft. Of great significance is undoubtedly the threat to national integrity. Sub-groupism is on the verge of [re] emerging, parallel to or even as a response to globalization, at the same time that the position of the central government is eroding. The use of force to deal with this problem is no longer adequate. Local nationalism springs up as a response to globalization and as the hold of older nation-states weakens. One should recognize that national disintegration is essentially attributed to the inability of the state to assert authority in a proper way.

The Indonesian state, which the military supports constitutionally, could possibly re-impose control. The loss of power it experienced is not a sign of organizational failings, but reflects the incapacity of its institutions. It is interesting to speculate how the *de facto* dominant-subordinate relations between the military and the civil bureaucracy would eventually evolve to a parallel-spheres-of-action model, where both will have their autonomous spheres of action. While the armed forces legitimately monopolized every issue related to security, the civilians are charged with developing the national economy. Yet, this scenario is stable only under the condition of a growing economy and internal and external stability and peace. In the Indonesian case, the transformation will be a long process due to doctrinal rigidity, on the one hand, and the fluidity of military politics on the other. It is possible that the military would be transformed from the praetorian soldier to that of guardian[38] – whose function is to protect a particular social and political order but will refrain from day-to-day intervention in politics.

The Military, Globalization, and Internal Developments

The dynamics of globalization has transformed the concept of security from a preoccupation with territorial protection to a concern for economic well being and social welfare. In conversations with the military elite, the following views were expressed: 'recourse to war across national boundaries is likely to be increasingly eschewed, because it becomes too expensive economically and politically'; and 'thanks to its natural barrier, Indonesia is not going to face conventional threat of military invasions in the immediate future'. Regional stability is perceived to be maintained at least in the near- and mid-term, and that prolonged disturbances or violent conflicts would certainly invite the intervention of larger powers, such as the

United States (US) or Japan that have profound interests in the region. Security questions will basically stem from military force build-up, spillover from adjacent regional conflict, sovereignty conflicts over maritime resources, and secure access to international waters.

What then is left of the military's role in defending the country against external threats? Again, this is not a simple question to answer. The confluence between democratization at the domestic level and the domestic vulnerabilities that result from globalization creates new security challenges. The military around the globe, including in the US, is trying to find a new role. The end of the cold war, the demise of the Soviet Union, and shrinking defense budgets are powerful reasons for what the Pentagon labels as 'military operation other than war' to justify American involvement in smaller conflicts and the wider spectrum of peacekeeping missions. A more professional army in Indonesia indeed could mean greater roles for the military. For the Indonesian military, professionalism is defined broadly to encompass administrative and even political functions as well as proficiency in arms. The military continues to believe that it has the responsibility of maintaining political stability, strengthening legitimacy and authority of the government, and maintaining social order. It is also important to note that it intends to use its 'idle capacities' in civic mission and peacekeeping missions.[39] Perhaps military professionalism in Indonesia will always be defined primarily in terms of the capacity to maintain domestic order. However, a new generation of professional military officers is emerging. Since it was not involved in the struggle for independence against the Dutch, it may not be able to claim a special political role.

Professionalism in defense affairs, in the more narrow sense of the word, is definitely on the rise within the Indonesian military. Australian and American analysts have detected this growing military professionalism during the first real strategic planning for the defense of the Natuna Islands and its incorporation in the broader defense of the nation. On the horizon, there seems to loom new operational strategies as a result of technical advances. The navy and the air force are at the forefront of developing new operational strategies. This suggests that there will be changes in weapons configurations and force structures.

These changes do not necessarily relate to globalization. Institutional changes within the military are caused more by domestic developments rather than changes in the external environment. The navy and the air force have always felt that they do not benefit from *dwifungsi*. To them, it is no more than the dual function of the army, those wearing the 'green uniform'. Furthermore, the nature of future conventional threats, the revolution in military affairs, and the conduct of modern war should enhance the role of the navy and the air force relative to the ground forces. The protection of exclusive economic zones (EEZs), the security of maritime resources, and the sustainability of access to international waters will have to depend heavily on the capability of the naval forces and the surveillance of the air force.[40]

The Indonesian military is no longer a single, cohesive body as it was in the past. Even within each service, there is a strong feeling that *dwifungsi* has benefited only the generals. For instance, business activities involving military agencies have been limited to some military generals. The need for the redistribution of wealth, assets, and economic benefits from *dwifungsi* seems prominent among and within the military services.

These trends do not necessarily strengthen factionalism within the military establishment. Quite possibly, the military headquarters, in trying to regain control and to make itself more efficient and effective,[41] will be able to manage well the hierarchy of command, while allowing for some kind of organizational diversification and dissolution of power and authority. A modern armed force will involve inter-service coordination rather than rivalry. To regain a sense of unity and integrity, military leaders need to find the appropriate institutional set-up and build the appropriate networks that effectively embody social capital. As Putnam suggests, 'horizontal ties' represent more productive social capital than 'vertical ties' of hierarchical command.[42]

Mounting pressures on the Indonesian military are leading to explicit definitions of the roles it wants to play, particularly with regard to internal security matters. There is also the need for rules of engagement and codes of conduct for the use of force in particular circumstances. The construction of democratic civil-military relations requires arduous work both from the civilian and the military. General Yoedhoyono himself has made the assertion that 'the role of an armed forces should not have been determined and formulated by the military alone'.[43] Ronald Spector may be wrong in stating that 'military people and politicians will never have the same responsibilities or concerns or the same vision of the world and its conflicts; and some measures of tension and misunderstanding will probably always exist in their relationship'.[44] The *dwifungsi* concept is well embedded in military thinking and could be useful in maintaining the unity of Indonesia. Nevertheless, in light of the internal reforms now taking place in the Indonesian military, global and civilian norms must be integrated in searching for solutions.

Concluding Note

Globalization presents challenges not only to the state but also to society and distinct social groups and corporate entities. The above discussion showed many morbid symptoms of Gramsci's interregnum[45] being learned by the Indonesian military. How they perceive and respond to global challenges do not confirm the Marxist notion that the economy is the determinant of both polity and culture, nor do they prove the Parsonian predilection that culture determines the other two realms. In fact, the Indonesian case reflects the Durkheimian notion that the dynamics of globalization in the economy, polity, and culture are structurally independent. This perspective helps us to understand why the Indonesian military has adopted some sort of flexible response to globalization. They have adopted a sort of cultural relativism in response to pressures that are perceived as representing global norms, such as human rights and liberal democracy. They endorse economic selectivity in economic liberalization. They also promote partial engagement in regional and global security arrangements.

Value and belief systems, politics, and professional interests play a significant role in shaping the military's perceptions and shaped its response to globalization. To the military mind, globalization presents serious challenges to the process of nation building, state building, and the internal cohesion of the military itself. Responses are varied; the response to globalization is not well defined and targeted. The response would depend on how globalization affects development and security, not only of the nation and the state but also of the regime, and of course the institutions of the military itself. Boundary strengthening in the economic, cultural, and international arenas is surprisingly not the military's preferred response to globalization. Yet it remained cautious about the overall impact of globalization.

At the national level, the Indonesian military's concerns include, among others, the integrity of a particular Indonesian brand of nation-craft from the possible 'infection' of global values. It sees itself as the institution responsible for Indonesian nation-craft. At the state level, the military is concerned with political stability. Political, corporate, and individual interests could well blend into a single and dangerous perception of equating national security with the security of the state, the regime, the government, and even an individual leader.

With this perspective in mind, some general trends must be highlighted. At the national level, the military's concerns revolve around security threats of global values rather than around dangers posed by economic liberalization. Global values may eventually engender the demand for more political space and participation. Meanwhile, geostrategic calculations and a strong sense of leadership entitlement remain embedded in military thinking. The monocentric alliance system will eventually be gone, superseded by the concept of a 'new world order' that accommodates the realities of interdependence and multilateralism and the ideal of pacific diplomacy.

Nevertheless, the Indonesian military remains wedded to the concept of state sovereignty and rejects the idea of intervention in another state's domestic affairs and political conditionality. Regardless of such nationalist sentiments, however, the military has not rejected international cooperation altogether. There is a limited commitment to deeper cooperation in defense matters, while accommodating the idea of multilateral security arrangements.

Globalization is both a differentiating and homogenizing process. The adequacy of the Indonesian military's response to globalization, however, will depend on its ability to adjust to increased global pressures that are likely to rise.

Pressures coming from global dynamics necessitate the reconstitution of civil-military relations. Neo-professionalism that is being asserted by subgroups of services within the military poses an enormous challenge. In Indonesia, civilians no longer view military action as the solution to national problems. Certainly, the military is not the only actor that is concerned with the unity of the country. Stability and social order are also the concerns of all the people. In the decades ahead, the path towards more democratic military governance is the only way for the Indonesian military to liberate itself from the bondage of Gramsci's interregnum.

Notes

1 These meetings were, among others, The Role of the Armed Forces: Threat Assessment, Security Planning, and Defense Procurement, organized by the military's College of Joint Staff and Command, Bandung, 11-12 May 1999; and one on conflict resolution, organised by the military's Institute of National Resilience, in Jakarta, 17-19 May 1999.

2 General Wiranto (1999), 'Paradigma Baru ABRI: Tantangan dan Tekad ABRI Sebagai Bhayangkari Negara' (New Paradigm of the Armed Forces: Challenges and Determination of a Guardian Army), *Widya Dharma*, special edition, College of Joint Staff and Command, Bandung, pp.107-115.

3 For civilian perception of and response to globalization, see contribution of Rizal Sukma in this collection.

4 Unlike their civilian counterpart, military establishment in the United States and Europe are the most conservative elements of the society to restrict globalization. The signing of Wassenaar Agreement and other non-proliferation regimes, which reflect strongly element of techno-nationalism, enjoyed full support and enthusiasm from the military.

5 For more theoretical exposures on the subject, see Rosenau, J. (1997), 'Globalization' and 'Fragmegration', in J. Rosenau, *Along the domestic-foreign frontier: Exploring governance in a turbulent world*, Cambridge University Press, Cambridge, pp.78-98 and 99-117, respectively.

6 Ministry of Defence and Security (1997), *The Policy of the State Defence and Security of the Republic of Indonesia*, Jakarta, pp.2.

7 *Merdeka*, 29 May 1991.

8 *Media Indonesia*, 3 October 1997.

9 *Angkatan Bersenjata*, 25 September 1992.

10 *The Policy of the State Defence and Security*, 1997, pp.11.

11 *Angkatan Bersenjata*, 25 September 1992.

12 *The Jakarta Post*, 8 February 1994.

13 Private discussion, 11 April 1999.

14 *The Policy of the State Defence and Security*, 1997, pp.2.

15 Private discussion, 28 August 1998.

16 Private discussion, 12 April 1999.

17 *The Policy of the State Defence and Security*, 1997, pp.1.

18 *Media Indonesia*, 3 October 1997.

19 *Suara Karya*, 4 April 1991.

20 *Suara Karya*, 12 March 1997.

21 *Angkatan Bersenjata*, 15 January 1993.

22 Just over 50 per cent of 82 participants to the College of Joint Staff and Command (Bandung), 73 per cent of 79 participants to the Naval College (Cipulir, Jakarta) are now in favor of having closer cooperation in defense matters, not only in security. Survey was conducted in Bandung on 11-12 April, and in Jakarta on 6 June 1999.

23 Private discussion, 28 August 1998.

24 Private discussion, 11 February 1999.

25 Anggoro, K. (1998), 'Strategic Changes in the Asia Pacific Region: The Dimensions of Military-Technology Diffusion and Proliferation', in J. Krausse and F. Umbach (eds), *Perspectives of Regional Security Cooperation in Asia Pacific: Learning from Europe or Developing Indigenous Models?* Forschungsinstitut der Deutschen Gesellschaft fur Auswartige Politik, E.V., Bonn, pp. 80-81.

26 Private discussion, 10 April 1999.

27 *Media Indonesia*, 13 April 1993; and *Angkatan Bersenjata*, 8 February 1993.

28 *The Policy of the State Defence and Security*, 1997, pp.2.

29 Many businesses of the military remain rent-seeking enterprises (for example those with logging enterprises or fishing licenses), or are tied to protected industries. One of the army's timber companies is a partner of PT Nusamba, the largest timber corporation in Indonesia. The army airline, PT Sempati, was a joint venture between the Army and Humpuss group owned mostly by Tommy Soeharto. PT Sempati and Air Force foundation have shareholdings in PT Batam Aircraft Maintenance along with the state's aircraft company (IPTN) and Singapore Aerospace. The Navy Foundation has joint venture interests in the Bintan Beach International Resort, the Karimun Kecil crude oil refinery, the Pulau Bayan Marina Club, and fish processing ventures.

30 For the business activities of the military, see Samego, I. (ed) (1998), *Bila ABRI Berbisnis*, (The Activities of Military Business), Peneerbit Mizan, Bandung, and Irwandi (1998), *Bisnis Militer Orde Baru* (The New Order's Military Bussiness), Penerbit Rosda, Bandung.

31 Buzan, B. (1991), *People, States and Fear: An Agenda for International Studies in the Post-Cold War Era*, second edition, Lynne Rienner, Boulder, pp.36-72.

32 For more elaboration of this point, see Ayoob, M. (1995), *The Third World Security Predicament: State Making, Regional Conflict, and the International System*, Lynne Rienner Publishers, London.

33 For example, Article 30 of the Constitution reads that 'every citizen shall have the right and duty to take part in efforts for the defense of the state'.

34 Private discussion, 11 April 1999.

35 Yoedhoyono (1999), 'Peran ABRI dalam Kehidupan Bangsa: Redefinisi, Reposisi dan Reaktualisasi' (Role of the Indonesia's Armed Forces: Redefinition, Reposition, and Reactualization), *Widya Dharma*, special edition, College of Joint Staff and Command, Bandung, pp.15.

36 *Ibid.*

37 Wiranto, 'New Paradigm of the Armed Forces: Challenges and Determination of a Guardian Army', 1999, especially pp. 109-110.

38 Daniker, G. (1995), *The Guardian Soldier: On the Nature and Use of Future Armed Forces*, Research Paper No.36, United Nations Institute for Disarmament Research, New York and Geneva.

39 Yoedhoyono, 'Role of the Indonesia's Armed Forces: Redefinition, Reposition, and Reactualization', 1999, pp.3; and Wiranto, 'New Paradigm of the Armed Forces: Challenges and Determination of a Guardian Army', 1999, pp.111.

40 Revision of operational doctrine of 'total people's defense' is now taking place in the navy and the air force, suggesting that defense procurements may, resources permitted, in the future become different from practice in the past. As an archipelagic country facing external threats of non-conventional security concerns, such as economic security, sea line of communication, maritime resources and globalization of information, the navy and air force should have more appropriate position and better equipped. The Department of Defence and Security indirectly mentioned this point in 'Peran ABRI dalam Kehidupan Bangsa', pp. 19.

41 Lt. Gen. Agus Widjaja (1999), *Management of [Political] Reform and Organizational Changes of Defense Institutions*, paper presented at the 'Chief of Defence Forces Forum', Jakarta, 11 March 1999, pp.10.

42 Putnam, R. (1993), *Making Democracy Work*, Princeton University Press, Princeton, especially chapter 6.

43 Yoedhoyono, 'Role of the Indonesia's Armed Forces: Redefinition, Reposition, and Reactualization', 1999, pp.3.
44 *The Washington Post*, 22 August 1999.
45 As understood by Stephen Gill, 'Theoretizing the Interregnum: The Double Movement and Global Politics in the 1990', in Hettne (ed.), *International Political Economy*, pp.65.

References

Anggoro, K. (1998), 'Strategic Changes in the Asia Pacific Region: The Dimensions of Military-Technology Diffusion and Proliferation', in J. Krausse and F. Umbach (eds), *Perspectives of Regional Security Cooperation in Asia Pacific: Learning from Europe or Developing Indigenous Models?* Forschungsinstitut der Deutschen Gesellschaft fur Auswartige Politik, E.V., Bonn, pp. 80-81.

Ayoob, M. (1995), *The Third World Security Predicament: State Making, Regional Conflict, and the International System*, Lynne Rienner Publishers, London.

Buzan, B. (1991), *People, States and Fear: An Agenda for International Studies in the Post-Cold War Era*, second edition, Lynne Rienner, Boulder, pp.36-72.

Daniker, G. (1995), 'The Guardian Soldier: On the Nature and Use of Future Armed Forces', *Research Paper No. 36*, United Nations Institute for Disarmament Research, New York and Geneva.

Irwandi (1998), *Bisnis Militer Orde Baru* (The New Order's Military Bussiness), Penerbit Rosda, Bandung.

Ministry of Defence and Security (1997), *The Policy of the State Defence and Security of the Republic of Indonesia* Jakarta, pp. 2.

Putnam, R. (1993), *Making Democracy Work*, Princeton University Press, Princeton, especially chapter 6.

Rosenau, J. (1997), 'Globalization' and 'Fragmegration', in J. Rosenau, *Along the domestic-foreign frontier: Exploring governance in a turbulent world*, Cambridge University Press, Cambridge, pp. 78-98 and 99-117.

Samego, I. (ed.) (1998), *Bila ABRI Berbisnis* (The Activities of Military Bussiness), Peneerbit Mizan, Bandung.

Widjaja, A. (1999), 'Management of [Political] Reform and Organizational Changes of Defense Institutions', paper presented at the Chief of Defence Forces Forum, Jakarta, 11 March, pp. 10.

Wiranto (1999), 'Paradigma Baru ABRI: Tantangan dan Tekad ABRI Sebagai Bhayangkari Negara' (New Paradigm of the Armed Forces: Challenges and Determination of a Guardian Army), *Widya Dharma*, special edition, College of Joint Staff and Command, Bandung, pp. 107-115.

Yoedhoyo (1991) 'Peran ABRI dalam Kehidupan Bangsa: Redefinisi, Reposisi dan Reaktualisasi' (Role of the Indonesia's Armed Forces: Redefinition, Reposition, and Reactualization), *Widya Dharma*, special edition, College of Joint Staff and Command, Bandung pp. 15.

Bibliography

'A Foreign Playing Field', *IBON Facts and Figures*, Vol. 20(9-10), May 1997, pp. 7.

'A Leader in Industrial Park', *Asiamoney*, February 1998.

Abramovitz, M. (1986), 'Catching Up, Forging Ahead, and Falling Behind', *Journal of Economic History*, Vol. 46, pp. 385-406.

Acharya, A. (1997), 'Sovereignty, Non-intervention and Regionalism', *CANCAPS Papier No. 15*, Centre for International and Security Studies, York University, Toronto.

Acharya, A. (1995a), 'Transnational Production and Security: Southeast Asia's "Growth Triangles"', *Contemporary Southeast Asia*, Vol. 17(2), September, pp. 172-185.

Acharya, A. (1995b), *Human Rights in Southeast Asia: Dilemmas for Foreign Policy*, Eastern Asia Policy Papers No. 11, University of Toronto-York University Joint Centre for Asia Pacific Studies.

Acharya, A., Lizée, P., Peou, S. (eds) (1991), *Cambodia – The 1989 Paris Peace Conference. Background Analysis and Documents*, Kraus International Publication, Millwood, New York.

Acharya, A., Soesastro, H., Gochoco-Bautista, M S., and Evans, P. (1995), 'Report of the Task Force on Globalization and Security', *Development and Security in Southeast Asia: Task Force Reports*, Canadian Consortium on Asia Pacific Security (CANCAPS) Reports, Centre for International and Security Studies, York University, North York, Ontario, Canada, pp. 1-47.

Agence France Presse (AFP) (1999), 'ASEAN under fire over Burma talks', *The Nation* (regional edition), 13 April, pp. 1.

Alagappa, M. (1987), 'Comprehensive Security: Interpretations in ASEAN Countries', in R. A. Scalapino, S. Satao, J. Wanandi and S. Han (eds), *Asian Security Issues: Regional and Global*, Research Papers and Policy Studies No. 26, Institute of East Asian Studies, University of California, Berkeley.

Alagappa, M. (1994), 'The Bases of Legitimacy', in M. Alagappa (ed.), *Political Legitimacy in Southeast Asia: The Quest for Moral Authority*, Stanford University Press.

Alagappa, M. (1998), 'Asian Practice of Security: Key Features and Explanations', in M. Alagappa, (ed.), *Asian Security Practice: Material and Ideational Influences*, Stanford University Press, Stanford, pp. 624.

Aldana, C. (1989), 'The garment industry in the Philippines: multinationals, subcontracting, homework and new technology', *New Labor Relations: International Developments in the Garments Industry and the Consequences for Women Workers*, Seminar Report, Dordrecht, The Netherlands, June, News from International Education Network Europe (IRENE), pp. 15.

Almonte, J. (1997-98), 'Ensuring Security the "ASEAN way"', *Survival*, Vol. 39(4), Winter 1997-1998, pp. 80-92.

Amin, A. and Thrift, N. (1994), 'Living in the Global', in A. Amin and N. Thrift (eds), *Globalization, Institutions and Regional Development in Europe*, Oxford University Press, Oxford, pp. 2.

Amsden, A. (1990), 'Third World Industrialization: "Global Fordism" or a New Model?', *New Left Review*, Vol. 182.

Ang Kalagayan ng Mga Manggagawa sa Cavite Export Processing Zone, Workers' Assistance Center, Rosario, Cavite, December 1996, pp. 8.

Angeles, L. (1992), 'Why the Philippines Did Not Become a NIC', *Kasarinlan*, Vol. 7(3-4).

Angeles, L., (1998a) *Beyond Golf Courses, Memorial Parks, and Prawn Farms: Globalization, Land Conversion and the Politics of Food Security in the Philippines*, paper presented at the 'Rural Sociological Society Meeting', Portland, Oregon, August.

Angeles, L. (1998b), 'Review of Soliman Santos' Papers of Party in the Making, and Working Papers, Working Group: NGO-PO Perspectives for the Local Government Code Review', *Pilipinas*, No. 30, Spring, pp. 109.

Anggoro, K. (1998), 'Strategic Changes in the Asia Pacific Region: The Dimensions of Military-Technology Diffusion and Proliferation', in J. Krausse and F. Umbach (eds), *Perspectives of Regional Security Cooperation in Asia Pacific: Learning from Europe or Developing Indigenous Models?* Forschungsinstitut der Deutschen Gesellschaft fur Auswartige Politik, E.V., Bonn, pp. 80-81.

Aquino, C. Jr. (1998), *When Tariffs Rule: Philippine Smallholder Agriculture under the GATT/WTO Tariff and Trade Liberalization Regime*, Philippine Peasant Institute, Quezon City.

'ASEAN inaction wreaking havoc throughout Asia', *Hong Kong Standard*, 6 October 1997.

'ASEAN urged to adjust in New World', *The Nation*, 19 August 1998.

'ASEAN caught on the horns of a dilemma', *The Nation*, 26 October 1998.

'ASEAN delays its surveillance system: Official', *The Jakarta Post*, 28 July 1998.

ASEAN Secretariat (1998a) *Handbook on Selected ASEAN Political Documents*, Jakarta, pp. 8.

ASEAN Secretariat (1998b), *Towards Peace, Freedom and Prosperity: An Introduction to ASEAN Agreements*, Jakarta.

Ashayagachat, A. (1997), 'Relaxed deadlines discussion for new recruits', *The Bangkok Post*, 2 May.

'At Labor's Expense', *IBON Facts and Figures*, Vol. 20(9-10), May 1997, pp. 9.

Austria, M. (1994), *Textile and Garment Industries: Impact of Trade Policy Reforms on Performance, Competitiveness and Structure*, Philippine Institute of Development Studies, Makati, pp. 7.

Axworthy, L. (1998), *Remarks for the Second Annual NGO Consultations on Peacebuilding*, Ottawa, 18 February.

Ayoob, M. (1995), *The Third World Security Predicament: State Making, Regional Conflicts, and the International System*, Lynne Rienner Publishers, Inc., London, pp. 28-32.

Baguioro, L. (1999), 'ASEAN to push free-trade plan as part of recovery', *The Straits Times*, 29 November.

Balisacan, A. (1995), 'Targeting Transfers to the Poor: The Case of Food Subsidies', *Essays in Social Science and Development: A Tribute to Gelia T. Castillo*, Philippine Institute of Development Studies, Makati.

Balisacan, A. (1999), *Poverty Profile in the Philippines: An Update and Reexamination of Evidence in the Wake of the Asian Crisis*, University of the Philippines School of Economics (unpublished manuscript).

Ball, D. (1998), *Regional Maritime Security*, paper prepared for a 'Conference on Oceans Governance and Maritime Strategy', Canberra.

Bangko Sentral ng Pilipinas (BSP) (1997), *Selected Philippine Economic Indicators*, BSP, Manila.

Barber, B. (1998), *A Place for Us: How to Make Society Civil and Democracy Strong*, Hill & Wang Publishers.

Bello, W. (1999), 'The Answer: De-Globalize', *Far Eastern Economic Review*, 29 April.

Berger, P. L. and Neuhaus, R. J. (1996), *To Empower People: From State to Civil Society*, AEI Press, Washington, DC.

Berger, M. T. (1997), 'Old State and New Empire in Indonesia: Debating the Rise and Decline of Soeharto's New Order', *Third World Quarterly*, Vol. 18(2), June, pp. 346.

Bernard, M. (1994), 'Post-Fordism, Transnational Production, and the Changing Global Political Economy', in R. Stubbs and G. Underhill (eds), *Political Economy and the Changing Global Order*, London, Macmillan.

Betts, R., Bresnan, J., Brown, F. Z., Worley, J. W., Zagoria, D. (1992), *Time is Running Out in Cambodia*, East Asian Institute, Columbia University, New York.

Bienefeld, M. (1988), 'The Significance of the Newly Industrialising Countries for the Development Debate', *Studies in Political Economy*, Vol. 25, Spring.

Birdsall, N., Ross, D., and Sabot, R. (1995), 'Inequality and Growth Reconsidered: Lessons from East Asia', *World Bank Economic Review*, Vol. 9(3), pp. 477-508.

Blaney, D. L. and Pasha, M. Kl. (1993), 'Civil Society and Democracy in the Third World: Ambiguities and Historical Possibilities', *Studies in Comparative International Development*, Vol. 28(1), pp. 3-24.

Bowles, P. (1998), 'Canada', in C. E. Morrison and H. Soesastro (eds), *Domestic Adjustments to Globalization*, Japan Center for International Exchange, Tokyo.

Boutros-Ghali, B. (1995), *An Agenda for Development*, United Nations, New York, pp. 44.

'Breaking a Taboo', *The Philippine Daily Inquirer*, 4 October 1998.

Brown, R. H. and Liu, W. T. (eds) (1992), *Modernization in East Asia: Political, Economic, and Social Perspectives*, Praeger Publishers, Westport and London.

Buchori, M. (1999), *Development of Civil Society and Good Governance in Indonesia*, paper presented at the Global ThinkNet Paris Conference on

'International Comparative Study on Governance and Civil Society' organized by Japan Center for International Exchange and Institut Francais des Relations Internationales, Paris.

Bunbongkarn, S. (1999), *Governance and Civil Society in Thailand*, paper presented at the Global ThinkNet Paris Conference on 'International Comparative Study on Governance and Civil Society' organized by Japan Center for International Exchange and Institut Francais des Relations Internationales, Paris.

Buzan, B. (1984), 'Economic Structure and International Security: The Limits of the Liberal Case', *International Organization*, Vol. 38(4).

Buzan, B. (1991), *People, States and Fear: An Agenda for International Studies in the Post-Cold War Era*, second edition, Lynne Rienner, Boulder, pp. 36-72.

Buzan, B. (1994), 'The Interdependence of Security and Economic Issues in the New World Order', in R. Stubbs and G. Underhill (eds), *Political Economy and the Changing Global Order*, McClelland & Stewart, Toronto, pp. 89-100.

Cai, P. (1996), 'Human Rights: A Chinese Perspective', in B. Nagara and C. S. Ean (eds), *Managing Security and Peace in the Asia-Pacific*, Institute for Strategic and International Studies, Kuala Lumpur, Malaysia, pp. 541-548.

Campanella, M. (1993), 'The Effects of Globalization and Turbulence on Policy-Making Processes', *Government and Opposition*, Vol. 28(2).

Canlas, C. (1994), 'GATT Issues, Gut Issues', *Kasarinlan*, Vol. 9(4), pp. 25-44.

Cañares, C. (1998), 'Erap a hit in open forum', *The Philippine Daily Inquirer*, 14 October.

Chew, M. (1994), 'Human Rights in Singapore: Perceptions and Problems', *Asian Survey* Vol. XXXIV(11), November, pp. 934-935.

Chew, L. K. (1998), 'Don't discard fundamentals', *The Straits Times*, 25 July.

Chipman, J. (1998), *Asian Security in the Context of the Asian Economic Situation*, lecture delivered to the 'Yomiuri International Economic Society', Tokyo.

Chongkittavorn, K. (1997a), 'Changing roles for the old players', *The Nation*, 25 July.

Chongkittavorn, K. (1997b), 'ASEAN accepts "open society" concept', *The Nation*, 14 December.

Chongkittavorn, K. (1998), 'Good ideas need discreet lobbying', *The Nation*, 29 June, pp. A4.

'Chuan to put "open society" idea to ASEAN', *The Nation*, 12 December 1997.

Clements, K. (1989), 'Common Security in the Asia-Pacific: Problems and Prospects', *Alternatives*, Vol. XIV, pp. 49-76.

Coleman, J. (1988), 'Social Capital in the Creation of Human Capital', *American Journal of Sociology*, supplement, pp. 95-120.

Commission on Global Governance (1995), *Our Global Neighborhood*, Commission on Global Governance, Geneva, pp. 10.

Conferido, R. (1998), 'Human Resource and Social Impacts of the Financial Crisis: The Philippine Experience', *Philippine Labor Review*, Vol. 23(1), pp. 27-50.

Constantino, R. (1985), 'The Transnationalisation of Communications: Implications on Culture and Development', in R. Pineda-Ofreneo (ed.), *The New International Information and Communication Order (NIICO): Implications for the Philippines*,

International Studies Institute of the Philippines, University of the Philippines Law Complex, Quezon City, pp. 8.

Cooper, R. (1968), *The Economics of Interdependence: Economic Policy in the Atlantic*, McGraw Hill, New York.

Corbo, V. and Hernandez, L. (1993), 'Macroeconomic Adjustment to Portfolio Capital Inflows: Rationale and Some Recent Experiences', in S. Claessens and S. Gooptu (eds), *Portfolio Investment in Developing Countries*, World Bank Discussion Paper No. 228.

Cornia, G. A., Jolly, R., and Stewart, F. (eds). (1987), *Adjustment with a Human Face*, Oxford University Press, New York.

Cortes, J. R. and Balmores, N. R. (1992), *State of Philippine Education: Tension Between Equity and Quality*, Centre for Integrative and Development Studies and University of the Philippines Press, Quezon City.

Cox, R. (1992), 'Global Perestroika', in Ralph Miliband and Leo Panich (eds), *Socialist Register*, The Merlin Press, London, pp. 26-41.

Cox, R. (1996), 'Multilateralism and World Order', in R. Cox and T. Sinclair (eds), *Approaches to World Order*, Cambridge University Press, Cambridge, pp. 517.

Cox, R. (1997), 'The Transformation of Democracy', in A. McGrew (ed), *Global Politics: Globalization and the Nation-State*, Polity Press, London.

Cronin, R. (1998), *Asian Financial Crisis: An Analysis of US Foreign Policy Interests and Options*, CRS Report for Congress 98-74F, CRS, Washington, DC.

da Cunha, D. (1998), 'Concerns Loom Over Security', *The Sunday Times (Singapore)*, 19 July, p. 44.

Dahl, R. (1992), 'Why Markets are not Enough', *Journal of Democracy*, Vol. 3(3), pp. 82-9.

Daniker, G. (1995), *The Guardian Soldier: On the Nature and Use of Future Armed Forces*, Research Paper No. 36, United Nations Institute for Disarmament Research, New York and Geneva.

David, C. (1995), 'GATT-UR and Philippine Agriculture: Facts and Fallacies', in *Essays in Social Science and Development: A Tribute to Gelia T. Castillo*, Philippine Institute of Development Studies, Makati.

David, C. and Balisacan, A. (1996), 'Agriculture and Food Security: Protection versus Liberalization', in C. Paderanga (ed.), *The Philippines in the Emerging World Environment: Globalization at a Glance*, University of the Philippines Press, Quezon City, pp. 156.

Davies, R. (1993), 'UNTAC and the Cambodian Economy: What Impact?', *Phnom Penh Post*, 29 January – 11 February, pp. 4-5.

de Dios, E. (1995), 'On Recent Financial Flows: Causes and Consequences', in R. Fabella and H. Sakai (eds), *Towards Sustained Growth*, Institute for Developing Economies, Tokyo.

de Dios, E. (1999), *The Economic Crisis and Its Impact on Labor*, Oxfam and the Philippine Center for Policy Studies, Quezon City.

de Dios, E., Diokno, B., Fabella, R., Medalla, F., and Monsod, S. (1997), 'Exchange Rate Policy: Recent Failures and Future Tasks', *Public Policy*, Vol. 1(1), pp. 15-41.

de Dios, E. and Villamil, L. (1990) (eds), *Plans, Markets and Relations: Studies for a Mixed Economy*, Philippine Center for Policy Studies, Manila, pp. 187.

Diamond, L. (ed.) (1991), *The Democratic Revolution: Struggles for Freedom and Pluralism in the Developing World*, Freedom House.

Department of Public Information (1992), *An Agenda for Peace: Preventive Diplomacy, Peacemaking and Peacekeeping*, United Nations, New York.

Department of Trade and Industry (1998), *Garments Industry Profile*, DTI, Cebu City.

Dewitt, D. (1994), 'Common, Comprehensive and Cooperative Security', *The Pacific Review*, Vol. 7(1), pp. 1-15.

Deyo, F. C. (ed.), (1987), *The Political Economy of the New Asian Industrialism*, Cornell University Press, Ithaca and London.

Dibb, P. (1997-98), 'The End of the Asian Miracle? Will the Current Economic Crisis Lead to Political and Social Instability', *SDSC Newsletter*, Spring 1997 – Summer 1998, p. 2.

Dibb, P., Hale, D., and Prince, P. (1998), 'The Strategic Implications of Asia's Economic Crisis', *Survival*, Vol. 40(2).

Dickens, D. (ed.) (1997), *No Better Alternative: Towards Comprehensive and Cooperative Security in the Asia-Pacific*, Centre for Strategic Studies, Wellington.

Donnelly, J. (1993), *International Human Rights*, Westview Press, Boulder, Colorado, pp. 19.

Dore, R. (1998), 'Crisis Stills Apologists for Corruption', *International Herald Tribune*, February 1998.

'Economic Zones: From Tough Sell to Hot Prospect', *Asiamoney*, February 1998.

Eichengreen, B. (1997), 'Is There a Monetary Union in Asia's Future?', *The Brookings Review*, Spring, pp. 33-5.

Eldridge, P. J. (1990), 'NGOs and the State in Indonesia', *Prisma*, Vol. 47, pp. 34-56.

Eldridge, P. J. (1995), *Non-Governmental Organization and Democratic Participation in Indonesia*, Oxford University Press, Kuala Lumpur.

Ernst, D. (1981), 'Recent Developments in the SemiConductor Industry: Implications for International Restructuring and Global Patterns of Technological Dominance and Dependence', based on a chapter of a larger study, *Restructuring World Industry in a Period of Crisis – the Role of Innovation: An Analysis of Recent Developments in the Semiconductor Industry*, UNIDO/IS 285, 17 December 1981, pp. 1-41.

Esguerra, E. F. (1996), 'Labor Standards in Open Economies and the Social Clause', C. Paderanga (ed.) *The Philippines in the Emerging World Environment: Globalization at a Glance*, University of the Philippines Press, Quezon City, pp. 173-175.

'Estrada protests arrest of Mahathir's deputy', *The Philippine Daily Inquirer*, 2 October 1998.

'Estrada-Mahathir face-off set', *The Philippine Daily Inquirer*, 23 October 1998.

Evans, P. M. (1994), 'The Dialogue Process on Asia Pacific Security Issues: Inventory and Analysis', in P. M. Evans (ed.), *Studying Asia Pacific Security*, University of

Toronto-York University Joint Centre for Asia Pacific Studies and Centre for Strategic and International Studies Jakarta, pp. 303.

Evans, P. (1987), 'Class, State, and Dependence in East Asia: Lessons for Latin Amerianists', in F. C. Deyo (ed.), *The Political Economy of the New Asian Industrialism*, Cornell University Press, Ithaca and London.

Fabella, R. (1996), 'Features of the Emerging World Economic Order: Implications on Growth Policy', in C. Paderanga, Jr. (ed.), *The Philippines in the Emerging World Environment: Globalization at a Glance*, University of the Philippines Press, Quezon City.

Feige, E. (1990), 'Defining and Estimating Underground and Informal Economies: The New Institutional Economics Approach', *World Development*, Vol. 18(7), pp. 989-1002.

Ferreira, A. J., Batalla, M. C. R., and Magallanes, N. (1993), 'Investments and TNCs in the Philippines: Towards a Balanced Local and Regional Development', *Regional Development Dialogue*, Vol. 14(4), Winter, pp. 79.

Flood, R. and Garber, P. (1994), 'Collapsing Exchange Rate Regimes: Some Linear Examples', *Journal of International Economics*, No. 17, pp. 1-13.

Fortuna, D. A. (1998), 'Indonesia: Domestic Priorities Define National Security', in M. Alagappa (ed.), *Asian Security Practice: Material and Ideational Influences*, Stanford University Press, Stanford, Ca., pp. 492.

Friedmann, J. (1988), *Life Space and Economic Space*, Transaction Books, New Jersey.

Friedmann, J. (1996), 'Modular Cities: Beyond the Rural-Urban Divide', *Environment and Urbanization*, Vol. 8(1), April, pp. 129-131.

Fujita, K. and Hill, R. C. (1995), 'Global Toyotaism and Local Development', *International Journal of Urban and Regional Research*, Vol. 19(1), pp. 19.

'Future Ambitions: Is the community of Southeast Asian nations ready for the 21st century?', *Asiaweek*, 12 December 1997.

'Future Cities and Habitat II', *Environment and Urbanization*, Vol. 8(1), April 1996, pp. 4.

Ganesan, N. (1998), 'Singapore: Realist cum Trading State', in M. Alagappa (ed.), *Asian Security Practice: Material and Ideational Influences*, Stanford University Press, Stanford, pp. 579-607.

Gardener, R. (1980), *Sterling-Dollar Diplomacy: The Origins and Prospects of Our International Economic Order*, Columbia University Press, New York.

Garnaut, R. (1996), 'The Asia-Pacific: Role Model and Engine of Growth', in *OECD Proceedings, Globalization and Linkages to 2000: Challenges and Opportunities for OECD Countries*, OECD, Paris, pp. 22.

Gatchalian, J., Gatchalian, M., Almeda, C., and Barranco, N. (1987), *The Nature, Consequences, and Prospects of Underground Employment in the Four Major Cities of Metro Manila*, University of the Philippines School of Labor and Industrial Relations, Quezon City.

Ghai, Y. (1994), *Human Rights and Governance: The Asia Debate*, Occasional Paper 1, November, The Asia Foundation's Center for Asian Pacific Affairs.

Giddens, A (1987), *The Nation-State and Violence*, University of California Press, Berkeley and Los Angeles.

Giddens, A. (1990), *The Consequences of Modernity*, Polity Press, Cambridge.

Giddens, A. (1999), *The Third Way: The Renewal of Social Democracy*, Polity Press.

Gill, S. and Law, D. (1988), *The Global Political Economy: Perspectives, Problems and Policies*, The Johns Hopkins University Press, Baltimore, pp. 92.

Gilpin, R. (1987), *The Political Economy of International Relations*, Princeton University Press.

Glyn, A. and Sutcliffe, B. (1992), 'Global but Leaderless? The New Capitalist Order', in R. Miliband and L. Panitch (eds), *Socialist Register 1992*, The Merlin Press, London, pp. 77-88.

Gochoco-Bautista, M. S. (1997), *Prospects and Adjustment Imperatives for Philippine Capital Markets*, study submitted to the Long-Term Planning, Research and Development Project, National Economic and Development Authority, Manila.

Goetz, A. (ed.), *Getting Institutions Right for Women in Development*, Zed, London, pp. 3-6.

Gono, C. (1997), *Peasant Movement-State Relations in New Democracies: The Case of the Congress for a People's Agrarian Reform (CPAR) in Post-Marcos Philippines*, Institute on Church and Social Issues, Quezon City.

Greider, W. (1997), *One World, Ready or Not: The Manic Logic of Global Capitalism* Simon and Schuster, New York, pp. 18.

'Growth From Without', *IBON*, Vol. 20(9-10), May 1997, pp. 2-3.

Haas, E. (1987), 'War, Interdependence and Functionalism', in R. Vayrynen (ed.), *The Quest for Peace: Transcending Collective Violence and War among Societies, Cultures and States*, Sage Publications, Beverly Hills.

Haas, M. (1973), 'The Asian Way to Peace', *Pacific Community*, No. 4, pp. 504.

'Habibie unveils grand I'nesia vision', *The Nation*, 6 October 1998.

Haggard, S. and Kaufman, R. (eds) (1992), *The Politics of Economic Adjustment*, Princeton University Press, Princeton.

Harris, S. (1995), 'The Economic Aspects of Security in the Asia/Pacific region', *The Journal of Strategic Studies*, Vol. 18(3), September, pp. 39.

Hassan, M. J. (1998), *Impact of Globalization on Political Change in Southeast Asia*, paper presented at 'ISEAS 30th Anniversary Conference on Southeast Asia in the 21st Century: Challenges of Globalization', Singapore, 30 July – 1 August, pp. 7.

Henrik-Holm, H. and Sorensen, G. (1995), 'Introduction: What Has Changed?', in H. Henrik-Holm and G. Sorensen (eds), *Whose World Order? Uneven Globalization and the End of the Cold War*, Westview Press, Boulder, CO.

Hernandez, C. G. (1995), *ASEAN Perspectives on Human Rights and Democracy in International Relations*, Peace, Conflict Resolution and Human Rights Occasional Papers Series 95-6, December, Center for Integrative and Development Studies and the UP Press Quezon City, Philippines, pp. 3.

Hernandez, C. G. (1996), 'Political Reform for Global Competitiveness: The Philippines in the 1990s', in W. S. Thompson and W. Villacorta (eds), *The Philippine Road to NIChood*, De La Salle University and Social Weather Stations, Manila, pp. 118-38.

Hiebert, M. (1997), 'ASEAN – All for One', *Far Eastern Economic Review*, 7 August 1997, pp. 26.

Higgott, R. (1998), *The Asian Economic Crisis: A Study in the Politics of Resentment*, CSGR Working Paper No. 02/98, Centre for the Study of Globalization and Regionalization, The University of Warwick.

Higgott, R. and Reich, S. (1998), *Globalization and Sites of Conflict: Towards Definition and Taxonomy*, Centre for the Study of Globalization and Regionalization Working Paper 01/98, March, Warwick University.

Hikam, M. A. S. (1999), 'Non-Governmental Organizations and the Empowerment of Civil Society', in R. W. Baker, M. H. Soesastro, J. Kristiadi and D. E. Ramage (eds), *Indonesia—The Challenge of Change*, Institute of Southeast Asian Studies, Singapore.

Hourn, K. K. (1999), *Emerging Civil Society in Cambodia: Opportunities and Challenges*, CICP Conference Working Paper Series No. 2, Cambodian Institute for Cooperation and Peace (CICP), Phnom Penh, pp. 32.

Ibrahim, A. (1997), 'Crisis Prevention', *Newsweek*, 21 July, pp. 13.

Ikhsan, M. and Tuwoi, L. D. (1997), 'Tinjauan Triwulanan Perekonomian Indonesia' (A Quarterly Assessment of Indonesia's Economy), *Ekonomi dan Keuangan Indonesia*, Vol. XLV(2), June 1997, pp. 195.

'Industry Features', *IBON Facts and Figures*, Vol. 20(9-10), May 1997, pp. 4-5.

'Industrial Estates: A Lure for Development?', *IBON Facts and Figures*, Vol. 13(23), December 1990.

'Investing on Exports', *IBON Facts and Figures*, Vol. 18(1-2), January 1995, pp. 4.

'Investing hit hard', *The Straits Times*, 2 April 1999.

Irwandi (1998), *Bisnis Militer Orde Baru* (The New Order's Military Business), Penerbit Rosda, Bandung.

Irvine, D. (1982), 'Making Haste Less Slowly: ASEAN from 1975', in Alison Broinowski, (ed.), *Understanding ASEAN*, Hong Kong, Macmillan, pp. 47-48.

Irvine, R. (1982), 'The Formative Years of ASEAN: 1967-1975', in A. Broinowski (ed.), *Understanding ASEAN*, Hong Kong, Macmillan, pp. 9.

Jacob, P. (1998), 'Estrada and Habibie to discuss APEC, ASEAN issues', *The Straits Times*, 14 October.

Jacob, P. and Baguioro, L. (1999), 'Stronger Asean ties with East Asia', *The Straits Times*, 29 November.

Jacob, P., Choo, T. L., Kassim, I., and Chan, R. (1992), 'ASEAN Prefers Soft Talk to Threats in Dealing with Yangon', *The Straits Times*, 26 August, pp. 27.

Job, B. L. (1999), *ASEAN Stalled: Dilemmas and Tensions Over Conflicting Norms*, paper presented at the 'Annual Meeting of the American Political Science Association (APSA)', Atlanta, 2-5 September, pp. 10.

Jose, V. R. (1985), 'Towards a New International Information and Communication Order' in R. Pineda-Ofreneo (ed.), *The New International Information and Communication Order (NIICO): Implications for the Philippines*, International Studies Institute of the Philippines, University of the Philippines Law Complex, Quezon City, pp. 31.

Kagan, D. (1995), *On the Origins of War and the Preservation of Peace*, Doubleday, New York.

Kausikan, B. (1992), 'Asia's Different Standard', *Foreign Policy*, Vol. 92, pp. 38.

Kelley, B. (1994), 'The Informal Sector and the Macroeconomy: A Computable General Equilibrium Approach for Peru', *World Development*, Vol. 22(9), pp. 1393-1411.

Keohane, R. and Nye, J. (1977), *Power and Interdependence: World Politics in Transition*, Little Brown, Boston.

Koh, T. (1998), 'East Asians Should Learn from Western Europe', *International Herald Tribune*, 10 July.

Korten, D. (1996a), 'Civic Engagement in Creating Future Cities', *Environment and Urbanization*, Vol. 8(1), April, pp. 38-39.

Krasner, S. (1982), 'National Security and Economics', in B. Thomas Trout and J. E. Harf (eds), *National Security Affairs: Theoretical Perspectives and Contemporary Issues*, Transaction Books, New Brunswick, pp. 313-328.

Krugman, P. (1979), 'A Model of Balance of Payments Crises', *Journal of Money, Credit and Banking*, No. 11, pp. 311-25.

Krugman, P. and Obstfeld, M. (1988), *International Economics: Theory and Policy*, McGraw Hill, New York.

Kumara, U. A. (1993), 'Investment, Industrialization and TNCs in Selected Asian Countries', *Regional Development Dialogue*, Vol. 14(4), Winter, pp. 16.

Kusuma-atmadja, M. (1993), *Some Thoughts on ASEAN Security Cooperation: An Indonesian's Perspective (Indonesia dan Kerjasama Keamanan Regional)*, Ministry of Foreign Affairs, Jakarta, pp. 15.

'Labor Only Contracting: The Permanence of Contractualization', *IBON Facts and Figures*, Vol. 19(9), 15 May 1996.

'Land Reform 2000: Gone With the Land' and 'What it Means: Lives and Livelihood', *IBON Facts and Figures*, Vol. 16(20), October 1993.

Leipzinger, D. M. and Thomas, V. (1997), 'An Overview of the East Asian Experience', in D. M. Leipzinger (ed.), *Lessons from East Asia*, The University of Michigan Press, Ann Arbor, pp. 4.

Lertcharoenchok, Y. (1997), 'ASEAN urged to rethink policy on intervention', *The Nation*, 22 August.

Levitt, T. (1985), 'The Globalization of Markets', in A. M. Kantrow, (ed.), *Sunrise Sunset: Challenging the Myth of Industrial Obsolescence*, John Wiley & Son, New York.

Levy, J. (1989), 'The Causes of War: A Review of Theories and Evidence', in P. E. Tetlock, *et al.* (eds), *Behavior, Society and Nuclear War*. Vol. 1, Oxford University Press, London.

Lim, J. (1998), *The Social Impact and Responses to the Current East Asian Economic and Financial Crisis: The Philippine Case*, country paper prepared for the United Nations Development Programme, Regional Bureau for Asia and the Pacific.

Lim, J. (1999), *The Effects of Globalization and the East Asian Crisis on Employment of Women and Men: The Philippine Case*, University of the Philippines School of Economics (unpublished manuscript).

Lipietz, A. (1987), *Mirages and Miracles: The Crises of Global Fordism*, Translated by David Macey, Verso, London, pp. 72.

Lizée, P. P. (1999), 'Testing the Limits of Change: Cambodia's Politics after the July 1998 Elections', *Southeast Asian Affairs 1999*, pp. 79-91.

'Love it, like it, hate it, adore it', *The Economist*, 15 May 1999.

Magno, F. A. (1999), 'Social Capital and Environmental Protection', *DSSEA Update*, No. 5.

'Malay daily blasts Surin', *The Nation*, 7 November 1998.

Manet, E. G. (1985), 'NIIO: Issues and Trends, 1983', *Democratic Journalist*, 8 July 1983.

Mann, M. (1988), *States, War and Capitalism. Studies in Political Sociology*, Basil Blackwell, Oxford and New York.

McBeth, J. (1999), 'Living Dangerously. Violence and Uncertainty Fuel Worries About the Forthcoming Timor Poll', *Far Eastern Economic Review*, 15 July 1999, pp. 16-17.

McGrew, A. (1992), 'Conceptualizing Global Priorities', in A. McGrew *et al.* (eds), *Global Politics: Globalization and the Nation-State*, Polity Press, Cambridge.

Mendoza, A. Jr. (1996), 'Impact on the Informal Sector', in C. Paderanga, Jr. (ed.), *The Philippines in the Emerging World Environment: Globalization at a Glance*, University of the Philippines Press, Quezon City, pp. 193-231.

Menon, J. (1998), 'The Expansion of AFTA: Widening and Deepening?' *Asia Pacific Economic Literature*, Vol. 12(2), November, pp. 10-22.

Ministry of Defence and Security (1997), *The Policy of the State Defence and Security of the Republic of Indonesia*, Jakarta, pp. 2.

'Mirrors of the Social Crisis', *IBON Facts and Figures*, Vol. 19(17), 15 September 1996, pp. 2.

Mittelman, J. H. (1994a), 'The Globalization of Social Conflict', in V. Bornschier and P. Lengyel (eds), *Conflicts and New Departures in World Society*, Transaction Books, New Brunswick.

Mittelman, J. H. (1994b), 'The Globalization Challenge: Surviving at the Margin', *Third World Quarterly*, Vol. 15(3), September, pp. 432.

Mittelman, J. H. (1995), 'Rethinking the International Division of Labor in the Context of Globalization', *Third World Quarterly*, Vol. 16(2).

Mittelman, J. H. (1996), *Globalization: Critical Reflections*, Lynne Rienner, Boulder, pp. 3.

Mochizuki, M. (1998), 'The East Asian Economic Crisis: Security Implications', *Brookings Review*, 22 June.

Möller, K. (1998), 'Cambodia and Burma: The ASEAN Way Ends Here', *Asian Survey*, Vol. XXXVIII(12), December, pp. 1088.

Monsod, S. (1998), 'The War Against Poverty: A Status Report', in D. Timberman (ed.), *The Philippines: New Directions in Domestic Policy and Foreign Relations*, ISEAS and The Asia Society, Singapore, pp. 85-110.

Montemayor, L. (1994), 'World Trade under GATT and the Filipino Peasantry', *Kasarinlan*, Vol. 9(4), pp. 74-82.

Montes, M. (1994), 'What is Wrong with Structural Adjustment Programs?', *Issues and Letters*, Vol. 3(4-5), January-February.

Montes M. (1997), 'Direct Foreign Investment and Technology Transfer in ASEAN', *Asian Economic Bulletin*, Vol. (14(2), pp. 181-183.

Montes, M. (1998), *Globalization and Capital Market Development in Southeast Asia*, paper presented at the 'ISEAS 30th Anniversary Conference on Southeast Asia in the 21st Century: Challenges of Globalization', Institute of Southeast Asian Studies, Singapore.

Moore, B. Jr. (1966), *Social Origins of Dictatorship and Democracy. Lord and Peasant in the Making of the Modern World*, Beacon Press, Boston.

Moreno, R., Pasadilla, G., and Remolona, E. (1998), *Asia's Financial Crisis: Lessons and Policy Responses*, Working Paper No. PB-98-02, Federal Reserve Bank of San Francisco, Center for Pacific Basin Monetary and Economic Studies.

Morrison, C. E. (ed.) (1997), *Asia Pacific Outlook 1997*, East-West Centre, Honolulu, Hawaii, pp. 101.

Na Thalang, J. (1999), 'EAEC launch set for Nov 28', *The Nation*, 26 November.

Neher, C. and Marlay, R. (1995), *Democracy and Development in Southeast Asia: The Winds of Change*, Westview Press, Boulder, pp. 85-88

Nelson, J. (1992), 'Poverty, Equity, and the Politics of Adjustment', in S. Haggard and R. Kaufman (eds), *The Politics of Economic Adjustment*, Princeton University Press.

Obstfeld, M. (1986), 'Rational and Self-fulfilling Balance of Payments Crises', *American Economic Review*, No. 76, pp. 72-81.

'Of Making Ends Meet', *IBON Facts and Figures*, vol. 19, no. 24, 31 December 1996, pp. 8.

Ofreneo, R. (1987), 'Transnationals and Industrial Restructuring: The Tasks Facing the Trade Union Movement in the ASEAN', *World Bulletin*, Vol. 3(2-3), March-June, pp. 72-73.

Olson, M., Jr. (1965), *The Logic of Collective Action*, Harvard University Press, Cambridge.

'Open and just society to be proposed for region', *Bangkok Post*, 12 December 1997.

Organization for Economic Cooperation and Development (OECD) (1994), *Globalization and Local and Regional Competitiveness*, No. 16, OECD, Paris, pp. 7-8.

Osteria, T. (1996), 'Implementation of the Local Government Code in the Philippines: Problems and Challenges', in T. Osteria (ed.), *Social Sector Decentralization: Lessons from the Asian Experience*, International Development Research Centre, Ottawa, pp. 16-83.

'PabiGATT!: NGO-PO Statement on the General Agreement on Tariffs and Trade', *Kasarinlan*, Vol. 9(4), pp. 141-3.

Pathan, D. (1999a), 'ASEAN to soul search in Singapore', *The Nation*, 20 July 1999.

Pathan, D. (1999b), 'ASEAN ministers stick to non-interference policy', *The Nation*, 24 July.

Patiyasevi, R. (1998), 'Ministers reaffirm ASEAN's non-intervention principle', *The Nation*, 24 July, pp. A1.

Payumo, F. (1994), 'Year-end Review and Prospects: A View from Congress', *Kasarinlan*, Vol. 10(2), pp. 25-46.

Peattie, L. (1987), 'An Idea in Good Currency: The Informal Sector', *World Development*, Vol. 15(7), pp. 851-60.

Pena, D. and Cardenas, G. (1988), 'The Division of Labor in Microelectronics: A Comparative Analysis of France, Mexico, and the United States', *Studies in Comparative International Development*, Summer, pp. 104-105.

Pereira, D. (1998), 'KL-Jakarta Ties "may be affected"', *The Straits Times*, 4 October.

'Perekonomian Indonesia: Harus Bisa Berselancar di Atas Ombak Globalisasi' (Indonesia's Economy: The Ability to Surf on the Wave of Globalization is Crucial), *Angkatan Bersenjata*, 16 August 1990.

Pineda-Ofreneo, R. (1985), 'The Garments Industry: Restructuring for Whom?', *World Bulletin*, Vol. 1(5-6), Sept-Dec, pp. 93.

Pitsuwan, S. (1998), *Thailand's Non-Paper on the Flexible Engagement Approach*, 27 July.

'Plan to set up regional crisis warning system', *The Straits Times*, 8 October 1998.

Polanyi, K. (1957), *The Great Transformation: The Political and Economic Origins of Our Time*, Beacon Press, Boston, pp. 133.

Przeworski, A. (1992), 'The Neoliberal Fallacy', *Journal of Democracy*, Vol. 3(3), pp. 45-59.

Putnam, R. (1993), *Making Democracy Work*, Princeton University Press, Princeton.

Rafinus, B. H. and Suryabrata, W. A. (1997), 'Tinjauan Triwulanan Perekonomian Indonesia' (A Quarterly Assessment of Indonesia's Economy), *Ekonomi dan Keuangan Indonesia*, Vol. XLV(3), September, pp. 373.

Raghavan, C. (1995), *What Is Globalization?*, paper presented at the University of Lausanne, reprinted in Third World Network, *http://www.twnside.org.sg/souths/twn/ title/what-cn.htm*.

Rajaretnam, M. (1999), 'Principles in Crisis: The Need for New Directions', in K. K. Hourn and J. A. Kaplan (eds), *Principles Under Pressure: Cambodia and ASEAN's Non-Interference Policy*, Cambodian Institute for Cooperation and Peace, Phnom Penh, pp. 44.

Richardson, M. (1997), 'Alliance prefers informal consensus', *The Globe and Mail*, 7 June, pp. A19.

Richardson, M. (1998), 'Applying the Brakes to "Crony Capitalism"', *The Straits Times*, 1 July.

Robinson, G. (1996), 'Human Rights in Southeast Asia: Rhetoric and Reality', in D. Wurfel (ed.), *Southeast Asia in the New World Order: The Political Economy of a Dynamic Region*, Macmillan Press, Ltd., London, pp. 85.

Robinson, J. (1962), *Economic Philosophy*, Cambridge University Press.

Robinson, W. I. (1996), *Promoting Polyarchy: Globalization, US Intervention and Hegemony*, Cambridge, Cambridge University Press, pp. 32.

Robison, R. (1996a), 'The Middle Class and the Bourgeoisie in Indonesia', in R. Robison and D.S. G. Goodman (eds), *The New Rich in Asia: Mobile Phones, McDonalds and Middle Class Revolution*, Routledge, London, pp. 79.

Robison, R. (1996b), 'The Politics of "Asian Values"', *The Pacific Review*, Vol. 9(3), pp. 312.

Rodrik, D. (1999), *The New Global Economy and Developing Countries: Making Openness Work*, Overseas Development Council, Washington, DC.

Rolfe, J. (ed.) (1995), *Unresolved Futures: Comprehensive Security in the Asia-Pacific*, Centre for Strategic Studies, Wellington.

Romm, J. (1993), *Defining National Security: The Non-Military Aspects*, Council on Foreign Relations Press, New York.

Root, H. (1996), *Small Countries, Big Lessons: Governance and the Rise of East Asia*, Oxford University Press (China) Ltd., Hong Kong.

Rosamond, B. (1997), *Reflexive Regionalism? Global Life and the Construction of European Identities*, paper presented for the 'Annual Convention of the International Studies Association', Toronto, 18-22 March, pp. 4.

Rosecrance, R., *et al.* (1977), 'Whither Interdependence', *International Organization*, Vol. 31(3).

Rosenau, J. (1996), 'The Dynamics of Globalization: Toward an Operational Formulation', *Security Dialogue*, Vol. 27(3), September, pp. 249.

Rosenau, J. (1997), 'Globalization' and 'Fragmegration', in J. Rosenau, *Along the domestic-foreign frontier: Exploring governance in a turbulent world*, Cambridge University Press, Cambridge, pp. 78-98 and 99-117.

Sakamoto, Y. (ed.) (1994), *Global Transformation: Challenges to the State System*, United Nations University Press, Tokyo, pp. 4.

Samego, I. (ed.) (1998), *Bila ABRI Berbisnis* (The Activities of Military Business), Peneerbit Mizan, Bandung.

Santos, S. (ed.) (1997), *Working Papers, Working Group: NGO-PO Perspectives for the Local Government Code Review*, Institute of Politics and Government, Quezon City.

Sayigh, Y. (1990), 'Confronting the 1990s: Security in the Developing Countries', *Adelphi Paper 251*, Summer, pp. 3.

Scalapino, R. (1994), 'Challenges to the Sovereignty of the Modern State', in B. Nagara and K. S. Baladrisnan (eds), *The Making of a Security Community in the Asia-Pacific*, ISIS Malaysia, Kuala Lumpur.

Schwarz, A. (1997), 'Indonesia After Soeharto', *Foreign Affairs*, Vol. 76(4), July-August, pp. 125.

SEIFI and SGV and Co. (1990), *The Semiconductor Industry*, Board of Investments, Makati.

Sjolander, C. T. (1996), 'The Rhetoric of Globalization: What's in a Wor(l)d?', *International Journal*, Vol. LI(4), Autumn, pp. 603.

'Soeharto used decrees to enrich family and friends, says group', *The Straits Times*, 18 October 1998.

Soesastro, H. (1997a), 'Harus Diupayakan Krisis Rupiah Berakhir' (The Rupiah Crisis Should be Ended), *Kompas*, 23 December.

Soesastro, H. (1997b), 'Challenges to AFTA in the 21st Century', in H. Soesastro (ed.), *One Southeast Asia in a New Regional and International Setting*, CSIS, Jakarta, pp. 87.

Soesastro, H. (1998), 'Long-term Implications for Developing Countries', in R. Garnaut and R. McLeod (eds), *East Asia in Crisis—From Being A Miracle to Needing One?*, Routledge, London.

Soesastro, H. (1999), 'Domestic Adjustments in Four ASEAN Economies', in C. E. Morrison and H. Soesastro (eds), *Domestic Adjustments to Globalization*, Japan Center for International Exchange, Tokyo, Japan, pp. 24-36.

Solidum, E. (1981), 'The Role of Certain Sectors in Shaping and Articulating the ASEAN Way', in R. P. Anand and P. V. Quisumbing (eds.), *ASEAN Identity, Development and Culture*, University of the Philippines Law Center, Manila and the East-West Center, Honolulu, pp. 130-148, 136.

Sopiee, N. (no date), 'Malaysia's Doctrine of Comprehensive Security', *The Journal of Asiatic Studies*, Vol. XXVII(2), pp. 259-265.

State Secretariat (1991), *Himpunan Pidato Presiden Republik Indonesia (A Collection of Speeches of the President of the Republic of Indonesia)*, Fourth Quarter, Jakarta.

Sternberg, R. (1996), 'Regional Growth Theories and High-Tech Regions', *International Journal of Urban and Regional Research*, Vol. 20(3), Figure 4, pp. 534.

Stone, D. (1997), *Networks, Second Track Diplomacy and Regional Cooperation: The Role of Southeast Asian Think Tanks*, paper presented at the '38th Annual Meeting of the International Studies Association (ISA)', Toronto, 16-22 March, pp. 20.

'Stripping the Garments Industry', *IBON Facts and Figures*, Vol. 20(9-10), May 1997, pp. 3.

Stubbs, R. (1995), *Legitimacy and Economic Growth in Eastern Asia*, University of Toronto – York University Joint Centre for Asia Pacific Studies Eastern Asia Policy Papers No. 10, pp. 12-14.

Sukma, R. (1997), 'Values, Governance, and Indonesia's Foreign Policy', a paper presented at the Conference on *Values, Governance and International Relations*, Tokyo, December.

Supratikno, H. (1991), 'Globalisasi Ekonomi Dunia, Peluang dan Strategi' (The Globalization of World Economy, Opportunities and Strategies), *Kompas*, 3 August.

Tang, E. (1998), 'Habibie concerned about Anwar's well being', *The Straits Times*, 5 October, pp. 25.

Tasker, R. and Hiebert, M. (1998), 'Dysfunctional Family', *Far Eastern Economic Review*, 23 July, pp. 20.

Tay, S. (1999), *Questioning Globalization*, paper presented at the 'Conference on Globalization and Regional Security', Asia-Pacific Center for Security Studies, Hawaii.

'Thai minister defends his gov't vocal criticism of Myanmar', *The Straits Times*, 30 July 1998.

'Thailand satisfied with debate', *The Straits Times*, 26 July 1998.

'Thais retract call for Asean intervention', *The Straits Times*, 27 June 1998, pp. 44.

Thayer, C. A. (1999), 'Southeast Asia: Challenges to Unity and Regime Legitimacy', *Southeast Asian Affairs 1999*, pp. 4.

'The game goes on: changing views in ASEAN', *The Economist*, 1 August 1998.

'The Garment Industry: Growth Potentials and Prospects', *Philippine Trade and Development*, August 1975, pp. 26.

The North-South Institute (no date), *Civil Society and the Aid Industry*, Canada.

Thomas, M. L. (1991), 'Social Changes and Problems Emanating From Industrialization in the ASEAN Region', *Regional Development Dialogue*, Vol. 12(1), Spring, pp. 3.

Thompson, M. (1993), 'The Limits of democratisation in ASEAN', *Third World Quarterly* Vol. 14(3), pp. 471-473.

Tilly, C. (1985), 'War Making and State Making as Organized Crime', in P. Evans, D. Rueschmeyer, T. Skocpol (eds), *Bringing the State Back In*, Cambridge University Press, Cambridge.

'Towards a common market', *The Nation*, 24 October 1997.

Tuaño, P. (1999), 'Labor: Bearing the Crisis Cross', *Politik*, Vol. 6(1), August.

Uerpaiojkit, R. (1997), 'ASEAN may scrap policy on Burma', *Thailand Times*, 4 July.

Uhlin, A. (1997), *Indonesia and the 'Third Wave of Democratization': The Indonesian Pro-Democracy Movement in a Changing World*, Curzon Press, Surrey, pp. 167-168.

United Nations Centre for Human Settlement (UNCHS) (1996), *An Urbanizing World: Global Report on Human Settlements*, Oxford University Press, Oxford.

United Nations Conference on Trade and Development (UNCTAD) (1999), *World Investment Report 1998: Trends and Determinants*, Geneva, UNCTAD, pp. 216.

United Nations Development Programme (UNDP) (1993), *UNDP and Civil Society*, UNDP, New York.

United Nations Development Programme (UNDP) (1994), *Philippine Human Development Report 1994*, UNDP, Makati.

United Nations Development Programme (UNDP) (1997), *Human Development Report 1997*, Oxford University Press, Oxford, pp. 82.

United Nations Development Programme (UNDP) (1999), *Human Development Report 1999*, Oxford University Press, New York.

United Nations Industrial Development Organisation (UNIDO) (1979), 'Industry 2000 – New Perspectives', *The UNIDO Joint Study on International Industrial Cooperation*, August, pp. 100.

United States Institute of Peace (USIP) (1998), *Beyond the Asian Financial Crisis: Challenges and Opportunities for US Leadership*, Washington, DC.

Vervoorn, A. (1998), *Re-orient—Change in Asian Societies*, Oxford University Press, Melbourne.

Wah, C. K. (1998), *Globalization and its Challenges to ASEAN Political Cooperation*, paper presented at 'ISEAS 30th Anniversary Conference on Southeast Asia in the 21st Century: Challenges of Globalization', Singapore, 30 July – 1 August 1998, pp. 2.

Waltz, K. (1983), 'The Myth of National Interdependence', in C. Kindleberger and D. Audretsch (eds), *The Multinational Corporation in the 1980s*, MIT Press, Cambridge, Massachusetts.

Walzer, M. (1992), 'The Civil Society Argument', in C. Mouffe (ed.), *Dimensions of Radical Democracy: Pluralism, Citizenship, Community*, Verso Books, London.

Walzer, M. (1997), 'The Concept of Civil Society', in M. Walzer (ed.), *Toward a Global Civil Society*, Berghahn Books, Oxford.

Wanandi, J. (1984), 'ASEAN Perspectives on International Security: an Indonesian View', in D. Hugh McMillen (ed.), *Asian Perspectives on International Security*, St. Martin's Press, New York, pp. 41.

Wardhanan, A. (1998), 'Economic Reform in Indonesia: The transition from resource dependence to industrial competitiveness', in H. S. Rowen (ed.), *Behind East Asian Growth: The Political and Social Foundations of Prosperity*, Routledge, London, pp. 135-139.

Waters, M. (1995), *Globalization*, Routledge, New York.

Weber, M. (1980), *The National State and Economic Policy* (Freiburg Address), translated and reprinted in *Economy and Society*, Vol. 9(4), November, pp. 438-439.

'What it Means: Lives and Livelihood', *IBON Facts and Figures*, vol. 16, no. 20, October 1993.

'Whither globalization?', *The Straits Times*, 22 September 1998.

Widjaja, A. (1999), 'Management of [Political] Reform and Organizational Changes of Defense Institutions', paper presented at the Chief of Defence Forces Forum, Jakarta, 11 March, pp. 10.

Wilson, P. (1997), 'Building Social Capital: A Learning Agenda for the Twenty-First Century', *Urban Studies*, Vol. 34(5), pp. 745-760.

Wiranto (1999), 'Paradigma Baru ABRI: Tantangan dan Tekad ABRI Sebagai Bhayangkari Negara' (New Paradigm of the Armed Forces: Challenges and Determination of a Guardian Army), *Widya Dharma*, special edition, College of Joint Staff and Command, Bandung, pp. 107-115.

Wolfe, A. (1991), *Whose Keeper? Social Science and Moral Obligation*, University of California Press.

Woo, Y. P. (1998), *State-led Civil Society at the Regional Level: The Case of the APEC Study Centers*, paper presented at the Conference on 'APEC and Civil Society', Universiti Sains Malaysia, Pulau Pinang, Malaysia.

World Bank and Energy Department (1990), *Garments: Global Subsector Study*, Working Paper, Industry Series Paper No. 19, World Bank, Washington, January, pp. 37.

World Bank (1997), *Private Capital Flows to Developing Countries: The Road to Financial Integration*, Oxford University Press.

Yoedhoyo (1991) 'Peran ABRI dalam Kehidupan Bangsa: Redefinis, Reposisi dan Reaktualisasi' (Role of the Indonesia's Armed Forces: Redefinition, Reposition, and Reactualization), *Widya Dharma*, special edition, College of Joint Staff and Command, Bandung pp. 15.

Yonekura, Y. (1997), 'The Emergence of Civil Society in Cambodia', *Cambodia Report* Vol. 3(1), May-June, pp. 10-17.

Yue, C. S. (1997), 'Singapore: Advanced Production Base and Smart Hub of the Electronics Industry' in W. Dobson and C. S. Yue (eds), *Multinationals and East Asian Integration*, IDRC and ISEAS, Ottawa and Singapore, pp. 32.

Yuen, K. F. (1998), *ASEAN's Collective Identity: Sources, Shifts and Security Consequences*, paper presented to the '94th Annual Meeting of the American Political Science Association', Boston, 3-6 September, pp. 10.

Zoellick, R. (1997-98a), 'Economic and Security in the Changing Asia-Pacific', *Survival*, Vol. 39(4), Winter 1997-1998, pp. 36.

Zoellick, R. (1998b), 'The Political and Security Implications of the East Asian Crisis'. *National Bureau of Asian Research Analysis*, Vol. 9(4).

Index

Council for Security Cooperation in the Asia Pacific (CSAP) 32, 106n

Crony capitalism 20, 29, 109n, 113n, 144

Cross-cultural differences 218

Cultural relativism 120, 272

Deeper integration 92, 105

Defense budget 265, 270

Defense spending 45, 50

Defense White Paper 25, 263, 265

De-globalization 22

De-industrialization 148

Democracy-building 26

Democratic consolidation 24, 25, 246

Democratic transition 24, 233, 246-247, 250

Democratization 7, 10, 23, 25-27, 30-31, 33-34, 54-55, 57, 90. 115, 119, 126, 196, 224, 242-244, 247, 251-252, 255n, 257n, 259, 262, 267, 270

Development and security nexus 3-4, 8, 12, 14n, 16n, 21, 23, 25, 27-30, 35, 42-43, 55, 77, 87-88, 104, 125, 141, 197n, 199n, 203-204, 209, 211-212, 219, 224n, 251, 272

vicious circle in 29

virtuous circle in 28

Development aggression 24

Developmental state 20, 28, 119

Dual function of the military 261; *see also* dwifungsi

Dwifungsi, 261, 268, 271-272; *see also* dual function of the military

East Timor 10, 15n, 26, 32, 69-70, 79, 81-83, 85n, 90, 93, 125-127, 248

Economic fundamentals 22, 139, 141, 143, 146-147, 149, 151, 158, 163-164, 166n, 248

Economic globalism 19, 254n, 63n, 65n

Economic hegemony 45-46, 108n, 113n

Economic interdependence 27, 41-45, 48, 55-56, 60n, 64n, 101, 264

Economic liberalization 22, 24, 29, 31, 45, 92, 103, 105, 144, 262, 264, 268, 267-273

Economic nationalism 49, 89, 239, 264, 266, 270, 273n

Economic regionalism 6, 20, 26, 51, 77, 83, 88-89, 91, 101, 105-106, 107n, 108n, 111n, 113n

Economic-security linkage 3-4, 8, 11-12, 15n, 27, 41-43, 45, 56, 82, 87, 129, 194, 203

Effective state 212

Electronics industries 203-204, 209, 214

Enabling environment 31, 221-222

Endogenous development 204, 219

Enhanced fundamentals 22

Enhanced interaction 79, 96, 98, 101, 104, 109, 166

Entrepreneurial agents 23

Ethnic conflict 142, 218, 248

Exchange rate policy 22, 140, 149, 155

Export-oriented industrialization 118, 205, 211

Export processing zones 187, 204, 213, 226n, 229n

Failed state 25, 117

Female workers 23, 206; *see also* women workers

Feminization of the labor force 218-219

Financial crisis 6-10, 12-13, 19, 21-22, 24-25, 60n, 62n-65n, 124-126, 129, 141, 144, 170n, 184, 190, 199n, 210n, 209-211, 214-215, 218, 245, 248

First track 33

Flexible consensus 91

Flexible engagement 52, 54, 78, 84n, 86n, 88, 93, 95-97, 99-100, 101-102, 104

Flexible specialization 207, 215, 221

Footloose investments 218

Foreign Direct Investment (FDI) 19-20, 30, 146-147, 167n, 203-205,